THE COMPLETE
JAPANESE JOINERY

THE COMPLETE
JAPANESE JOINERY

Japanese Woodworking by *Hideo Sato*
Japanese Joinery by *Yasua Nakahara*

Translated by
Koichi Paul Nii

Hartley & Marks
PUBLISHERS

Published by Hartley & Marks Publishers Inc.

400–948 Homer Street
Vancouver, BC V6B 2W7
Canada

PO Box 84332
Seattle, WA 98124-5632
USA

Original Japanese Edition of *Japanese Woodworking* © 1967
by Rikogashuka Ltd.
Translation © 1987, 1995 by Hartley & Marks Ltd.
Illustrations © 1987, 1995 by Hartley & Marks Ltd.

Original Japanese Edition of *Japanese Joinery* © 1967
by Rikogashuka Ltd.
Translation © 1983, 1990, 1995 by Hartley & Marks Ltd.
Illustrations © 1983, 1990, 1995 by Hartley & Marks Ltd.

Front cover photograph © Eli Wakan/PRSB.

ISBN 978-0-88179-121-1

Printed in the United States of America

Contents

Foreword

I must admit that when I was first asked to act as an advisor to the publisher in the translation and technical aspects of what follows, I was a bit skeptical. I assumed then, as I still do, that the manual deals with a subject, the depth and sophistication of which can hardly be grasped by the uninitiated through a book alone. When I first went to Japan, before I was the recipient of so much kindness from my teachers and sponsors there, I hardly could have guessed at the complexity of Japanese carpentry technique and the sheer (almost bottomless) depth of knowledge and tradition tied up with it.

Japanese carpentry, as so many of the crafts of Japan, did not spring fully developed from the mind of some genius. Rather, Japanese carpentry and architecture are the products of 1500 years (in Japan alone, not to mention China, their origin) of cumulative knowledge, collected and passed on from teacher to disciple. In my case, the transmission was directly to me from my teacher, over a five year period, working 70–80 hours per week. I might add this was thought minimal, but enough to get the basics down. Fifteen years is considered necessary for becoming a temple carpenter, the equivalent of 30 years at 40 hours a week.

Many many more books would be necessary to deal with the basics. I refer to manuals on tool use, layout, architectural styles, not to mention teahouses or temples.

I strongly suggest that one enter into this work with a kind of boldness and take the plunge, but I also caution the reader that one cannot learn alone. One can learn something, and that is good, but by the use of this manual alone one will not become a Japanese carpenter.

Also I should add that becoming good—really good—takes a lot of time. This manual is analogous to sheet music. To an accomplished musician who doesn't have to think about how to play an instrument, sheet music is valuable, but owning the sheet music will not teach one how to play. Constant practise, for years, of repetitive tasks alone develops a sense of square and straight and leads to a fluency with tools, as with learning a foreign language, which in turn leads to a freedom to make things as one wants them.

All this is not to say that this manual is of no use. There is much to use in this book and much one can borrow. I would hope that Westerners see what is useful and applicable to their needs and then to use it. Just as the Japanese in the past borrowed extensively from China and the West, and also have been able to forge distinctive versions of their own, I would hope that North Americans would, in turn, be able to do the same. There is great room for innovation, particularly where new technologies are now available to deal with architectural problems.

The diagrams of joints will probably elicit the greatest response. However, it is interesting to note that the design of the joints is really quite simple and that, of all the things in the book, layout is considerably more difficult.

This work is physical. The layout, also, is physical. Western geometry is the product (as far as I know) of an intellectual process, a process for which I have great respect. This Japanese layout, however, is experiential—it is "hands on"—and deals with a carpenter's ability to visualize on a three-dimensional scale. Though "recipes" for layout are included, I would urge the reader to try to understand the *why* on a *perceptual* level.

In this book, I want to draw attention to the importance of the center line (⌀). All joints *must* be drawn and laid out, from the center line outwards in both directions. Otherwise confusion will almost certainly result in pieces whose length is off. All distances and spans are made from center line to center line. Then, where joints are used, the carpenter works back from the center line, if necessary. In the same way, spans broken into segments are broken on the center line. Such a system is necessary, especially when constructing a building, as there simply are too many joints to keep track of. So always go from the center line, even if it seems an extra step.

One final note. Those joints which are structural must be very tight. They alone hold up the roof, and the roof is both heavy and dangerous. A loose joint cannot be trusted, especially if it serves a critical structural purpose.

This book, it seems to me, can be either an interesting excursion or it can be the start of a lifetime study. Either way, I think, it has great value, and I sincerely hope it is used.

April 29, 1983
Len Brackett
Nevada City, Ca.

Introduction

A word of encouragement: curiosity
A word of caution: sharp
A word to the wise: learn how to learn

The modern world affords opportunities for us to gain insight and understanding of other peoples of the world. This perspective can be gained by eating their food, listening to their music and enjoying the fruits of their unique crafts. Occasionally, one finds a bridge strong enough to support contact, seemingly, back through time itself. Japanese woodworking is one of these special continua that has survived by striving to refine one of the basic works of the world.

For centuries at a time without major interruptions, the tricks of the trade have been passed from *sensei* to apprentice. Finished buildings were the only public exposure of accumulated trade secrets. Only after years of practice and work did the apprentice develop a complete sense of the task at hand. Today, there are a handful of professionals working in the Western world, still doing it the old fashioned way. Some are building traditional structures while others infuse their designs with contemporary taste and inclination. The work changes, as the world changes, but the resolution of these craftspeople and the quality of their work remain.

Japanese Woodworking attempts to lay the ground in basic preparations and attitudes that, when mature, can produce the kind and quality of work presented in *Japanese Joinery* by Nakahara. *Japanese Woodworking* offers more scope about the work itself—and it *is* work—and about basic tool operations. Personal work habits should be forged and tempered like fine steel tools until they are effective, are performed with control, and are as safe as possible. Then, they *can* be enjoyable and result in good work.

Learning begins with the basics in this tradition—*doing*, not reading!—and lasts a lifetime. One's own experience must begin to establish the context for work preparations and procedures. Learning and skill accumulate through experience, soak in by repetition, and become second nature over time.

The text of *Japanese Woodworking* has been clarified and expanded to offer encouragement to Western woodworkers and would-be woodworkers not familiar with the versatility and extent of joinery possible through skilled handwork. Basic woodworking processes and set-ups have been stated in a straightforward manner that can be applied to woodworking in any style. There are fine points of technique that are developed only with hands-on experience, but each of these has its feet, hands, heart and head rooted in the Basics. The attention to detail and the refinement of skills in the initial chores of simple sharpening and tool care are crucial to the work reaching its peak in the more complicated forms of joinery.

Another major area of this work that needs comment is the joinery itself. A clear mental picture of the layout, geometry and space configurations involved in each joint must be built up from the simpler to the more complex configurations. Start work with the most elementary joinery. Once skill in creating these becomes accurate and predictable, it can be applied to the compound joints and practiced until it becomes a reflex. When building joinery it is very helpful to visualize and fabricate it from the inside out, instead of removing the easy, obvious parts first from the outside. This approach helps to determine the proper sequence for mortising and sawing. In this way error and inefficiency resulting from reworking the layout lines can be greatly minimized. The work can thus proceed in a speedier and more organized fashion.

The opportunity to contribute to an effort such as this book has drawn upon my years of experience as a professional Japanese-style woodworker, tool demonstrator and teacher of Japanese tools and joinery processes.

The diversity and originality of Japanese woodworking provide insight into the complexity of relationships with Nature which reflect and shape the character, value and practices of Japanese culture. As a fellow Kentuckian, Wendell Berry, has noted, the universal law of Song is that one must enter singing. It is hoped that even if you cannot sing the lead yourself with certainty, with the help of this book you can at least hum along.

Jay van Arsdale
The Pull of the Saw
South Oakland, Ca.

Author's Preface to *Japanese Joinery*

Though there is greater utilization of steel and reinforced concrete in modern structures, wood construction remains among the most important, maintaining its long tradition in Japanese architecture. Regretfully however, with the passing of time, the splendid tradition of Japanese wood construction has become stagnant and is losing its driving force.

Though it is essential for architects and builders to understand traditional Japanese wood construction, texts on the subject are woefully limited. This could be due to the difficulties of describing and illustrating the actual woodwork, but there are other limiting factors as well. In many cases, a wood member serves a dual purpose as a structural member and as a finished decorative piece. Also, different methods are used in each school, such as the Kennin Temple sect, Shintennoji sect, and Kyoto sect. Moreover, different methods are stressed even within the same school by such master carpenters as Hiruuchi, Kira, Kiuchi, and Tsuru. Then, there are alterations in detailing methods brought about by changes in the style of periods such as the Asuka [ca 700 A.D. – 800 A.D.], Momoyama [ca. 1550 A.D.–1600 A.D.], and Edo [ca. 1600 A.D.–1860 A.D.] periods. There are further differences in technique in styles such as the *Karaya* [Chinese style], *Tenjikuyo* [Indian style], *Wayo* [Japanese style], *Shoinzukuri* [study room style], *Sukiyazukuri* [free style], and the *Chashitsu* [tea room style]. Lastly, there are regional differences on such things as *uchinori* [inside face], *tatami* [straw mat], and *kiwari* [proportion].

It is not an easy task to incorporate all these conditions. This book was written using my own practical experience combined with information from available resources, and from documents on various methods of wood construction compiled during the time I was teaching at the Occupational Training Center.

At present, there are numerous publications on new details. However, as in the proverb, "onko chishin" (not to throw the baby out with the bath water), it is first necessary to review the past development and progress of wood construction before creating new methods.

I write this book in the hope that it will be of use to the reader, not only to architects and to carpenters, but also to students, and the lay person.

I wish to express my gratitude to Professor Tamaoki, Toyojiro, Professor of engineering, for his guidance, and to the editing department of Rikogakusha for its invaluable assistance.

December, 1967   Yasuo Nakahara

JAPANESE WOODWORKING
A Handbook of Japanese Tool Use & Woodworking Techniques

CHAPTER 1

THE WORKPLACE

The Work Area

Sufficient space is all that is needed for a work area. No special set-up is required. However, a flat site free from wind is preferable. It is also important that work be done out of direct sunlight. Exposure to sunlight may cause wooden plane bodies to warp and twist, and sharpening stones will dry out and crack. When out of doors, work in the shade of a tree or other building. Indoors, the work area should be well lit, but still, care should be taken to prevent direct light from the sun striking work surfaces.

The work area should be clean and orderly, to avoid hazards. The floor of the work area should be covered with carpeting or *tatamis*. This makes standing more comfortable and protects sensitive tool blades from damage should they drop to the ground.

Clothing

Clothing should be comfortable to work in and made of a material that is easily washed and cleaned. It should allow for free movement of the arms and legs, since Japanese carpentry involves much physical movement, squatting and bending over. Balance and control of bodily motion are all important, so restrictive clothing would not be comfortable.

2 The Workplace

The Work Table

Having a work table makes the work easier and less tiring, and is a must when working with small pieces. The work surface should be slightly higher than waist height, allowing for movement of the shoulders without restriction. The work table is generally used for laying out or marking pieces, or for gluing. Sawing and planing are done either on saw horses or on the planing bench. Although not used traditionally, a vice may be attached to a corner of the table, though this is not necessary when working on framing members such as posts and beams.

The Planing Bench

The height of a planing bench should be determined by the dimensions of the workman's body. The top of the planing surface should graze the knuckles of the workman's hand when he is standing erect. Most of the effort in planing is made with the leg and stomach muscles, with the shoulders being used for the follow-through, so a work surface at about hip height is preferable. When setting up the planing bench, one should adjust it to a height which feels natural and comfortable. The wood for the bench top should be free of warp or twists and should be absolutely flat to allow even pressure throughout the stroke of the plane. The work surface can sit on saw horses and should be well braced throughout its length, so that it does not bow or bend when pressure is applied. For stability, the legs of an outdoor planing bench may be set into the ground (see Figure 1.1).

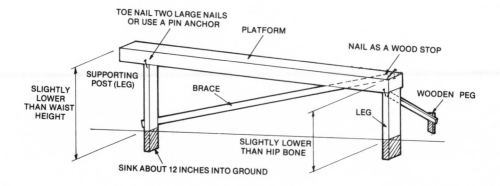

Figure 1.1. The planing bench.

The basic structure of a planing bench is one planing board and two legs. The legs should match the planing board; if it is a 4×4 then the legs should also be 4×4's. The width for the bench top will depend on the dimension of the wood that is to be worked on. A shallow angle from end to end of the working surface may be comfortable for some, but care should be taken to ensure that this does not interfere with the workman's ability to maintain a level, even stroke through the length of the board being planed.

A wood stop or even just nails, hammered into the end of the board toward which the plane will be drawn, should be sufficient to hold the board in place while it is being planed. Clamps may be used, but they are seldom necessary.

Japanese woodworking saws.
(from left: kyoto *dozuki*, crosscut *dozuki*, rip *dozuki*, 4 different sizes of *ryoba*, *yokobiki*).

CHAPTER 2

TOOLS AND THEIR CARE

Artisans should keep in mind that their tools are their livelihood. Tools should always be used and maintained with the greatest care. When professional-quality cutting tools are purchased, they are rarely ready to use immediately. Blade sharpening or other adjustments may need to be done to put them in working order. Once sharpened, blades of edged tools should be wiped with oil after each use. In Japan, camellia oil is used. Walnut oil is also good because it will not become sticky or tacky, while vegetable oils become gooey and so should be avoided. Petroleum-based oils should not be used, since they will stain wood. Only a light film of oil is necessary, and any residue or dirty oil should be wiped off.

Woodworkers and carpenters use many different kinds of tools, and there are many variations among them, depending on the type of construction being done. However, the carpenter's square (used to make measurements in addition to being a square), saw, plane, chisel, hammer, awl, and whetstones are a carpenter's basic working tools.

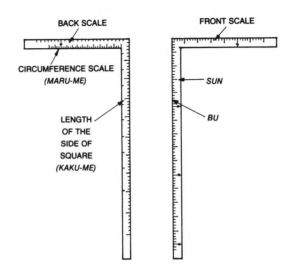

Figure 2.1. Carpenter's square.

The Carpenter's Square

Traditionally, the carpenter's square was made of copper. However, stainless steel is used today. In either case, the material of which it is made should be flexible. The cross-section of the square is shown in Figure 2.2a. Figure 2.2b shows how the square is easily pressed down onto the object being measured by depressing the middle part with the thumb. Both ends of the cross-section are tapered so that the square doesn't smear ink when using it with a pen or *sumisashi*. Figure 2.3 shows the relationship between the scales on the front and back side. The scales on the front, calibrated in *sun* (about 1 inch) and *bu* (about ⅛ inch), are used for linear measurement. The scales on the back can be used to determine the length of the side of the square of the largest beam which can be made from a log, or the circumference of the log itself.

(a)

(b)

Figure 2.2. Using the square.

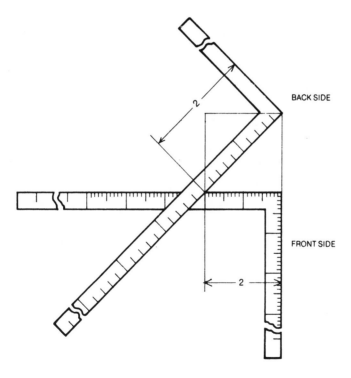

BACK SIDE

FRONT SIDE

Figure 2.3. Relationship between front and back scales of square.

The types of saws

Unlike Western saws, which are rated by the number of teeth per inch, Japanese saws are graded according to length, with the number of teeth, especially in crosscut saws, being roughly constant. Thus, a smaller, shorter saw has finer teeth than a longer saw.

The following are the different types of saws and their functions:

Tatebiki—Rip saw.   Used for cutting with the grain.

Yokobiki—Crosscut saw.   Used for cutting across the grain.

Ryoba - Double-edged saw.   This saw has both ripping and crosscutting sides. For finishing work, a smaller double-edged saw is used.

Dozuki - Back saw.   Used to cut joints requiring absolutely flat surfaces. It is used for very fine finish work. Since the saw blade is very thin, the back of the blade is slipped into a channel to strengthen and reinforce it. There are both rip and crosscut back saws. Crosscut *dozuki* are used for cuts up to 45° from the perpendicular to the grain; rip *dozuki* are used from this point on.

Keyhole saw.   Used to cut out round and various other shapes. The blade tapers to a point.

Hacksaw.   Used for cutting bamboo and hardwoods.

Sawyer's saw.   Used for rough rip-cutting large pieces of lumber or trees.

Lumber saw.   Used for rough crosscutting large pieces of lumber or trees.

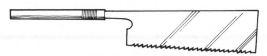

Figure 2.4. *Tatebiki*—rip saw.

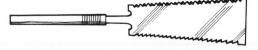

Figure 2.6. *Ryoba*—double-edged saw.

Figure 2.5. *Yokobiki*—crosscut saw.

Figure 2.7. *Dozuki*—back saw.

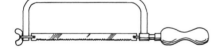

Figure 2.8. Keyhole saw.

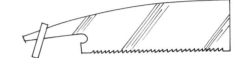

Figure 2.10. Sawyer's saw.

Figure 2.9. Hacksaw (Western style).   Figure 2.11. Lumber Saw.

Both the sawyer's saw and the lumber saw have bigger, coarser teeth and a thicker blade than regular saws because they are used for cutting green wood which tends to bind.

The above are some of the most common saws. Aside from these, the marking gauge (*kebiki*) also severs wood. This tool, shown in Figure 2.12, comes in many sizes and is preferable to the European type because of its sharp blade which will not scratch or tear the grain and which makes a very fine cut. Although it is not a saw, by increasing the size of the blade, it can be used to split thin boards by scoring them parallel to the grain. First, the blade is set at the gap required to cut the board to the desired size. Then, as shown in Figure 2.13*a, b,* the tool is placed at an edge of the board and pulled, scoring the board. Similar incisions are made on both sides of the board. By utilizing the edge of another object and striking gently on the protruding portion of the board, the extra width is removed, as shown in Figure 2.13*c.*

Aside from this use, the marking gauge is also used by carpenters and cabinetmakers to dimension a piece of timber for planing. The line made with the gauge is different from one made with a pencil. Since the gauge line is a shallow cut, when the plane reaches the line, the shaving peels off like paper, indicating the line has been reached. The line, however, must be drawn with care because the tool tends to follow along the grain.

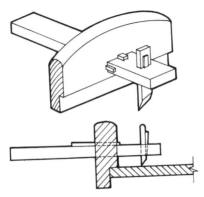

Figure 2.12 Marking gauge (*kebiki*).

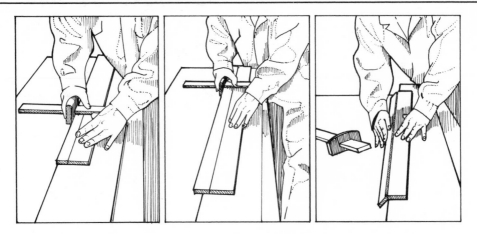

Figure 2.13 Using the marking gauge.

Japanese saws are pulled with a slight angle instead of pushing at a steep angle. If the saw is pulled in direction *A* of Figure 2.14, the wood is cut parallel to the grain. This is called ripping.

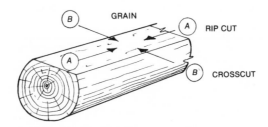

Figure 2.14. Ripping and crosscutting.

When the saw is pulled in direction *B,* the wood is cut across (perpendicular to) the grain, giving greater resistance to the cutting. This is called crosscutting. Saw teeth are made either for ripping or for crosscutting, and are shaped accordingly. The tips of both types of teeth flare outward slightly so that the cutting surface of the saw is wider than its body, thereby preventing binding. (See Figures 2.15 and 2.16.)

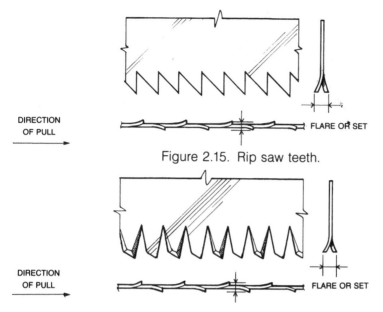

DIRECTION
OF PULL
FLARE OR SET

Figure 2.15. Rip saw teeth.

DIRECTION
OF PULL
FLARE OR SET

Figure 2.16. Crosscut saw teeth.

The parts of the saw

The different parts of a saw are shown in Figure 2.17.

BODY
HANDLE
CUT
ANGLE
FOOT
END TEETH
MAIN TEETH
LENGTH
NECK
EXTENSION OF
NECK IN HANDLE
(TANG)

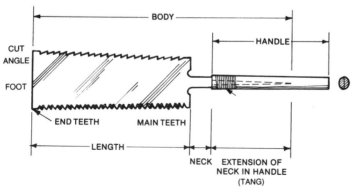

Figure 2.17. The parts of the saw.

The body.   The body of a saw was traditionally made by softening and stretching a ball of steel; modern saws are made from a sheet or ribbon of steel ground to the desired configuration. If the steel is too hard it will break or the teeth may chip. If it is too soft it will not hold an edge. The thickness of the body is tapered with the end teeth thin and gradually becoming thicker near the handle. This serves to strengthen the saw and make the pulling easier.

The teeth of a hardwood saw have a small, squat, and stable triangular profile. Saws for cutting soft wood have a tooth profile consisting of a longer, more sharply pointed triangle. The shape of the teeth of a rip saw used in sawing hardwood is shown in Figure 2.18a. The top angle of each tooth is from 40° to 45° and back side is 90° to the body. Figure 2.18b shows the shape of teeth on saws used for cutting softwood. The top angle is from 30° to 35° and the back, about 75°. Saws for crosscutting softwood have teeth with the top at an angle of about 75° and the back angle at 90°, while the angle at the tip is about 30° (see Figure 2.19).

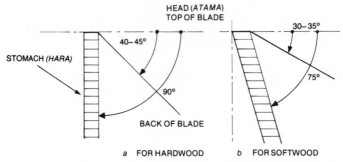

Figure 2.18. The angles of rip saw teeth.

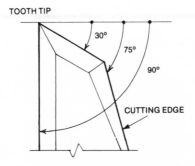

Figure 2.19. The angles of crosscut saw teeth.

The handle.   The handle of a saw is generally made of *kiri* wood (paulownia) or *ho* (poplar). Pieces with a minimum of warpage or cracks are selected. The weight of the saw handle should balance the weight of the saw blade. Two identical, grooved pieces are glued together, as shown in Figure 2.20. Then the end where the body is inserted is securely wrapped with rattan. The tang of the blade may be held in place with pine tar, but it is not glued.

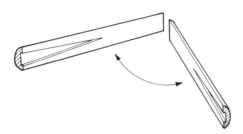

Figure 2.20 The saw handle (before being assembled).

Care of the saw

Sharpening the teeth.   When used properly, saw teeth need sharpening less frequently than Western saws. When they do, however, in Japan they are generally brought to a professional sharpener, since this is a task which requires great skill and exacting precision. The teeth are sharpened with a special sharpening file called a feather file (Figure 2.21). The body of the saw is pressed up tightly against a block of wood slightly larger than a common post, and the teeth are sharpened one at a time, as illustrated in Figure 2.22. Often a sharpening vice is used, as shown in Figure 2.23.

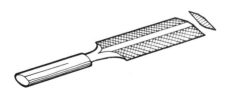

Figure 2.21. Feather File.

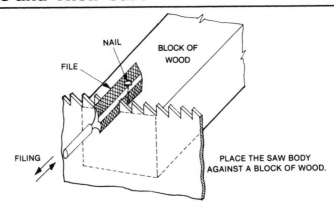

Figure 2.22. Simple method for bracing when sharpening saw teeth.

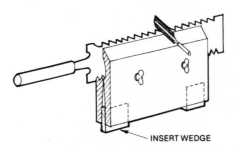

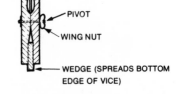

Figure 2.23 Sharpening vice.

The set of the teeth.   Inability to saw straight is due either to lack of skill, improper saw maintenance, or the set of the teeth not being even, right and left. If the sets on both sides are not evenly aligned, the cut will be crooked, favoring the side with the greater set (see Figure 2.24). This may be determined by sighting along the length of the tooth edge or sighting along the length of the blade.

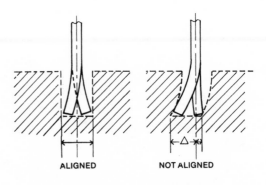

Figure 2.24 The set of the teeth.

To set the teeth, the *hazuchi* (a special hammer) and set aligner are used (see Figures 2.25–26). First, the teeth are straightened by pounding with the *hazuchi* (Figure 2.27), then they are set (Figure 2.28).

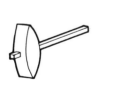

Figure 2.25. *Hazuchi* hammer.

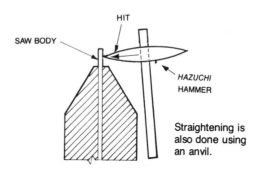

Figure 2.27. Straightening the teeth with the *hazuchi*.

Figure 2.26. Set aligner.

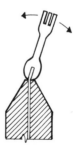

Figure 2.28. Aligning the set.

Oiling the saw.   Saw blades are composed of high-carbon steel and will rust very quickly if they come into contact with water, perspiration, or moisture from wood. They should be wiped with oil after use before being stored away, or they will corrode, increasing friction when cutting. Again, camellia oil is best. Saws should not be used in the rain or around water; if this cannot be avoided, make sure the saw is cleaned and dried after use.

The Plane

Planes are classified according to the angle of the blade in the block (*kannadai*) and mouth opening in the block (*dai*) in front of the blade. They are referred to as rough (preliminary), medium (smoothing), or finishing (burnishing) planes, depending upon their performance. Thus, a finishing plane would be used for the final planing and to remove any ridges left by earlier blade strokes.

A rough plane is seldom used and is not necessary if a board has already been machine-planed or put through a jointer. A medium plane is used to condition lumber, truing and smoothing it prior to layout; it will yield a shaving 2–3/1,000ths of an inch thick. After joinery has been cut into a board, the finishing plane is used for a final clean-up and to remove layout lines; it yields a shaving with a thickness of about 1/1,000th of an inch.

The type of planes and their functions

The following are the more common types of planes used:

General purpose plane: Used for smoothing and truing the dimensions of a board. *Jointing plane:* Used for jointing, it performs the same function as a machine jointer, though much more smoothly. *Toothing (scraper) plane:* Used to manually correct the conditioning of the body of a plane. Its blade is set perpendicular to its body, and it scrapes across the grain. It is used to correct any slight warp or twist. *Compass plane:* The bottom face of this plane's body is either concave or convex. It is used to plane circular or rounded pieces. *Rabetting plane:* Used to make the groove in the track for a

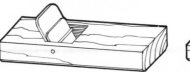

Figure 2.29. General purpose plane.

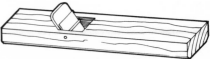

Figure 2.30   Jointing plane.

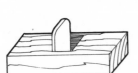

Figure 2.31 Toothing plane.

Figure 2.32. Compass Plane.

sliding door. *Side plane:* Used to shave the sides of a groove to widen it, or for finish planing. *Plowing plane:* This plane has a built-in guide and is used to cut a groove into a board. It also has side cutters so that it can go in either direction, against or with the grain.

Figure 2.33. Rabetting plane—for rough finish.

Figure 2.34. Rabetting plane—for smooth finish.

Figure 2.35 Side plane.

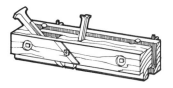

Figure 2.36. Plowing plane.

The parts of the plane

The parts of a plane are shown in Figures 2.37 and 2.38.

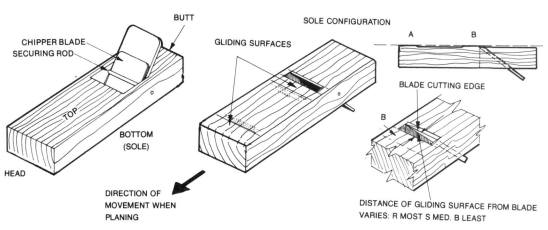

Figure 2.37. The parts of a plane.

The blade.   The blade is made from two types of steel. The back is of soft steel, and the front, a very hard, high-carbon steel. In this way, the strength and resilience of the softer steel combine with the edge-holding capability of the harder steel to meet the special requirements of this tool.

If the steel is too hard, the blade will chip easily. On the other hand, if the steel is too soft, the blade will not hold an edge. Because of this, when acquiring a plane, it is important to first consult with someone who knows tools. Evidence of handwork, such as carbon specking or an unevenness at the line where the two pieces of steel are laminated together, is often an indication of a high-quality blade.

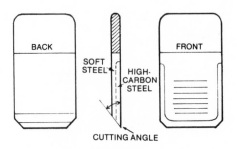

Figure 2.38. The blade.

Softwood is easier to plane with harder steel. The planing quality is also affected by the angle at which the blade is set in the plane body. To plane hardwoods or extremely highly figured woods, 45–55° is the most efficient angle, and for softwoods, 30–35° is ideal. Very soft woods, such as *kiri* (paulownia) or balsa, may require 22°–30°. Most North American woods work well at an angle of 32°–35°. Generally, the harder the wood, the steeper the angle required to plane it. Some denser woods, such as maple or exotic hardwoods, may require a blade angle as steep as 55–60°. Through experience, a craftsman will learn the proper angle for use with each type of wood.

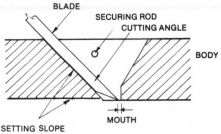

Figure 2.39. Angle of blade tip.

The single-blade plane, shown in Figure 2.40, is used for finishing. The mouth of its blade must be kept at a minimum in order to not tear the grain. This is a very difficult plane for the layman to use.

The rough and medium planes, with their larger mouth, have a tendency to bite into the wood's surface. A wider mouth means that the pressure of the gliding surface is farther away from the cutting surface of the blade; this allows more wood to be lifted or torn before being sheared or cut off. To a certain extent, this can be reduced by adjusting the throat opening between the gliding surface of the block and the cutting edge of the blade. To prevent torn grain, a chipper blade is used (see Figure 2.41). This type of plane is called a double-blade plane. The edges of the blade and the chipper blade are placed back to back, as shown in Figure 2.42. Dimension *a,* shown there, should be .020 inch for a rough plane, .013 inch for a medium plane, and .010 inch ± for a finishing plane. The chipper blade should r t be advanced beyond the cutting edge, or shavings will clog the blade.

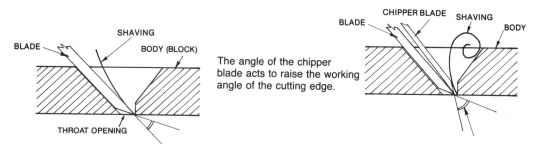

The angle of the chipper blade acts to raise the working angle of the cutting edge.

Figure 2.40. Single-blade plane.

Figure 2.41. Double-blade plane.

Figure 2.43. Cross-section of plane body.

Figure 2.42. Relationship of blade to chipper blade.

The plane body.   Hardwood, being more durable, is preferred in making the plane body. Heartwood (the portion without knots) of white or red oak are good choices. Wood from the root end of a tree and the wood near knots should not be used because these tend to warp. The outside-of-the-tree side of the wood should be used for the bottom face of a plane, so that any warpage will occur at the edges and be more easily corrected. The side of the wood closer to the root should be used for the head of a plane. The grain of the block will then run more smoothly upon the grain of the board being planed. The direction of movement should be with the grain itself and *not* against the grain pattern of the block.

Adjusting the blade

Setting the blade.   To set the blade, check it coming out from the head end of the base, as in Figure 2.44. Gently hit the top of the blade with a small metal hammer. This must be done gradually, for if the blade is hit too hard, the body will crack because of the way the blade is inserted in it. The blade should be hit squarely and at the center, otherwise it will be set crooked. To allow for this adjustment, the slot in which the blade rests must be slightly wider (about ⅛") than the blade itself.

Figure 2.44. Setting the blade.

Retracting the blade.   To retract the blade back into the plane body, gently hit the top of the heel with a hammer parallel to the direction of the blade, as shown in Figure 2.45. Make certain the bottom portion of the heel is not struck. If it is, the heel corner may crack or splinter away, preventing the blade from coming down flat on the surface when planing.

When storing the plane, the blade should be recessed from the bottom surface, or sole, of the body to protect it.

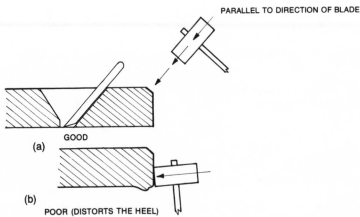

Figure 2.45. Retracting the blade.

Correcting blade gap. The cutter blade and chipper blade of a Japanese plane must be perfectly flat. This is essential to its proper functioning. When these are not precisely matched, shavings collect in the space between them and will very quickly close the mouth of the plane. To correct this, sharpen both blades, and adjust the unequal protuberance on the back of the chipper blade by pounding it with a hammer against an anvil.

To check whether the blades are flat, place the blades together in the position shown in Figure 2.46a. Next, the fingers are placed on the lettered positions shown in Figure 2.46b: the thumb on a, the index finger on b, the middle finger on c, and the little finger on d. Then apply pressure on each corner separately as shown in Figure 2.46c. If you hear a click, the blades are still not flat, and the chipper blade should be adjusted.

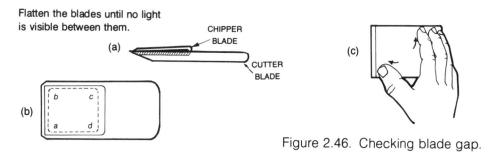

Figure 2.46. Checking blade gap.

Adjusting the plane body

There is a legend in which two boards planed by Hidari Jingoro adhered to each other when placed together. This happened because the two planed surfaces were so perfectly flat that air could not enter between them. Accurate planing depends on the proper care of the plane body. Adjusting the body of the plane entails checking the shape of the sole with a straight edge and adjusting the bottom surface of the body for easier planing. Make certain the blade is retracted into the block before commencing. The straight edge should be placed in the positions indicated in Figure 2.47, and the sole checked for flatness by holding it at eye level (Figure 2.48). The surface can then be corrected by scraping with a toothing plane, as shown in Figure 2.49. Check first the throat and then the front or nose, since flatness in all other directions should be based upon the relationship of these two gliding surfaces.

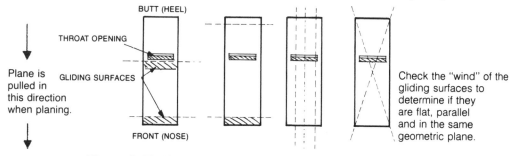

Figure 2.47. Where the straight edge should be placed.

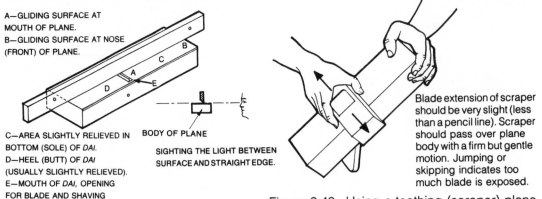

A—GLIDING SURFACE AT MOUTH OF PLANE.
B—GLIDING SURFACE AT NOSE (FRONT) OF PLANE.

C—AREA SLIGHTLY RELIEVED IN BOTTOM (SOLE) OF *DAI*.
D—HEEL (BUTT) OF *DAI* (USUALLY SLIGHTLY RELIEVED).
E—MOUTH OF *DAI*, OPENING FOR BLADE AND SHAVING CONTACT

BODY OF PLANE

SIGHTING THE LIGHT BETWEEN SURFACE AND STRAIGHT EDGE.

Figure 2.48. Checking flatness with straight edge.

Blade extension of scraper should be very slight (less than a pencil line). Scraper should pass over plane body with a firm but gentle motion. Jumping or skipping indicates too much blade is exposed.

Figure 2.49. Using a toothing (scraper) plane.

Adjusting the rough plane.   The mouth, though naturally wider than that of the other planes, should be as small as possible. Figure 2.50 shows the procedure for adjusting this plane. Since the rough plane's shavings are rather thick, a great deal of force has to be exerted when planing with it. Therefore, the size of the plane should be somewhat narrow and comfortable to hold.

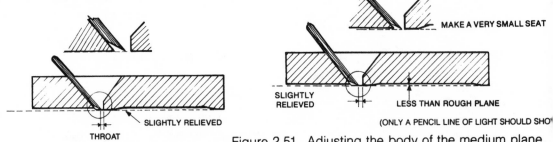

MAKE A VERY SMALL SEAT

SLIGHTLY RELIEVED

SLIGHTLY RELIEVED

THROAT

LESS THAN ROUGH PLANE

(ONLY A PENCIL LINE OF LIGHT SHOULD SHOW)

Figure 2.50. Adjusting the body of the rough plane.

Figure 2.51. Adjusting the body of the medium plane.

Adjusting the medium plane.   The mouth of this plane should be less than .060 inch. (Plane blades are available in 50 to 70 mm widths.) Ideally, the plane itself should be slightly wider than the rough plane. The body should be adjusted as indicated in Figure 2.51.

Adjusting the finishing plane.   The sole of the finishing plane should be almost perfectly flat. The portion closest to the heel of the plane should be sloped up just enough to allow a sheet of paper to be placed under it. The mouth opening should be less than .020 inch ±. The plane can be of a size which can be held with one hand. The smaller its mouth, the better. However, if the mouth is too narrow, the shavings will get stuck, rendering the plane unusable (see Figure 2.52). In time, when the mouth gets wider, due to numerous adjustments, a wooden inlay can be inserted to close it up, as shown in Figure 2.53.

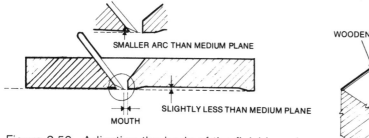

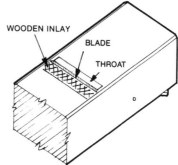

Figure 2.52. Adjusting the body of the finishing plane.

Figure 2.53. Wooden inlay.

The Chisel

The types of chisels and their functions

The timber mortising chisel.   This chisel is used for timber work. It is large and sturdy, the blade about ½ inch thick, and the edge angle approximately 32°±.

Finishing chisel.   Compared to the timber mortising chisel, the blade of the chisel is thin (about ¼ inch) and the edge angle is approximately 20°.

Paring chisel.   This chisel's handle is about 2 to 2½ times longer than the two preceding chisels, and it does not have a crown ring at the top. Relatively speaking, the blade is thin (less than ⅛ inch) and narrow, and the edge angle is 15–20°. It is used in cleaning up mortises and for bringing joints down to the line. While the above two chisels are striking chisels, this one is never to be struck. It is a push chisel.

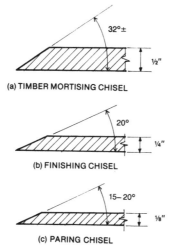

Figure 2.54. Blade angle and thickness.

Experience will teach the proper angle for use in cutting different woods. A harder wood needs a steeper angle to have more material supporting the cutting edge. Softer woods need a flatter angle, less than 32°, so that the wood is cut before it is compressed too much.

The parts of the chisel

The parts of a chisel are shown in Figure 2.55. The chisel blade is made of two pieces of steel, a softer steel at the back with harder steel laminated on the top and bent around to form the cutting edge. The softer steel absorbs the shock of hammer blows; the tang inserted into the handle is part of this piece. The handle is usually made of red or white oak or other hardwood. At the top, a crown ring (or ferrule), which is inserted about ¼ inch from the struck end the handle, prevents the handle from splitting when struck by a hammer.

It is very important that the handle and blade of a chisel be aligned. Otherwise, it is difficult to sense how one is cutting.

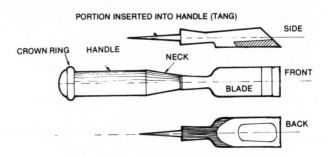

Figure 2.55. The parts of the chisel.

Adjusting the crown ring.   As the top of the handle wears down, the crown ring becomes more exposed and may be struck directly by the hammer, causing its inner top portion to bend and the ring to wobble (Figure 2.56). When this happens, the crown ring should be removed and its irregularities filed away. It can then be reinserted in the handle.

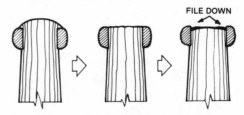

Figure 2.56. Wearing down of the crown ring.

Sharpening Stones

In daily use, cutting edges become dull or may chip, and must be sharpened. This can be done anywhere that is well lit and free of dust. Since a carpenter's job site is not fixed, blades are often sharpened outside, away from direct sunlight which will dry the stone. However, those who work indoors, such as millworkers and cabinetmakers, should have a counter where they can sharpen blades. The counter should be constructed so that the top face of the sharpening stone will be slightly below waist height when placed on the counter. Or, one may kneel before the stone placed on a low bench or level board. In both cases, the working height should be adjusted so that balance and flexibility in the arms and shoulders are optimal.

The types of sharpening stones and their functions

Sharpening stones are classified as coarse, medium, and finish stones, and are used in sequence when sharpening blades. Japanese sharpening stones should be used with water only, never oil. The water lubricates the action of the stone and flushes away the metal rubbed from the blade. Manmade stones should be soaked in water for a few minutes before each use, but natural stones must *never* be soaked.

A rough manmade stone made of silicon carbide, aluminum carbide, or aluminum silicate is used to remove chips from blades. The coarse stone, made of sandstone, is used to begin any sharpening practice except daily maintenance, in which only the medium and finish stones are used. The medium stone is made of shale and is dark blue in color. When used, it follows the coarse stone, after which the blade is applied to the finish stone.

There are manmade finish stones and naturally formed ones. The finest edges are obtained from the natural stones. Manmade stones are often too soft and, generally speaking, the harder a finish stone is, the sharper the edge it will produce. The best Japanese stones are Honyama stones, found near Kyoto. They are beige in color and tend to be quite expensive, especially the larger ones. Better natural stones have an even texture and no inclusions of grit or other foreign matter in the sharpening surface.

When a blade has been sharpened on a medium or coarse stone, a burr of metal appears on the front side of the blade. This "wire edge" can be felt by running a finger along the top side of the blade edge off the front. Do not break this off; remove it with the next finest stone. The finish stone will not leave a wire edge.

How to use sharpening stones

When blades are sharpened on a rough or coarse stone, the hollow grind begins to appear at the cutting edge and the edge must be made flat again. For this, a steel plate, the top surface of which is perfectly flat, is used (Figure 2.60). In the case of planes, the blade is tapped out. Chisels, however, are never to be pounded; they should only be ground.

Using the steel plate.   When a blade has been chipped as in Figure 2.57, it must be sharpened on a rough stone, or very carefully ground on an electric waterwheel grinder, until the chip disappears (Figure 2.58). If an electric grinder is used, the blade should be constantly cooled with water in the course of grinding, so that the temper of the steel is not lost. After grinding, the cutting edge, instead of being a straight line, will be curved like a bow where the hollow ground of the back of the blade has been penetrated. This must be flattened out so that it can bear a straight cutting edge. Therefore, a flat edge, about ⅛ inch wide (a white shiny strip) has to be created beyond the hollow ground.

In the case of a plane, first gently tap the cutting edge on the edge of the steel plate, as shown in Figure 2.59a. When it is struck, the recessed portion protrudes, as shown in Figure 2.59b, across the width of the blade. This protrusion should be hardly noticeable—just enough to see the lump when the blade is held horizontally at eye level. Then, sprinkle some emery powder and water, or oil, on the steel and the blade surface. Place the back surface of the blade on the steel plate and move it back and forth with pressure, as shown in Figure 2.60, until you have a mirror finish, as flat as a piece of glass. Be careful not to let any emery powder or water contaminated with it come into contact with the polishing stones. Make sure that you press down at the edge of the blade only. Most plane maintenance is limited to using the medium and finishing stone to maintain a sharp cutting edge.

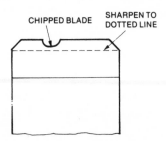

Figure 2.57. Blade damage.

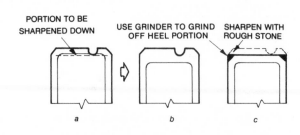

Figure 2.58. Grinding a damaged blade.

*NOTE: *Rationale* This narrow flat surface at the cutting edge should not be created by simply grinding down the top surface of the blade. Grinding this top surface reduces the thickness of the wedge shape of the blade itself and requires the blade to be set too deep in the *dai* before it is held in proper tension (compression in the outside slots) and position. Thick shavings or paper shims can be added to the area on the *dai* that is in contact with the back of blade to tighten fit.

Grind gently on the cutting edge itself. This leaves the existing angle in proper set. Removing large amounts of blade by grinding the angled level surface only tends to lead to contortions in the flatness of that surface.

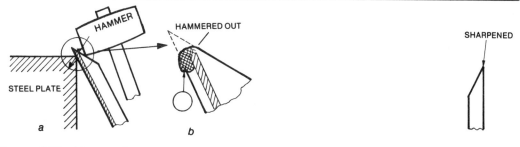

Figure 2.59. Hammering out a new cutting surface.

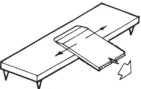

Figure 2.60. Using the steel plate.

In the course of creating a new cutting edge, the "ears" (beveled corners) may have become too small and, in the case of a plane blade, should be ground out until the width of the blade is the same size or just a little less than the width of the mouth of the plane. If this is not done, wood shavings will jam up the plane mouth; ears allow them to escape.

Using the rough stone.   Once the back his been fixed, use the rough stone to grind the cutting edge until the chip disappears completely, as explained previously.

Using the coarse stone.   When the blade has become very rounded, the edge appears as a white line as light reflects off it. In such a case, sharpen the blade with a coarse stone until a wire edge is produced across the full width of the blade.

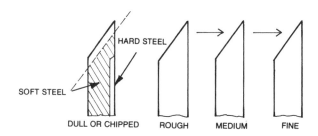

Figure 2.61. Sharpness obtained using progressively finer stones.

Using the medium stone. Even after the blade has been sharpened on a rough or coarse stone, the cutting surface will still appear dull, and needs to be sharpened on the medium stone to decrease the roughness and straighten the edge. The blade is sharpened on the medium stone until it has luster and a finer wire edge.

Using the fine finish stone. The finish stone is used to remove the wire edge and to polish the smoothed edge still further. As shown in Figure 2.62a, the back side of the blade is run back and forth several times with slight pressure to remove the wire edge. Then the angled portion of the blade is polished repeatedly (Figure 2.62b). These steps are repeated until the wire edge is removed, gradually decreasing pressure and increasing the number of strokes as the final finishing is approached.

As described above, the wire edge can be felt with the fingers, but it should not be forcefully removed by them, since this will tear away parts of the cutting edge. When the wire edge has been successfully removed, the white gleam will no longer be visible when the blade's front face is reflecting light at eye level. Finally, wipe the blade with camellia oil or any refined or non-coagulating oil, and store it.

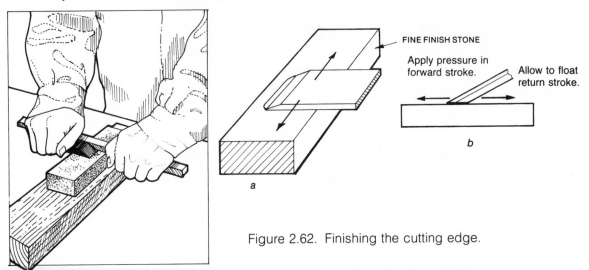

Figure 2.62. Finishing the cutting edge.

Sharpening technique

Posture. The single most important factor in sharpening is balance. The surface on which blades are to be sharpened should be lower than the waist, and one's posture should allow for free, horizontal movements of the arms. Never assume a posture with the shoulder at the center of the motion, resulting in rounded movements of the arm, for this will cause the blade's edge to be sharpened to a curve. The posture must provide for a horizontal movement with even pressure from the fingers on the blade. (See Figure 2.63.)

Pressure to sharpen the blade is applied only on the push stroke; on the return, the angle of the blade to the stone is retained but without pressure. Each stroke will measure about 6 to 7 inches, extending over the full flat length of the stone. The blade is held in both hands to steady it. A slight flex in the wrists will help to maintain a constant angle through the length of the stroke. A steady, slight "wave" or ripple in the water in advance of the blade as it is pushed foward is a good indication of a smooth, even stroke in which the proper angle has been maintained. The consistent sound of metal-to-stone contact is another key to proper technique.

If one is rushed, or the mind wanders, or the heart is not in it, the blade cannot be sharpened accurately. The blade must be sharpened with complete concentration for ten to fifteen minutes. As one becomes proficient, a blade can be sharpened in just a few minutes.

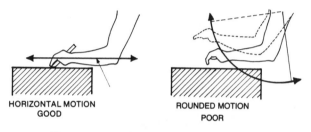

HORIZONTAL MOTION
GOOD

ROUNDED MOTION
POOR

Figure 2.63. Sharpening technique.

The surface of the sharpening stone.   The surface on which the blade is to be sharpened must be perfectly flat. However, the front and back ends of the coarse and medium stones should have a slight bevel, as shown in Figure 2.64. To obtain and maintain this slope, the blade should be pushed over the front end once every three times it is pushed forward. The front and back ends of the stone should be reversed after using it, so that the front becomes the back. If this is consistently done, the proper bevel will always be maintained. The entire flat surface of the stone should be used evenly, so that a depression is not created in the center of the sharpening surface. If depressions or distortions appear on the stone's surface, the cutting edge of the blade cannot be sharpened to a straight line. To remove distortion or depressions from the surface of the stone, rub the water-soaked surface back and forth on a hard, flat surface such as concrete until the stone is flat. If concrete alone does not work well enough, add some sand onto the surface of the concrete, and repeat the rubbing.

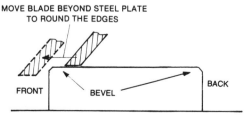

MOVE BLADE BEYOND STEEL PLATE
TO ROUND THE EDGES

FRONT   BEVEL   BACK

Figure 2.64. Sharpening through the bevel.

From time to time, fresh water must be added to the surface of the stone, to prevent a build-up of metal paste, formed by the grindings from the blade and stone, which will make it difficult to determine the accuracy of the sharpening stroke, as well as leading to uneven contact between blade and stone. This water should be kept clean to avoid the possibility of contamination. In order to prolong the stone's life, a wooden base should be made for it, making sure that the inside-of-the-tree side of the board faces up. The stone may be inset into this base but should not be glued to it, since warpage or contraction of the wood block could crack the stone. Natural stones are susceptible to water damage, so all sides except the sharpening surface should be coated with paint or paper to restrict absorption.

After sharpening is complete, all impurities should be wiped or washed from the surface of the stone, and the stone should be dried, out of sunlight, before being stored.

Other Tools

Awls or gimlets

Awls, by their twisting action, can pierce holes in wood. Pilot holes are made with an awl (Figure 2.65a) to prevent nails from slipping and boards from splitting. They are also used for making holes through which wires and other thin objects are to pass (Figure 2.65b); as a countersink for recessing the head of a nail or screw (Figure 2.65c); and for boring still deeper and larger holes (Figure 265d). They are extremely handy in awkward positions and in locations where an electric drill or brace and bit is inconvenient.

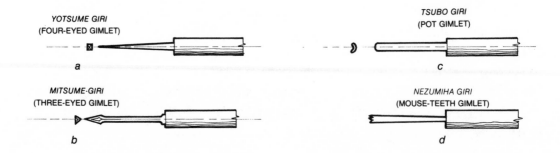

Figure 2.65. Awls or gimlets.

Hammers

All Japanese quality hammers are laminated just like the other tools. They have a very hard, tempered steel face and a mild steel body. The *genno* (Figure 2.66) is a special hammer with two faces which appear, at first glance, to be the same. However, one face is flat and the other, slightly convex. The flat face of the *genno* is used to drive large nails. The other end, with its slightly rounded face, is used with chisels and is used to "kill the wood". When, for instance a mortise and tenon joint is made very tight, in order to be able to introduce the pieces without too much stress on them, the wood (the tenon piece) is pounded very carefully with this rounded face of the *genno,* depressing the surface of the wood. During the next six to twelve hours, after the tenon has been inserted, the compressed wood returns to its original size, coming up very tight. Care must be taken to used the rounded face of the *genno,* for killing the wood with the flat face would cut the fibers and ruin it.

The *kanazuchi* (Figure 2.67) is used for driving small nails, and its pointed end can be used as a set, as well as for making pilot holes in rough surfaces. Traditionally, it was used for the latter purpose by roofers to make holes in shingles. As a rule, the size and weight of hammer used should be in relationship to the size of the work to be done.

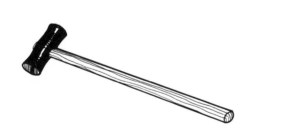

Figure 2.66. *Genno* hammer.   Figure 2.67. *Kanazuchi* hammer.

A Word on Machine Tools

Power tools are of extreme value to the Japanese carpenter in removing, or hogging out, large quantities of wood. While machine tools can rarely match handwork in versatility and acute precision, much time and labor can be saved by employing them wherever they can be used without decreasing the quality of the work.

Stack of pieces with finished joinery, wrapped for protection.

CHAPTER 3

CHARACTERISTICS OF WOOD

Understanding Wood

Wood is alive. Even after trees have been cut, wood continues to respond to environmental conditions. Before, during, and after construction, changes in the wood's characteristics can have serious consequences for the integrity of a structure. With proper understanding, mishaps can be foreseen and avoided.*

Selecting Wood

Wood for use in any structure should be properly seasoned. Most lumber today is kiln dried, a process which bakes the cells on the outer layer of a board, damaging their plasticity. Often the wood beneath this surface layer has a higher moisture content. Become familiar with your wood suppliers, whether they be lumber yards or custom mills. The methods they use in seasoning wood will affect its performance when it is used in a structure.

Because wood is so susceptible to its environment, one should allow it sufficient time to adjust to the climate in which it is to be used. This is especially true for wood imported from another country or another region. If possible, lumber, particularly structural members, should be stored close to the site on which they are to be used for a year or more, in order to allow them to adjust to seasonal variation in temperature and humidity.

*For an excellent treatment of the subject, see R. Bruce Hoadley, *Understanding Wood: A Craftsman's Guide to Wood Technology* (Newtown, CT: Taunton Press, 1980).

Recycled lumber can be useful, since it has had time to become acclimated after being cut and finished; its behavior under stresses has also been tested.

In Japan, as in North America, there are a number of regional variants within a given species, such as cedar or cypress, each with its own characteristics. A workman should become familiar with the different woods available which have the features desired for each use. One good way to identify local woods which are suitable for use in wood frame construction is to visit local heritage buildings. The craftsmen who built them were generally limited in their selection of materials to those available locally, so the woods they used for certain applications, and their joinery methods, can be instructive.

Types of wood typically used in constructing Japanese houses are listed in Table 3.1.

Table 3.1: Selecting Wood for Use

Use	Desirable Characteristics	Types of Wood
mudsill (*dodai*)	Water resistant, tight grain, abundant pitch and oil, reddish to conceal soiling.	Japanese cypress (*hinoki*), Japanese cedar (*sugi*) *North American equivalents:* Port Orford cedar (sim. *hinoki*), Alaskan yellow cedar (sim. *sugi*), redwood, pressure-treated fir
post (*hashira*)	No or minimal warp and twist. Beautiful surface grain. Non-structural member should have pitch and structural should be pitch-free.	Japanese cypress, Japanese cedar, zelkova (*keyaki*), paulownia (*kiri*)—also known as Princess tree in U.S.
beams and girders	Almost all will be used for structural purposes, so	black pine (*kiromatsu*), hemlock spruce (*tsuga*),

(*hari* and *keta*)	select lumber that is flexible and ductile, clear, without knots. Preferably, select a board with grain lines of the load-bearing surface on edge, not flat (see Figure 3.1).	Japanese cypress *North American equiv.:* Douglas fir

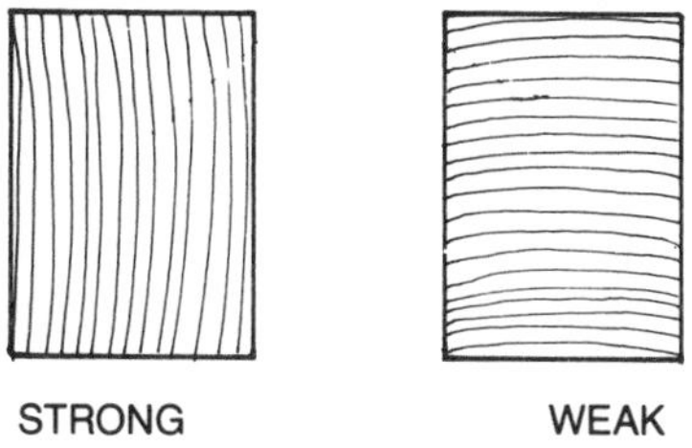

STRONG   WEAK

Figure 3.1 End grain for beams and girders

finishing lumber (trim, siding)	Non-load-bearing members. Free of pitch and knots, good grain and smooth surfaces. Free of warp or distortion. Very moisture resistant.	Japanese cypress, Japanese cedar, lauan (*Shorea*), mahogany *North American equivs.:* fir, Western red cedar
floor boards	Free of knots, smooth, clear surfaces. Strong resistance against friction or rubbing.	Japanese cypress, Japanese, cedar, pine, hemlock spruces *North American equivs.:* oak, beech, red cedar
moldings and jambs (*shikii*)	Select hard wood to resist friction from doors and *shoji*.	Japanese cypress and Japanese cedar, with a hardwood (cherry, oak) for tracks

Storing Finished Lumber

To protect lumber from the rain and sun, a temporary roof made of corrugated metal or wood planks should be constructed on the job site. Nailing should be kept to a minimum, so that lumber used to build this shelter can be reused. Sawn pieces, such as structural and finished wood, particularly if they are damp or green, will warp and split if they are stored in direct sunlight or left exposed to the wind. Therefore, a low and shady place should be selected to store the wood. The roof and enclosure should be built according to need, and lumber should be stacked in a sloped pile, in an orderly manner.

If wood is placed directly on the ground, dirt will penetrate it, which will then ruin tool blades. Also, moisture from the ground will soak into the wood, thereby destabilizing it. To avoid this, 4×4's should be used to support the wood above the ground. These supports can be positioned as needed to ensure that boards lie flat and level throughout their length. Sticks should be placed between the layers of wood in a stack to allow proper air circulation. These sticks should be placed 3 to 5 feet apart (or otherwise, depending upon the dimensions and stability of the lumber) and should be directly above one another in a vertical line down to the support, to prevent warping (see Figure 3.2).

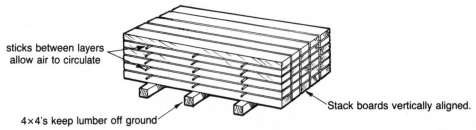

sticks between layers
allow air to circulate

Stack boards vertically aligned.

4×4's keep lumber off ground

Figure 3.2. A sawn-lumber stack.

In the workshop, wood should be stacked on the north side of the room, where there is less direct sunlight and less range in temperature.

The Moisture Content of Wood

By and large, all warpage, expansion, contraction, swelling, and shrinkage in wood is a function of its moisture content, and this can vary considerably depending on the humidity in the air. Lumber with the heart center, the core wood containing the initial annual ring, is the most affected by this. From a single tree, there is only one piece with the heart center; the other pieces cut will suffer less distortion the further they are from the center. The relation of a board to the heart center can be determined by examining its end grain (see Figure 3.3).

BEAM MADE
FROM HEARTWOOD

Figure 3.3. Heartwood.

BEAM MADE
FROM PITH WOOD
(OUTSIDE GRAIN)

Using Heartwood to Advantage

When a board is split in half through the heart center, the two pieces will often bend like a bow (Figure 3.4). This is particularly true in a log which has been partially dried. The sapwood, having a higher moisture content, tends to have a higher rate of contraction than the heartwood. This phenomenon can be used to good advantage in obtaining shaped lumber for curved structures.

Even a badly warped piece, as long as it is not cracked, may be saved for a use which requires a bend or curve. In Japan, wood for braces is often taken from the part of the tree at which a branch meets the trunk. The natural curvature of its grain makes for greater strength in this use.

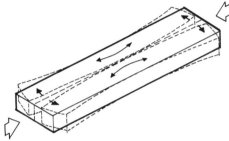

Figure 3.4. Lateral warpage.

Warpage

The most common distortions in lumber are shown in Figure 3.5. The outside-of-the-tree side of a board will tend to become concave, while the inside-of-the-tree side of the board will tend to become convex. In the past (and still somewhat today) this tendency was counteracted by leaving cut logs to soak in the water at the mill for as long as one or two years, during which time the sap and water interact and the sap is removed. Lumber left in water dries more evenly, and is more stable and easier to work. Wood used for cabinetry, sculpture, and furniture, where distortion cannot be permitted, must be properly air dried or kiln dried at low temperature for a long period after soaking to considerably reduce the moisture content.

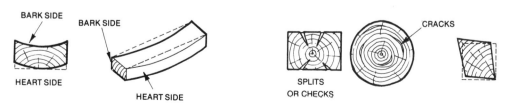

Figure 3.5. Forms of warpage.

Correcting warpage

The concave face of a warped plank (Figure 3.6a) is difficult to plane because the center area is lower than the edges. With thin boards, the warpage can be temporarily corrected by pouring water on the concave face of the board, as shown in Figure 3.6b. The soaked board should then be placed upside down on a flat surface, and in a few minutes the board will be ready for planing. However, never plane a soggy board, since the wet fibers will bind, preventing a smooth finish, and the wetness will damage the plane blade and body.

Warpage in a beam or other larger member can be reduced by cutting a shallow saw kerf along the length of the board on a side which will not be exposed when the building is completed. Small wedges should then be inserted to keep the kerf open. Forces which could result in warping or checking will tend to be absorbed by the kerf.

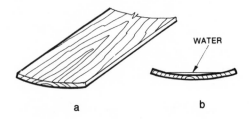

Figure 3.6. Correcting warpage.

Working with warpage in wood

The outsides of floor boards should be placed facing upward, as shown in Figure 3.7. The grain on the outside of the board is finer, its pattern is more pronounced, and it overlaps and will not rise, so that even when the floor is wiped it will not splinter. With use and the passage of time, the force of people walking on a board used in this manner will tend to flatten the warpage without cracking the board.

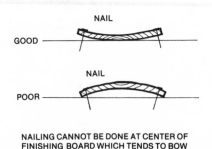

NAILING CANNOT BE DONE AT CENTER OF
FINISHING BOARD WHICH TENDS TO BOW

Figure 3.7. Working with warpage in nailing.

Defects in Wood

The most common defect in wood is the knot—the cross-section of a branch appearing on the board surface. There are two types of knots: dead, where the wood in the knot has dried out more than the surrounding board and will often drop out of the knot hole, and live, where the grain of the knot is simply an imperfection in the grain of the board. If at all possible, they both should be avoided, since knots decrease the strength of the material and contribute to instability and the likelihood of the wood warping. Joints should not be cut in a knot or knot hole. The denser wood of the knot will damage tool blades, and the unstable grain leads to weakness in the joinery.

Other common defects are splits, burls, pitch pockets, and ingrown bark. Their presence should be permitted only where structural soundness and esthetics will not be adversely affected. In some feature boards or detail work, the variable grain of such defects can lend a pleasing appearance to such pieces as paneling or cabinet doors.

Treatment of the Lumber

In traditional construction, wood is used in its natural form. Weathering of exterior boards adds luster to the natural grain and color of the wood. Wood stains or paints are seldom used. If circumstances require it to prevent soil, termite, or other insect damage, as well as dry rot due to moisture, the wood may be treated.

Methods of Treatment

In the course of construction, two methods are used to prevent finished pieces from becoming dirty or discolored.

Oils

After the finishing planing, before the wood can become soiled, it is rubbed with a transparent oil. Any smudges can then be easily wiped off. The oil should be rubbed onto the wood with a cloth wrapped around a cotton ball. Camellia oil, made from the berries of the black camellia bush, is often used for this purpose, as are some oils derived from seaweed. Once the structure is completely assembled, the oil may be washed or wiped off.

Paper or cloth wrapping

In strong sunshine natural woods will burn and their surfaces will discolor. To prevent this, boards for interior use are wrapped with paper or cloth after they have been cut, planed, and chiselled. This wrapper is later removed when construction is completed. In the case of wall members, it is not removed until mud or plaster has been applied.

Wood finishes

In most traditional Japanese structures, paints, varnishes, or other finishes are seldom used, except for some decorative purposes in temples, or occasionally to prevent moisture penetration on, for example, beam ends. Coal tar or creosote may be applied to the base of posts or other footings to resist water damage. One method of finishing sometimes used is scorching with a torch of logs or posts. This seals off the cells of a porous grain and also darkens and highlights the grain pattern.

Termites

Since termites will enter the wood at the cut ends and eat their way up along the pitch, the cut ends should not be set directly on soil or concrete. The ends should be protected as shown in Figure 3.8, wrapped with a metal sheet, or placed on a wood base in such a way that the end grain is not facing the ground. Then, the protected end or base should be set upon a rock or concrete slab, never in soil. In cases where damage is anticipated despite precautions, a short piece may be joined, using a splicing joint (*kanawa tsugi*), to the end of a post. This piece may then be removed and replaced should damage occur.

   Since termite damage will not be visible on the exterior surface, careful inspection is necessary. When a structure is harboring termites, a hollow sound is produced when eaten wood is tapped; in this way the damaged areas can be detected.

   Some species of cedar and cypress have a natural insecticide which discourages termites and other insects from entering the wood.

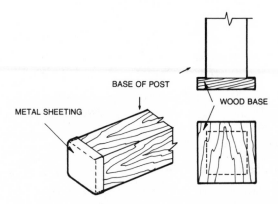

Figure 3.8. Protecting the post from moisture.

Another way to protect lumber is to paint or soak it with creosote, but this process cannot be used in *shiraki zukuri* (natural wood) construction.

Moisture and Ventilation

Where there is considerable moisture, or poor ventilation which will prevent the lumber from drying, rot due to bacteria will develop and gradually weaken the structure. If a waterproofing solution is applied to the base members of the structure up to 3 feet from the ground, this will prevent moisture from entering into the wood.

Other Considerations

The primary source of damage to wood construction is fire. A second problem results from the increased use of stucco as an exterior finish. Stucco serves as an exterior skin which decreases ventilation and causes dry rot. A third cause of damage to wood construction has an economic basis: heart wood is used less frequently in order to reduce construction costs. Lastly, construction work is no longer being done with sufficient care, as it once was.

For reasons such as these, the wooden buildings constructed before World War II had a life expectancy of one hundred years, while those built after the war have an expectancy of only about twenty years. In addition to the practices discussed, with the timely repair of leaks, waterproofing, and regular maintenance, buildings can be cared for to make them last longer.

CHAPTER 4

LAYOUT

Layout refers to drawing on the lumber the cuts that will be made in order to asemble the building. The implements used by Japanese woodworkers for doing layout work are the ink marker (*sumisashi*) and ink container (*sumitsubo*).

Ink Markings (*Sumizuke*)

Ink applied with a bamboo ink marker (*sumisashi*) is preferable to pencil for a number of reasons: it makes a finer, more accurate line; it doesn't get dull nearly as quickly as a pencil; it leaves only a surface mark, rather than penetrating and cutting the wood as a pencil does; and it is highly visible and will not rub off.

The Ink Container (Sumitsubo)

The ink container consists of a pot which holds ink, a long string with which to mark out lines, a wheel on which to rewind the string, ink-saturated balls of raw silk or cotton through which the string is pulled when it is rewound, and a pin or hook at the end of the string for securing it in place (see Figure 4.1). Though these containers may vary slightly in their

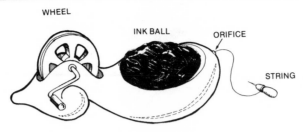

Figure 4.1. *Sumitsubo* (ink container).

shape, depending on personal preference, they are usually made from zelkova wood. The ink ball is made of raw silk or cotton which will not shed, retains moisture for a long time, and will not harden after contact with the ink. Ink stick chips (or ink in a condensed form) are placed in the bottom of the box, and on top of them, fluffy raw silk or cotton balls in two layers. String is placed in between the layers. The string should be one continuously long, strong silk line.* If the ink balls harden, sprinkle some water on them while poking the wad with the pointed end of the bamboo ink marker (*sumisashi*). This will dissolve the ink chip and, at the same time, soak the wad with ink while softening it.

Sumi ink is used, which is indelible once it dries. For marking a surface which will later be exposed, reddish-orange vermillion power or ground charcoal is substituted; these may be washed off after serving their purpose.

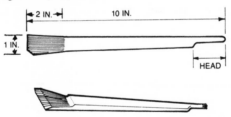

Figure 4.2. *Sumisashi* (ink marker).

The Ink Marker (*Sumisashi*)

The ink marker (Figure 4.2) functions as either pencil or brush. The pointed end is used for marking grid letters, while lines are drawn with the split end. *Sumisashi* are made from dried bamboo stalks cut into 10 inch lengths, and widths of about one inch, then shaped until they are comfortable to hold. Next, the bamboo is soaked in water until it is saturated, at which time it is split. The interior surface, which is pithy and soft, is removed. (With bamboo, the absolute exterior is the hardest.) The line-drawing end is split with a chisel (*hira nomi*) or razor at intervals of 1/16 to 1/32 inch, to a depth of about 2 inches (Figure 4.3). Then, it is tapered to a sharp edge, using a chisel. The head has a final width of about 2 inches. The tip is pounded with a hammer to form bristles like a brush, as shown in Figure 4.4.

*To get a superfine line, Dacron® sail thread is ideal.

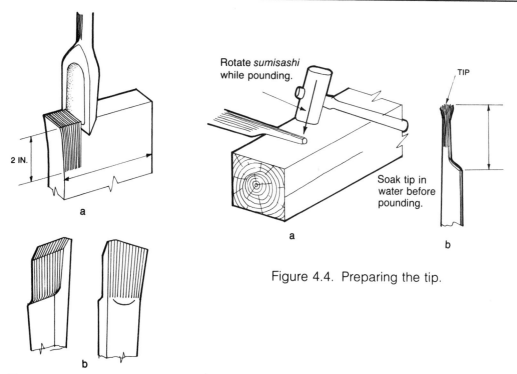

Figure 4.4. Preparing the tip.

Figure 4.3. Splitting the line-drawing end.

The lines and markings are made by using the stick in the manner shown in Figure 4.5. The line-drawing end is charged with ink by dipping it into an inkpot; the splits retain ink. It is then used in much the same fashion as a quill pen. A mark is made by starting away from the body and pulling the *sumisashi* towards you. The drawing edge will blunt with use; it may be resharpened using a chisel.

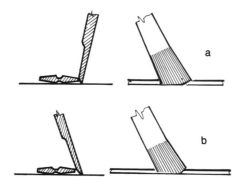

Figure 4.5. Drawing lines with the *sumisashi*.

Using the ink line and container (*sumitsubo*)

The wood should always be marked with a center line, which is then used as the reference from which measurements are taken. This practice is essential when using logs. The ink line and container (*sumitsubo*) is used for this, as shown in Figure 4.6a. First the hook or pin is stuck into the center of one end of the timber. Then the string, soaked with ink, is pulled to the center of the other end. The string is pulled taut and held as far away from the pin as the arm can comfortably reach (see Figure 4.6b). It is pulled upward 2–4 inches then released so that the inked string hits the surface of the board, marking it with a clear line. Care should be taken to maintain the proper consistency in the ink, so that it is fluid enough to leave a mark, but not so liquid as to drip or spray when the string is snapped.

Figure 4.6. Marking a line with the *sumitsubo*.

To mark a line perpendicular to the center line, place a carpenter's square on it, as in Figure 4.7. If the center line needs to be extended onto the end or opposite side of the timber, use two carpenter's squares (as in Figure 4.8).

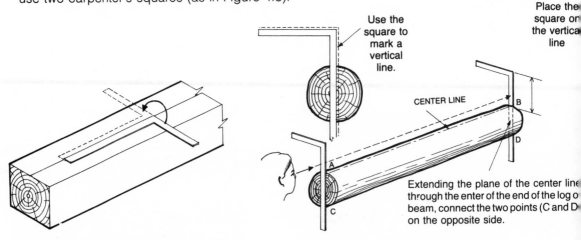

Use the square to mark a vertical line.

Place the square on the vertical line

CENTER LINE

B

D

A

C

Extending the plane of the center line through the center of the end of the log or beam, connect the two points (C and D) on the opposite side.

Figure 4.7. Taking measurements from the center line.

Figure 4.8. Squaring the ends.

Suggestions for marking oblique lines

When drawing oblique lines for the *tsugite* (end joints) and the *shiguchi* (right angle joints), if the degree of obliqueness is kept constant throughout, fewer mistakes will be made when drawing out the male and female joint parts. Figures 4.9 and 4.10 give examples of the oblique lines for dovetail, gooseneck, and other joints using the width on the carpenter's square scale. The carpenter's square is 5 *bu* wide, which corresponds to a 15 mm mortising chisel.

As illustrated below, the reference point set in making a joint has to be changed in relation to the type of joint, but if the width of the carpenter's square is used as a constant, or as a unit by using its multiples, the work becomes simpler. The slope angle of the joint will vary according to use (1 in 5 or 1 in 8 is common for a dovetail). Using reference points and the constant width of the carpenter's square allows the angle to be more easily replicated on both the male and the female pieces.

The *sumi* line (guide line) also serves as a finishing line, therefore the work must be done in such a way as to leave a faint line, which may then be finish-planed away. The method for assembling connecting members must also be considered. Very great skill is required to assemble pieces in such a way that initially loose connections end up as a tight and secure unit.

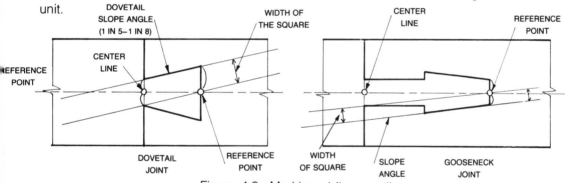

Figure 4.9. Marking oblique cutlines.

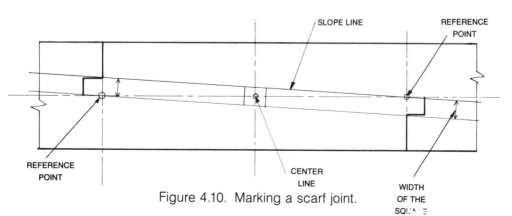

Figure 4.10. Marking a scarf joint.

Board drawings

Blueprints are inconvenient at a job site because they tear easily and are damaged by wind and rain. For this reason, board drawings are used. These are ink drawings showing the predominant structural aspects of a house (usually the floor plan), on thin plywood or other similar board. Ordinarily, floor plans and structural plans are simply drawn, and grids with numbers and letters are assigned, as shown in Figure 4.11.

The grid letters and numbers identify the location and directional orientation of structural members such as posts, beams, girders, and footings. Starting at the bottom left corner of the floor plan, letters (A), (B), (C) . . . up and numbers (1), (2), (3) . . . across, are assigned to the grid, with the side with the entry way closest to the viewer. With these symbols, a column located at the intersection of grid lines C and 3 can be identified as column C3. Each grid marking is spaced to represent intervals of 3 feet.

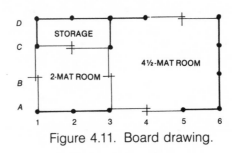

Figure 4.11. Board drawing.

Taking post C3 as an example, further attributes of this post can be delineated. Of the four surfaces of the post, the surface facing the bottom of the drawing, and entry way, is called the *banzukemen,* and is the face upon which grid identification C3 is marked. Since this surface faces the opening between a 4½-mat and a 2-mat room, both lintel and lower track must be attached. Also the surface 90 degrees to the *banzukemen* on the left, will accept more lintels and lower tracks, since it faces the opening to the storage space. The face 90 degrees to the *banzukemen* on the right, will be facing the 4½-mat room. The surface opposite the *banzukemen* will butt a wall, so holes for ties must be provided. A drawing of the four surfaces of the post will be similar to Figure 4.12. Using grid identification, structural members can be located and identified, and the function of each of its surfaces ascertained.

To avoid confusion in the case of buildings with multiple floors, the floor number is marked on the bottom left side, thus 2F3.

Horizontal structural members such as beams and girders are marked in a similar fashion. A beam running up and down the board drawing will be marked vertically, as in Figure 4.13. There, the beam spans between posts A3 and D3. In the same way, a beam running across the drawing will be marked horizontally, as in Figure 4.14, where the beam spans between posts A1 and A6.

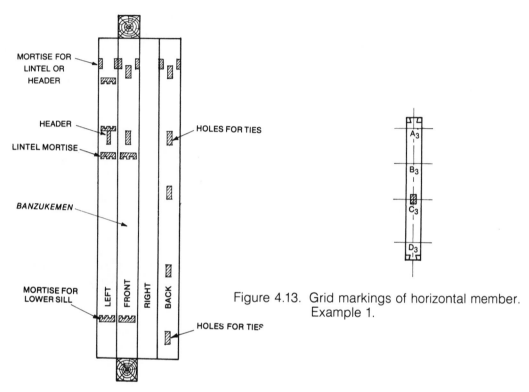

Figure 4.13. Grid markings of horizontal member. Example 1.

Figure 4.12. The four surfaces of a post.

Figure 4.14. Grid markings of horizontal member. Example 2.

A Japanese carpenter's tools, arrayed for use.

CHAPTER 5

WORKING THE WOOD

Good work cannot be produced unless the work is enjoyable; making a thing should bring pleasure, not pain. The work must never be rushed to completion, but done with care and patience. Above all, one should truly enjoy one's work. It is also important to remember that wood is a living thing—one must understand its properties and not oppose them. Whenever work is forced, it either ruins the piece, damages the tools, or injures the worker, so work must always be done with the utmost care.

Sawing

In this section, sawing method will be explained.

Japanese saws are made to cut when pulled. The pushing is done without force, but force is applied in pulling the saw. Good sawing requires a consistent rhythm in these forward and backward movements.

If a work bench is to be used, it should be at about hip height. Otherwise, saw horses are placed on the ground and the materials are sawed on them.

Figure 5.1. Preparing to saw.

Sawing posture

(1) As shown in Figure 5.1, the piece to be cut is steadied by the left hand, and the cut line it-self is set in front of the right hand. When sawing small pieces a work table is used, while larger pieces such as framing members are cut on saw horses. Thus the height at which the lumber is cut will vary, but the pulling force is more easily applied at a lower position. When using a saw on a work table, the wood is held firmly in place with the left hand, and the saw is pulled with the right hand. Large pieces are cut by securing them with the left foot and pull-ing the saw with both hands.

(2) In one-handed sawing, the grip is such that force is applied using the thumb of the right hand on top of the handle, aligned with the direction of the cut, while the forefinger acts as a fulcrum underneath. The other fingers stabilize the saw, using a light grip. (For left-handed people, this is reversed.)

With larger saws, both hands are used. The right hand firmly grips the saw's handle near its butt, while the left hand clasps the handle lightly near the neck (see Figure 5.2). While pulling, force is applied with the right hand; while pushing, the force is decreased. Little force is required in comparison to using a Western saw, since the weight of the saw blade, which is wider and heavier near the tip, assists the cut. If sawing is done in this manner, there will be less damage to the saw teeth, less fatigue, and the cut will be more accurate. Figure 5.3 and 5.4 show the correct stance for cutting a larger piece with a rip and crosscut saw.

Figure 5.2. Holding the saw.

Figure 5.3. Correct position for crosscutting.

Figure 5.4. Correct position for rip cutting.

With smaller saws, only one hand, the right for right-handed people, is used. The grip for one-handed sawing is adjusted to balance the saw relative to the thickness of the piece being cut. When cutting a smaller piece, the handle is gripped nearer to the blade for more control. With a larger piece, the grip is farther back on the handle and the stroke is longer.

Figure 5.5. Starting to saw.

Sawing procedure

Hikikomi----hikikata----hikiowari
Starting----continuing----finishing

When starting to saw (especially with a rip saw) the first cut is difficult to make at the exact location desired, because the saw tends to get caught in the lumber. To make the first incision at the desired location, place the thumb next to it, bend the thumb, placing the saw against the thumb joint and its teeth at the desired location, as shown in Figure 5.5. Begin by making small sawing movements while the saw remains against the thumb. This procedure for making the initial cut is called *hikikomi*. *Hikikata* is the term which describes the main actions of sawing. As described above, continue to saw with care and consistency, using the *honba* (teeth near the handle).

Hikiowari describes the correct manner of sawing when nearing the end of the cut. If *hikikata* were continued until the end, the wood being cut would break, splitting the end of the piece, or else the force applied would become uncontrollable, carrying the saw into the saw horse, into the ground, or into one's clothes. Instead, when nearing the end of the cut, it is important to slow down the sawing, holding the piece being severed with one hand, and continuing to saw gently until the cut is completed.

When cutting through a piece, after a shallow cut has been made on the first side, rotate the piece away from you and continue cutting. The saw cut always advances toward you. Continuing this procedure until the piece is cut through allows a clean cut to be made, without splintering. Unlike Western sawing procedure, the piece is supported on both sides of the cut, whether on a bench or on saw horses, so that the cut end will not fall, risking tearing.

Suggestions for sawing

(1) At times sawing becomes difficult because when the saw is cutting into the wood it goes further in than half the depth of the saw. This occurs most frequently when cutting wood with irregular grain (*atezai*). Before cutting, the grain is in a balanced condition, but when such wood is cut, the grain is severed, and the side with fibers having more force presses against the saw. This phenomenon, where sawing becomes laborious, is called *tsuru*. When sawing wood that is thicker than the width of the saw, cutting becomes very difficult, especially when ripsawing. At such times, pound a wedge into the mouth of the incision to hold the cut open for easier sawing (see Figure 5.6). When ripping longer boards, it is advisable to tilt the board slightly, with the end away from you elevated. In this way, gravity and the taper of the blade aid the cut of the saw more directly, pulling the teeth against the wood to be cut. Always advance the cut you are making toward you, never away from you, where you cannot see it. Control of the saw cut is most effective when the blade is tensioned and the cut guided by the pull toward you.

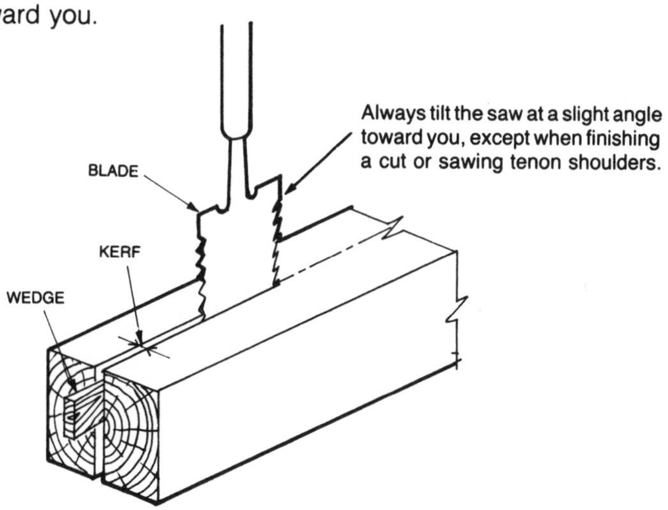

Figure 5.6. Rip sawing.

(2) When sawing a piece thicker than 4 inches or longer than 4 inches, it must be cut from both top and bottom surfaces in order to be cut squarely and under control. This is to take into account the worker's left or right side bias, and to compensate for any incorrectly set teeth, both of which will cause inaccurate cutting. When selecting a crosscut saw to cut a particular board, a general rule is to not cut a board which is thicker than half the length of the saw blade. This allows for a longer, more controlled stroke.

Planing

Whether a carpenter can do a good job of planing or not can largely depend on the quality of the board being planed. To plane well, all conditions, including the sharpness of the blade, proper height of support, and the others mentioned previously must be satisfied. Since the care of the blade and body have already been discussed, only the planing itself is explained here.

SUE OR *SUEGUCHI*
(TIP)

MOTO
(BUTT)

Figure 5.7. The ends of the tree.

Working with different types of wood

In order to plane properly, the characteristics of the wood must first be known. Even with a top quality plane the planing cannot be done successfully without first determining if the surface to be planed is the front or back side, or whether it is an *atezai*. The difference between a professional and an amateur is the ability to distinguish between them.

The *kiura* (back) and *kiomote* (front) sides are shown in the drawings below. The base of the tree is called *moto* (butt), and the top of the tree is called *sue* or *sueguchi* (tip) (see Figure 5.7). When squared lumber is cut from a log (see Figure 5.8), the side closer to the *zaishin* (pith) is the *kiura* (back side), and the side further away from it is the *kiomote* (front side). On carefully inspecting the grains on the front side they are seen to run up from the

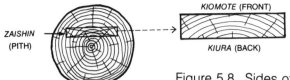

ZAISHIN (PITH)

KIOMOTE (FRONT)

KIURA (BACK)

Figure 5.8. Sides of the board.

butt end to the tip. Examination of the overlapping grains shows that they grow outward as they overlap the pith. On the back side the grain runs in the opposite direction, from the outside towards the center, with the grain closest to the center at the very top. The direction of planing is determined by these conditions. The planing directions are called either *oime* or *sakame*. The *kiomote* (front side) of a board should be planed from the tip to the butt, and the back side should be planed from the butt to the tip. This is called *oime* planing (Figure 5.9), while planing in the opposite (wrong) direction is called *sakame* (Figure 5.10). When wood is planed in the *sakame* direction, the plane blade cuts into the grain and gouges out bits of the surface. The surface can never be planed smoothly in this way. To correct such a surface, the *kasaneba* (chipper blade) mentioned above, has to be used.

Planing should be in the *oime* direction, but there remains the problem of knots. Knots are cross-sections of branches and are always present in lumber with pith. The grains around the knot run in different directions and thus the direction of planing becomes inconsistent. At such times, the planing direction will have to become *sakame*. Furthermore, since knots grow towards the tip, the planing of knots must be done towards the tip as well. This type of planing is called *oifushi*.

When a hard knot is planed with *sakame,* the cutter's edge may chip. Since the direction of the plane cannot be changed at each knot, the blade should be exposed as little as possible, with the tightest throat opening possible, and a chipper blade should be used. Always plane carefully and tenaciously at knots.

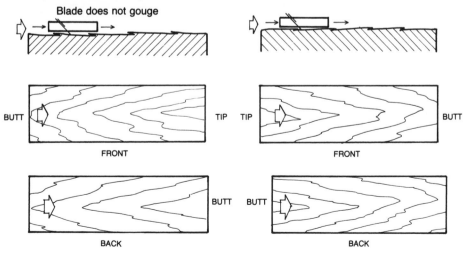

Figure 5.9. Planing *oime* (correct).   Figure 5.10. Planing *sakame* (wrong).

Body movements in planing

(See Chapter 2 for methods
of setting the plane blade.)

(a) CORRECT POSITION

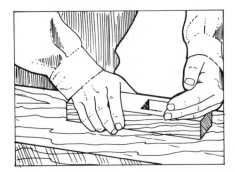

Figure 5.11. Correct way to hold the plane.

(b) BEGINNING PLANING

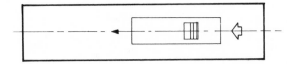

Figure 5.13. Direction of the planing stroke.

(c) END OF PLANING

Figure 5.12. Planing sequence.

As shown in Figure 5.11, the head of the cutter is held very gently with the left hand cupped against it, while the body of the plane is grasped firmly with the right hand about half-way between the butt end of the body and the cutter. Next, as shown in Figure 5.12, put the weight of your body on the left leg and stretch forward. With both arms stretched well forward, but remaining well balanced and under control, pull the plane back, at the same time extending the right leg straight back and transferring your weight onto the right leg—all in one motion. A piece is planed by repeating this movement and stepping back until the end is reached. Most important is to keep the plane always basically parallel to the piece being planed and to apply pressure consistently throughout the length to be planed (see Figure 5.13). Some carpenters hold the plane at an angle to the wood. Though pulling becomes easier due to the decreased friction between plane stock and surface, the work is made more difficult later while using the finishing plane, when the surface cannot be planed absolutely flat. When the material requires only rough finishing, the plane may be held at an angle, but this is not a good practice.

When planing a wide piece, move the plane towards you after each movement. After the whole width has been planed, start over again from the side away from you, after stepping back, as shown in Figure 5.14. The final pass should be one continuous stroke.

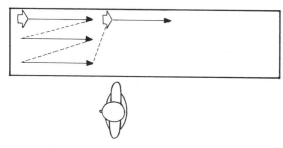

Figure 5.14. Planing a wide board.

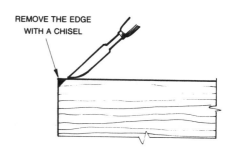

REMOVE THE EDGE WITH A CHISEL

Figure 5.15. Preparing the board end.

Before starting to plane, shave the end of the piece with a chisel, as shown in Figure 5.15, to remove any sand or particles which may cause the plane blade to chip. To plane knots with sap or with a sheen, soak the board in water for about 3 to 5 minutes to soften, because such a board surface consists of fibers running in different directions which will cause the blade to chip. One must work hard to plane such boards flat. After planing in this fashion, dry your tool, to prevent rusting of the blade or warpage of the block.

To plane producing shavings of a constant width which match the width of the cutter, and which are of continuous length from the beginning to the end of the cut, is considered a sign of the highest skill in planing.

At the end of the work always recess the blade into the body of the plane, and lay the plane on its side—not on its sole.

Chiseling

Uchikomi—striking the chisel

When using a chisel, start sitting on the piece being chiseled so that it will be on your left, and hold the chisel in the left hand and a hammer in the right, as shown in Figure 5.16. Alternate your position frequently while you work to balance the tension in your back muscles. This will allow you to work longer, more comfortably and with more control. The chisel should be held gently just below the crown, and the hammer should be held lightly near the end of the handle. In striking, apply the force while watching both the blade edge and the crown. Strike the end of the chisel with the head of the hammer flat, so that force is applied in a straight line. When swinging the hammer up, make sure that no one is nearby. Below are listed the essentials of chiseling:

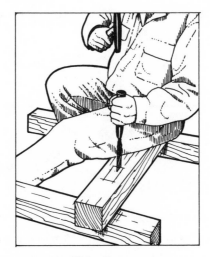

Figure 5.16. Chiseling posture.

(1) When striking parallel to the wood grain, there will be a tendency for splitting to occur along the fibers. For this reason the chisel should not be struck hard (see Figure 5.17).

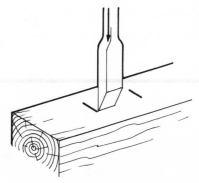
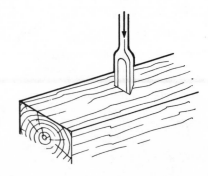

Figure 5.17. Striking parallel to the wood grain.   Figure 5.18. Striking across the grain.

(2) When striking across the grain, strike hard (see Figure 5.18).

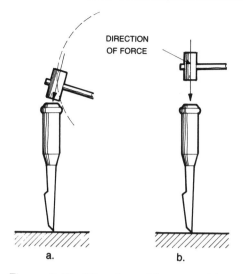

DIRECTION
OF FORCE

a.

b.

Figure 5.19. Direction of hammer blow.

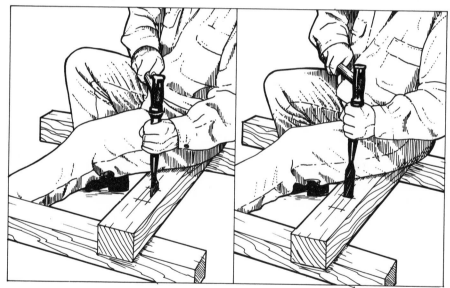

Figure 5.20. Striking parallel
to the grain.

Figure 5.21. Striking perpendicular
to the grain.

(3) When hitting the chisel, strike the crown straight and follow the steps shown in Figures 5.19 to 5.21.

(4) If the area to be chiseled has a knot, do not try to remove it with a hard blow since this will chip the blade's edge. It should be chiseled out in small pieces, as shown in Figure 5.22.

(5) When the chisel is struck, it moves backwards as shown in Figure 5.23. This is due to the wedge shape of the back of the blade. Except when finish chiseling a hole, the chisel's front face should be placed near the edge of the hole to be chiseled out.

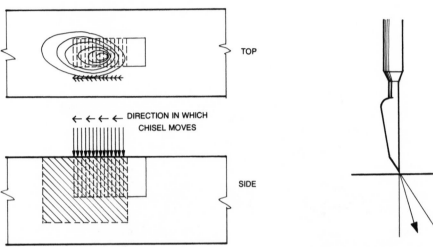

TOP

DIRECTION IN WHICH
CHISEL MOVES

SIDE

Figure 5.22. Chiseling around a knot.

Figure 5.23. Chisel movement when struck.

(6) Chiseling should be completed right up to the drawn line (leaving a thin line on the wood). Those allows small adjustments for clean up and fit.

Chiseling procedures

(1) Wood fibers are severed just inside the cut line using the *usunomi* (thin chisel), as shown in Figure 5.24 (1).

(2) Next, repeat procedures (2) through (8) of Figure 5.24. At the end, strike the chisel in to remove the remaining piece as shown in Figure 5.24(9).

(3) Using the *usunomi*, carve the hole out squarely, leaving the cut line on the piece as shown in Figure 5.24(8). Take special care as to the amount of cut line to remove since this will affect the fit of the connection when the members are assembled.

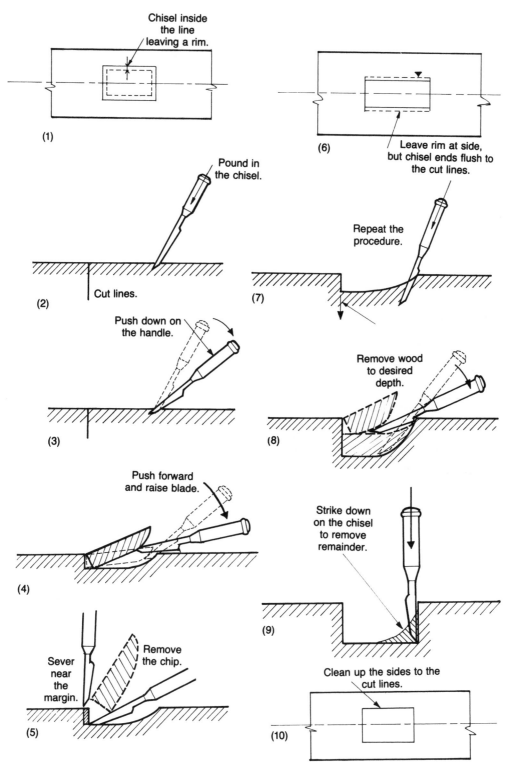

Figure 5.24. Chiseling a mortise.

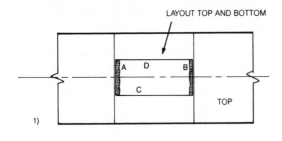

LAYOUT TOP AND BOTTOM

A   D   B

C

TOP

1)

Alternative mortising technique

A + B are STOP CUTS across end grain just inside layout 1/16″– 1/8″ deep. C + D are score lines along grain direction

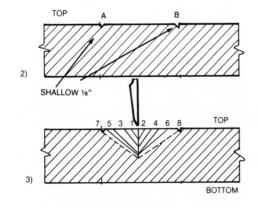

TOP   A   B

2)

SHALLOW ⅛″

ALL STOP CUTS made to control and limit wood removal to mortise layout.

7 5 3 1 2 4 6 8   TOP

3)

BOTTOM

Start cuts at center of mortise layout taking out a chip (⅛″) moving from center cut alternating sides till hole is ½ depth from top surface.

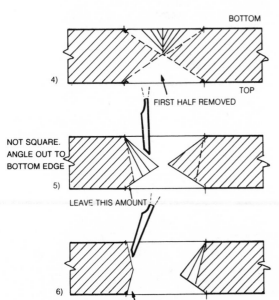

BOTTOM

4)

FIRST HALF REMOVED

TOP

Turn piece over and repeat same procedure until a hole is through from bottom to top in center of mortise.

NOT SQUARE. ANGLE OUT TO BOTTOM EDGE

5)

LEAVE THIS AMOUNT

Start at tip towards center of mortise and cut off at angle until top edge is flush and surface is angled towards bottom. Turn board over and repeat procedure.

6)

At this point top and bottom of mortise should be flush to lay out line, with any bulge only at center. Clean up this inside face from top to bottom so this is flat. Clean up all surfaces to be flush to layout lines; this procedure is similar to digging a hole with a shovel. Start digging in the middle and work to edge enlarging hole—not from outside in to middle.

In case mortise is not square through board, this technique is more reliable and consistent method to produce accurate and efficient mortising.

*All mortising should be done with angled side of chisel against shoulder to be cut. Flat side chisel (with hollow grind) is used for paring and clean up only.

To measure the depth of a hole that has been chiseled, insert a chisel or small stick perpendicularly into the hole. Locate the top of the hole on the stick with the fingers and remove the stick from the hole. Then measure the depth with a ruler. When chiseling a hole right through a board, roughly chisel to about half the depth then chisel from the other side. When the hole has been made, a square or a similar tool is used to check the verticality and smoothness of the cut surface, as shown in Figure 5.25. Then the hole is squared and smoothed to finish it.

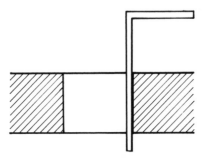

Figure 5.25. Checking squareness of a hole.

Another practical method for making holes is to use a brace or gimlet as shown in Figure 5.26. By roughly boring a hole of the required size and depth with a brace or gimlet, and then squaring and finishing it with a chisel, a hole can be made quite easily.

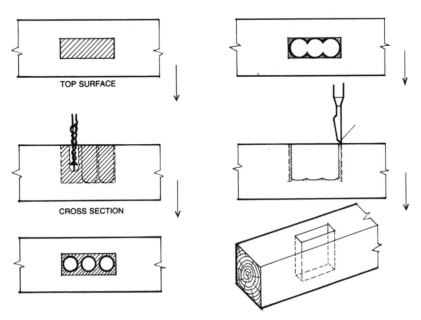

Figure 5.26. Boring holes to ease chiseling.

Hatsuri—Chipping

Hatsuri is the method used for removing a thick piece of wood by chipping most of it out. In modern times, due to lumber mills producing completed pieces, *hatsuri* work has become limited to special construction and log work. But as *hatsuri* work is also done when correcting warpage and other distortions, a basic explanation is provided. In *hatsuri* work, a *chona* (adze) and an *ono* (hatchet) are generally used (Figures 5.27 and 5.29).

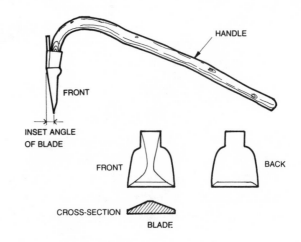

Figure 5.27. *Chona* (adze).

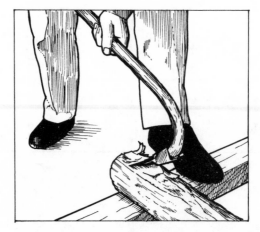

Figure 5.28. Chipping with an adze.

Chona—adze

An adze is used to trim and shape surfaces, such as in carving out a portion of a post surface, making a flat surface on a log, providing a flat area on a *koya bari* (roof beam) for the *koya tsuka* (end post), for end joint surfaces on a *nagekake bari* (beam), and for V-slanted connecting surfaces of joints such as the *daimochi tsugi, shippasami tsugi,* and *okkake daisen tsugi.* The adze is worked while securing the lumber with the left foot, with the toes extended beyond the piece as shown in Figure 5.28, and striking with the blade at a slight angle and in front, instead of straight into the material. This requires tremendous skill and is difficult to do unless one has quite a lot of experience. The shavings or chips are called *koppa.* Thin and long *koppa* rather than thick ones indicate the skillfulness of the carpenter.

Since there are only a few widely scattered people who can do good *hatsuri* work, much of this kind of work is done with a chisel imitating the finishing work of an adze.

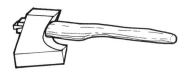

Figure 5.29. *Ono* (hatchet)

Ono—hatchet

The hatchet is used to split wood. This is easily achieved by striking a piece and relying on its characteristic of splitting when it is struck parallel to the grain. The hatchet is also used to sharpen the ends of pegs, to trim the corners of squared pieces, and to shape logs.

Woodworking Procedures

The pieces are shaped in the following sequences:
(1) Select manufactured square lumber.

(2) Place a level at each end of the piece, as shown in Figure 5.30, then look at the tops of the levels to see if they align. If they do not align, the wood is warped. In this case, plane it, removing the warp difference gradually, until the piece is flat. Next, using the *sumitsubo,* mark a length of 4 inches from each end of the piece.

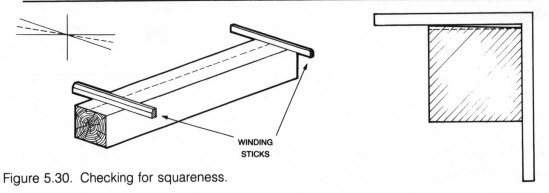

Figure 5.30. Checking for squareness.

Figure 5.31. Using carpenter's square to check squareness

(3) Plane one surface at each end up to the line marked. Place a carpenter's square on the planed surface as shown in Figure 5.31 to check for squareness. Repeat this procedure until each of the four surfaces at both ends has been planed, checking with the square until the piece has been squared.

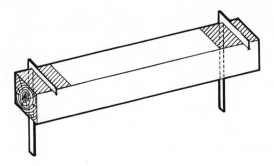

Figure 5.32. Make a squared surface at each end to be used as a reference.

(4) After the end surfaces are squared, using the ink line mark a line between the two squares on both sides of the piece, as shown in Figure 5.32. Plane the surface up to the lines to make one side of the piece completely square. Repeat this procedure until all sides have been squared.

(5) The piece is now prepared for joinery.

Commonly Used Joints

A description of simple and commonly used end joints and right angle joints follows.

The *tsugite* (end joint) is used to extend a piece in its axial direction. Some of the common end joints are *inro tsugi* (half blind mortise and tenon), *koshikake tsugi* (lapped joint), *sogi tsugi* (scarf joint), *ari tsugi* (dovetail joint), *kama tsugi* (gooseneck joint), and *okkake daisen tsugi* (dadoed and rabbetted scarf joint).

Shiguchi are joints which change the direction of axis (right angle joints). Some examples are *ari shiguchi aigaki, watari ago* (dadoed cross lap joint) and *hozo sashi* (mortise and tenon joint).

On single story residences, the end joints most commonly used on mudsills and beams are *koshikake ari tsugi* and *koshikake kama tsugi*.

Below, end joints and right angle joints for mudsills and beams are explained in the order of construction procedures:

(1) *Koshikake kama tsugi* (lapped gooseneck joint): An end joint used on mudsills, *obiki* beams, *moya* beams, and on other simple members.

(2) *Koshikake ari tsugi* (lapped dovetail joint): This end joint is used on larger members.

(3) *Kanawa tsugi* (blind dadoed and rabbetted and keyed scarf joint): An end joint used on girders and at the base of columns.

(4) *Kabuto ari* (end lap joint with dovetail joint): A right angle joint used on various types of beams, including *do sashi* beams and mudsills.

(5) *Eriwa kone hozo sashi wari kusabi uchi* (collared haunch mortise and tenon joint with a wedge): A right angle joint for the outside corners of a mudsill.

(6) *Sumidome hozo sashi:* A right angle joint used in the same way as the one above, except that it is of higher quality.

Sumizuke for and making of end joints

(1) *Koshikake kama Tsugi*—Lapped Gooseneck Joint

(i) *Sumizuke*

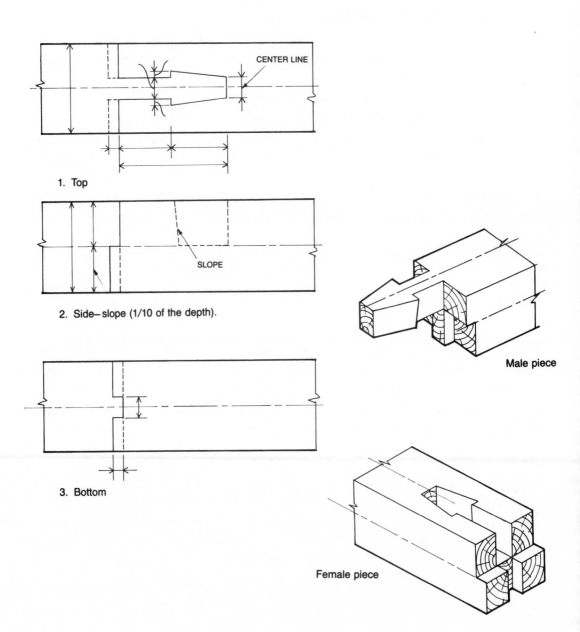

CENTER LINE

1. Top

SLOPE

2. Side–slope (1/10 of the depth).

3. Bottom

Male piece

Female piece

(ii) Procedure for making the male piece

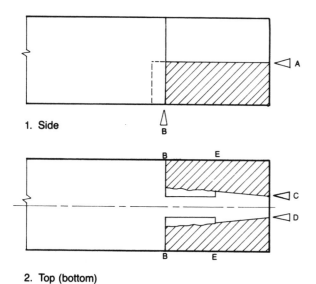

1. Side

2. Top (bottom)

First, draw the shape or cut lines.

(1) With a rip saw, cut along line A to intersect line B.

(2) With a rip saw, cut along lines C and D to intersect line B.

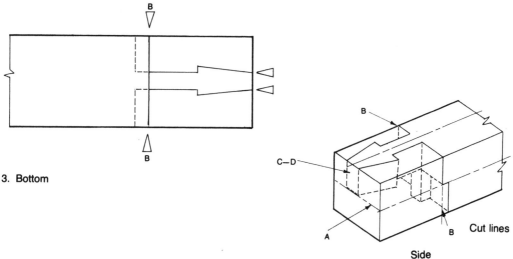

3. Bottom

Side

(3) With a crosscut saw, cut along line B on bottom to intersect line A.

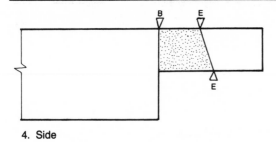

4. Side

(4) Saw from each side to the neck of the male piece along lines B and E with a crosscut saw.

(5) Insert a chisel into the kerf made in (4) and remove the diagonally marked portion.

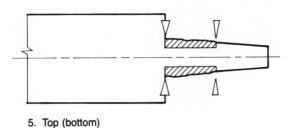

5. Top (bottom)

(6) Make kerfs with a rip saw along lines F and G and with a crosscut saw along line H.

The last step is to remove the diagonally marked portion with a chisel.

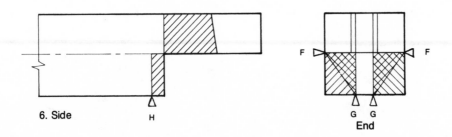

6. Side   H

G   G
End

(iii) Procedure for making the female piece

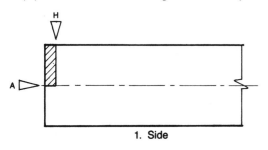

1. Side

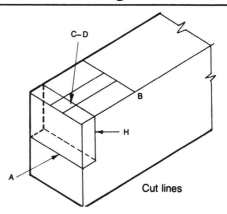

Cut lines

First draw the cut lines.

(1) With a rip saw, cut along line A to line H.

(2) Cut with a crosscut saw along line H and remove shaded portion.

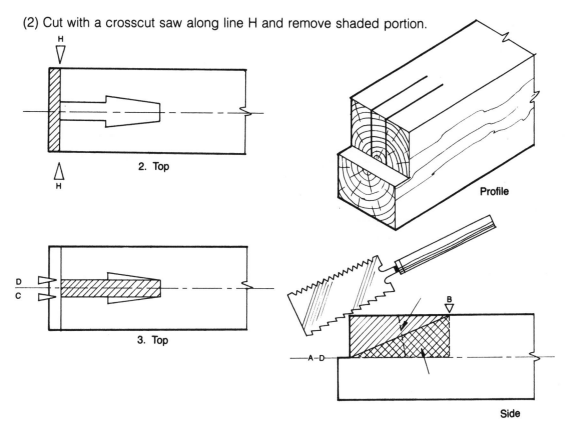

2. Top

Profile

3. Top

Side

(3) Along lines C and D make kerfs with a rip saw from line B to line A.
Chisel out diagonally marked section between lines C and D.

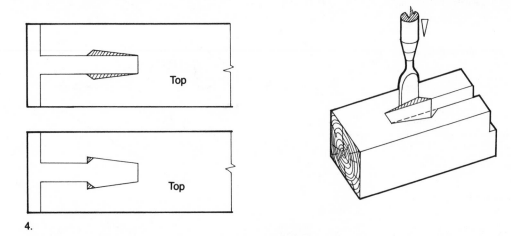

4.

(4) Chisel off the shaded portion by repeatedly carving
out. Remember to allow for the slope on the tenon.

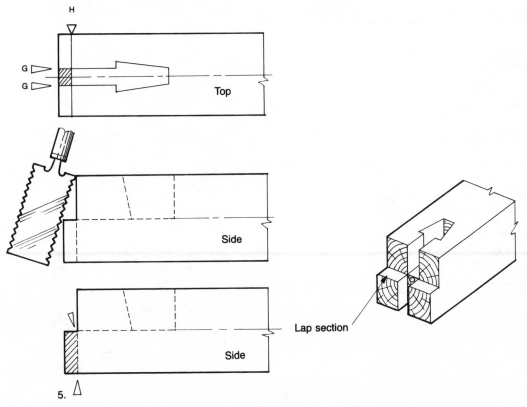

5.

(5) With a rip saw, cut in from the end along lines G to intersect with line H. Finally, chisel out
between these two cuts.

(2) *Koshikake Ari Tsugi*—Lapped Dovetail Joint

(i) *Sumizuke*

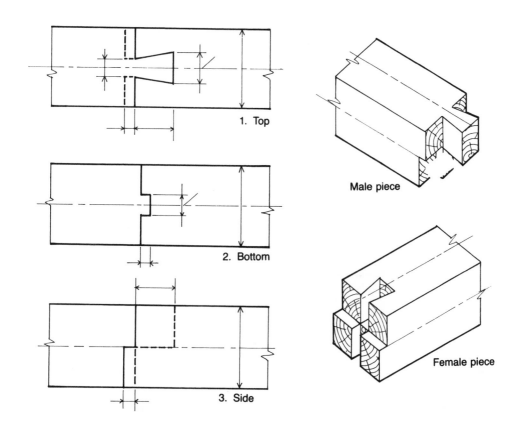

1. Top

2. Bottom

3. Side

Male piece

Female piece

(ii) Procedure for making the male piece

First, draw the cut lines.

(1) Make kerfs with a rip saw: along line A to intersect line B; along lines C and D to intersect line B.

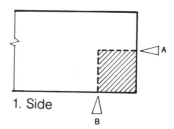

1. Side

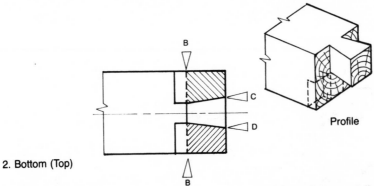

2. Bottom (Top)

(2) Cut along line B with a crosscut saw: on either side to intersect lines C and D; on bottom to intersect line A.

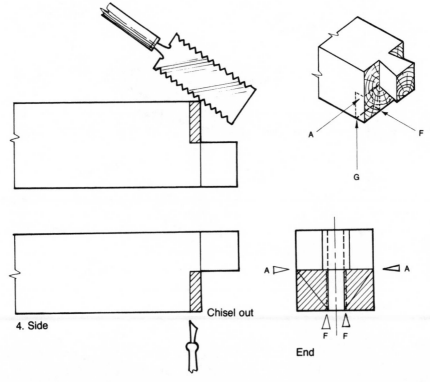

4. Side

Chisel out

End

(3) Make kerfs with a rip saw along lines A and F to line G, on both sides of the dovetail. With a crosscut saw, make kerfs on both sides along line G to intersect lines A and F.

(4) Chisel out the diagonally marked section on both sides between lines A and F until the haunch is squared.

(ii) Procedure for making the male piece

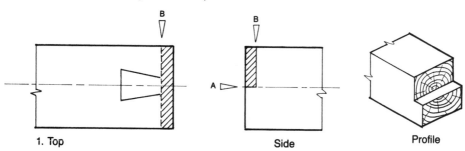

1. Top   Side   Profile

First, draw the cut lines.

(1) Cut with a rip saw along line A to intersect line B.
     Cut with a crosscut saw along line B to intersect line A.

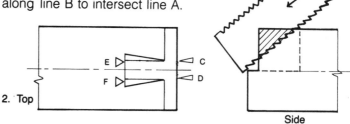

2. Top   Side

(2) Make rip saw kerfs from C–E and D–F.

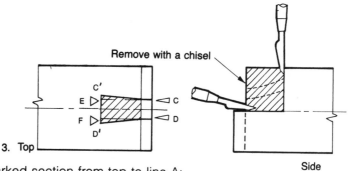

Remove with a chisel

3. Top   Side

(3) Chisel out diagonally marked section from top to line A:
     first, the area between E–C and F–D;
     then, finish to C′–C and D′–D.

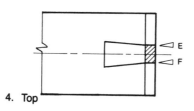

4. Top

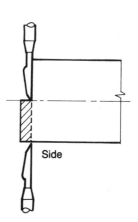

Side

(4) Make a rip saw kerf along lines E and F.
     Chisel off this portion.

(3) *Kanawa Tsugi*—Blind dadoed, rabbetted and keyed scarf joint.
In this joint, the two joined ends are identical.

(i) *Sumizuke*

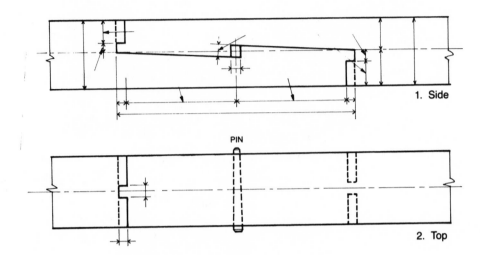

1. Side

PIN

2. Top

A pin is used to lock the two finished pieces together.
Or, two wedges may be used, giving greater play for
tightening and adjusting.

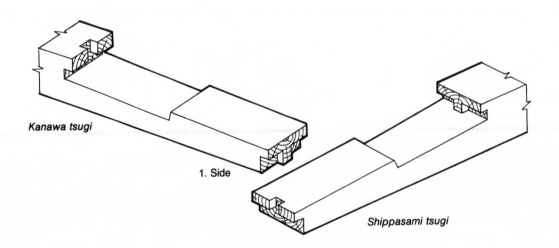

Kanawa tsugi

1. Side

Shippasami tsugi

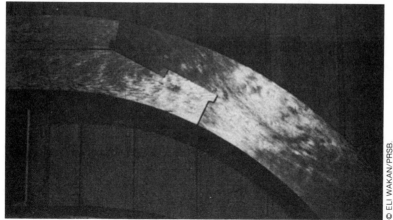

A variant of the *kanawa tsugi*.

(ii) Procedure

First, draw the cut lines.

(1) Make a ripsaw kerf along line A, at the proper angle, to intersect line B.

(2) With a crosscut saw, cut down along lines B and C to intersect line D.

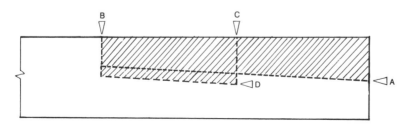

(3) Chisel out diagonally marked portion from C to B. Then make a rip saw kerf at E and finish chiselling out the notch to line F.

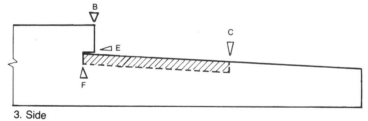

3. Side

(4) Make a sloping kerf with a rip saw on both sides: along line G to intersect lines H and I; along line I to intersect lines G and H. Chip away with a chisel the diagonally marked section.

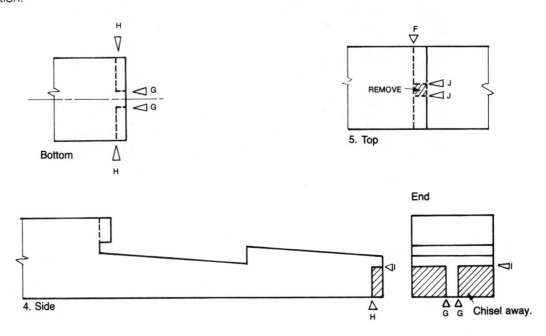

(5) Make a rip saw kerf along lines J to intersect line F. Chisel out the diagonally marked section.

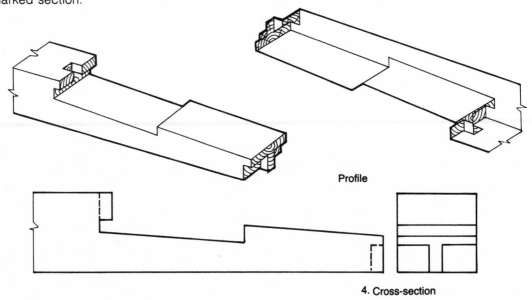

Sumizuke for and making of right angle joints

(1) *Kabuto ari*—End lap joint with dovetail joint.

   (i) *Sumizuke*

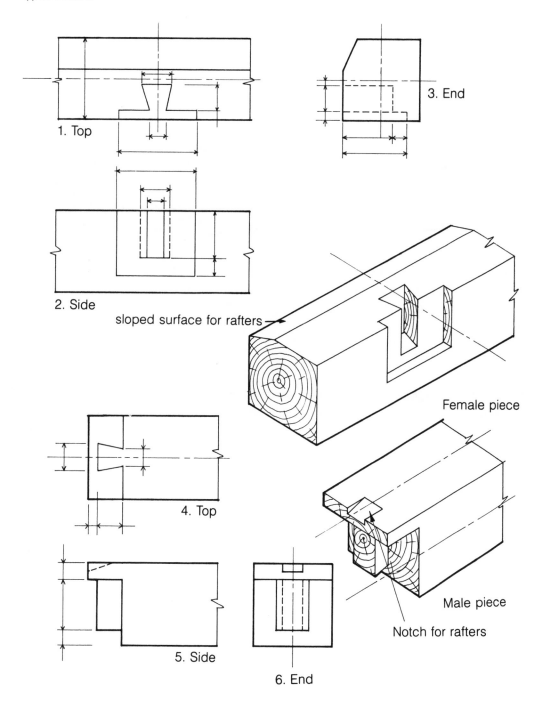

1. Top

2. Side

3. End

sloped surface for rafters

Female piece

4. Top

5. Side

6. End

Male piece

Notch for rafters

(ii) Procedure for making the female piece
Draw the cut lines first.

(1) Make a shallow, angled crosscut saw kerf at A and B to intersect lines D and E. Make an incision with a chisel between A–C and B–C on the inside of the cut line, and chip away until this area is square and flush to line D.

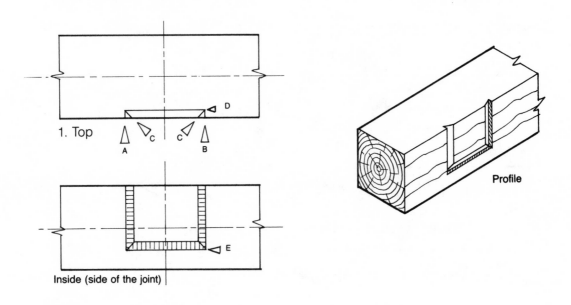

(2) With a rip saw, make angled kerfs at G to intersect lines F and H. Chisel out the diagonally marked section.

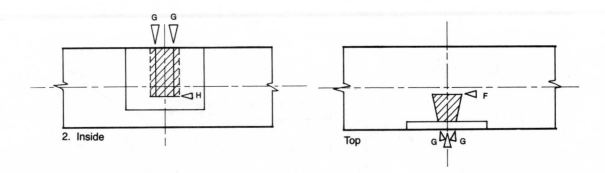

(3) Plane a sloping surface for the *kuchiwaki* (rafter slope cut into the outer edge) or a notch for the rafters (*taruki bori*) to match the slope of the roof.

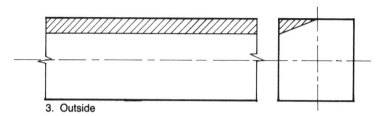

3. Outside

(iii) Procedure for making the female piece

(1) With a rip saw make one cut at A to intersect line D. Make another rip cut at B to intersect line C. Then, make cuts with a crosscut saw at C and D to intersect B and A, respectively.

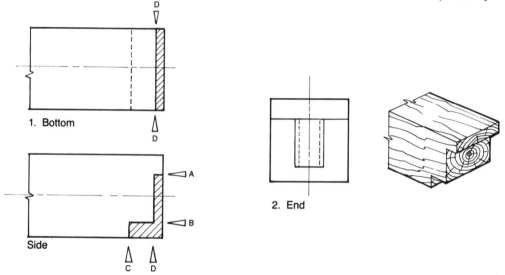

1. Bottom

Side

2. End

(2) Draw the cut lines for the dovetail section at the end of the piece.

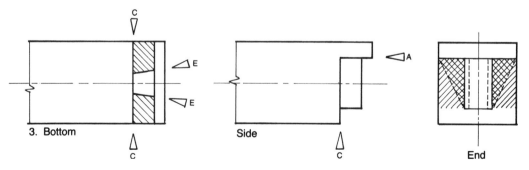

3. Bottom

Side

End

(3) Make a rip saw kerf at E, penetrating diagonally half-way into the piece. With a crosscut saw, make a kerf at C. Chisel out the remaining portion.

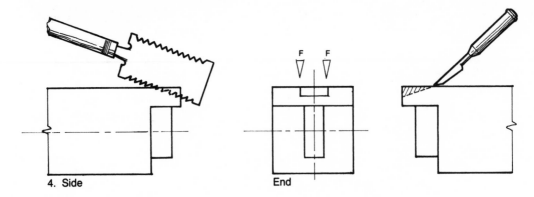

4. Side   End

(4) Make rip saw kerfs at F for the *taruki bori* (notch) and chisel out the notch.

(2) *Eriwa kone hozo sashi wari kusabi uchi*—Collared Haunch Mortise and Tenon Joint with a Wedge

(i) *Sumizuke*

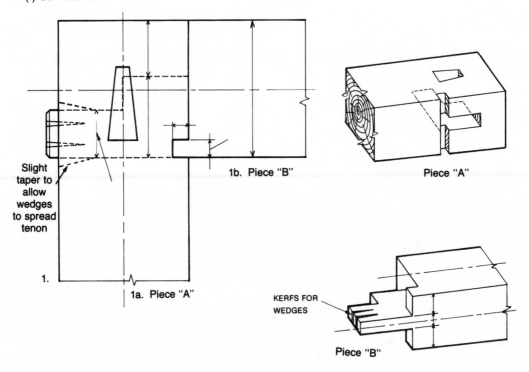

Slight taper to allow wedges to spread tenon

1.   1a. Piece "A"   1b. Piece "B"   Piece "A"

KERFS FOR WEDGES   Piece "B"

(ii) Procedure for making piece "A"
  Start by drawing the cut lines.

(1) Make crosscut saw kerfs at A and B to intersect line C. Chisel off from both sides of the piece.

(2) Chisel out the diagonally marked section to form a mortise to the depth of the center line.

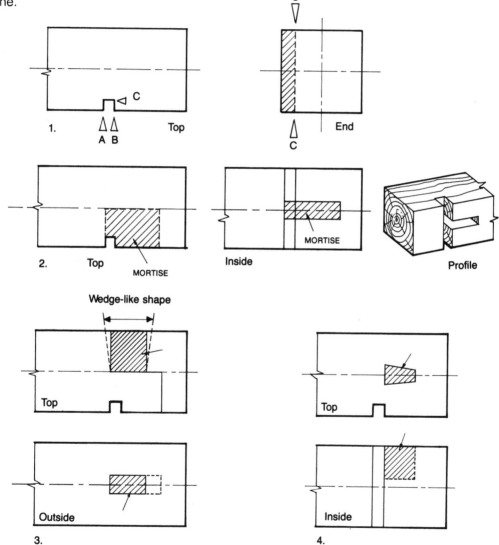

(3) From the other side, chisel through the rest of the mortise, angled slightly into a wedge shape as shown.

(4) From the top, chisel out a fan-shaped hole as shown.

(iii) Procedure for making piece "B"

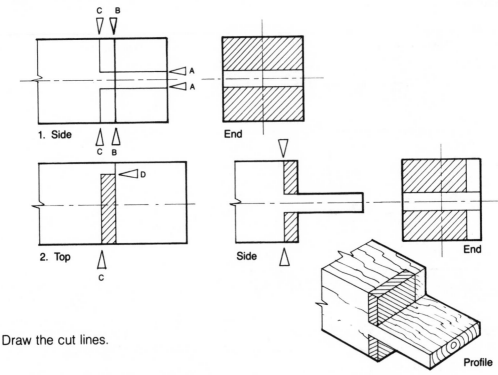

1. Side

End

2. Top

Side

End

Profile

Draw the cut lines.

(1) Make rip saw kerfs at A to intersect line B.

Make crosscut saw kerfs at B on both sides to intersect lines at A.

(2) Make a crosscut saw kerf at C on both sides to intersect lines D and A.

Make rip saw kerfs on both sides: at A to intersect lines D and C; at D to intersect lines A and C. Remove the diagonally marked section with a chisel.

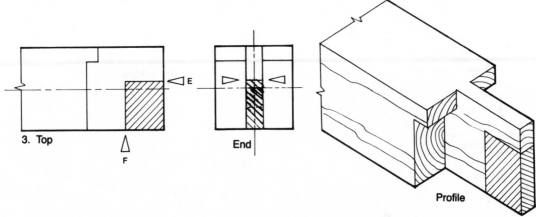

3. Top

End

Profile

(3) Make a rip saw kerf at E to intersect line F. Make a crosscut kerf at F to intersect line E.

(4) Make a rip saw kerf at G to intersect line C. Make a crosscut kerf at C to intersect line G.

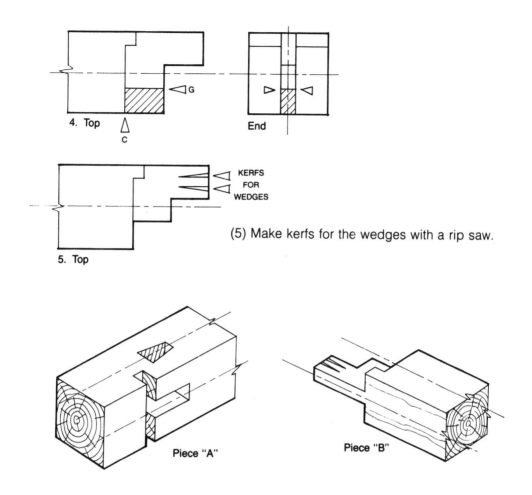

4. Top

C

End

KERFS FOR WEDGES

(5) Make kerfs for the wedges with a rip saw.

5. Top

Piece "A"

Piece "B"

When the joint is secured in position, the end of the tenon with wedges that protrudes past the outside face of Piece "A" is sawed off and planed flush so as not to interfere with exterior applications of other building materials.

(3) *Sumidome Hozo sashi*—Tongue and Groove Shoulder Miter Joint

(i) *Sumizuke*

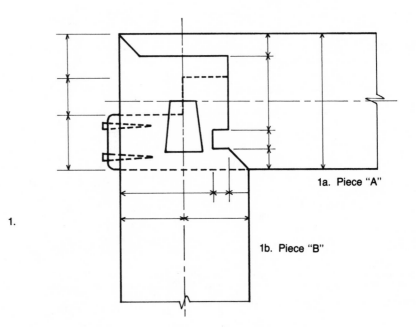

1a. Piece "A"

1.

1b. Piece "B"

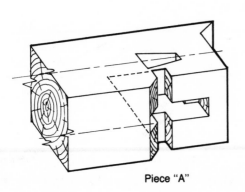

Piece "A"

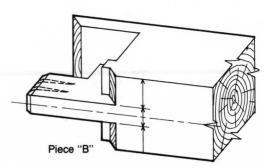

Piece "B"

(ii) Procedure for making piece "A"

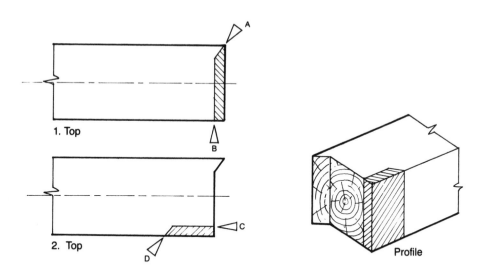

1. Top

2. Top

Profile

Draw the cut lines.

(1) Saw with a rip saw at A to intersect line B. Saw with a crosscut saw at B to intersect line A.

(2) Saw with a rip saw at C to intersect line D. Saw with a crosscut saw at D to intersect line A.

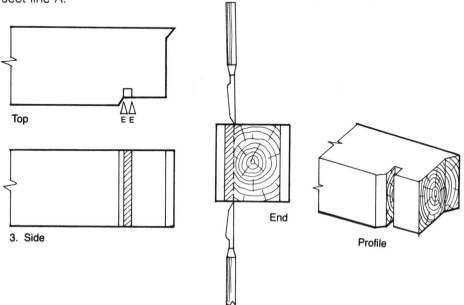

Top

3. Side

End

Profile

(3) Saw kerfs with a crosscut saw at E. Remove the wood between the kerfs with a chisel (chiseling from both sides).

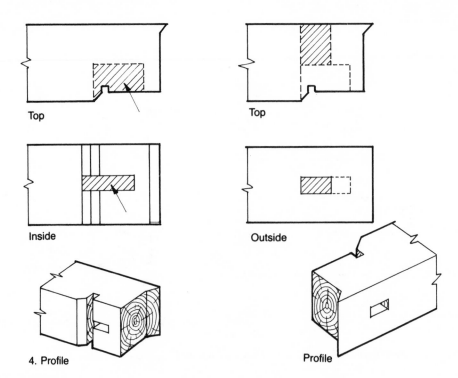

Top

Top

Inside

Outside

4. Profile

Profile

(4) Chisel a through mortise in two stages as shown:
a) mortise all the way through top shaded area;
b) enlarge inside area that is ½ through and widen.

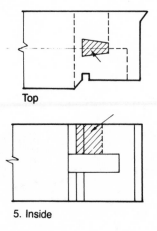

Top

5. Inside

(5) Finish by carving out a fan-shaped mortise.

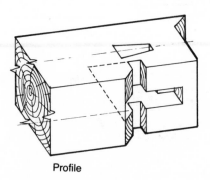

Profile

(iii) Procedure for making piece "B"

Draw the cutlines.

(1) Make a rip saw kerf sloping diagonally half-way into the piece from A to intersect lines B and C. Make another rip saw kerf sloping diagonally half-way into the piece from B to intersect lines A and C. Make a crosscut saw kerf sloping diagonally half-way into the piece from C to intersect lines A and B. Remove remaining wood with a chisel.

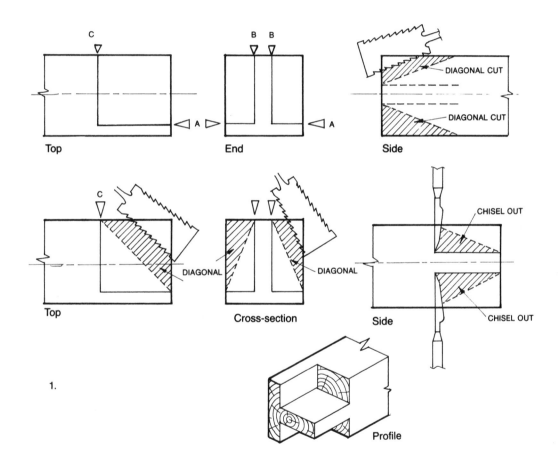

1.

(2) Make shallow rip saw kerfs at D and E. Chisel out the diagonally marked section.

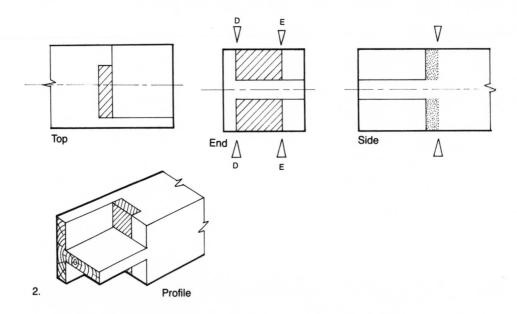

2.   Profile

(3) On both sides, make a shallow rip kerf at F and a shallow crosscut kerf at G. Chisel out the diagonally marked section.

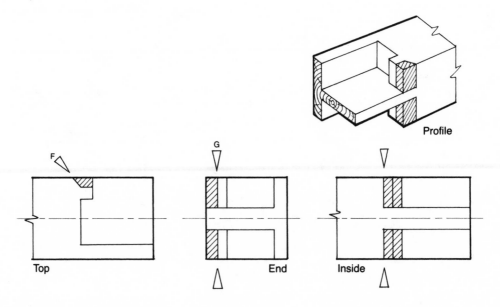

3.

(4) With a rip saw, make cuts at H. Brace the tongue on a wooden support to prevent it breaking. Chisel out the diagonally marked section.

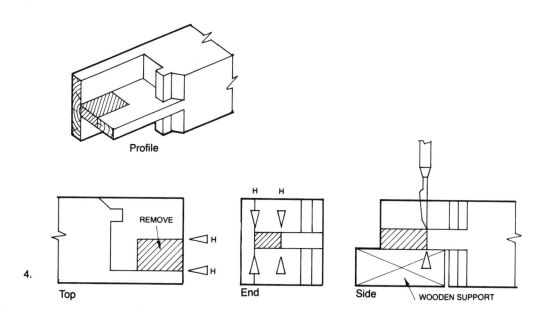

Profile

REMOVE

4.

Top   End   Side   WOODEN SUPPORT

(5) Make two rip saw kerfs at I. Remove diagonally marked section with a chisel.

Top   End   Top

5.

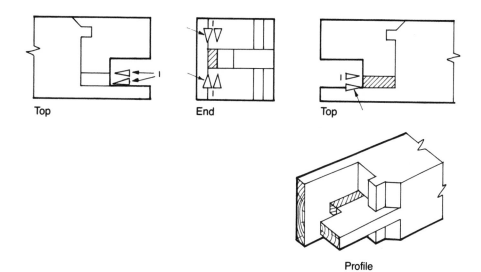

Profile

(6) Remove slope at an angle of 45° with a crosscut saw

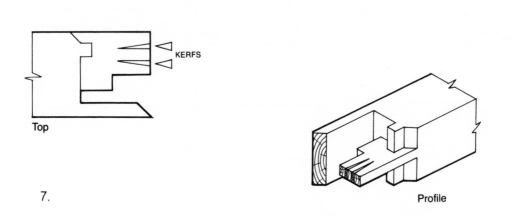

Top

45°

End

Profile

6.

Top

KERFS

Profile

7.

(7) Make kerfs for the wedges with a rip saw.

CHAPTER 6

THE FUNCTIONS OF VARIOUS MEMBERS

Chapter 5 explained the making of various major end joints and right angle joints as well as ways of working with the materials. In this chapter, using wooden residential structures as examples, the functions of end joints and right angle joints on major structural and architectural members will be discussed.

There are two framing methods used in Japanese construction: *okabe,* in which all framing members are concealed at both the exterior and interior by the wall finishing materials (sheet rock or lath); and *shinkabe,* in which major structural members such as posts and beams are exposed and treated as finishing materials.

Jiku Gumi—Axial Framing

The skeletal framing of the walls is called *jiku gumi.* As shown in Figure 6.1, the main members of *jiku gumi* are the mudsills, posts, beams, girders, and headers (in the case of two stories). There are two types of *jiku gumi:* the Japanese and the Western style.

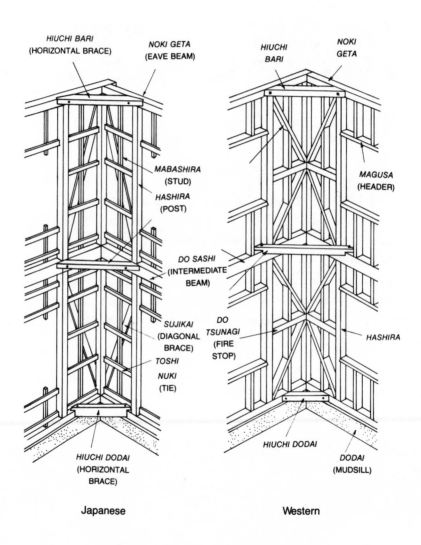

Figure 6.1. Styles of framing (*Jiku Gumi*).

Dodai—Mudsills

The mudsill is the skeletal framing member which rests on the footing, ties the posts, and transfers the load to the foundation.

(1) Materials

Since mudsills are placed close to the ground, raised on a post or stone foundation, they are susceptible to moisture and rot. Mudsills are usually made of pith wood, preferably a reddish wood. Cherry, chestnut, Japanese cypress, and fir, which resist moisture well, are all used, but Japanese cypress and fir are most frequently used due to their ease of milling.

(2) Measurements.

The mudsills should be large enough for the posts to sit on the inside of the beveled edges, as shown in Figure 6.2. Today, mudsills often are of the same dimension as the posts. Generally, a single story house uses 4×4 mudsills, while a two-story house requires a larger beam.

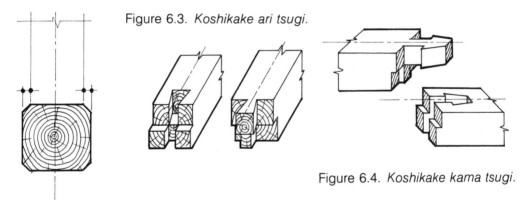

Figure 6.3. *Koshikake ari tsugi.*

Figure 6.4. *Koshikake kama tsugi.*

Figure 6.2. Beveled edges.

(3) End joints.

The end joints of mudsills should be as follows:

(i) Standard quality: *Koshikake ari tsugi* (see Figure 6.3) or *koshikake kama tsugi* (see Figure 6.4).

(ii) Select grade: *Okkake daisen tsugi* (see Figure 6.5) or *kanawa tsugi* (see Figure 6.6).

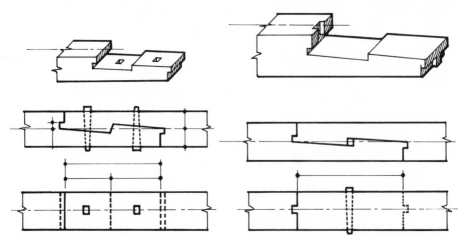

Figure 6.5. *Okkake daisen tsugi.*　　Figure 6.6. *Kanawa tsugi.*

(4) *Shiguchi*—right angle joints.

The right angle joints of mudsills include inside corner joints, outside corner joints, T-shaped, and cross joints. They should be used as explained below.

(i) *Dezumi no shiguchi:* outside corner joints.

(a) For simple construction: *Ari otoshi* (dadoed, half lapped, half blind dovetail with full mortise and tenon) (see Figure 6.7).

(b) For standard construction: *Eriwa kone hozo sashi wari kusabi uchi* (see Figure 6.8).

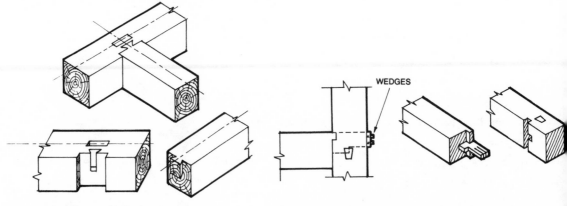

Figure 6.7 *Ari otoshi*　　Figure 6.8. *Eriwa kone hozo sashi wari kusabi uc*

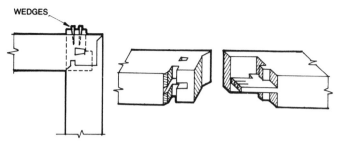

Figure 6.9. *Sumidome hozo sashi wari kusabi uchi.*

(c) Quality construction: *Sumidome hozosashi wari kusabi uchi* (see Figure 6.9).

Where mudsills are parts of finished members and are exposed, it is undesirable that their ends should be exposed. In this circumstance the *bintadome eriwa kone hozo sashi wari kusabi uchi* (haunched mortise and tenon with quarter mitered joint secured with a wedge) joint should be used (see Figure 6.10).

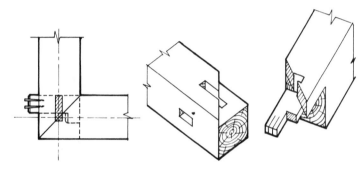

Figure 6.10. *Bintadome eriwa kone hozo sashi wari kusabi uchi.*

(ii) *Irizumi no shiguchi* — inside corner joints.

(2) Simple construction: *Oire ari otoshi* (see Figure 6.11).

(b) Standard construction: *Nuki hozo sashi wari kusabi uchi* (see Figure 6.12).

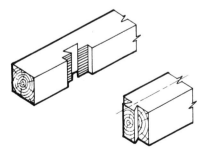

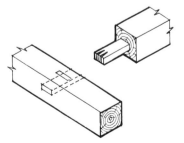

Figure 6.11. *Oire ari otoshi.*   Figure 6.12. *Nuki hozo sashi wari kusabi uchi.*

(iii) *Tyi* or *juji toriai*—T-shaped or cross joints.

(a) Simple construction: *Ari shikake* (see Figure 6.13).

(b) Quality construction: *Saotsugi shachisen uchi* (dado with cross tenon lap joint secured with a key) (see Figure 6.14).

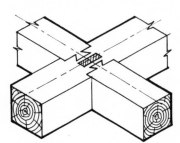

Figure 6.13. *Ari shikake.*

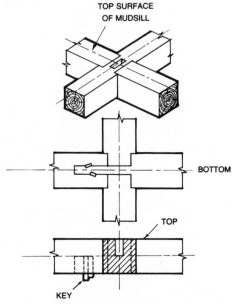

Figure 6.14. *Saotsugi shachisen uchi.*

(5) Construction Techniques

Paint a waterproofing solution (e.g., Creosote) on the bottom and the two sides of the mud-sills.

The placement of the end joints should not conflict with the locations of anchor bolts, of posts, or of vents (see Figure 6.15). If milled and manufactured pieces are to be used, the placement of posts, anchor bolts, and vents must be considered beforehand.

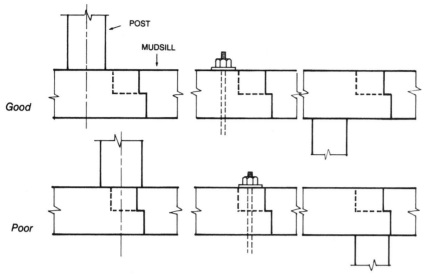

Figure 6.15. Location of end joints relative to bolts and posts.

Hiuchi dodai—angle braces for mudsills

In order to prevent horizontal distortion of mudsills, braces must be installed at the corners (see Figure 6.16).

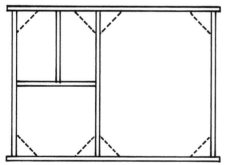

Figure 6.16. Corner braces.

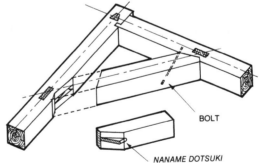

Figure 6.17. Joining corner braces.

(1) Material: The wood should be the same as that of the mudsills. The most common size is 3½ in. square, however a size equivalent to ½ to ⅓ the thickness of the posts can also be used.

(2) Installation: When a brace with ½ the post's thickness or more is used, the end surface must be enlarged to resist forces, as shown in Figure 6.17. The joint used should be

naname dotsuki or *naname dotsuki tan hozo sashi* secured with a ½ in. or ¾ in. bolt. When a 3½ in. square piece is cut or a thin board is used, notches to accept the braces are made onto the surface of the mudsill. They are secured by two nails at each end (Figure 6.18).

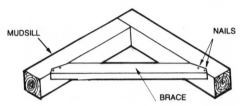

Figure 6.18. Securing a thin brace.

(3) Method of construction: Do not make too deep a notch on the mudsill. The depth should be just enough to prevent the brace from loosening.

Hashira—Posts

Posts are very important framing members since they serve to transfer the weight of loads onto the ground and to support the walls. They also resist the lateral forces of wind and earthquake. In a two-story house, a single piece that goes from the ground floor to the roof is called a *toshi bashira* (a continuous post). Posts terminating within one floor are called *kuda bashira* (discontinuous posts). The vertical members erected between the posts which support the walls are called *ma bashira* (studs). (See Figure 6.19.)

(1) *Toshi bashira*—continuous posts.
In the past, wooden houses with many continuous posts and with long walls were considered sturdiest. Since beams must be connected at each post when many continuous posts are used, such posts must be kept to a minimum. Usually, continuous posts are used only at the four corners, and where T- or cross-shaped girders intersect.

(i) Material: Japanese cypress or cedar with pith.

(ii) Dimensions: These should be slightly larger than those recommended in *Kenchiku Kijunho* (Architectural Standards)*, and slightly bigger than the *kuda bashira* (discontinuous posts).

*Translator's note: Equivalent to the North American Uniform Building Code.

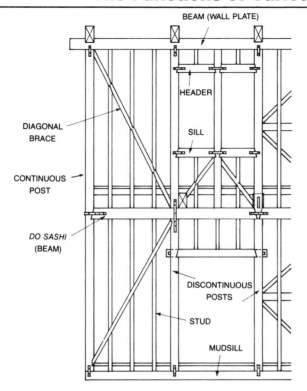

Figure 6.19. Wall framing members.

(iii) Right angle joints: For quality work, the mortise and tenon joint to use at both the lower and upper ends is a *naga hozo sashi komisen uchi* (long tenon with pin) (Figure 6.20a). When a *tan hozo* (short tenon) is used, secure the joint with a pin anchor (Figure 6.20b). An *ogi hozo* (fan-shaped tenon) must be used on the outside corner post (Figure 6.20c). At ends of the mudsills, the joint to use is an *ari otoshi kasugai uchi* (dadoed, half lapped, half blind dovetail joint, secured with a pin anchor) (Figure 6.20d).

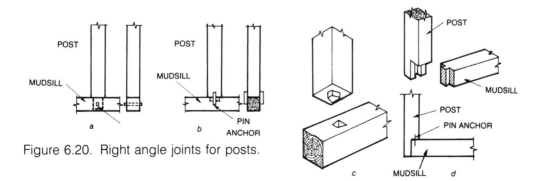

Figure 6.20. Right angle joints for posts.

(iv) Construction practice: Construction of a wall longer than 35 in. using a diagonal brace secured to continuous posts resists lateral forces (earthquake and wind) well, and is quite sound.

(2) *Kuda bashira*—discontinuous posts.
These posts support the loads above, and are also used at the ends of partitions. In a two-story structure, although the first and second floor posts do not have to align it is a good practice to align them wherever possible.

(i) Material: In the Japanese framing method, these posts are usually exposed and are part of the finished work, so they should be free of knots and pitch. They should be of either edge-grained (quarter sawn) or flat-grained (plain sawn) wood. Usually zelkova, cherry, pine, Japanese cypress, and cedar are used. Their surfaces should be beautiful, with a sheen. Most commonly used are Japanese cypress and Japanese cedar. In some cases, peeled and polished logs are used.

(ii) Dimensions: Generally 4×4's are used on single-story houses, and somewhat larger square posts are used for two-story houses.

(iii) Right angle joints: The most commonly used mortise and tenon joint at both the top and bottom of the posts is the *tan hozo* (short tenon) with a pin anchor, but in places with heavy winds, or where quality work is desired, a *hozo sashi komisen uchi* is used. If the bottom joint fits tightly, the work of construction is made easier since the posts will not sway.

Right angle joints connecting posts to other members are described below. In all cases, the cut lines are located using the *kenzao* scales. (See Appendix 3.)

(a) Gooseneck joints on the bottom face of the eave joists (Figure 6.21).

(b) The joint for eave beams and beams supporting rafters is shown in Figure 6.22a.

(c) Holes for the *nuki* (bridging or ties) on *shinkabe* framing (Figure 6.22).

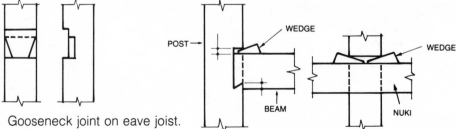

Figure 6.21. Gooseneck joint on eave joist.

Figure 6.22. Joints for eave and rafter beams.

(iv) Construction practice: If a post with pith is being used for finished work, a kerf must be made along the center of a vertical face other than the exposed one to relieve stresses which might cause warpage. To be effective, the kerf must be cut to the depth of the pith, and be held open with small wedges.

When cutting the posts, determine which are the butt and tip ends, and always place the butt end at the bottom. Also, do not use posts with *atezai* (abnormal grain.)

(3) *Mabashira*—studs. These are members which form and support the walls. It must be noted that, structurally, they are non-bearing members.

(i) Material: This should be wood without pith or abnormal grain. Even though studs are non-bearing members, do not use warped pieces.

(ii) Dimensions: For *okabe* framing, the studs should be about ⅓ the size of the posts. For *shinkabe,* studs equalling the size of the rafters are used.

(iii) Right angle joints: A *tan hozo sashi* joint (short tenon mortise and tenon) reinforced with two nails is used at both the bottom and top connections to the studs.

(iv) Construction practice: In *okabe* framing, where a stud intersects with the diagonal bracing, the stud is cut off and secured to the brace as shown in Figure 6.23a. In *shinkabe* framing a notch is chiseled out for the brace on the stud and they are nailed together (Figure 6.23b).

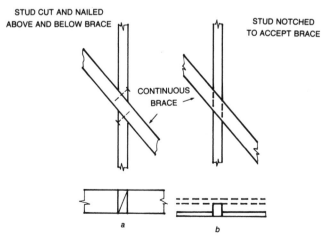

Figure 6.23. Intersecting studs.

Noki geta—Eave Beams

The *noki geta* transfer the load on the *koya bari* (roof joists) to the continuous posts, as well as connecting the ends of the posts. The *noki geta* also are called *hanamoya*.

(1) Material: Lumber with pith from pine, Japanese cedar, zelkova, and Japanese cypress are used. The most commonly used are pine, Japanese cypress, and Japanese cedar.

(2) Dimensions: The width of the *noki geta* (eave beams) should match that of the *dodai* (mudsills). It should also be wider than the post by the width of the bevels on both sides of the post. The depth of the beam is determined by the length of the span and the load it supports; usually it is anywhere from 1.2 to 1.6 times its width.

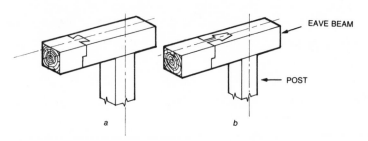

Figure 6.24. Simple end joints for eave beams.

(3) End joints: The end joints of the *noki geta* occur beyond the posts and away from intersecting beams, except in *shiraki zukuri* (exposed framing construction). The various types of joints are described below:

(i) Simple construction: A *koshikake ari tsugi* (Figure 6.24a), or *koshikake kama tsugi* (Figure 6.24b).

(ii) Quality construction: A *kanawa tsugi* (see Figure 6.6), *okkake daisen tsugi* (see Figure 6.5), and a *shippasami tsugi* (see Figure 6.25).

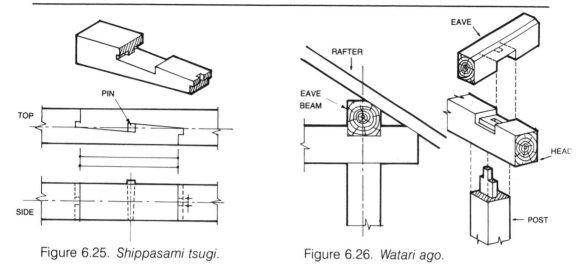

Figure 6.25. *Shippasami tsugi.*

Figure 6.26. *Watari ago.*

(4) Right angle joints.

(i) *Orioki gumi* (*orioki* framing method): In the framing method where the top of the post is a stacked tenon on which the *noki geta* and *koya bari* are inserted, a *watari ago* (stacked tenon) joint is used (Figure 6.26).

(ii) *Kyoro gumi:* In this framing method where the joint occurs beyond the post, a *kabuto ari* (end lap joint with a dovetail) is used (Figure 6.27).

(iii) *Yosemune* (hip roof): Where there is an *irimoya* (hipped gable) roof, a *neji gumi* (two step tenon) joint is used (Figure 6.28).

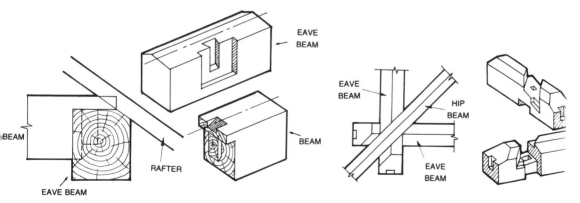

Figure 6.27. *Kabuto ari.*

Figure 6.28. *Neji gumi.*

(5) Construction practice: The *noki geta* beams must always be framed so that the back side of the wood is on top, and the beam will bow upward. This is very important in order to prevent deflection of the *kamoi* (the headers with grooves for two-paneled sliding doors).

Do Sashi—Subsidiary Beams

Do sashi beams are used on the exterior walls of two-story houses. They are placed on the second floor level and serve to connect the discontinuous posts, and to support the second floor joists and beams. These structurally important members are also known as *hariuke* (beam supporters).

(1) Material: Lumber with pitch from pine, Japanese cypress, and Japanese cedar are used, though pine and Japanese cedar are used most widely.

(2) Dimensions: The width should match that of the posts, but the depth must be determined by the spacing of its supporting posts.

(3) End joints: Though it is preferable to have a single continuous *do sashi* beam between two continuous posts, when a long span requires that two pieces must be joined, a joint is made between them, and between two discontinuous posts. The following joints are used.

(i) Standard construction: *koshikake ari tsugi* (Figure 6.3).

(ii) Quality construction: *okkake daisen tsugi* (Figure 6.5).
In each case metal connectors should be used to reinforce the joints.

(4) Right angle joints.

(i) For connection with a continuous post: *Kashigi oire tan hozo sashi* (oblique dado with blind stub mortise and tenon) with a metal strap secured with a bolt (Figure 6.29).

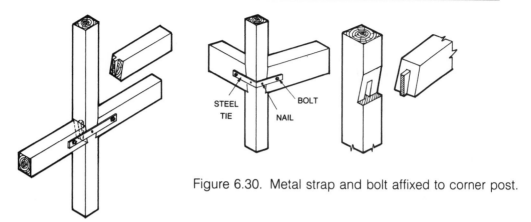

STEEL TIE   NAIL   BOLT

Figure 6.30. Metal strap and bolt affixed to corner post.

Figure 6.29. Metal strap and bolt
             affixed to continuous post.

(ii) For connection with a corner post: *Kashigi oire tan hozo sashi* with a metal strap or metal angle secured with a bolt (Figure 6.30).

(5) Construction practice: When using the *shinkabe* framing, the *do sashi* will be exposed in the staircase and in a clerestory room. In such cases the same care must be taken as on the outside faces on exterior walls. It is also important to take into account that when wood expands and contracts, causing movement, a joint tightened with wedges or keys will be stronger than one reinforced with metal connectors.

Sujikai—Diagonal Bracing

To prevent distortion of an axial frame, diagonal members are placed between two posts. This member is placed in such a way as to counter either compressive force or tensional force. The general practice is to place the member to resist compressive force. The strength of a diagonal brace is not determined by its size, but rather by the method of connection at its end. Careful attention must therefore be given to this connection. The installation of diagonal braces should not be limited only to the framing of exterior walls. It is preferable to place such braces on the interior partitioning walls as well.

(1) Materials: It is best to use lumber with pith. However, if the bracing is made by splitting a post into thirds, then the lumber must be free of pith.

The diagonal bracing for large buildings should be the same size as the posts. In smaller structures, or in *shinkabe* framing, the thickness should be either one half or one third of the posts.

(2) Framing

At each of the corners of a frame, the diagonal brace is connected with the joint, *kashigi oire* (obliqued dado), secured either by a pin anchor or by large nails to both a post and a beam (Figure 6.31).

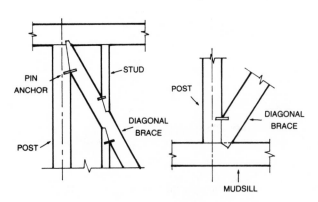

Figure 6.31. Securing diagonal bracing.   Figure 6.32. Joining intersecting braces.

When intersecting with posts and studs, always notch out the posts and studs to accept the diagonal brace. Where two diagonal braces intersect, make one continuous; secure the other halves onto it with a pin anchor or with two large nails at each end (Figure 6.32).

(3) Construction practice: If the diagonal brace is connected only to a post as shown in Figure 6.33a, only the tenon acts to resist forces. For this reason, the diagonal brace should be connected to both a post and a mudsill or beam, as shown in Figure 6.33b. Since the external forces acting on a structure (i.e., wind and earthquake) are never constant, the ideal framing practice is to install intersecting diagonal braces. However, due to wall framing methods, involving various types of underlayments for different types of wall finishes, such as stucco, board and batter, etc., there are many instances where only a single brace can be installed. In such cases, install the braces as shown in Figure 6.33b, balancing the left and right sides.

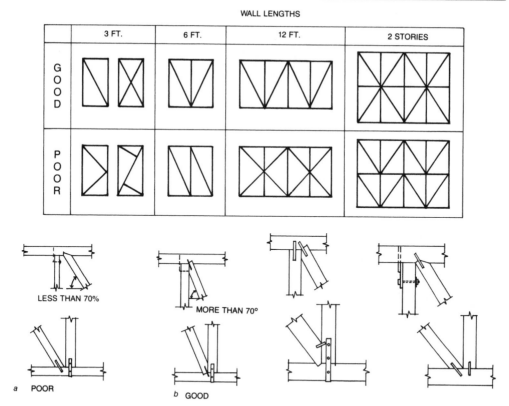

Figure 6.33. Bracing patterns.

Kabe Nuki—Wall Bridging or Ties

Kabe nuki's function is to support the bamboo lath for plastering over *shinkabe* framing. The different varieties of *kabe nuki* shown in Figure 6.34 are described below:

(1) *Chi nuki:* This tie is place above the mudsills (*dodai*).

(2) *Uchinori nuki:* This tie is placed where there are openings in the wall. It is used especially to support thin *kamoi* (headers) and is also called *chikara* (strengthening) *nuki*. It has a larger cross-section than the other *nuki*.

(3) *Do nuki:* This tie is placed at the midpoint between the *chi nuki* (bottom bridging) and *tenjo nuki* (ceiling bridging).

(4) *Tenjo nuki:* This tie is placed at the edges of the ceiling.

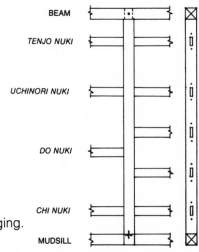

Figure 6.34. Wall bridging.

(1) Materials: Cedar or cypress that is free of pith should be used. *Atezai* wood should never be used.

(2) Dimensions: For *uchinori nuki* (*chikara nuki*), the thickness should be from 1¼ in. to 1½ in. and the width 4 to 4¾ in. All other common *nuki* should be from about 1 in. thick, and from 2 to 3½ in. wide.

(3) Framing

(i) Quality construction: Ends should be connected with a *shitage kama* (blind half dovetailed stub mortise and tenon) with a wedge (Figure 6.35), while the joints in-between should be *watari ago* with a wedge (Figure 6.36). In higher quality construction, a pin is inserted in the middle of the post.

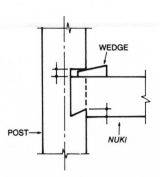

Figure 6.35. *Shitage kama.*

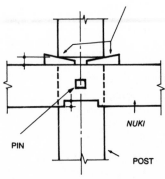

Figure 6.36. *Watari ago* with wedge.

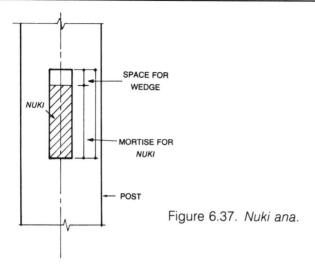

Figure 6.37. *Nuki ana.*

(ii) Standard construction: The *nuki ana* (hole) for the *nuki* is made from ¼ to ½ in. larger than the depth of the *nuki* and wedges are used to secure the *nuki* (see Figure 6.37).

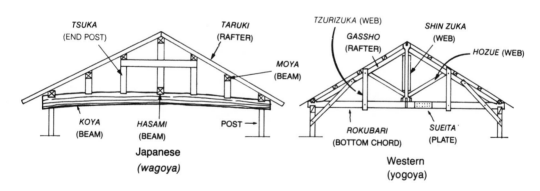

Figure 6.38. Styles of roof framing.

Koya Gumi — Roof Framing

The skeletal frame which forms the triangular shape of the roof is called *koya gumi* (roof frame). There are two types of roof framing, as shown in Figure 6.38. One is *wagoya* (Japanese roof framing) and the other is *yogoya* (western roof framing). *Wagoya* is widely used for small structures because is is simple to construct. However, *yogoya* is preferable in larger structures, where the beam span is greater than 20 feet. In this book only *wagoya* will be explained.

Koya bari—Roof beam

Koya bari is the bottom member of the triangular roof frame. Generally, it is one continuous member, but when the span is long, the pieces are joined above shiki bari (see Figure 6.38).* This type of koya bari is called negakake bari.

*Translator's Note: Shiki bari differ slightly from the koya beam in that they are used in a hip instead of a gable roof. They are located between the eave beam and the beam supporting the end post which supports the end of the ridge beam.

(1) Materials: Lumber with pith is preferable but pine or Japanese cedar logs are quite often also used. When a peeled log is used, the end is shaped to connect with a taiko otashi joint. The dimensions have to be determined by the span. However, where clay shingles are used for roofing, the end diameter of the log should be a minimum of 7 5/16 in.

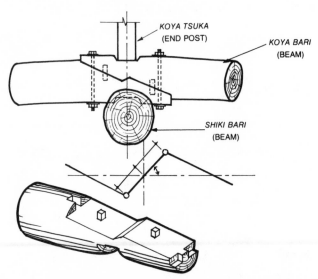

Figure 6.39. Koyadaimochi tsugi.

(2) End joints: The end joints of a nagekake bari (beam supporting the end post which supports the end of the ridge beam) should be on top of the supporting beam (shiki geta or majikiri geta), and should be either daimochi tsugi secured with a bolt, or daimochi tsugi reinforced with a pin anchor on both sides (Figure 6.39).

(3) Right angle joints: The joints for *koya bari* and *noki geta* should be either *kabuto ari kake* or *watari ago kake* secured with a strap bolt (Figures 6.40 and 6.41.)

When the *koya bari* is a log, the places where posts and end posts will attach should be notched and flattened (Figure 6.42.)

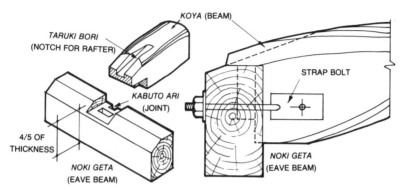

Figure 6.40. *Kabuto ari kake.*

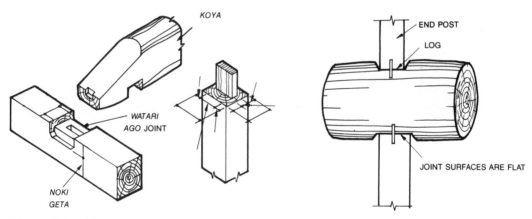

Figure 6.41. *Watari ago kake.*   Figure 6.42. Securing a log *koya bari.*

(4) Construction practice: The *koya bari* should be installed with the back of the lumber as the top surface so that it will bow upwards. When connecting two logs, they should be arranged in the *okuri tsugi* manner (Figure 6.43a) or the *yukiai tsugi* manner (Figure 6.43b). *Wakari tsugi* (Figure 6.43c) is generally considered undesirable, so avoid using this form of attachment. (Connecting butt to butt is undesirable; connecting butt to tip and tip to tip are considered good practice).

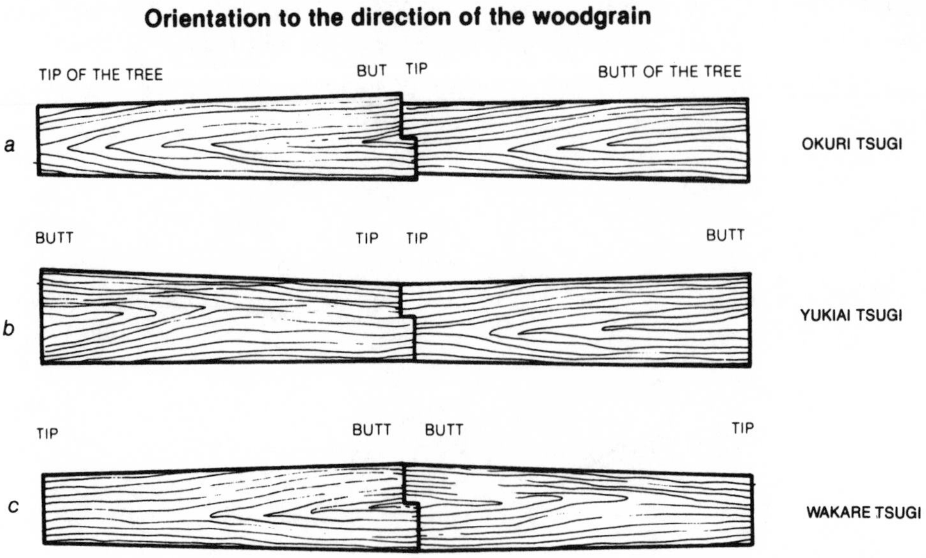

Orientation to the direction of the woodgrain

TIP OF THE TREE   BUT   TIP   BUTT OF THE TREE

a   OKURI TSUGI

BUTT   TIP   TIP   BUTT

b   YUKIAI TSUGI

TIP   BUTT   BUTT   TIP

c   WAKARE TSUGI

Figure 6.43. Joints for connecting two log beams.

Hiuchi bari—brace on a horizontal plane: See section above on *hiuchi dodai* for explanation.

Koya Tsuka—End Post

Tsuka is the term used to describe a short post. The *koya tsuka* is installed on top of the *koya bari* and supports the *munagi* (ridge beam), or the *moya* (intermediate beam which supports rafters—a purlin). (See Figure 6.45.)

(1) Materials: Most widely used are Japanese cedar or pine with pith.

(2) Dimensions: Generally it is 4×4 in. square, but for the *muna tsuka* (end post supporting ridge beam), it is about ½ to ¾ in. larger.

(3) Right angle joints: The joints for *koya bari* and *noki geta* should be either *kabuto ari kake* or *watari ago kake* secured with a strap bolt (Figures 6.40 and 6.41.)
the *koya bari* should be a *tan hozo sashi* (short tenon) reinforced with a pin anchor. Where there is a *niju bari* (spaced beam), a *ju hozo* (stacked tenon) is used.

(4) Construction practice: The length, or longer side, of the tenons on both the top and the bottom of the end post runs parallel to the beams they are connecting, as shown in Figure 6.44. This is done so that the width of the beam (its shortest dimension) is not weakened. Always orient the length of the mortise with the length of the grain.

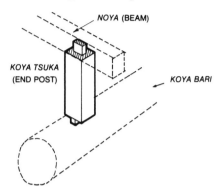

Figure 6.44. Tenons run parallel to beams.

Koya Sujikai and *Keta Yuki Sujikai*—Roof Bracings

The function of both braces is to tie and secure the end posts. As shown in Figure 6.45, *koya sujikai* runs parallel to the rafters and *keta yuki sujikai* runs parallel to the *moya* (purlin).

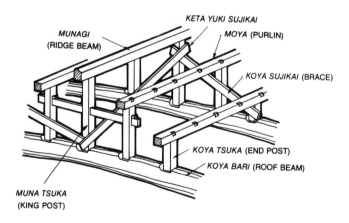

Figure 6.45. Roof bracing members.

(1) Materials and dimensions: Japanese cedar with the dimension ½–¾ in. × 3½–4 in. is the most widely used.

(2) Right angle joints: The *tsuka soitsuke* is used, secured with two nails. The bottom of *koya sujikai* is carved into the log beam and secured with two nails.

Munagi—Ridge Beams and *Moya*—Purlins

These are horizontal members placed at the apex of the triangular frame and 35 in. apart along the slopes to support the rafters.

(1) Materials and dimensions: Generally pine and Japanese cedar with pith are used. The *munagi* are 3½ in. wide × 4¼ in. deep, and the *moya* are 3½ × 3½ in.

(2) End joints: The joint is usually *koshikake ari tsugi* secured with two nails, placed about 60 in. beyond the center line of the *tsuka* (end post). For a fine joint, *okkake daisen tsugi* is used.

(3) *Shiguchi:* At a "T" shaped junction, *oire ari kake* is used, reinforced with a pin anchor on the top surface. In order to accept the rafter, one of the following types of notches is chiseled out: *uwaba kogaeshi kezuri* or *atari kaki,* or *taruki bori* for superior grade work (see Figure 6.46).

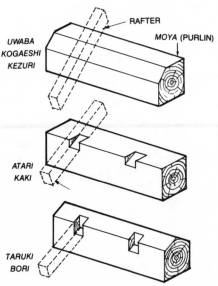

Figure 6.46. Notches for rafters.

(4) Construction practice: The end joints of the *munagi* and the *moya* should not align with each other. Instead, they should be placed scattered at random to prevent any sagging of the roof where the joints are located. This practice should also be applied in the connection of the *neda* (joists), which is discussed in a later section.

Taruki—Rafters and *Nojiita*—Roof Sheathing

These are the elements which shape the roof and are the first layer of the roofing materials.

(1) Materials: Pieces with pith are considered to be best for rafters. Due to the shortage of such materials and other current factors, the most common practice is to use thin pieces of pine, about 2 in. × 1½ in. The material used for the *nojiita* is usually Japanese cedar, about ½ in. thick and may be of random size.

(2) End joints: The joints for the rafters on top of the *moya* are either *sogi tsugi* (scarf joints), or the *tsuki tsuke tsugi* (lap joints) secured with nails. The top end is cut at an angle, and the rafters are connected to each other on top of the ridge beam with a *hame komi* (dado) joint secured with nails (see Figure 6.47).
    The *nojiita* are nailed on to the rafters, every tenth board having a *rantsugi* (random joint). The eave edges should be as in either a *suberiba* (scarf) or an *ai jakkuri* (shiplap) joint.

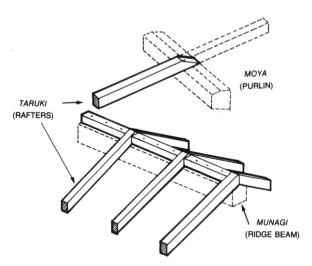

Figure 6.47. Connecting rafters.

(3) Construction practice: The size of the rafters is determined by the eaves' depth, which in turn is determined by the roof tile. Make sure that the dimension of the roof is a multiple of the roof tile so that cut tiles need not be used.

Floor Framing

The floor framing supports the floor and consists of the *obiki* (beams), *neda* (joists), *neda kake* (beams) and *yuka tsuka* (floor posts) (see Figure 6.48). For two-story construction, a *nikai bari* beam (second story beam) is added.

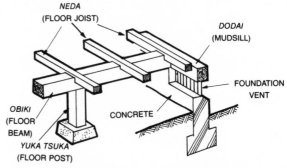

Figure 6.48. Floor framing members.

Obiki — Beams Supporting Floor Joists

These beams are placed on top of the *yuka tsuka* and supports the joists. *Obiki* are usually placed 35 in. apart on center.

(1) Materials: Generally 3½ in. square Japanese cedar with pith is used. For quality construction 4¾ in. square pieces are used. Japanese cypress is also used at times.

(2) End joints: *Koshikake ari tsugi* joints are used, reinforced with nails 6 in. beyond the center line of the *yuka tsuka* (floor post).

(3) Right angle joints: Use an *oire tan hozo sashi* joint (dadoed full short tenon) when connecting to the post, and for connecting to a *dodai* (mudsill), use a *nosekake* (or *koshikake*) joint (full tenon) secured with nails.

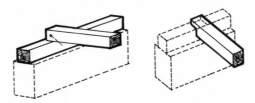

Figure 6.49. Joining *obiki* to mudsill.

(4) Construction practice: The *obiki* for the first floor should be framed so that the back of the lumber is the bottom face and the beam bows downward. If the *obiki* were installed the other way around it might separate from the *yuka tsuka* (floor post) causing irreparable damage.

Yuka Tsuka—Floor Posts

This is the structural member which stands on the stone footing and supports the *obiki*.

(1) Materials: 3½ in. square pine or cedar with pith is used most widely.

(2) Right angle joint: The top end should be connected to the *obiki* with a *tan hozo sashi* (short tenon) or a *michikiri hozo* (rabbet) secured with two nails. (As shown in Figure 6.50, the width of the tenon is equal to the full width of the male piece.) The bottom of the *yuka tsuka* is connected with a butt joint to the footings; sometimes a pin is used to hold this in place.

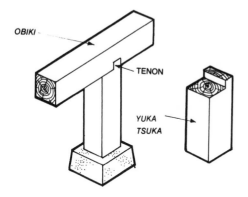

Figure 6.50. Joining floor post to beam.

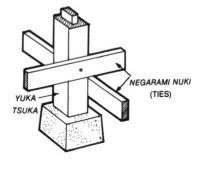

Figure 6.51. Ties to support floor post.

(3) Construction practice: In a house with a high crawl space, *negarami nuki* (ties) (see Figure 6.51) are installed to prevent swaying of the *yuka tsuka* (floor posts). *Negarami nuki* are usually made of Japanese cedar, about ½ in. × 3½ in. The *negarami nuki* that run parallel to the *obiki* (beam) are secured to each post with two nails. (This applies only to floors more than 3 feet above ground.)

Neda (or *Neda Kake*)—Joists

The members which run perpendicular to the *obiki* and which directly support the flooring are the *neda* (joists). *Neda kake* is an *obiki* at the exterior wall on which the ends of the joists are supported.

(1) Materials: The *neda* support a large load in relation to their size, so they are made of strong materials such as pine, Japanese cypress, and Douglas fir. They are either 2 in. square or 1½ in.×1¾ in., and they are usually spaced 18 in. apart. Most *neda kake* are about 1¾ in.×4 in. and are made of Japanese cedar.

(2) End joints: The joists should be connected randomly on top of the *obiki* with a *tsuki tsuke* (butt) joint or *sogi tsugi* (scarf) joint (Figure 6.52). The *neda kake* are joined at the center line of all the posts with a *tsuki tsuke* joint. In quality construction, the joint used is *watari ago kake uke,* secured with two nails at each post.

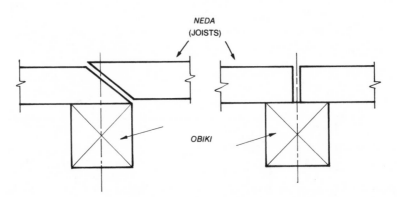

Figure 6.52. Connecting joists over a beam.

(3) Right angle joints: The *neda* (joists) are usually placed on top of the *obiki* and secured to them with nails. However, when joists are more than 3½ in. deep, a *watari ago kake* joint is used. The joists are secured with nails on top of the *neda kake* (beam), or else they are connected by a *nosekake oire* (shoulder) joint or by a *watari ago kake* and are all secured with nails.

Nikai Yuka Bari—Second Floor Beams

Second floor framing consists of the *do sashi, nikai yuka bari,* and *neda* (joists). As shown in Figure 6.53, there are two second floor framing methods: *tan yuka gumi* (single frame) and *fuku yuka gami* (multiple frame). Most widely used in residences and other small structures is the *tan yuka gumi* framing.

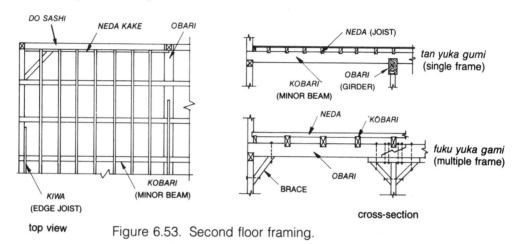

Figure 6.53. Second floor framing.

(1) Materials: since much force will act upon this beam, pith lumber is used from hemlock spruce, black pine, zelkova, or Japanese cypress. The size will be determined by the span.

(2) End joints: Each beam should be one continuous piece with no joints within a span. Joints should be made at the center line of the supporting member and should be either an *okkake daisen tsugi,* or a *daimochi tsugi* joint secured with bolts, as shown in Figure 6.54. If the two members being joined are of different depths, a *daimochi tsugi* joint secured with two bolts is used, keeping the top surfaces of both beams flush. Another method of joining two beams of different depths is to extend the deeper beam out about 6 in. beyond its supporting member, and to use a *koshikake ari tsugi* joint, reinforced with a metal strap on both sides and secured with two bolts (Figure 6.55.)

(3) Right angle joints: Between a *nikai bari* and a post the joint used is *kashigi oire tan hozo sashi,* secured with a strap bolt (Figure 6.56). Another method is to use a metal hanger secured with a bolt.

   The joint used between a *nikai bari* and a *do sashi* (beam) is an *ari shikake* joint secured with a strap bolt (Figure 6.57).

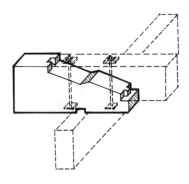

Figure 6.54. *Daimochi tsugi* secured with bolts.

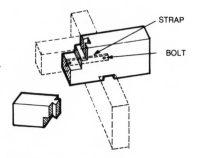

Figure 6.55. *Koshikake ari tsugi* reinforced with straps and bolts.

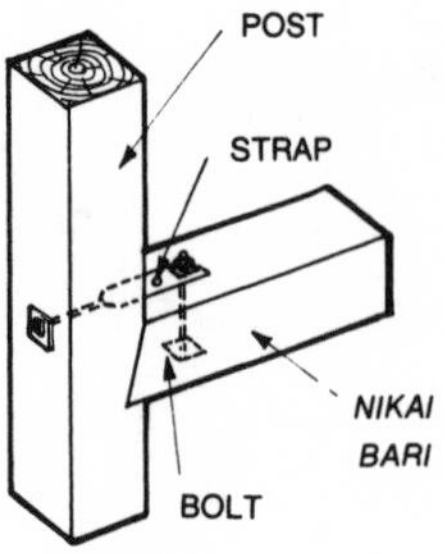

Figure 6.56. *Kashigi oire tan hozo sashi* secured with bolt.

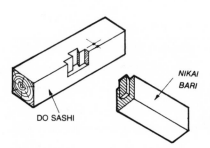

Figure 6.57. *Ari shikake* secured with strap bolt.

(4) Construction practice: In framing, usually braces are included along a horizontal plane to prevent distortion of the horizontal shape due to lateral force. However, in the case of *nikai bari* (second-floor framing) beams, especially in standard framing, very strong framing can be constructed if the beams in the *nikai bari* direction and in the *koya bari* direction are tied perpendicularly.

Shitaji—Supports

Supports to which finishing materials such as floors, walls, and ceilings are attached are called *shitaji*. An explanation of wooden *shitaji* follows:

Yuka Shitaji—Subfloors

The nature of the finished flooring, such as *tatami* (straw mat), vinyl tiles, flooring blocks, sheet flooring, and others, will determine the type of floor supports.

(1) A subfloor for *tatami* is usually made of ½ in. thick pine or Japanese cedar boards placed side by side, the ends being butt jointed and secured to the joists with nails. In quality construction, the boards are also shiplapped along their sides.

(2) The subfloor for linoleum and vinyl or plastic tiles is usually made of ½ to ¾ in. thick waterproofed plywood, secured to the joists with nails every 4 in. The length of the nails should be from 2 to 2½ times the thickness of the plywood. If the plywood were to bend as a result of people walking over it or because of other loads, the tiles would become loose. Because of this the plywood should be as thick as possible—the thicker the better.

(3) Subflooring for wood block floors.
The block flooring pieces are usually 9½ to 12 in. square and ¾ in. thick, and made of oak or beech. The pieces are usually joined by a form of edge joint. The subflooring for block floors is similar to that in (2). Today there are also plywoods veneered with block flooring patterns. With this type of material, the veneered plywood is placed directly over the joist in the same way as the subflooring plywood in (2).

(4) Subflooring for carpeting and other covering materials.
The installation for this type of subflooring is similar to that in (2), except that here the plywood subfloor is installed below the top surface of the *shikii* (headers) and *kutsuzuri* (baseboards) to allow for the thickness of the covering material.

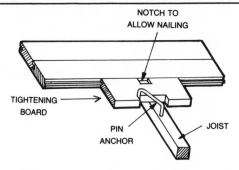

Figure 6.58. Installing wood strip flooring.

(5) Wood strip flooring.

Because of its close relation to subfloors a brief explanation of wood floors follows.

Wood flooring is usually made of ¾ in. thick and from 4 to 4¾ in. wide boards with tongue and groove edges. Various types of wood flooring are available. The boards are tightly attached to each other by using a tightening board as shown in Figure 6.58. They are then secured in place by nails. At the edge of the floor, the boards are shaped to accept posts as shown in 6.59. The edge board is pushed by the other boards until it is installed flush against a post. Then it is secured with a pin anchor.

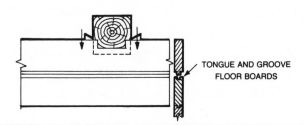

Figure 6.59. Floor board cut to fit post.

Kabe Shitaji—Wall Underlayments or Wall Sheathing

Among the wall underlayments are *komai* (furring strips), *kizuri* (traditional wood lath), *rasu* (Westernized lath) and *rasu bodo* (Westernized lath board) underlayment.

(1) *Komai* (bamboo) underlayment is the traditional Japanese lathing method. Green bamboos are split about 1¼ in. thick and are tied to wall bridgings with strings to form a mesh. Then clay mixed with straw is plastered on both sides of this bamboo lath. After the application of a scratch (first) coat, smoothing (second) and a brown (third) coat, a finishing coat of mud, sand, or plaster is applied.

Today it is common practice to put a finishing coat over the brown coat, which in turn is applied over a scratch coat which has been applied over wood or metal lath.

(2) Wood lath underlayment.

Wood lath is commonly made of thin, long cedar boards, about 1¼ to 1½ in. wide and ¼ in. thick, which are secured to the studs with a slight space as shown in Figure 6.60a. The wall is finished by applying plaster or stucco over the lath.

The boards are randomly butt-joined in groups of six to ten pieces. Laths are spaced about ⅜ in. apart and secured to each stud with two nails. At inside corners, the laths are secured to a nailing board as shown in Figure 6.60b.

Where tile is applied on either outside or inside walls, the lath board is usually about ½ in. thick by 3 in. wide. The term which describes the lathing for tile is *nakanuki* (instead of *kizuri*).

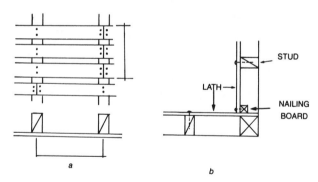

Figure 6.60. Wood lath underlayment.

(3) Lath underlayment which is made of metal is backed with asphalt felt (paper-backed lath) which is installed on top of the wood lath. The most commonly used finish with this type of underlayment is sprayed integral-colored mortar over regular mortar.

The wood lath is randomly butt-joined in groups not exceeding 5 pieces which are secured with nails to the studs or other receiving boards. On top of this lath, the asphalt felt and metal lath are attached with staples every 12 in. in both vertical and horizontal directions.

(4) Lath board underlayment is plaster board with small holes or indentations on its surface. Since it is fire resistant, the boards are used as underlay for walls in kitchens and bathrooms.

To install this plaster board, the necessary *dobuchi* (ties or bridges) must be put in place. On them, the plaster boards are secured with special large flat-head nails.

In *shinkabe* construction, the insulation is framed into the wood and used to prevent separation and cracks where plaster has filled the grooves especially made on the post to receive the lath boards (Figure 6.61a).

In *okabe* construction, notches are carved out on vertical framing members such as the posts and studs to secure the *dobuchi* ties flush. Their end joints are randomly set (Figure 6.61b).

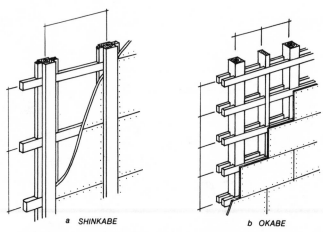

a SHINKABE   b OKABE

Figure 6.61. Securing plaster board underlayment.

(5) Underlayment for prefinished plywood panels.

With advances in the manufacture of plywoods, numerous textured and colored prefinished plywood panels have been introduced which are now widely used as interior finishing materials. Prefinished plywood paneling includes the following:

(i) Printed veneered paneling: Wood grain prints are glued to a plywood surface.

(ii) Real wood paneling: Thin wood veneers are glued to the plywood surface.

(iii) Vinyl surfaced paneling: Vinyl sheets are glued to plywood.

The plywood base varies from ¼ in to ⅝ in. in thickness. Thin boards should be avoided since they will bend. The underlayment for these panels is similar to that in (4) above. Adhesives are applied to the *dobuchi* or *nuki* (ties or bridges) and the panels are attached to them.

Ceiling Underlayments

Ceiling styles include the *saobuchi,* the *hari,* and the *nuri* ceiling. In each case, the ceiling is attached to the bottom of the *nobuchi* (ceiling joists) which are suspended by *tsuriki* (hangers). (See Figure 6.62.)

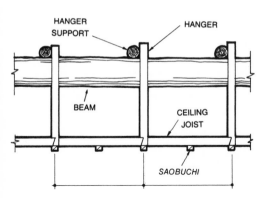

Figure 6.62. Ceiling underlayments.

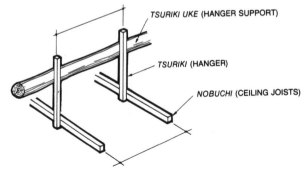

Figure 6.63. Ceiling hangers and joists.

(1) The *saobuchi* ceiling underlayment: *Tsuriki uke* (hanger supports) are placed perpendicularly on the beams, at about 36 in. intervals. (Usually a 2¾ in. diameter log is used.) To secure the hanger support on the beams use the *najimi kakinose kake* joint secured with a pin anchor or nails. The hangers (about 1 in.×1¼ in.) are hung from these members at intervals. The hangers are nailed onto the hanger supports at one end, and in turn at the other

end are connected to the *nobuchi* or *urasan* (ceiling joists) with a *kata ari* (half dovetail) joint secured with nails. (Ceiling joists are about 1½×2 in. They are called *urasan* only with a *saobuchi* ceiling.)

(2) Fiberboard ceiling underlayment.
Sound absorbent fiberboards or acoustic tiles are installed as shown in Figure 6.64. The *nobuchi* (ceiling joists) are hung onto them 18 in. on center, and the underlayment boards (about ⅝ in.×4 in.) are attached perpendicularly with a spacing equal to the width of the acoustic tiles. In between the boards, another board half the width of the underlayment boards is installed. These board underlayments are nailed to the underside of the ceiling joists.

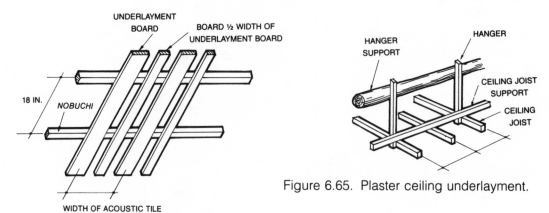

Figure 6.65. Plaster ceiling underlayment.

Figure 6.64. Fiberboard ceiling underlayment.

(3) Ceiling board underlayment.
The ceiling joists for securing the lath boards, particle boards, or plaster boards are attached to the beams with a lap joint and secured with nails (Figure 6.66).

(4) Plaster ceiling underlayment.
The ceiling joists are nailed parallel to each other and 18 in. apart (measuring from the inside face of one to the outside face of the next joist), onto the bottom face of the beam. Wooden laths are attached to the bottom of the ceiling joists, as for wall lathing (Figure 6.65).

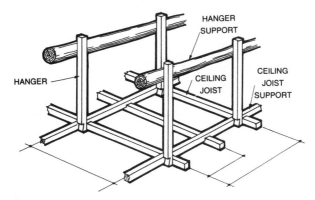

Figure 6.66. Ceiling board underlayment.

Interior Construction

Interior construction here includes the finishing around openings, ceilings, walls, and all other parts of the interior space. Since most of these are exposed, the selection of materials and the construction have to be done with special care. As there are numerous ways to finish the interior space and all its parts, only the main parts will be discussed here. An explanation of stair construction follows in a separate section.

Uchinori—Headers, Jambs, and Sills

Generally *uchinori* refers to the finished framing around an opening.

(1) *Shikii*—grooved sill for sliding doors.

(i) Materials: Usually Japanese cypress and pine are used, but sometimes Japanese cedar is also used. For all these, select wood with edge (vertical) grain from pieces which have been quarter-sawn. Place with the front side of the wood on the top and plane or dado out the grooves or tracks.

(ii) Size: The sill should be of the same thickness as the *tatami* mats. Its width should be as shown in Figure 6.67. On the *tatami* mat side (*A*), its edge should be flush with the edge of the post, and on the *engawa* (exterior corridor) side (*B*) its edge should butt the inner side of the bevel of the post.

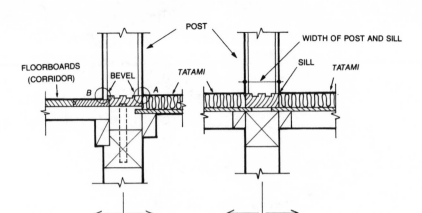

Figure 6.67. Relation of sill to *tatami* and floor boards.

(iii) Dimensions of the grooves or tracks: Depending on the number of sliding doors to be used and how they are to operate (whether in a single groove or in three grooves) the grooves should be ⅛ in. wider than the *mikomi* thickness. The *mikomi* is the rabbetted edge on the bottom or top of the door that fits into the groove or track. For a *fusama* door* the track width should be ¾ in. and the space between the tracks, called the *hibata*, should be ⅜ in.

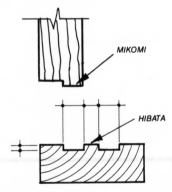

Figure 6.68. Grooves for *shikii*.

*Translator's note: A *shoji* is a light, translucent door while a *fusama* is a solid door. Usually, *shoji* doors are located between a *tatami* mat room and an *engawa* (exterior corridor), while *fusama* doors are used between two *tatama* mat rooms or between an inner hall and a room.

(iv) Joints between the *shikii* and posts: There are numerous joining methods, but the one most commonly used has one end of the *shikii* connected by a *yokohozo sashi* (half blind mortise and tenon) joint, and other end connected with a *yokosen uchi* (spline) joint and secured with nails as shown in Figure 6.69. Figures 6.70–6.72 show the superior grade joints. Between the bottom of the *shikii* and the joist tops, wedges are placed about 20 in apart and secured with nails, to maintain straightness and prevent sagging.

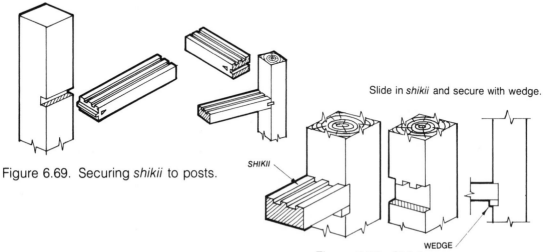

Figure 6.69. Securing *shikii* to posts.

Slide in *shikii* and secure with wedge.

SHIKII

WEDGE

Figure 6.70. *Shikii* as tenon.

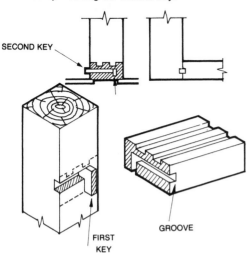

Shikii is introduced from above onto first key,then locked by inserting the second key.

SECOND KEY

FIRST KEY

GROOVE

Figure 6.71. Securing *shikii* with keys.

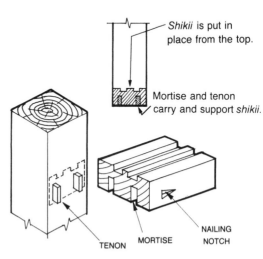

Shikii is put in place from the top.

Mortise and tenon carry and support *shikii*.

TENON   MORTISE   NAILING NOTCH

Figure 6.72. Tenons inset in post.

(v) Construction practice: The grooves or tracks on the *shikii*, as well as on the *kamoi* (grooved headers), must be made on the front side of the wood. If the back side were used there could be distortion, and the grain would come up, causing splinters.

N.B. In a Japanese house, the threshold should never be stepped upon; instead, it should be stepped *over*.

(2) *Kamoi*—grooved header for sliding doors.

(i) Material: This should be of the same wood as the posts, and should be select grade edge (vertical) grain lumber.

(ii) Size: Usually *kamoi* are 1½ in. thick, but in quality construction they are made from 0.4 to 0.6 times the post size. The *kamoi's* width should match the inside (i.e., shorter) dimension between the beveled edges of the post.

(iii) Dimensions for *shikii* (grooves or tracks): The width of the grooves is usually ⅝ in.

(iv) *Kamoi* and post joint: It is common practice to have a mortise and tenon joint at one end as shown in Figure 6.73*a* and to blind nail the other end, in order to simplify assembly. There is also a more sophisticated joint for this purpose, as shown in Figure 6.73*b*.

(v) Construction practice: This will be the same as the *shikii*.

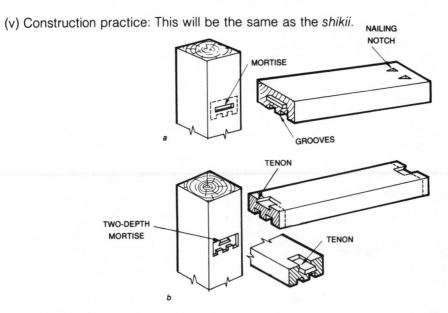

Figure 6.73. Joints for securing *kamoi*.

(3) *Tsukegamoi* or *tsukekamoi* (molding) and *tatamiyose* (base trim).

Tsukegamoi refers to a horizontal wood trim on plaster walls placed at the same height as the *kamoi*. *Tatamiyose* refers to the wood trim which runs flush with the *tatami* matting around the room at the base of the plaster walls. For each of these, the material should be the same as that for the *shikii* and the *kamoi*. How to install them is shown in Figures 6.74a and *b*.

The *tsukegamoi* are joined at one end by a half blind mortise and tenon joint, and at the other end they are blind nailed.

The *tatamiyose* are blind nailed to the posts at both ends. Wedges are placed at the bottom of the *tatamiyose* and are then nailed to the subflooring.

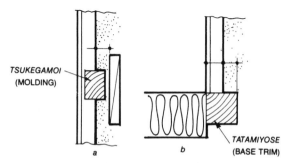

Figure 6.74. *Tsukegamoi* (header molding) and *tatamiyose* (base trim).

(4) *Uchinori nageshi*—frieze trim.

This traditional trim is rarely used today. In its place another trim, called simply *nageshi,* is used.

Nageshi is a wood trim placed above the *kamoi* and the *tsukegamoi* on all the walls of a room. Traditionally there were various types of trims. Today, however, *nageshi* usually refers to the trim shown in Figure 6.75. Also, there are many modern methods of *tatami* room construction which entirely omit the *nageshi*.

(1) Materials: It is preferable to match the wood used for the *kamoi,* but edge (vertical) grain Japanese cedar is also widely used.

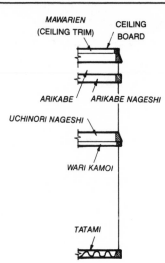

Figure 6.75. *Nageshi* (trim).

(2) Size: The *nageshi's* width should be from about 0.7 to 0.8 of the post's size, and its depth from about 1⅜ to 2in. Its shape is trapezoidal and is referred to as *nageshibiki.* (A rectangular piece is sliced diagonally in half as shown in Figure 6.76.) Today, commercial trims are being used more and more frequently.

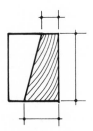

Figure 6.76. Pattern for cutting *nageshi.*

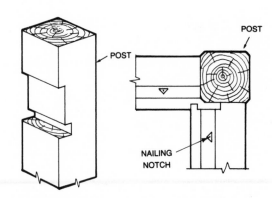

Figure 6.77. Joining and securing *nageshi.*

(3) Joining the post and the *nageshi:* the post must be notched with an *eriwa kaki* (collar ring) notch. A nailing notch is carved out in the *nageshi* at 12 in. intervals and it is then nailed to the *kamoi* (see Figure 6.77). At the inside corners, a *shitaba dome mechigai ire* joint

(mortise and tenon locked at bottom) is used. At the outside corners a *mitsuke dome* (blind miter) joint is used (Figure 6.78).

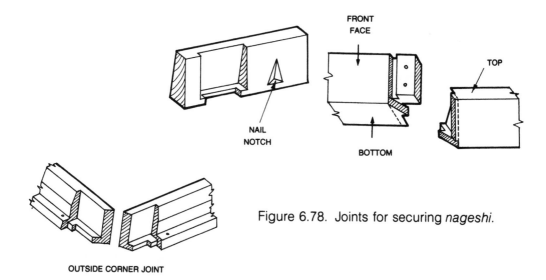

Figure 6.78. Joints for securing *nageshi*.

Tenjo Mawari—Ceilings

There are numerous styles of ceiling, but here only the most common Japanese ceiling, called *saoen tenjo* (*saoen* ceiling) will be discussed. *Saoen tenjo* consists of *mawarien* (ceiling trim) at the junction of ceiling and walls, and *saoen* (the exposed ceiling joists) supported by the *mawarien* and the *tenjo ita* (ceiling boards).

(1) *Mawarien*—ceiling trim.

(i) Materials: It is preferable to use the same material as is used for the *nageshi*, but Japanese cypress and Japanese cedar are also widely used.

(ii) Size: The width should be from about 0.4 to 0.5 of the post's size, and the depth of the bottom should be from about 1½ to 2 in. *Mawarien* extends from ¼ to ⅜ in. beyond the surface of the post (Figure 6.79).

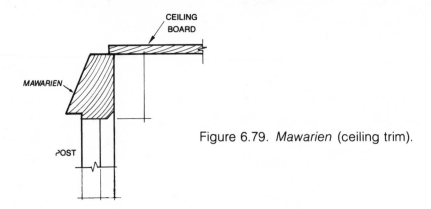

Figure 6.79. *Mawarien* (ceiling trim).

(iii) *Shiguchi*—right angle joints: For the post an *eriwa kaki* (collar dovetail notch) joint is used, and for the *mawarien,* an *ari kaki* (dovetail notch) joint firmly set in by wedges and secured with nails is used (Figure 6.80). For the inside corners, a *shitaba dome* joint (mortise and tenon locked at bottom) is used, and at the outside corners, an *odome* (blind miter) joint is used (Figure 6.81).

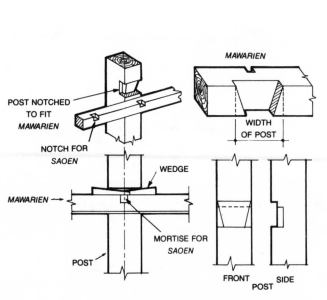

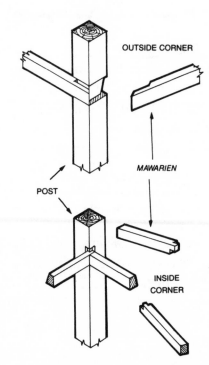

Figure 6.80. Joining *mawarien.*

Figure 6.81. Corner joints for *mawarien.*

(2) *Saoen*—exposed ceiling joists.

(i) Materials: Usually the wood used is the same as for the *mawarien,* but sometimes small peeled or unpeeled logs, or bamboo poles are used.

(ii) Size: A rule of thumb is to use material that is about 0.6 the thickness of the *mawarien.* However, pieces 1 ¼ × 1 in. or 1 ⅜ × 1 1/16 in., shaped as shown in Figure 6.82, are also commonly used.

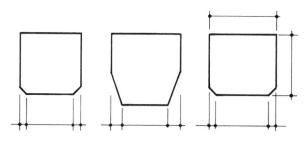

Figure 6.82. Cross-sections of *saoen.*

(iii) *Shiguchi*—end joints: The *mawarien* is joined by the *oire* method (the *mawarien* is notched out to support the *saoen*) and secured with nails (see Figure 6.83).

(iv) Construction practice: The following points should be considered when deciding the location of the *saoen:*

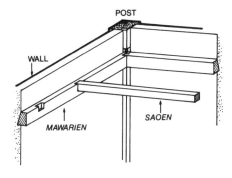

Figure 6.83. Joining *saoen.*

(a) In a room with a *tokonoma* (an alcove where a scroll is hung and/or an *ikebana*—a formal flower arrangement—is kept), the *saoen* should be installed parallel with it.

(b) In a room without a *tokonoma,* the *saoen* should be placed parallel with the entrance. However, in a *tsuginoma* (annex) the *saoen* should be placed to match the ones in the *shunoma* (main room).

(c) In a hall, they should be placed to run lengthwise.

(3) *Tenjo ita*—ceiling boards

(i) Materials: Edge (vertical) grain as well as half-round grain boards of Japanese cedar, Japanese cypress, and pine are all used. Today, veneered boards of these species are widely used.

(ii) Size: The *tenjo ita* (ceiling boards) are usually from ¼ to 5/16 in. thick. They are usually 12 in. wide, and 13, 10, 9 or 8 boards are used, depending on the size of the room.

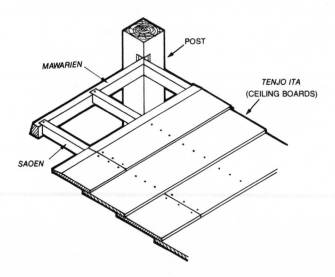

Figure 6.84. Securing ceiling boards.

(iii) Construction method: Make a gentle bevel along one edge of the boards so that their edge thickness is about ⅛ in. Overlap the next board about 10 in., and then secure to the *saoen* and *mawarien* with nails (see Figure 6.84). In superior construction, the top of the overlapping board is grooved as in Figure 6.85a. This method is called *wagaeshi*. The over-lapping boards are joined with nails or pins as shown in Figure 6.85b and c.

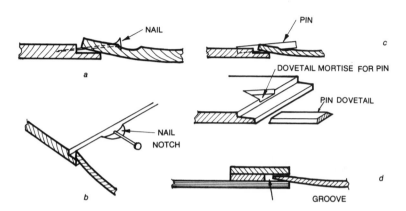

Figure 6.85. Detail of superior quality ceiling attachment.

Where a ceiling board connects to plywood or to other artificial boards, a groove, as shown in Figure 6.85d, is made and the ceiling board fits into it. The ceiling boards are placed in a room so that the edges are seen as one looks into the room from its entrance.

(iv) Construction practice: When a ceiling is placed absolutely flat, the center of the ceiling usually appears to sag, due to an optical illusion. To correct this illusion, the ceiling must be slightly raised towards the center. (The pitch should be about ⅛ in. rise every 6 ft.)

Kaidan—Stairs

In providing vertical access, stairs must not only be placed at a convenient location, but consideration must be given to their design and decorative qualities. Their specifications are spelled out in the architectural building code, and they must be built accordingly. However, as the code only sets minimum requirements, care must be taken to build them in such a way that they can be used comfortably from day to day (see Figure 6.86).

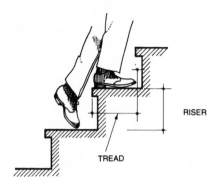

Figure 6.86. *Kaidan* (stairs).

Hako kaidan—box stairs

The *hako* stair is walled on both sides and runs straight or is "L"-shaped. It is very common in residences. The stair is composed of *soku ita* (stringers), *fumizura* (treads), *uraita* (soffits), and at times risers (see Figure 6.87). Stairs are usually from 30 to 32 in. wide, since they are generally placed between posts that are 36 in. apart at their centers.

(1) Materials: Pine, Japanese cypress, zelkova, and at times *ruan* (lauan) mahogany all without pith are used. However, it is advisable not to use *ruan* because it usually is worm-eaten.

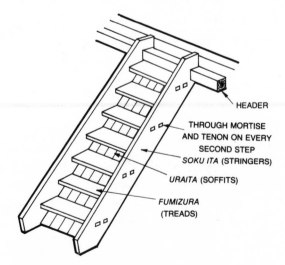

Figure 6.87. *Hako kaidan* (box stairs).

(2) Dimensions: Stringers and treads should be from 1¼ to 1¾ in. thick. The width of the stringers should be 2⅜ in. more than the height resulting from the pitch of the riser and tread (see Figure 6.88). The soffits are usually made of Japanese cedar from ⅜ to ⅝ in. thick. The width is an equally divided dimension between the inside faces of the stringers. Sometimes plywood is used for making soffits.

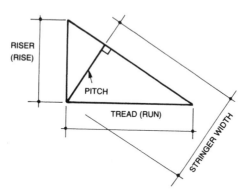

Figure 6.88. Width of stringer relative to riser and tread.

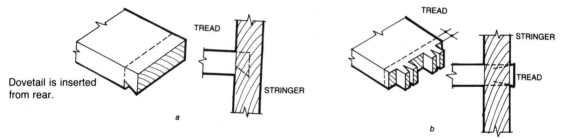

Figure 6.89. Joints for attaching treads.

(3) *Shiguchi*—end joints.

The treads are connected to the stringers with every other tread having a *kata ari suitsuki* (half dovetail dado) and the others having two *kaki hozowari* (split tenons) which are secured to the stringers with wedges (see Figure 6.89).

The soffits are joined to the underside of the treads with an *ai jakkuri* (shiplap) joint and secured with nails. When the risers are installed, the soffits are removed. The risers are connected to the undersides of the upper treads with a *fumita uwaba koanahori oire* (dado) joint, and secured with nails to both the stringers and the lower treads.

(4) Construction practice: To prevent splinters when walking on or wiping the stairs, the *kiura* (back side) of the board must always be used.

Katageta kaidan—beam framed stairs

These are bigger than the *hako* stairs, with more complex parts such as newel posts, railings, carriages, and metal fasteners. (see Figure 6.90).

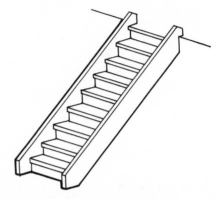

Figure 6.90. *Katageta kaidan* (beam framed stairs).

(1) Materials: These are the same as those used for *hako* stairs. However, though zelkova, oak, and pine are also used, special consideration is given to the finishing.

(2) Dimensions: The treads and stringers are similar to those in *hako* stairs. The riser is about ¾ in. thick. The posts are about 4 in. square except for those that are exposed as architectural parts of the stair, and these are about 6 in. square.

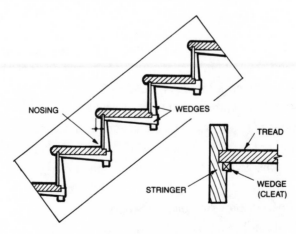

Figure 6.91. Detail of stair members.

(3) *Shiguchi*—end joints.

(i) Stringer: The stringer is routed to receive treads, risers, and wedges. This kind of routing is called *sasara hori* (Figure 6.92). Where extra thick treads are used, a carriage is placed under each tread to prevent warpage (see Figure 6.93). The joints connecting stringers and posts and/or beams of the building frame are usually *aikaki* (lap) joints secured with nails.

The top of the stringer is connected to the supporting member with a *kageiri ari otoshi* (dovetail stop lap joint) and secured with a strap bolt (see Figure 6.94).

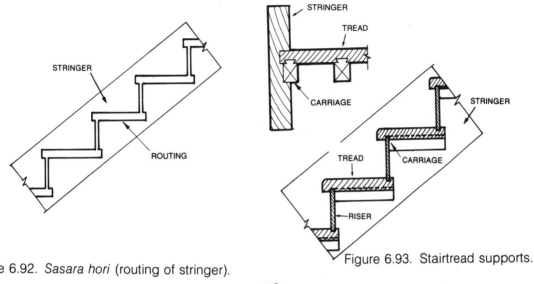

Figure 6.92. *Sasara hori* (routing of stringer).

Figure 6.93. Stairtread supports.

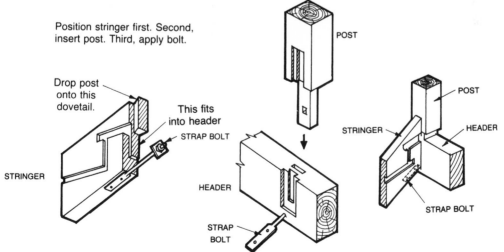

Figure 6.94. Securing top of stringer to supporting members.

(ii) Newel post: The baluster and newel posts are joined to the stringer with a long tenon secured with a pin (see Figure 6.95). The joint used to connect the handrail to the newel post is a *naga hozo sashi* (long tenon) reinforced with a metal fastener on a *jigoku hozo sashi* ("hell" tenon). Another method for connecting the balusters to both the handrail and the carriage is to use a *tan hozo sashi* joint (short tenon), or to use a long tenon secured with a pin on every other baluster and a short tenon on the remaining ones (see Figure 6.96).

(4) Construction practice: Since a stair is composed of many parts requiring various joints, it is important to construct it without torque or warp. The quality of a stair's construction is judged by the alignment of the nosings (the parts of the stair treads projecting beyond the risers) to each other.

Figure 6.96. Alternating short and long tenons.

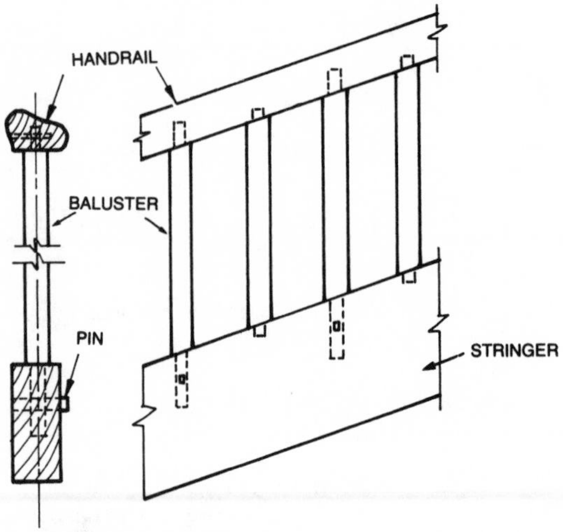

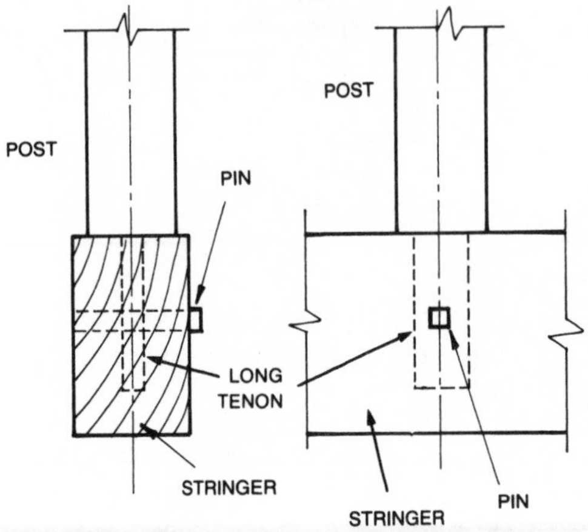

Figure 6.95. Long tenon used to secure balusters and newel posts.

Exterior Construction

Since all the exterior construction materials are exposed to rain, Japanese cypress, *sawara,* and *hiba* should be used—or any other woods which can resist the effect of moisture. Also, special consideration must be given to weatherproofing.

Hisashi Mawari—Eaves

Eaves are usually placed over windows and doors for protection against rain, snow, and sun. There are many ways to construct eaves, but the most common method is to use an *udegi* (bracket).

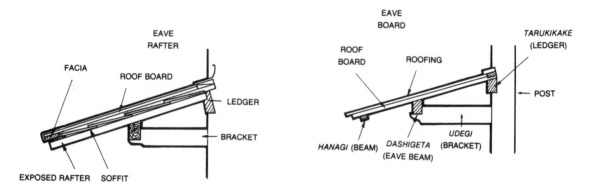

Figure 6.97. Eave members.

(1) Material: Usually Japanese cypress that is free of cracks is used.

(2) Size: The *udegi* (bracket) and *dashigeta* (eave beam) are usually from 1¾ to 2⅜ in. wide and from 2⅜ to 4 in. deep. Sometimes a log is used for the *dashigeta.* Its diameter is usually from 2⅜ to 3 in., or about the same size as the *udegi.* The *hakake,* or *taruki kake* (both are names for the ledger), is from 1¼ to 1½ in. wide. Its depth should be the same as that of the *dashigeta.* The width of the rafters is determined by the projection of the eaves, but a width from 1¼ to 1½ in. will usually suffice. The boards used for eave soffits are usually from 11/16 to 1¼ in. thick.

(3) *Shiguchi*—end joints.

The joints to be used between the *udegi* (brackets) and posts are *shitage kama* (notched full tenons) secured with wedges (Figure 6.98). Figure 6.99 shows the joint used for connecting the *udegi* to a beam. To connect the *taruki kake* (ledgers) to the posts either an *eriwa kaki* joint (cross lap with collar) or an *aikaki* (cross lap) joint is used (Figure 6.100).

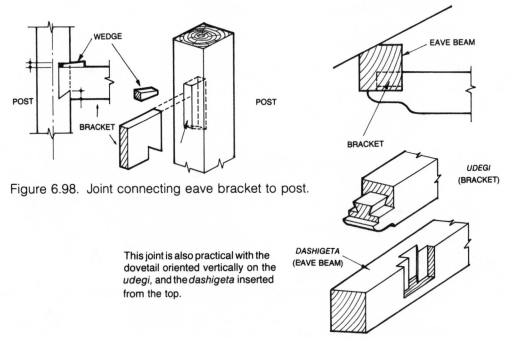

Figure 6.98. Joint connecting eave bracket to post.

This joint is also practical with the dovetail oriented vertically on the *udegi,* and the *dashigeta* inserted from the top.

Figure 6.99. Joint connecting eave bracket to beam.

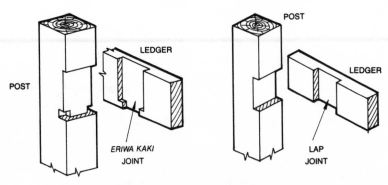

Figure 6.100. Joint connecting ledger to post.

(4) Construction practice: When installing the *udegi,* tilt it slightly upward as illustrated in Figure 6.101. This is done to compensate for its natural tendency to sag slightly after completion of construction. Throughout the construction period a temporary support or underpinning should be put in place (see Figure 6.102).

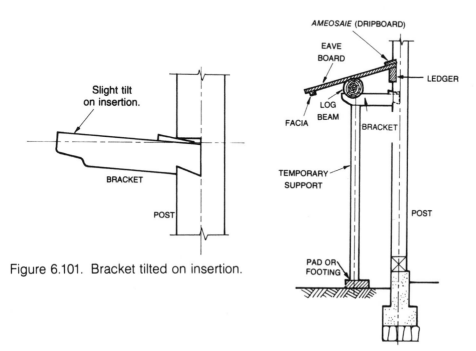

Figure 6.101. Bracket tilted on insertion.

Figure 6.102. Temporary bracket support.

Amajimai—Weather Proofing

To prevent rainwater or other waters that have been driven against the exterior walls from running down and seeping into the side, the proper drips and joints must be used where connections are made.

(1) Material: Japanese cypress boards without pith are used.

(2) Dimensions: The drip board's size is determined by the exterior finishing material as follows: Width of drip board = exterior finishing material + depth of nosing + depth of notch on post.

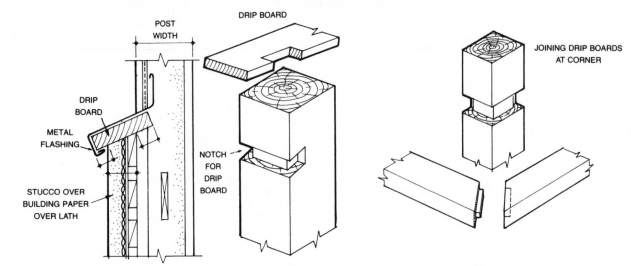

Figure 6.103. Joinery for weather proofing.

(3) Method of connection: The joint used at the post is an *eriwa kaki* (cross lap with collar) secured with nails, and at the corner post an *odome mechigai ire* (large stop mortise and tenon) is used, secured with nails (see Figure 6.103).

(4) Construction practice: Provide a slope for drainage, and wrap it with galvanized sheet metal (metal flashing) to make it completely waterproof.

Single Groove *Shikii* (Sills) and *Kamoi* (Headers)

These *shikii* and *kamoi* are used for the *amado* (shutters).

(1) Material: Japanese cypress without pitch is used. Select only straight boards since any warpage will make it difficult to slide the shutters.

(2) Dimensions: The width should be 1⅞ in. and the depth about 0.45 of the post's size.

(3) Method of construction: The *shikii* groove's depth will be determined by the size of the rollers (wheels) to be installed on the shutters. Both the *kamoi* and *shikii* are usually nailed on, and the nail holes plugged. In quality construction an *inrobame* joint (a variety of tongue

and groove joint) is used (see Figure 6.104). The stop is connected to the header groove with a *tsuno nobashi* joint (a form of mortise and tenon) and secured to the post with nails spaced from 6 to 7⅞ in. apart. The nail holes should then be plugged.

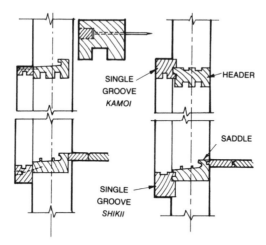

Figure 6.104. *Shikii* and *kamoi* for shutters.

(4) Construction practice: Another method of installing shutters is to replace the grooved tracks with metal rails. The grooved tracks are necessary for protection against burglary or vandalism. Weep holes should be provided to allow rainwater to drain off.

Tobukuro—Shutter Housings

The shutters are stored in the *tobukuro*. In the designing of Japanese houses, the *tobukuro* pose a decorative problem, and their material is chosen primarily for its esthetic qualities. Since the *tobukuro* are built onto the exterior of the house, Japanese cypress without pith is the most suitable wood. Sometimes cherry and Japanese cedar are also used.

Types of *tobukuro:*

(1) *Saraita tobukuro:* This housing, used on rural houses having two or three shutters, consists only of a bottom platform. It has neither a *moki ita* (front panel) nor *tsuma ita* (end panels) (see Figure 6.105).

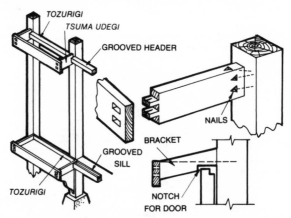

Figure 6.105. *Saraita tobukuro* (simple shutter housing).

(i) Construction practice: The *tsuma udegi* (cantilevered outrigger) is placed at an angle, so that the end connected to the post is ⅜ in. higher than the other end. The *tsuma udegi* is toe-nailed to the post with large nails. The facia connected to the other end is joined with a *nimai hozonuki wari kusabi uchi* (wedged mortise and tenon) joint. Between the posts which support the *tobukuro, tozurigi* (guide pieces) are placed from ¾ to 1¼ in. beyond the posts at the header and the sill at the proper heights for the grooved tracks.

(2) *Tsumaitadate tobukuro:* This is the standard housing and is composed of front and end panels, a bottom platform and ceiling, and a grooved headerguide (see Figure 6.106)

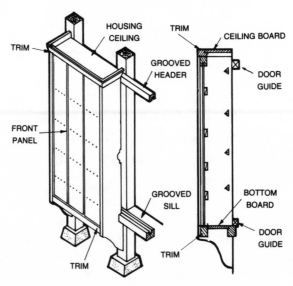

Figure 6.106. *Tsumaitadate tobukuro* (standard shutter housing).

(i) Construction practice: The joint used to connect the end panels and the top frame is a *kodotsuki ariotoshi* joint (dovetail dado with haunch on both sides) (Figure 6.107a). A *kata ari* (half dovetail) joint secured with nails is used to join the end panel and the bottom platform. The end panel and the bottom frame are joined with a *nimai hozonuki kusabi uchi* (double-wedged tenon) joint (Figure 6.107b) The end panel is connected to the post with *koanaire* (dado and rabbet) joint and is then toe-nailed. (Figure 6.107c).

(3) *Hashiradate tobukuro:* When there are a great number of shutters, this housing is used, but is is become very rare (see Figure 108).

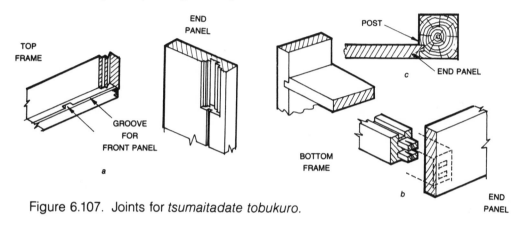

Figure 6.107. Joints for *tsumaitadate tobukuro.*

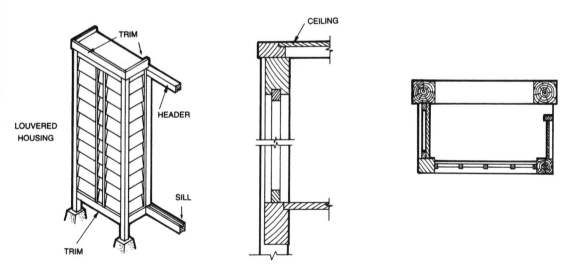

Figure 6.108. *Hashiradate tobukuro* (complex shutter housing).

The post and top frame are connected with a *kodotsuki ariotoshi* joint (dovetail dado with a haunch on both sides) secured with a steel pin anchor (Figure 109*a*). The same joint but using a pin connects the post to the bottom frame (Figure 109*b*). At the access edge a *hodate bashira* (small edge post) is used.

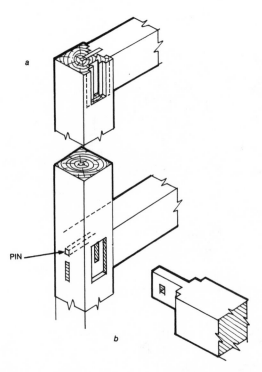

Figure 6.109. Joints for *hashiradate tobukuro*.

CHAPTER 7

FRAMING AND SECURING

Basic to wood frame construction is the connection of the wooden members. The quality of this construction will affect not only the exterior appearance but also the structural strength of the building.

Since the strength of a building is determined by the quality of its framing, simply using large, strong materials will not provide the best framing. Methods for resisting external forces such as compression, tension, and torque must be taken into account, and pieces should not be notched indiscriminately. Thin materials can resist only a small amount of force. Where a large member is required, the appropriate joint and securing method must be considered. With proper securing, members will adhere to each other and will be able to resist external forces. The framing itself should be simple and should not cause damage to any members. Once they are framed in place each member should act as part of the whole, permitting no loosening of any parts. In order to achieve these standards, *kusabi* (wedges), *shachisen* and *hanasen* (keys), and *komisen* (pins) were used in the past. Today, metal fasteners are more commonly used.

Metal Fasteners

Kugi—nails

Nails are the simplest of connectors. There are many types of nails made of a variety of materials, such as bamboo, wood, and metal. The length of the nails for a particular job should be about 2.5 or 3 times as long as the thickness of the boards to be secured.

(1) *Kugiuchi*—nailing.
When nailing twice on the same piece of edge (vertical) grain lumber, a split may connect to one that occurred on the previous nailing, easily causing a crack. When such a crack occurs, the nailing will become ineffective. Therefore, nails should be spaced at least 4 in. apart. As nails are usually aligned, it is best to pre-drill nail holes where the nailing has to be done on the same grain. Nails should be nailed at an angle to the surface as in Figure 7.1*b*, because with perpendicular nailing (Figure 7.1*a*), the nails more readily become loose. As nailing parallel to the grain is ineffective, nails should be toe-nailed, as shown in Figure 7.2.

As shown in Figure 7.3, when a thick piece has to be nailed to a thinner one, a nailing notch should be chiseled out on the thicker piece.

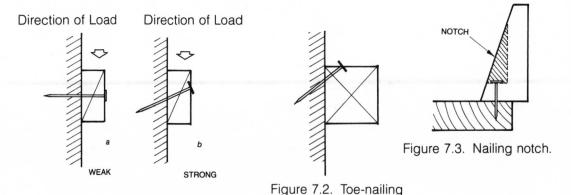

Figure 7.3. Nailing notch.

Figure 7.2. Toe-nailing

Figure 7.1. Correct angle for nailing.

(2) *Uchikomi*—hammering.

As shown in Figure 7.4, the hammer head should be aligned with the axis of the nail. If this is done the nailing is easily accomplished without any excessive use of force. The different types of nailing are shown in Figures 7.5 and 7.6.

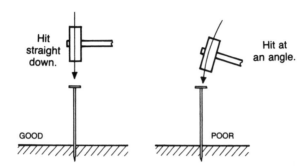

Figure 7.4. Alignment of hammer head with nail.

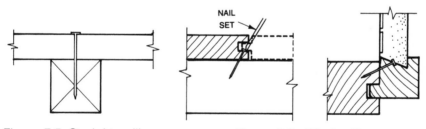

Figure 7.5 Straight nailing.   Figure 7.6. Blind nailing.

(3) Other nailing methods: As shown in Figure 7.7, nails can be hidden by countersinking the nail heads. The use of wood screws will simplify taking pieces apart. To prevent nails from coming out, *gyakume* (bent head nails) should be used. To prevent their loosening, *kaku kugi* or *funa kugi* nails (see Figure 7.8) should be used. These nails are also commonly used by roofers. Also there are *aikugi* (double pointed nails) and *namako kugi* (corrugated metal fasteners) to join two thick boards.

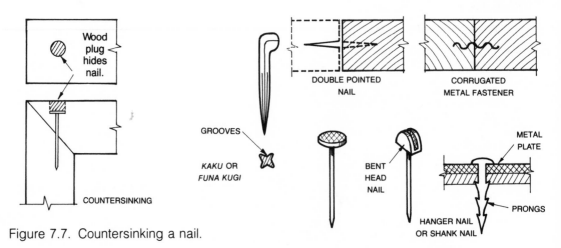

Wood plug hides nail.

COUNTERSINKING

Figure 7.7. Countersinking a nail.

DOUBLE POINTED NAIL

CORRUGATED METAL FASTENER

GROOVES

KAKU OR *FUNA KUGI*

BENT HEAD NAIL

METAL PLATE

HANGER NAIL OR SHANK NAIL

PRONGS

Figure 7.8. Other nailing methods.

Kasugai—anchors

Anchors are used to tie two pieces together to resist any pulling (tensional forces). Figures 7.9–7.11 show the various types of anchors.

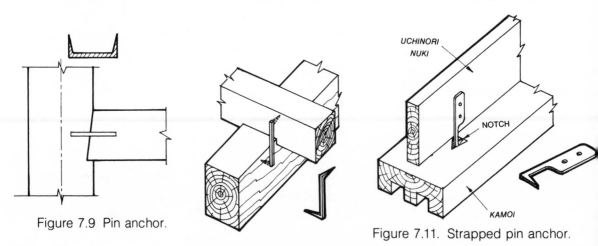

Figure 7.9 Pin anchor.

Figure 7.10. Twisted pin anchor.

UCHINORI NUKI

NOTCH

KAMOI

Figure 7.11. Strapped pin anchor.

Boruto—bolts

Bolts are used in tying and framing pieces.

Jiberu—split rings and shear plates

In this age of steel frames, many truss beams are made of steel, and split rings are rarely used. However, when wood trusses were still widely used, split rings and bolts functioned as an essential unit. The torque acting as a tensional force on the axis of the bolt is reversed by the rotation of the split ring (see Figure 7.12).

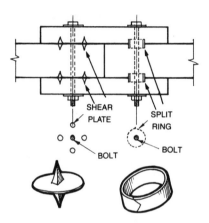

Figure 7.12. Shear plate and split ring.

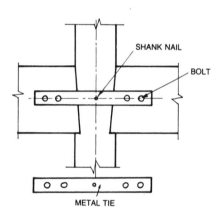

Figure 7.13. Metal tie.

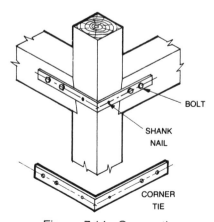

Figure 7.14. Corner tie.

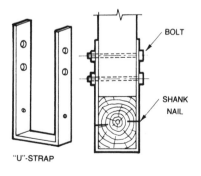

Figure 7.15. "U"-strap.

Other metal fasteners and adhesives

Other metal connectors are metal ties, corner ties, and "U"—straps. (Their applications are shown in Figures 7.13–7.15.) Adhesives are used mainly on thin and finishing materials to avoid the use of nails and exposed nail heads. However, glues usually lose their adhesive quality when exposed to moisture and humidity.

Preparation for Framing

Mizumori—leveling and *yarikata*—staking

(1) Leveling equipment: Leveling is done when surveying the site in order to obtain a horizontal plane. Unless this is done accurately, even where vertical adjustments are made when installing the posts, the beams will not sit perfectly level, and this will interfere with the proper functioning of the doors, as well as the correct fit of additional elements.

According to ancient records, horizontal planes were once determined using rain water gutters and folding screens.

(i) *Suitoi* level. As shown in Figure 7.16, projections of equal height are made at each end of the groove. A level plane is obtained by filling the groove with water and adjusting the tool so that the water will cover the projection tips (points A & B).

A modern leveling tool has at its center a curved glass tube filled with just enough water or clear oil to leave a small air bubble (see Figure 7.17). By tilting the level until the air bubble is centered, the bottom of the tool becomes level. This level is also used in plumbing, for pipe installation, and in masonry construction and tile work.

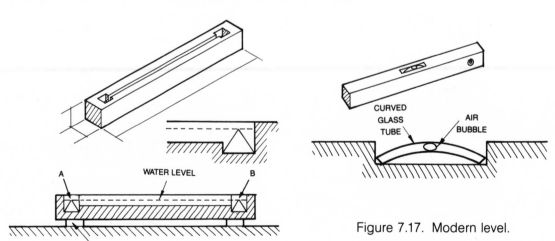

Figure 7.16. *Sutoi* (water level).

Figure 7.17. Modern level.

(ii) *Byobu* — screen

Byobu is a type of door, called a screen. By aligning the screen (the four corners of which are at right angles to each other) to a plumb line, and using the top or bottom edge as a guide, a horizontal line can be drawn (see Figure 7.18).

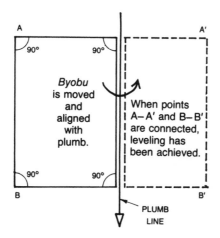

Figure 7.18. Plumbing a *byobu* (screen).

(iii) *Mizuso* — water tank. By placing a tank full of water at the center of the site, a level can be obtained by pumping the glass tube with a thumb until water appears on the glass tube (see Figure 7.19). The water at the end of the hose will seek the same level as the water in the tank. Thus, a constant level throughout the site may be obtained. This procedure is based on capillary action, and the fact that water seeks its own level in a closed system.

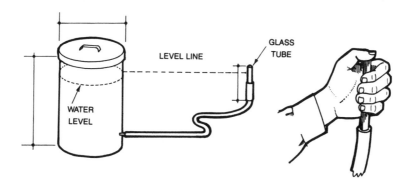

Figure 7.19. Leveling with a *mizuso* (water tank).

(iv) *Suijungi*—transit or theodolite.

A transit is comprised of a telescope, level, and level adjuster, and is set on top of a tripod (see Figure 7.20). First the front leg of the tripod is set firmly at about the center of the work site. The other two legs are then spread and adjusted so as to set the top as level as possible. The transit is then attached to the tripod and is further adjusted with the leveling screws. Since the attached level favors the higher side, two of the three leveling screws must be turned simultaneously in opposite directions, as shown in Figure 7.21. Then the telescope is rotated 120° and a new pair of leveling screws are worked. This process is repeated until the transit is set as close to perfectly level as is possible.

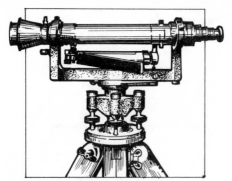

Figure 7.20. Transit.

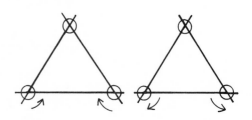

Figure 7.21. Adjusting leveling screws.

(2) *Yarikata*—batter boards.

A batter board is a temporary marker indicating a horizontal plane, as well as the center of a wall or post, obtained from a benchmark (see Figure 7.22).

The *suigui* (stakes) are 1¼ in. square and about 36 in. long. They are staked around the building location, off-set from the actual building position (see Figure 7.23). The tops of the *suigui* are formed in one of the shapes shown in Figure 7.24: (*a*) *yahazu* or (*b*) *isuka*. These shapes are used to discourage anything being placed on top of a stake, and to make it easier to spot if the stakes have been pounded after they have been set.

The *mizunuki* (ties) are boards about ¾ in. thick, 3½ in. wide, and 48 in. long, and are free of warps or twists. Usually Japanese cedar is used. The tops of the ties are planed.

There are two types of *yarikata* (batter board): the *sumi yarikata* (corner board), and the *hira yarikata* (straight board). To construct a corner board, three stakes and two tie boards are required. There are two types of straight board. One is to indicate the location of the center line of a wall center, the other is to support the taut line and to keep it from sagging when spanning a long distance. To construct a straight board, two stakes and one tie board are required.

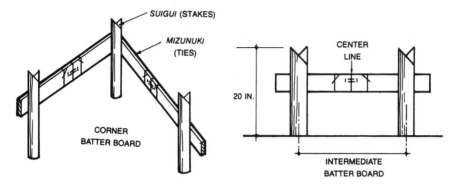

Figure 7.22. *Yarikata* (batter boards).

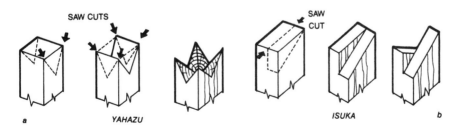

Figure 7.23. Location of batter boards.

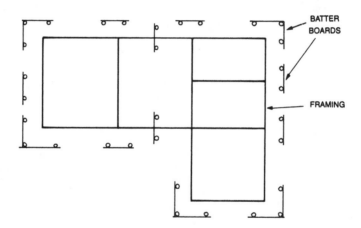

Figure 7.24. Tops of *suigui* (stakes).

(3) Leveling and staking:

(i) *Nawabari*—outlining the building. Outlining the perimeter of a building is done to establish the exterior boundary of a building, and to determine the locations for batter boards. This is accomplished by placing stakes at all outside and inside corners of the building.

(ii) Staking: After the outlining, stakes for the batter boards are placed about 36 in. away from the building's foundation line, and about 20 in. above grade. The tops of the stakes are cut in either *isuka* or *yahazu* shapes.

(iii) Marking elevations: Using levels and other equipment, elevations are marked on the exterior faces of the stakes.

(iv) Using the *mizuso* (water-tube leveling) method: The glass tube is capped with a finger and placed on a stake. The tube is placed in such a way that the water level in it will be at the tank's water height. When it settles, the stake is marked. This is repeated until all the stakes are marked.

Next, the height is verified by checking the first stake to see if the levels are aligned.

(v) If there are no discrepancies, the next phase begins, using the transit. The top of the foundation is determined by calculation from the bench marks. A leveling rod is placed at an arbitrary setting 4 in. plumb above the top of the foundation. This scaled rod is about 1¼ in. square and about 6 ft. long. The center lines of the horizontal and vertical lines in the transit are set at the height of the level rod. This height is kept constant as the rod is placed on each stake, and its bottom location is marked on the stakes (see Figure 7.25). On these marks, the bottoms of the ties are aligned, and then nailed to the outside face of the stake with two nails (about 1½ in. long).

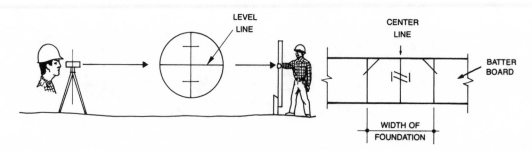

Figure 7.25. Using the transit.

Next, using the bench marks, the center lines of posts and walls are calculated and are marked on the inside faces of the batter boards, together with the foundation width. These marks are also placed on the outside faces. On these lines taut lines are securely set. The same process is repeated for the perpendicular lines. To prevent errors when matching marking on opposite faces, a string is wrapped around the board.

After the taut lines have been set in both directions their squareness is confirmed using a large square (see Appendix 2) or the 3:4:5 right triangle legs concept, and the locations for the temporary placement of the taut lines are marked. When three corners have been found to be square, the job of setting up the batter boards has been completed.

Using the taut lines, two types of carpenter's squares called *shojiki* and *baka* are made. They are used for footings, and for foundation and concrete work.

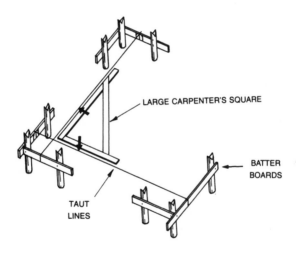

Figure 7.26. Setting up batter boards.

Determining the height of a king post

(i) Basic concept. The position of roof framing members is determined by the height of the king post.

In Figure 7.27, a horizontal line passes through the pivot point, which is an intersection of the vertical center line of a post and the bottom surface line of a rafter. If you draw a line from pivot point to pivot point across a room or building, it is called a "base line." The dimension *a* is the distance from the pivot point to the location of the king post, and *b* equals *a* x roof slope. (*C* equals the length of a rafter segment above length *a*, or $c = \sqrt{a^2 + b^2}$. Once we know the slope of the roof and distance *a*, the height of the king post can be determined.

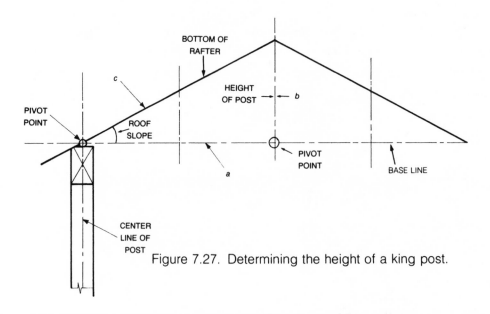

Figure 7.27. Determining the height of a king post.

Example: In a case were *a* = 36 inches and the roof slope equals 5/10 (using Figure 7.28) then *b* = 36 × 5/10 = 18 and *c* = $\sqrt{36^2 + 18^2}$ = 40.25 inches.

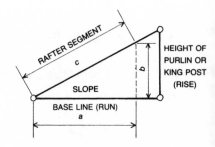

Figure 7.28. The basic triangle.

Kyoro framing: The top surface of the spanning beam in *kyoro* framing is usually higher than the base line. Since the king post sits on the spanning beam, the length of the king post at point *A* is determined by deducting the distance between the base line and the top surface of the spanning beam and the height of the purlin from length *b,* which was determined before, An example of this is given in Figure 7.29.

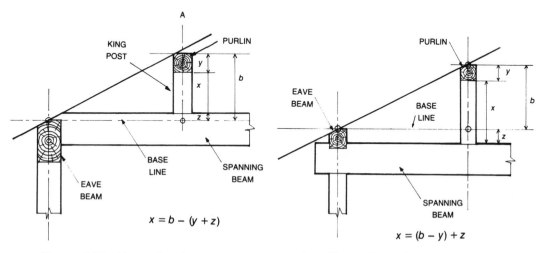

$$x = b - (y + z)$$

Figure 7.29. *Kyoro* framing.

$$x = (b - y) + z$$

Figure 7.30 *Orioki* framing.

Orioki framing: The top surface of the spanning beam in *orioki* framing is generally lower than the base line. To determine the length of the king post, the distance from the top surface of the beam to the base line must be added to length *b* in Figure 7.30 since the king posts rest on the top surface of the beam. Next, the depth of the purlin—the distance from the king post pivot to the bottom of the purlin—has to be deducted from length *b.* Since the purlin is a common member in either kind of framing, its depth must be deducted from length *b* in both cases.

Where the spanning beam or purlin is a log, the method for determining the lengths of the king posts is identical to the one explained above. However, the depth of the log at point *A* will not be a constant. For this reason each depth is noted on a board drawing, as part of a grid system, and the depth at point *A* is determined accordingly.

(ii) The return slope
Architects refer to the angle of the roof slope as a proportion of rise to run. The horizontal length or run is in units of either 1 or 10. The rise is the vertical distance and is the dimension which can be adjusted to obtain the desired slope. The greater the rise, the greater will be

the slope. The slope of the roof is obtained from the rise and run. This term is only applicable to the roof slope obtained when the horizontal length or rise is used as a reference line. However, to determine the slope of the face of the beams on which the rafters will rest (mentioned in previous examples), the vertical center line of the beam is used as the reference line. The slope obtained from the vertical line in this way is called the return slope (see Figure 7.31). This is based on the theory of the triangle, that the sum of the angles of a triangle is equal to 180°. This method of obtaining the slope is called *kikujyutsu*.

Kikujyutsu is the name of the method used to obtain various parts of the joints and structures with the use of the carpenter's square and the *sumitsubo*. Its usage is widespread, and an understand of *kikujyutsu* is necessary for all carpenters.

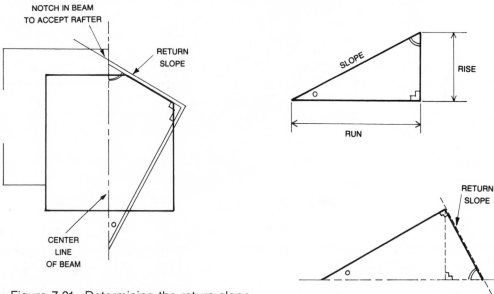

Figure 7.31. Determining the return slope.

Tatekata—Construction

After the footings, posts, beams, and roof framing members have been prepared, they are delivered to the site. The framing of these members is called *tatekata* (or *tatemae*). After the ridge beam is placed and the slope of the roof has been determined, a ceremony called *joto* or *muneage* is performed. (See Appendix 4 for further explanation.) In *tatekata,* the utmost care must be given to the correct sequential marking of the members, otherwise a partially built frame may have to be completely disassembled in order to fit in a piece that was marked incorrectly. The construction supervisor must take every precaution to prevent such an error.

Tatekata (construction) sequence:

(1) Placing the *dodai* (mudsill): After cleaning the top surface of the foundation wall, the exterior mudsill face location, obtained from the batter boards, is marked. If the center line were marked, it would be covered when the mudsill was set in place and would therefore serve no purpose. Instead, the line of the mudsill's outside face is marked and the mudsill aligned to it.

Next, the locations of the anchor bolts are marked and holes are drilled for them. Then the mudsill is secured to the foundation.

(2) *Erection:* The scaffolding is constructed set back about 24 in. from the exterior walls.

Placing the posts: The posts are placed according to the marking sequence. The *ashigatame* beams (bottom plates), *sashigamoi* beams (headers), and others which are connected to the posts with mortise and tenon joints are then assembled on the ground and raised to set the posts in place. In the case of a single story residence, the *noki geta* (eave beams) and the *tsuma bari* (full width) beams are inserted into the posts' tenons, and, using long members such as ties for temporary diagonal braces, the house is constructed starting from one corner.

In the case of a two story residence, the *do sashi* (equivalent to the top plates) are secured to the *toshi bashira* (continuous posts), and at the same time inserted into the top tenon of the *kuda bashira* (single story floor posts). Then the temporary diagonal brace is put in place. For the installation of the second floor *obari* and *kobari* (beams), the same procedure is followed as in single floor construction. After the axial members are framed, *tateokoshi* (plumbing) follows.

(3) *Tateokoshi*—plumbing posts: This is a method for plumbing posts using a *sage furi* (a type of guide), rope, turnbuckle, jacks, and other pieces (see Figure 7.32).

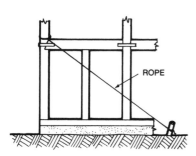
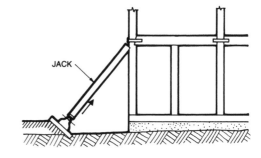

Figure 7.32. *Tateokoshi* (plumbing posts).

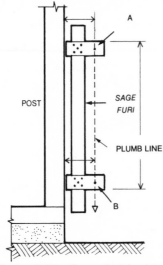

Figure 7.33. *Sage furi* (guide).

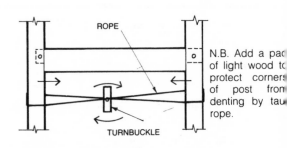

Figure 7.34. Using a turnbuckle.

The *sage furi* is a guide tool made at the site from readily available materials such as those used for the *nuki* (ties). It is shown in Figure 7.33, where A − B = about 10 in. The guide tool is placed along a post and a plumb bob is dangled from point A. When point B is aligned with the string, the post is plumbed.

To adjust members so that they are square one another, place a rope around them as shown in Figure 7.34, and with a stick at the middle twist the tope to pull the members towards each other.

During *tateokoshi* (plumbing) notch out members for the placement of the diagonal braces. Secure these braces with large nails or pin anchors. When the *juku gumi* (wall framing) is completed the roof framing can begin. Framing horizontal members such as the *nakabiki bari* and *chimune* beams in sequence, and setting the *koya bari* beam at the end, roof members such as the *koya tsuka* (end posts), and *niju bari* (headers) are put in place. Framing is completed when the ridge beam is installed.

The assembling of members for Western roof framing (the truss system) is done on the ground; bolts and pin anchors are used to secure the members.

To raise the truss and large beams, a single crane, called a *bozu,* is constructed at the site. The *bozu* is made of a tall log erected vertically and secured with four ropes tied to the top, with their other ends attached to pegs in the ground. A pulley is placed on the top of the pole and a rope is passed through it. Heavy members are then tied to this rope, raised gently, and secured to the attaching members one at a time. In doing so, the proper placement of pins, anchors, wedges, bolts, and other connectors must not be forgotten.

JAPANESE JOINERY
A Handbook for Joiners and Carpenters

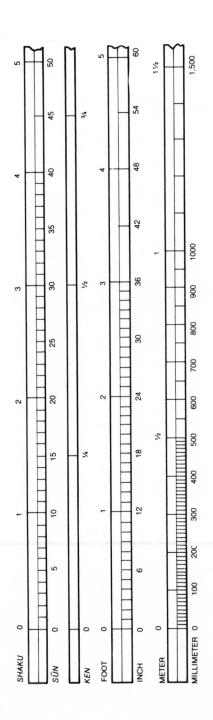

Measurement Comparisons

1 mm	= 0.039 inches	= .33 *bu*
10 mm	= 0.397 inches	= 3.3 *bu*
100 mm	= 3.937 inches	= 33 *bu*
1000 mm	= 39.37 inches	= 33 *sūn*
10 cm	= 3.937 inches	= 33 *bu*
100 cm	= 39.37 incehs	= 33 *sūn*
1 meter	= 39.37 inches	= 33 *sūn*
1 inch	= 25.4 mm	= *8.3 bu*
1 foot	= 304.8 mm	= 100 *bu*
1 *bu*	= 0.12 inches (1/10 inch)	= 3.03 mm
1 *sūn*	= 1.19 inches (1/10 foot)	= 30.3 mm
1 *shaku*	= 11.93 inches (1 foot)	= 303 mm
1 *ken*	= 5.97 feet (2 yards)	= 1,818 mm

To get approximate English dimensions, divide millimeters by 3 and multiply the answer by $\frac{1}{8}$.

For example $\frac{12\ mm}{3} = 4 \times \frac{1}{8} = \frac{1}{2}''$.

Tsugite—End Joints

In order to determine the type of *tsugite* (end joint), or *shiguchi* (right angle joint), the amount of load that it will bear must first be known. Then joints can be constructed accordingly to resist loads.

Generally speaking, in most Japanese architecture, a wood member serves a dual purpose as both structural member and as finishing material. As a structural member, it must be durable and the joint tightly fitted, and as a finishing material, it must be aesthetically pleasing. As a result there are many problems in the construction of *tsugite* and *shiguchi*.

The numerous joints require expert technique to construct. They also give the impression of having been designed strictly for appearance by a master craftsman. However, *tsugite* and *shiguchi* were developed on the basis of structural principles, to resist shear, bending, and moment during an era when metals were scarce.

Orientation to the direction of the woodgrain.

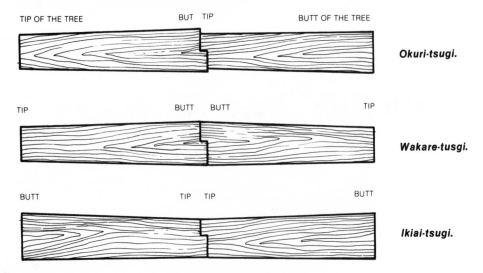

Okuri-tsugi.

Wakare-tusgi.

Ikiai-tsugi.

Wakare tsugi (divorce joint) is widely believed to bring ill fortune, especially when used on ridge beams, so it is inadvisable to use it.
Motoguchi, butt. (This term describes the end of lumber that is closest to the root or base.)
Sueguchi, tip. (This term describes the end of lumber that is closest to the tree top.)

Taking into account the location of the end joint (*tsugite*).

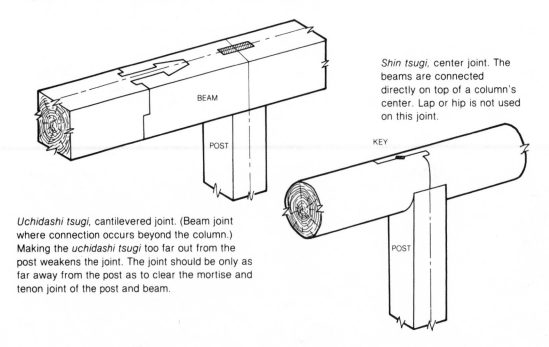

Shin tsugi, center joint. The beams are connected directly on top of a column's center. Lap or hip is not used on this joint.

Uchidashi tsugi, cantilevered joint. (Beam joint where connection occurs beyond the column.) Making the *uchidashi tsugi* too far out from the post weakens the joint. The joint should be only as far away from the post as to clear the mortise and tenon joint of the post and beam.

Ari tsugi—Half lapped dovetail joint.

Mudsills and roof joists are generally extended with this joint, although the joint below is better for mudsills.

Lap or hip is made at the midpoint of lumber's depth.

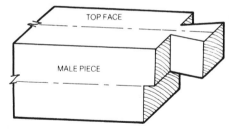

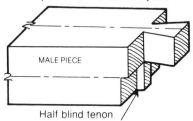

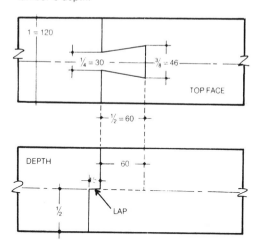

Koshi-ire mechigai-zuki ari tsugi—Half-lapped, half blind tenoned dovetail joint.

Construction method of the dovetail joint

Cut along the center of the drawn cut-line at the top surface of the female portion of the dovetail joint.

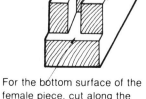

For the bottom surface of the female piece, cut along the outer edge of the drawn cut-line.

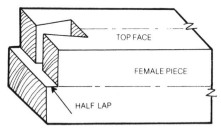

Half blind tenon.

For the top surface of the male portion of the dovetail, cut along the outer edge of the drawn cut-line.

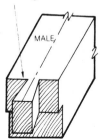

Chamfer edges for easier insertion.

Alternative size of dovetail tenon.

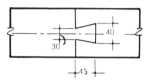

For pieces under 105 mm in width, the joints are usually constructed with the dimensions shown on the drawing. The dimensions noted on the drawing are in millimeters.

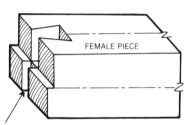

Half blind tenon counteracts moment or twisting force.

Kama tsugi—Half lapped gooseneck joint.

The sizes of the joints vary according to the size of materials. All measurements are proportional.

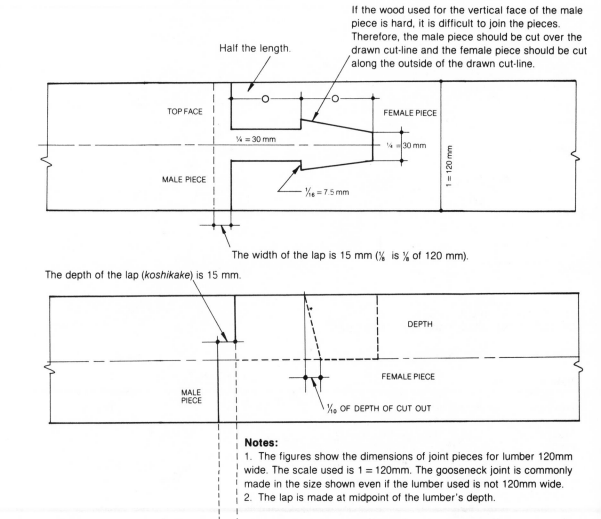

If the wood used for the vertical face of the male piece is hard, it is difficult to join the pieces. Therefore, the male piece should be cut over the drawn cut-line and the female piece should be cut along the outside of the drawn cut-line.

Half the length.

TOP FACE

FEMALE PIECE

¼ = 30 mm

¼ = 30 mm

1 = 120 mm

MALE PIECE

1/16 = 7.5 mm

The width of the lap is 15 mm (⅛ is ⅛ of 120 mm).

The depth of the lap (*koshikake*) is 15 mm.

DEPTH

MALE PIECE

FEMALE PIECE

1/10 OF DEPTH OF CUT OUT

Notes:

1. The figures show the dimensions of joint pieces for lumber 120mm wide. The scale used is 1 = 120mm. The gooseneck joint is commonly made in the size shown even if the lumber used is not 120mm wide.
2. The lap is made at midpoint of the lumber's depth.

30 mm

MALE PIECE

There are different size gooseneck joints according to their lengths: 120mm, 150mm, or 180mm. Most commonly used lengths are 150mm and 180mm. The 120mm length is used for mudsills and roof joists.

Mechigai hozotsuki kama tsugi—Half blind mortised and tenoned gooseneck joint.

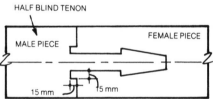

HALF BLIND TENON

MALE PIECE

FEMALE PIECE

15 mm   15 mm

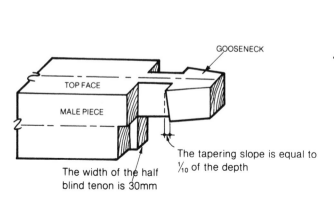

GOOSENECK

TOP FACE

MALE PIECE

The tapering slope is equal to $\frac{1}{10}$ of the depth

The width of the half blind tenon is 30mm

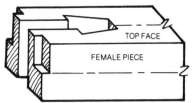

TOP FACE

FEMALE PIECE

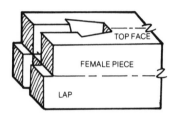

TOP FACE

FEMALE PIECE

LAP

In order to prevent moment or twisting motion at the end joint, a half blind tenon is made at the bottom half as well as the top half of the lumber. The width of the upper tenon is 15 mm. The half blind tenon at the top face of the joint is on the female piece and the one at the bottom face is on the male piece.

Drawing method.

Place the carpenter's square as shown so that the distance between the end of the neck and the end of the head is 15 mm longer than their horizontal length.

Place the carpenter's square at the center of the head's width

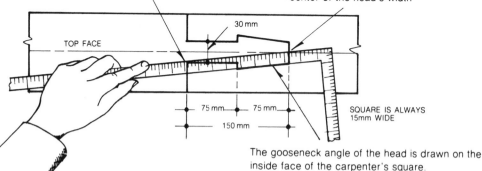

30 mm

TOP FACE

75 mm   75 mm

150 mm

SQUARE IS ALWAYS 15mm WIDE

The gooseneck angle of the head is drawn on the inside face of the carpenter's square.

Metric to English conversions:
1 mm = 0.04 inches; 10 mm = 0.4 inches; 100 mm = 4 inches; 1 metre = 39.3 inches.
   To get approximate English dimensions, divide millimeters by 3 and multiply the answer by $\frac{1}{8}$.
For example $\frac{12\,mm}{3} = 4 \times \frac{1}{8} = \frac{1}{2}$ ".

Okkake daisen tsugi—Dadoed and rabbetted scarf joint.

Wari tsugi is another name for this end joint. Both male and female pieces are identical except for the joint shapes being exact opposites of each other.

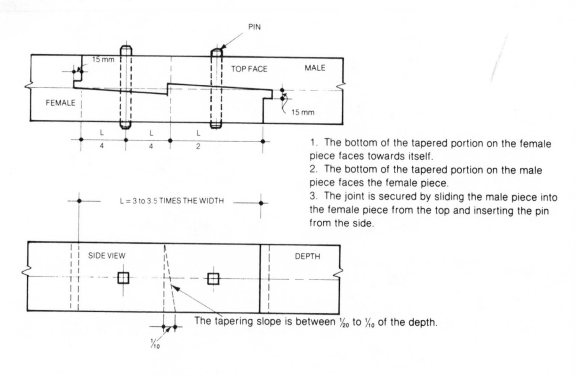

1. The bottom of the tapered portion on the female piece faces towards itself.
2. The bottom of the tapered portion on the male piece faces the female piece.
3. The joint is secured by sliding the male piece into the female piece from the top and inserting the pin from the side.

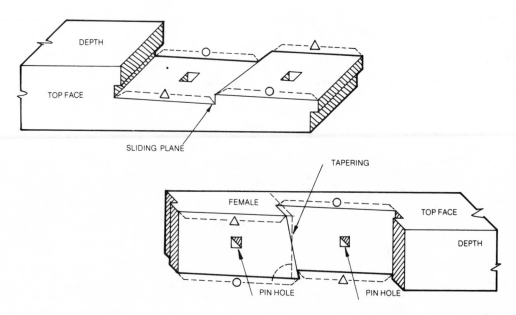

Kanawa tsugi—Half blind tenoned, dadoed and rabbetted scarf joint.

Since there is a T-shaped half blind tenon at the joint ends of *kanawa tsugi* and *shiribasami tsugi*, the connecting pieces cannot slide together as in *okkake daisen tsugi*. Thus the length of the oblique surfaces of the joint is decreased by the width of the dado on the end of the female piece. After the male and female pieces are placed together, a pin is inserted in the opening at the joint center.* Two wedge shaped pins can be used instead of the one-piece pin, which results in a tighter joint. The illustrations are examples of the joint using 120mm wide wood.

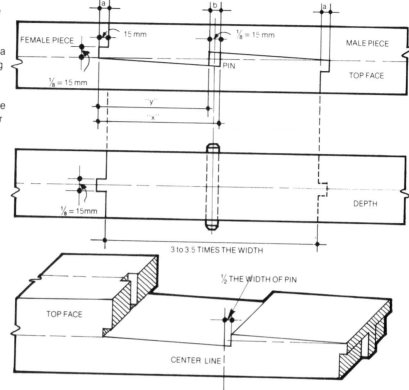

* If a joint were made such that the length of the oblique surface were "x" instead of "y," the pieces cannot slide into each other because of the protrusion "a" (dado). In order to slide the pieces together, the length of the oblique surface has to be "y." The open space "b" created due to the short length where the pieces are joined is filled with a pin. This locks the connection.

Drawing method.

The same method is used for outlining the *okkake daisen tsugi, kanawa tsugi,* and *shiribasami tsugi.*

For the bottom half, draw the line on the right side of the carpenter's square.

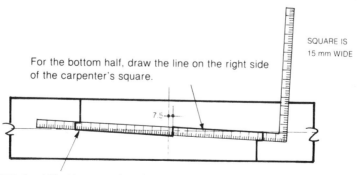

The top half of the figure should be drawn on the left side of the carpenter's square.

Shiribasami tsugi—Blinded and stubbed, dadoed and rabbetted scarf joint.

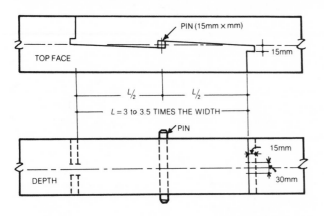

1. There is a T-shaped mortise and tenon joint member in the *shiribasami tsugi*, but unlike the *kanawa tsugi*, it is not visible on the surface of the wood.
2. The female and male pieces are identical.

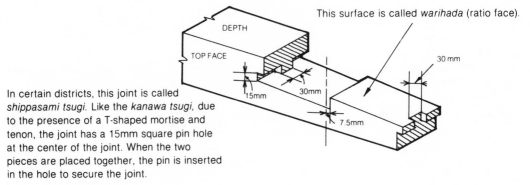

This surface is called *warihada* (ratio face).

In certain districts, this joint is called *shippasami tsugi*. Like the *kanawa tsugi*, due to the presence of a T-shaped mortise and tenon, the joint has a 15mm square pin hole at the center of the joint. When the two pieces are placed together, the pin is inserted in the hole to secure the joint.

Comparison of the similarity of mortise and tenon members.

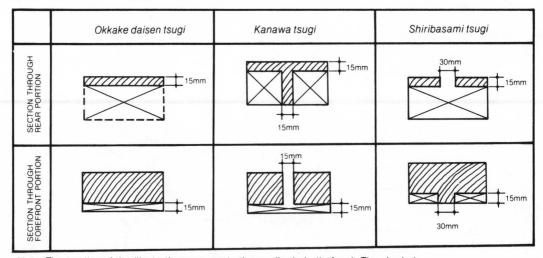

Note: The top line of the illustration represents the *warihada* (ratio face). The shaded areas indicate projected portions.

Shachi tsugi—Key haunch mortise and tenon.

Like the *kama tsugi* (half lapped gooseneck joint), the *shachi tsugi* joint is used where it is impossible to join the pieces by sliding them into each other. This joint is also used where its parts cannot be shaped from one piece of wood but have to be made from different pieces instead.

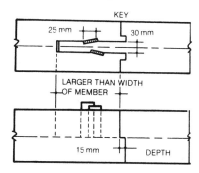

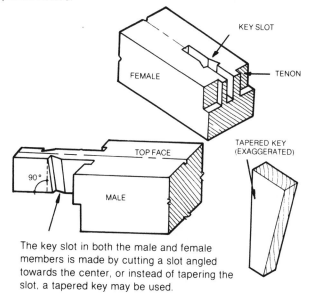

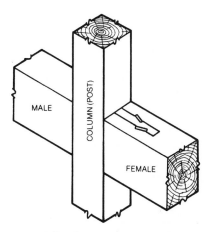

The key slot in both the male and female members is made by cutting a slot angled towards the center, or instead of tapering the slot, a tapered key may be used.

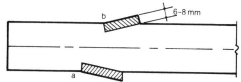

There are three ways to make keys. As shown under a, the key has a parallelogram shape and is made to fit perpendicularly to the lumber. Or keys can be made as under b, with a rectangular shape, or tapered as shown above.

Construction Method of the Key Slot

The four methods of making the slot are as illustrated:

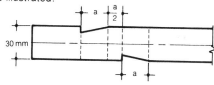

a. Offset.

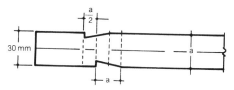

c. Staggered at half point.

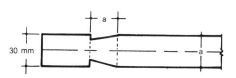

b. Aligned.

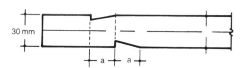

d. Fully staggered.

Daimochi tsugi—Stub tenon scarf joint.

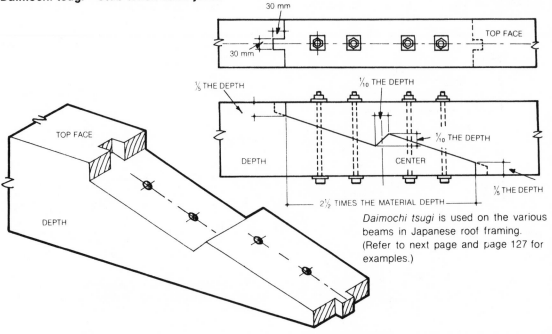

30 mm

30 mm

TOP FACE

⅕ THE DEPTH

⅒ THE DEPTH

⅒ THE DEPTH

DEPTH

CENTER

⅕ THE DEPTH

2½ TIMES THE MATERIAL DEPTH

TOP FACE

DEPTH

DEPTH

Daimochi tsugi is used on the various beams in Japanese roof framing. (Refer to next page and page 127 for examples.)

Sogi tsugi—Scarf joint.

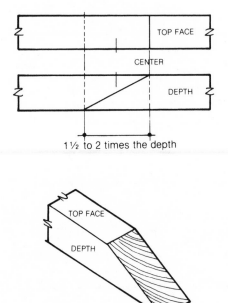

TOP FACE

CENTER

DEPTH

1½ to 2 times the depth

TOP FACE

DEPTH

This joint is commonly used on rafters and joists.

Jyuji mechigai tsugi— Cross shaped mortise and tenon joint.

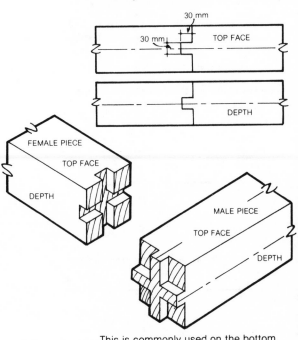

30 mm

30 mm

TOP FACE

DEPTH

FEMALE PIECE

TOP FACE

DEPTH

MALE PIECE

TOP FACE

DEPTH

This is commonly used on the bottom and top cord of monoplaner wood trusses.

***Koyadaimochi tsugi*—Log beam stub tenon scarf joint.**

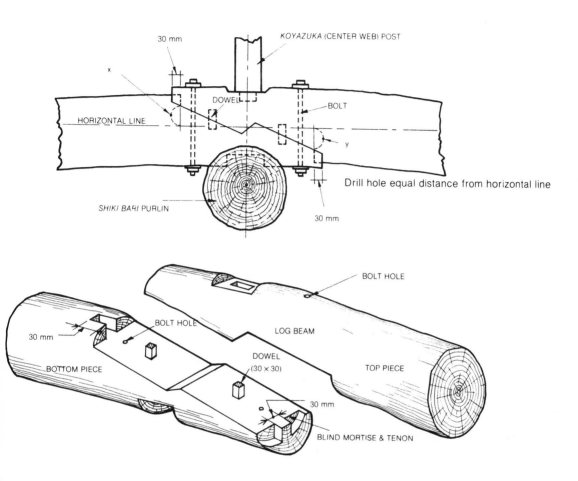

30 mm

KOYAZUKA (CENTER WEB) POST

x

DOWEL

BOLT

HORIZONTAL LINE

y

Drill hole equal distance from horizontal line

SHIKI BARI PURLIN

30 mm

BOLT HOLE

BOLT HOLE

LOG BEAM

30 mm

DOWEL
(30 × 30)

TOP PIECE

BOTTOM PIECE

30 mm

BLIND MORTISE & TENON

The construction method of *koyadaimochi tsugi* is similar to *daimochi tsugi,* shown above. However, due to variations such as the presence of purlins or different shapes of beams, it is essential that the distance from the horizontal line to points x and y is identical. Furthermore, the dowels must be placed vertically, parallel to the beam depth, instead of perpendicular to the cut joint surfaces.

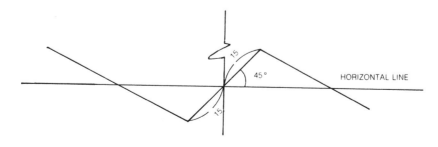

15

45°

HORIZONTAL LINE

15

Isuka tsugi—**Halved scarf joint**

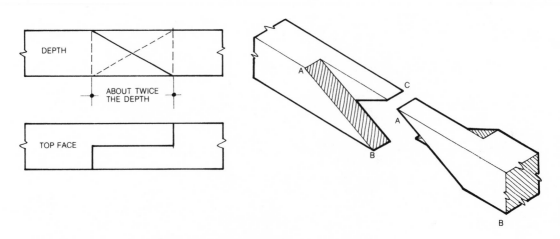

1. This joint is used on fence headers [top beams] and on exposed ceiling joists.
2. A pin is, at times, installed through the top face. However, when pinned, the pieces have a tendency to slide apart. If a pin must be installed, the joint called *miyajima tsugi* or *sumikiri isuka tsugi* (rabbetted half scarf joint) is used.

Sumikiri isuka tsugi—**Rabbetted halves scarf joint.**

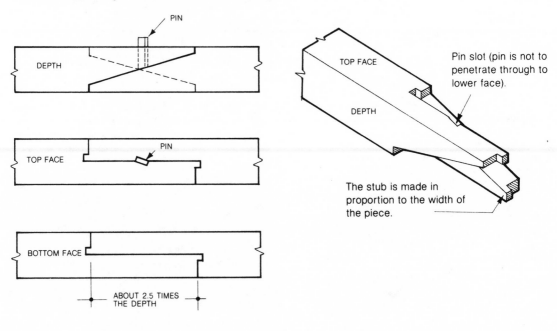

Sumi isuka tsugi—Corner splice joint.

A very good joint which is relatively easily made.

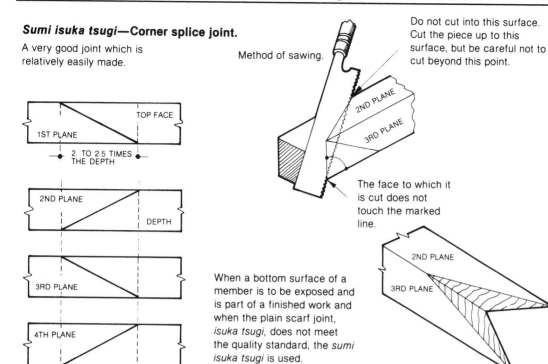

TOP FACE

1ST PLANE

2. TO 2.5 TIMES THE DEPTH

2ND PLANE

DEPTH

3RD PLANE

4TH PLANE

Method of sawing.

Do not cut into this surface. Cut the piece up to this surface, but be careful not to cut beyond this point.

2ND PLANE

3RD PLANE

The face to which it is cut does not touch the marked line.

When a bottom surface of a member is to be exposed and is part of a finished work and when the plain scarf joint, *isuka tsugi*, does not meet the quality standard, the *sumi isuka tsugi* is used.

2ND PLANE

3RD PLANE

Miyajima tsugi—Rabbetted half scarf joint.

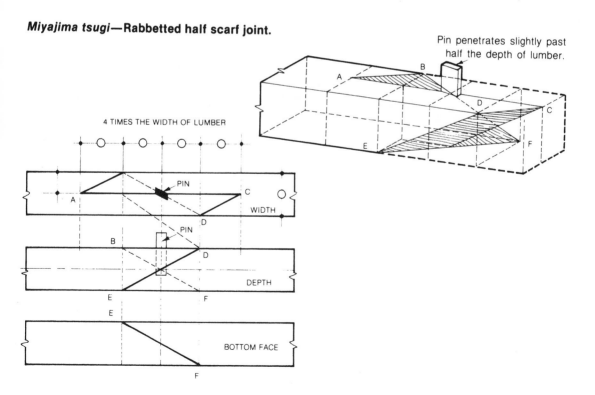

Pin penetrates slightly past half the depth of lumber.

4 TIMES THE WIDTH OF LUMBER

PIN

A

C

WIDTH

D

PIN

B

D

DEPTH

E

F

E

BOTTOM FACE

F

Western style joints.

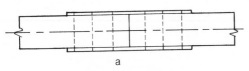

a

Tsuki tsuke—Butt joint.

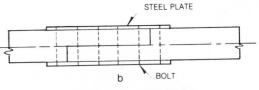

STEEL PLATE

b

BOLT

Aigaki tsugi—Half lap joint.

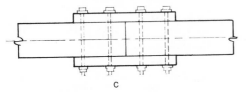

c

Tsuki tsuke—Butt joint.

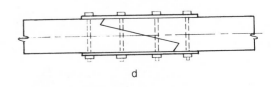

d

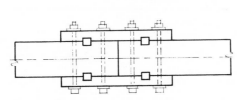

e

PIN

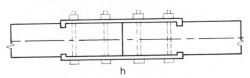

f

Daimochi tsugi—
Pinnned stub tenon oblique splice joint.

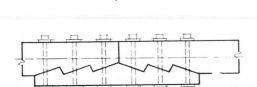

g

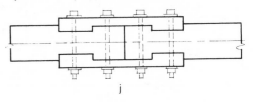

h

Since the steel plate grips into the wood, this joint is strong against a pulling force.

i

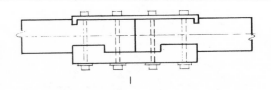

j

k

l

These are commonly used for joining beams.
1. For joints (a) through (d), the force is resisted by steel plates and bolts.
2. For joints (e) through (g), steel plates and bolts, as well as the joint itself, resist force.
3. For joints (h) through (l), force is counteracted by an extra piece between the wood and the steel plates, and by bolts and plates.

Kakushi kanawa tsugi—Blind dadoed and rabbetted scarf joint.

Like *hako michigai tsugi*, this joint is used whenever two faces of the wood are to be exposed.

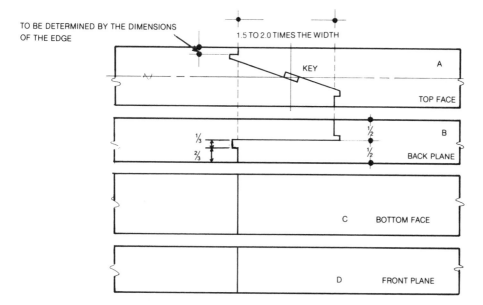

TO BE DETERMINED BY THE DIMENSIONS OF THE EDGE

1.5 TO 2.0 TIMES THE WIDTH

KEY

A

TOP FACE

⅓

⅔

½

½

B

BACK PLANE

C   BOTTOM FACE

D   FRONT PLANE

= CENTER LINE

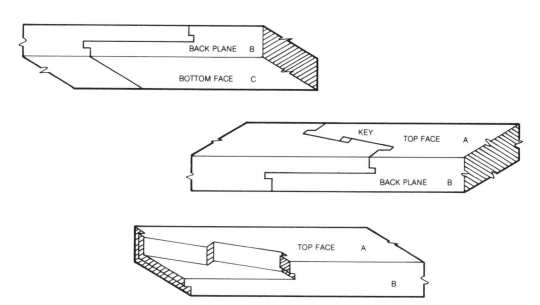

BACK PLANE   B

BOTTOM FACE   C

KEY   TOP FACE   A

BACK PLANE   B

TOP FACE   A

B

Construction of the *kanawa* (scarf) portion of this joint is similar to that of the common *kanawa tsugi*. The angle of the scarf portion is determined by the distance between the mortise and tenon portion of the joint and the cut plane they form.

Kai-no-kuchi tsugi— X-shaped ship (or open) end joint (French style).

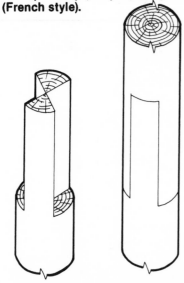

In France, this joint, reinforced with a steel collar, is used on piles.

Kai-no-kuchi tsugi— X-shaped ship (or open) end joint.

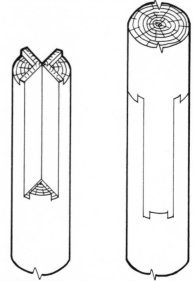

This joint is used on the main column of towers.

Saobiki dokko—Stacked tenon with keys.

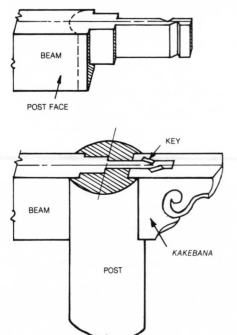

Shingiri daimochi tsugi— Dadoed and rabbetted squared scarf joint.

Commonly used to connect beams. The width of the beam should be $\frac{1}{3}$ of the column width. The depth of beam should be $\frac{8}{10}$ of column width.

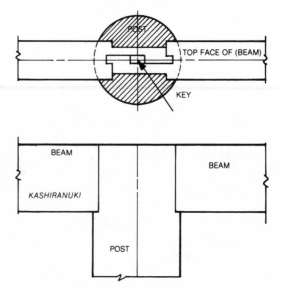

Noge tsugi—Dadoed gooseneck joint with scarf.

Since this joint is used to connect *kayaoi*, it is also called *kayaoi kama tsugi*.

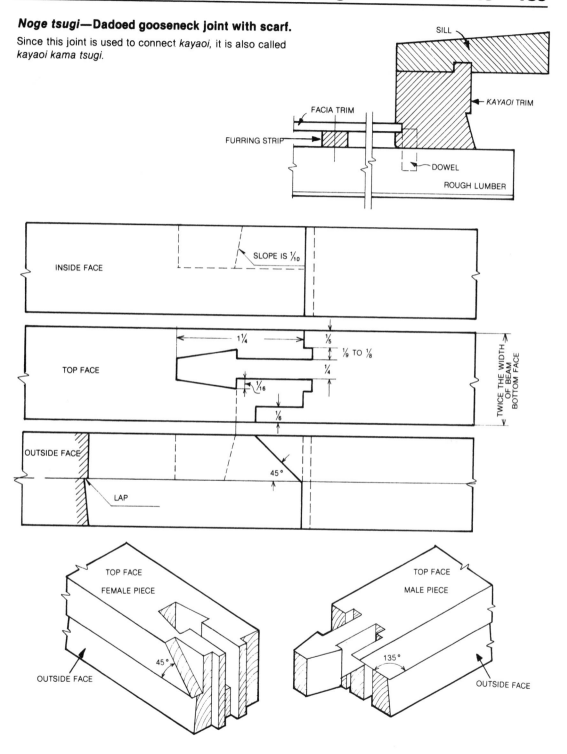

SILL

KAYAOI TRIM

FACIA TRIM

FURRING STRIP

DOWEL

ROUGH LUMBER

INSIDE FACE

SLOPE IS $\frac{1}{10}$

TOP FACE

$1\frac{1}{4}$

$\frac{1}{5}$

$\frac{1}{9}$ TO $\frac{1}{8}$

$\frac{1}{4}$

$\frac{1}{16}$

$\frac{1}{6}$

TWICE THE WIDTH OF BEAM BOTTOM FACE

OUTSIDE FACE

45°

LAP

TOP FACE

FEMALE PIECE

45°

OUTSIDE FACE

TOP FACE

MALE PIECE

135°

OUTSIDE FACE

Shihō kama tsugi—Four faced gooseneck joint.

This joint is commonly used at the foot of columns of bell towers and the sanctified wells of shrines and temples. Since the joint also serves as decoration, it is usually incorporated into the original construction. As shown in the illustration below, this joint is made by sliding the pieces diagonally into each other. It is a joint exposing the gooseneck on the four surfaces of a column.

UNIT OF MEASUREMENT: MILLIMETER

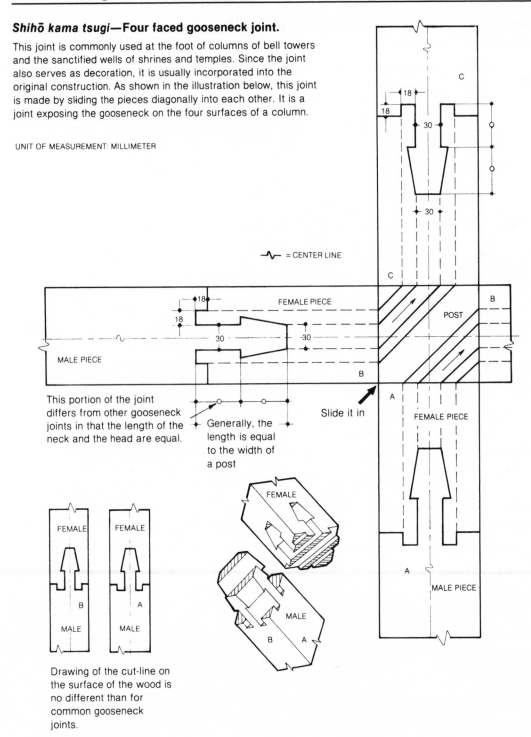

= CENTER LINE

FEMALE PIECE

MALE PIECE

POST

This portion of the joint differs from other gooseneck joints in that the length of the neck and the head are equal.

Generally, the length is equal to the width of a post

Slide it in

FEMALE PIECE

MALE PIECE

FEMALE

MALE

FEMALE

MALE

Drawing of the cut-line on the surface of the wood is no different than for common gooseneck joints.

Hako tsugi—**Blind and stub diagonally cut half lap joint.**

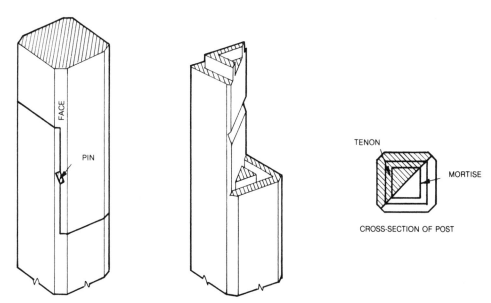

TENON

MORTISE

CROSS-SECTION OF POST

Hakodai-mochi tsugi—**Shipped and pinned and halved half lap joint.**

This is one of the *hako-mechigai tsugi*—L-shaped shipped and tenoned half lap joints. It is similar to *kakushi kanawa tsugi*—blind dadoed and rabbetted scarf joint.

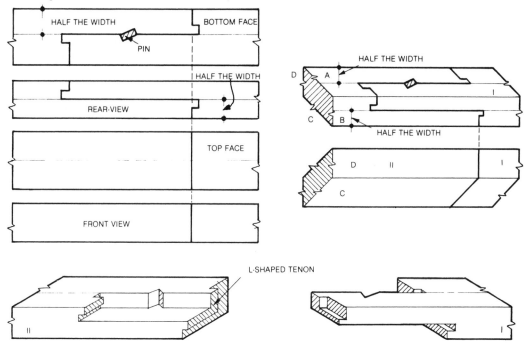

Hakosen tsugi—L-shaped dadoed and rabbetted scarf lap joint.

This joint is used on edge trim with its two surfaces exposed.

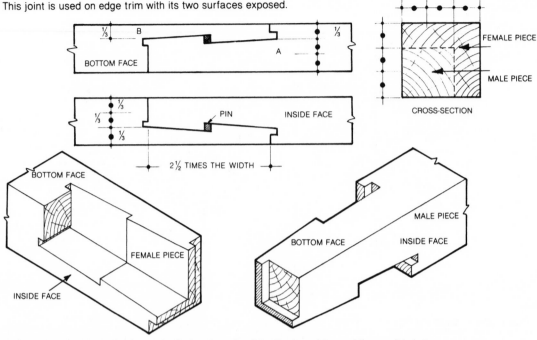

Hako shachi tsugi—L-shaped, dadoed and rabbetted and keyed lapped joint.

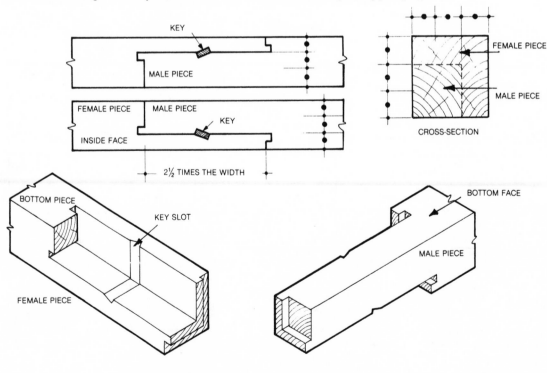

Mechigai tsugi—Mortise and tenon joint.

The mortise portion of the joint, *mechigai ire*, is commonly called *mechi ire* or *inro tsugi*. The tenon portion of the joint is commonly called *mechi hozo*. *Hako mechigai tsugi*—blind U-shaped stubbed mortise and tenon joint and *kaneori mechigai tsugi*—L-shaped half blind mortise and tenon joint are special cases.

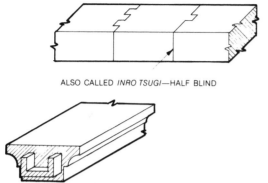

ALSO CALLED *INRO TSUGI*—HALF BLIND

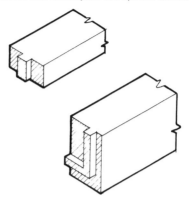

Hako mechigai tsugi—Blind & U-shaped stub.

Kaneori mechigai—L-shaped half blind. This joint has the most twist resistance.

Chigiri tsugi—Spline joints.

Below are different types of spline joints corresponding to the shape of the spline. This type of joint is also known as *kusabi tsugi*.

Ari kata—Butterfly spline.

Kine kata—Bow-tie spline (2 types).

Are kata—Dumb-bell. Not used for architectural construction. [But used for cabinetry in the west.]

Nami-kata—Corrugated metal fastener. The spline is corrugated metal, about 15 mm long. Used for cabinet work and furniture construction.

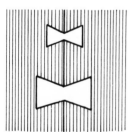

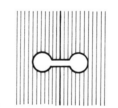
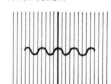

Spline joint variations.

Example of bow-tie spline.

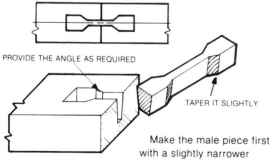

PROVIDE THE ANGLE AS REQUIRED

TAPER IT SLIGHTLY

Make the male piece first with a slightly narrower bottom than top. Scribe to cut out the female. Chamfer edges on bottom surface and then slide together.

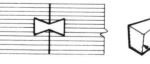

TAPER SLIGHTLY

Example of butterfly spline.

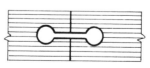

When the spline is to be installed parallel to the grain it is made longer than when it is to be placed perpendicular to the grain.

End joints of columns.

There are various types of end joints and right angle joints, but in this age it is important to select a joint which can be constructed with machine tools. This is necessary to solve the modern problems of lack of skilled and qualified craftsmen, and of the need to keep the construction period to a minimum. The following points should be considered:

1. Consider shapes which can easily be fabricated utilizing machine tools and electrical power tools.
2. Simplify the construction method. Utilize mechanical reinforcement such as screws, bolts, clips, split rings, and shear plates. Also use an adhesive.
3. Consider joints which anyone can make by using machine tools.

Cut as required to accept adhesive.

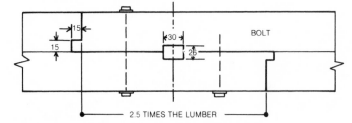

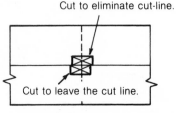

Cut to eliminate cut-line.

Cut to leave the cut line.

Construction method for pin-hole.

An example of end joint which can be made by using power tools.

Construction method of column end joints.

Figure (a) shows the method utilizing *shiribasami tsugi* (blinded and stubbed, dadoed and rabbetted scarf joint).

Figure (b) shows the method utilizing *shachi tsugi* (keyed haunch mortise and tenon joint).

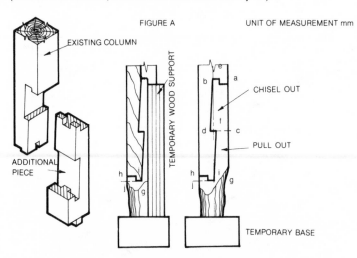

FIGURE A   UNIT OF MEASUREMENT mm

EXISTING COLUMN

TEMPORARY WOOD SUPPORT

CHISEL OUT

PULL OUT

ADDITIONAL PIECE

TEMPORARY BASE

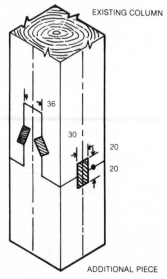

FIGURE B

EXISTING COLUMN

ADDITIONAL PIECE

1. At lines (a), (b), (c), and (d), cut inside the cut-line.
2. Chisel out a mortise at (e).
3. When the length between (f) and (g) is cut, half of the end joint is made. To it, attach a piece as shown on figure A.
4. Cut from point (h) to (j) and from point (j) to (g) to make lower mortise.

   This joint is sometimes used to connect a wooden post to a stone post.

Various types of edge joints.

Imohagi—Butt joint. Boards are butted together.

Aijakkuri—Shiplap joint. Also known as *chigai hagi*.

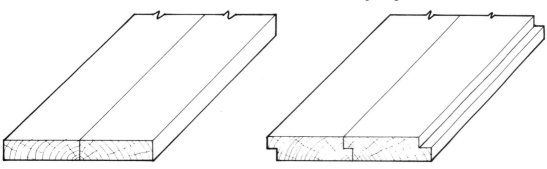

Honzane hagi—Tongue and groove joint. Also called *sane hagi* and *inro jakkuri*.

Hibukura hagi—V-grooved joint. This is one of the *sane* or *zane* (groove) joints.

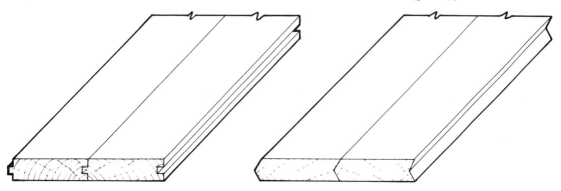

Yatoizane hagi—Spline joints.

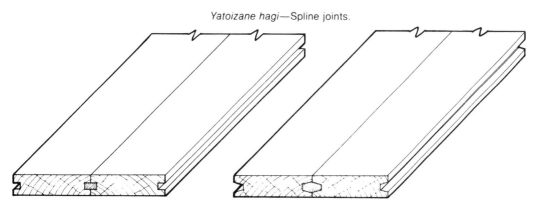

2

Shiguchi—Right Angle Joints

Shiguchi is a system of joints which connects pieces perpendicular or at an angle to each other. There are various right angle joints such as mortise and tenon, lap, dovetail, spline, miter, rabbet, and dado. Usually, these joints are applied and used in a myriad of combinations.

Since *shiguchi*, like *tsugite*, must resist various forces such as shear, bending and moment, the construction of joints requires exceptional skill.

The joints always use wooden pins, a key or wedge, metal connectors or clamps. It is also very common to use only metal connectors.

In future, *shiguchi* should be made simpler, relying on metal connectors as much as possible. It is necessary to investigate into a reinforcing member which will not cause the wood to chip or to leave cracks as wood expands and contracts.

Different types of tenons.

This surface is called *usuzoko* or *koshi tsuki*.

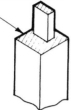

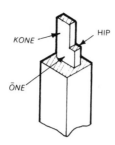

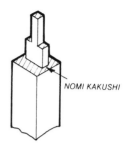

Hira hozo—Full tenon. According to the length of the tenon, there are *tanhozo* (short tenons) and *nagahozo* (long tenons).

Kone hozo—Haunch tenon.

Jyu hozo—Stacked tenon. Also called *kasane hozo*.

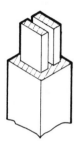

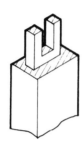

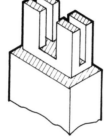

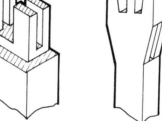

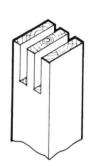

Nimai hozo—Double tenon.

Yonmai hozo—Quadruple tenon.

Wanagi hozo—A type of finger tenon.

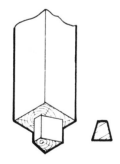

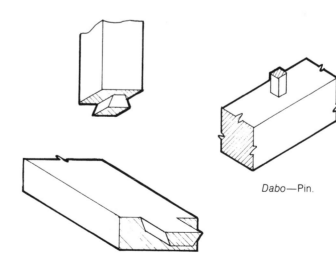

Oogi hozo—Fan shaped tenon. Cross section of tenon.

Dabo—Pin.

Ari hozo—Dovetail tenon.

Different types of tenons.

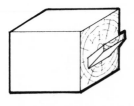

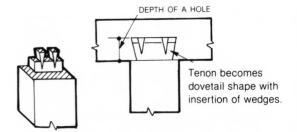

DEPTH OF A HOLE

Tenon becomes dovetail shape with insertion of wedges.

Shakushi hozo—Ladle tenon. The angle of slope illustrated is slightly exagerated.

Jigoku hozo—Hell tenon. The tenon is a regular full tenon cut to receive wedges. The bottom of the tenon is enlarged such that its cross section looks like a dovetail. When the tenon is inserted, the wedges expand the full tenon to a dovetail shaped tenon. The term, hell, comes from the fact that once it is inserted, it cannot be removed.

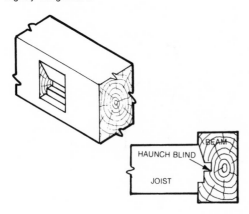

HAUNCH BLIND

BEAM

JOIST

Kiba hozo—Haunched blind tenon.

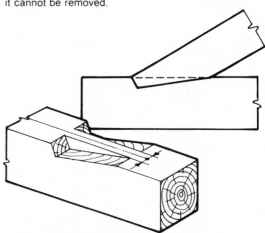

Kurakake hozo—Oblique dadoed tenon. This is similar to *nagare hozo* but is a variation of *wanaida* (finger tenon).

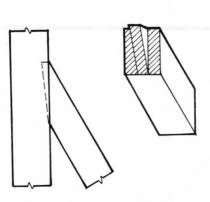

Nagare hozo—Sloped tenon.

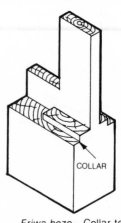

COLLAR

Eriwa hozo—Collar tenon.

L-shaped and T-shaped mortise and tenon joints.

Sumidome hozo sashi—Haunch blinded and collared tongue and groove miter joint.

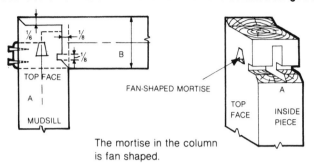

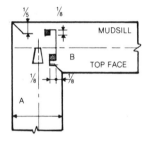

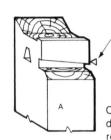

FAN-SHAPED MORTISE

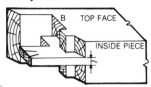

The mortise in the column
is fan shaped.

Notes:
1. The dimension shown on illustrations is
at scale of 1 = 120 mm.
2. In common practice, the fraction, ½,
always corresponds to 30 mm, regardless
of the size of the piece.
3. Similarly, the fraction ⅛ corresponds to
15 mm. It is the width of *sashi gane,* the
carpenter's square.

Daiwa dome—Full tenoned tongue and groove miter joint.

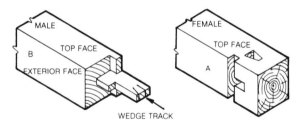

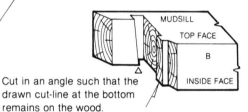

This indicates the dado.

Cut in an angle such that the
drawn cut-line at the bottom
remains on the wood.

Eriwa kone hozosashi—Collared haunch mortise and tenon joint.

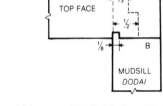

Wanagi komi—Ship (or open) mortise and
tenon joint.

Jaguchi hozosashi—Rabbet and half blind
mortise and tenon joint.

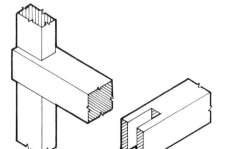

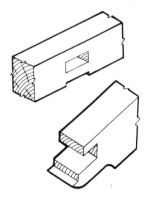

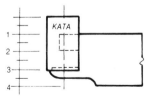

The top mortise is sometimes
made as a full or through
mortise.

Ari otoshi or *ari kake*—Dadoed, half lapped, half blind dovetail with full mortise and tenon.

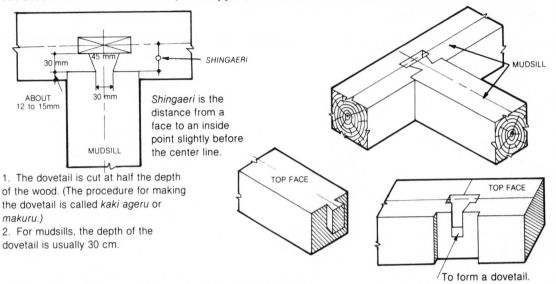

SHINGAERI

Shingaeri is the distance from a face to an inside point slightly before the center line.

MUDSILL

TOP FACE

TOP FACE

To form a dovetail.

1. The dovetail is cut at half the depth of the wood. (The procedure for making the dovetail is called *kaki ageru* or *makuru.*)
2. For mudsills, the depth of the dovetail is usually 30 cm.

Bintatsuke ari otoshi—Dadoed quartered dovetail joint.

The construction method is similar to the one for the *kabuto ari kake* joint.

When drawing the cut-line using the carpenter's square, the lines must be perpendicular to the top face of the beam. Also, the joist must be slightly tapered at the bottom to obtain a tight connection.

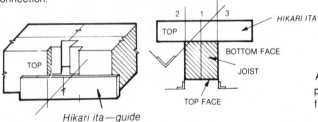

HIKARI ITA

TOP

BOTTOM FACE

JOIST

TOP FACE

Hikari ita—guide

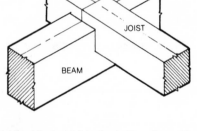

JOIST

BEAM

Apply *hikari ita* (guide) to the bottom face. (See pages 55–56 for illustration). The cut-line is drawn from center to outside.

Ari kake—Half lap dovetail joint.

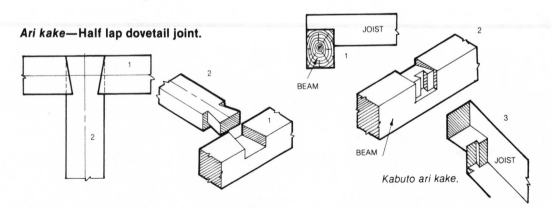

JOIST

BEAM

BEAM

JOIST

Kabuto ari kake.

Jyujikei—Crossed right angle joints.

Watari ago—Dadoed cross lap joint.

This joint is used for cantilevered beams.

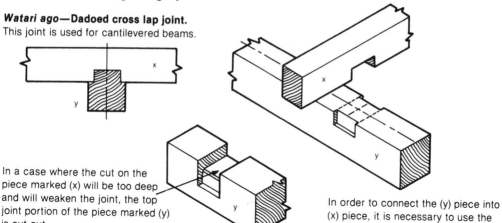

In a case where the cut on the piece marked (x) will be too deep and will weaken the joint, the top joint portion of the piece marked (y) is cut out.

In order to connect the (y) piece into (x) piece, it is necessary to use the *hikari ita* (guide).

Tasuki kake watari ago—Double mitered cross lap joint.

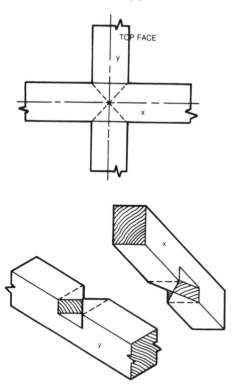

Saw along the cross and chip out the joint with a chisel.

Watari kaki—Stop dadoed cross lap joint.

The difference between *watari ago* is that piece "x" sits on the notch of piece "y" while *watari kaki* has piece "x" sitting on the whole surface of piece "y"; there is no notch on piece "y".

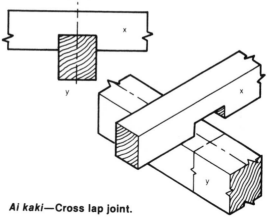

Ai kaki—Cross lap joint.

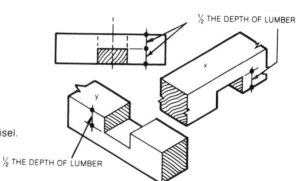

T-shaped right angle joints.

Ooire hozo sashi—
Dadoed full (or through)
mortise and tenon joint.

Toshi hozo sashi—
Full (or through) mortise
and tenon joint.

Tsutsumi hozo sashi—
Blind and stub mortise and
tenon joint.

ABOUT 15 mm

The center line is measured from
the dado's face. Measuring from
the face of the piece will be
inaccurate since its thickness will
vary.

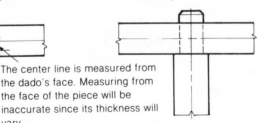

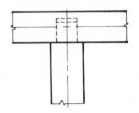

***Kashigi ooire hozo sashi*—**Oblique
dadoed full mortise and tenon joint.

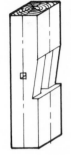

Instead of using a pin,
the joint can be
clamped together.

Unless there is
about 3 mm off-set,
the pin will not pull
the tenon tight
against the
attached piece.

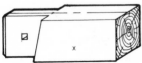

x

ABOUT 15 mm

OFF SET
ABOUT 5 mm

PIN HOLE

Location of pin.

Shinuchi—
at the center.

Shingaeri—off-set.
(A face of the pin
is flush with the
center line.)

Locate pin at a distance of the pin
width away from center line.

Shinmatagaeri—
off-set.

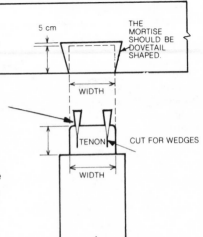

***Jigoku hozo sashi*—**Hell tenon.

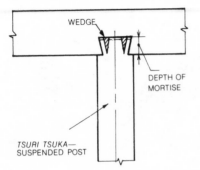

WEDGE

DEPTH OF
MORTISE

TSURI TSUKA—
SUSPENDED POST

When the wedge hits the
bottom of the mortise, and
when the tenon is pounded
into the mortise and touches
its bottom, the tenon
becomes fan shaped. Due to
this enlargement of the
tenon, it cannot be removed.
The mortise is cut so that the
bottom is larger than the top,
making its cross-section
shaped like a dovetail.

5 cm

THE
MORTISE
SHOULD BE
DOVETAIL
SHAPED.

WIDTH

TENON

CUT FOR WEDGES

WIDTH

Yatoi hozo—Right angle joint with spline tenon. (Condition 1.)

The spline tenon is installed into the horizontal member before connecting it to a post. This system is commonly used when the horizontal member is not long enough to include a tenon. The joint has very little shear resistance.

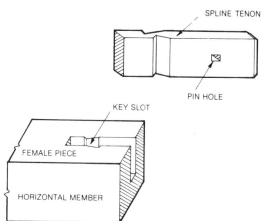

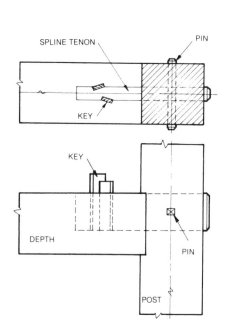

The spline tenon is used under the following conditions:

1. Where the material is not long enough to include the tenon.
2. Where mortise and tenon cannot be joined. In such cases, the construction method is similar to condition 1. The column is dadoed, and the tenon is inserted into the mortise and locked with a pin.
3. In situations where a pin or key cannot be used, similar to condition 2, the spline tenon is made with a dovetail at the end which will be inserted into the column. The spline tenon is first connected to the column, then to the horizontal member and secured with keys.

Yatoi hozo—Right angle joint with spline tenon. (Condition 2.)

This is a method in which the spline tenon is shaped with a dovetail at the end which will be connected to a column. The spline tenon is first inserted into a column, then lifted up to fit into the dovetail mortise. The beam is inserted into the other end of the spline tenon and then secured with keys.

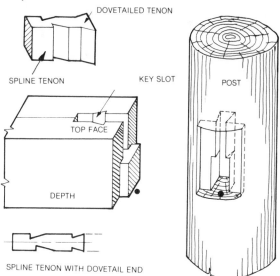

This is an example where a dovetail is made within the width of the spline tenon. Such a tenon is usually 35mm to 40mm wide.

L-shaped right angle joints.

Tome—
Plain miter

Han tome—
Shoulder miter

Tsuki tsuke—
Lap

Tsutsumi uchi tsuki tsuke—
Shoulder

Eri wa—
Dado and rabbet

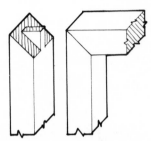
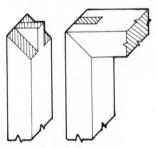
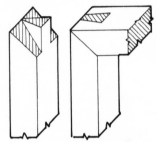

Kakushi-domekata sanmai hozo—
Blind and stub miter

Tomekata sanmai hozo—
Ship miter

Tome ari kata sanmai hozo—
Through single dovetailed miter

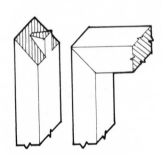
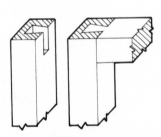
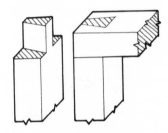

Kakushi-dome ari sanmai hozo—
Blind dovetailed miter

Kakushi ari kata sanmai hozo—
Half blind dovetail

Ari kata sanmai hozo—
Through single dovetail

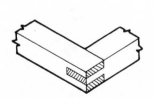
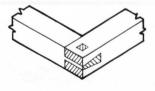

Kanegata sanmai hozo—
Ship (or open) mortise and tenon

Ari kata sanmai hozo komisen uchi—
Through single dovetail with pin

Otoshigama (also known as *sagekama*)—
Half blind dovetail mortise and tenon

3

Various Types of Fasteners

Traditionally, various fasteners such as keys, wedges, and pins have been used to secure and tie down pieces at their end and right angle joints. Their size and nomenclature differs according to their use. These fasteners are made from hard wood. When they are used, the hole or slot which is to accept them must be constructed so that the fasteners, when being installed, will pull the pieces together tightly.

Today, metal fasteners have in certain situations replaced the traditional wooden ones. These reinforcing fasteners, if used properly, can simplify the design of end joints and right angle joints, and can also increase their efficiency.

Various types of metal fasteners.

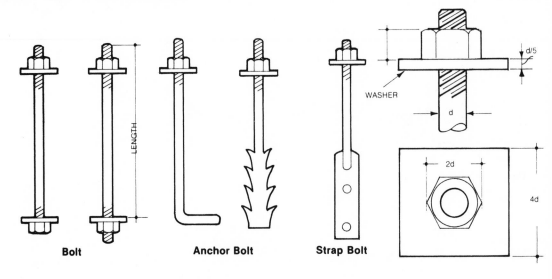

Bolt

Anchor Bolt

Strap Bolt

WASHER

d/5

d

2d

4d

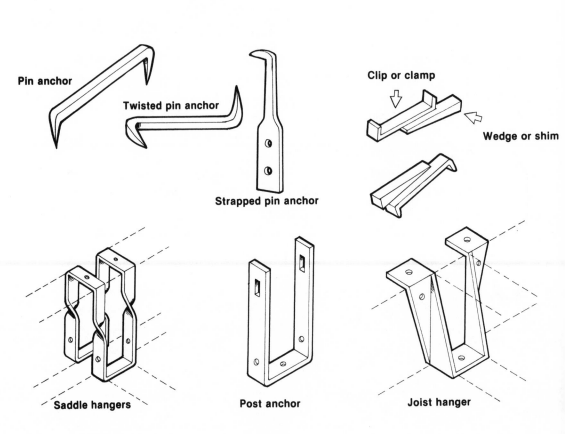

Pin anchor

Twisted pin anchor

Strapped pin anchor

Clip or clamp

Wedge or shim

Saddle hangers

Post anchor

Joist hanger

Various types of metal fasteners.

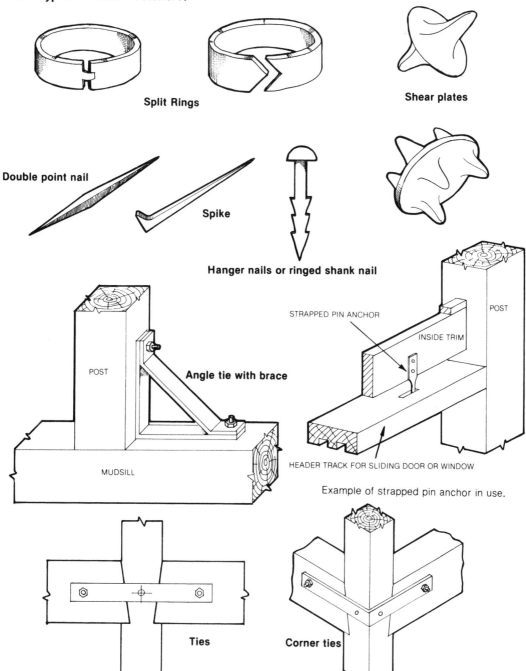

Split Rings

Shear plates

Double point nail

Spike

Hanger nails or ringed shank nail

POST

Angle tie with brace

MUDSILL

STRAPPED PIN ANCHOR

INSIDE TRIM

POST

HEADER TRACK FOR SLIDING DOOR OR WINDOW

Example of strapped pin anchor in use.

Ties

Corner ties

Sumi-kanamono—L-shaped *kanamono*

Various types of shear plates.

Section is T-shaped

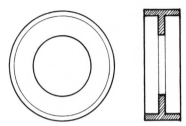

Section is L-shaped

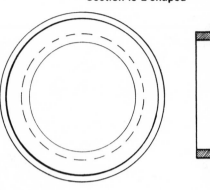

Shear plates

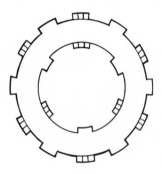

Shear plate with wings

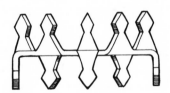

Toothed ring

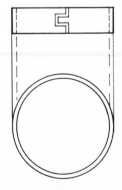

Split ring

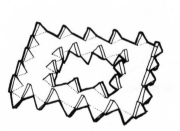

Flat clamping plate

Various types of shear plates (continued).

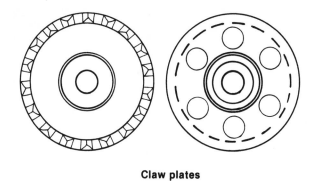

Claw plates

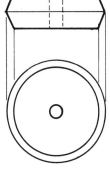

Kubler shear plate

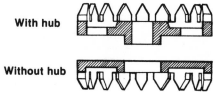

With hub

Without hub

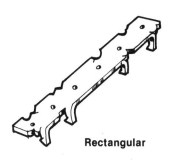

Rectangular

Angle

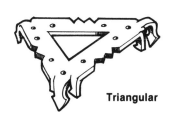

Triangular

Twisted

Twisted corner

Various reinforcing pins.

Komisen (Daisen)—Pin

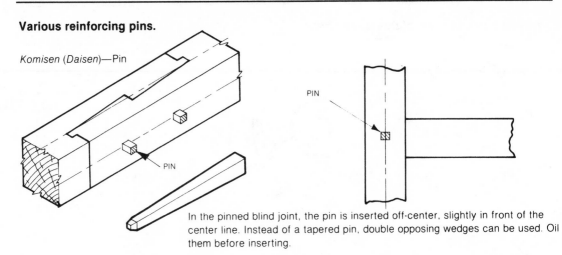

PIN

PIN

In the pinned blind joint, the pin is inserted off-center, slightly in front of the center line. Instead of a tapered pin, double opposing wedges can be used. Oil them before inserting.

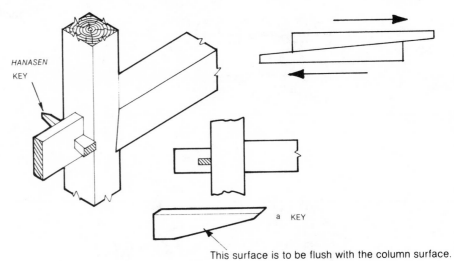

HANASEN KEY

a   KEY

This surface is to be flush with the column surface.

The point or tip of the key is shaped as indicated by (a) to eliminate the possibility of the point's penetrating into the column.

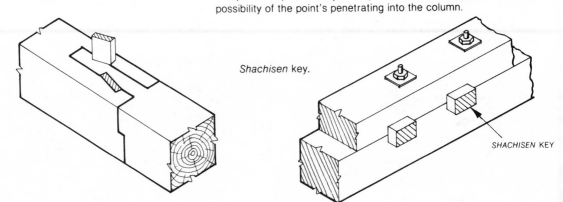

Shachisen key.

SHACHISEN KEY

Various reinforcing pins.

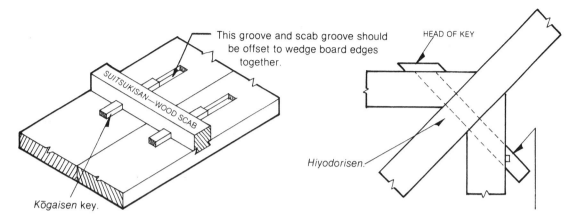

This groove and scab groove should be offset to wedge board edges together.

SUITSUKISAN—WOOD SCAB

Kōgaisen key.

HEAD OF KEY

Hiyodorisen.

The grooved guide for the *hogaisen* key of the *suitsukisan* scab must be made such that when the key is inserted, it pulls the board and the scab tightly together.

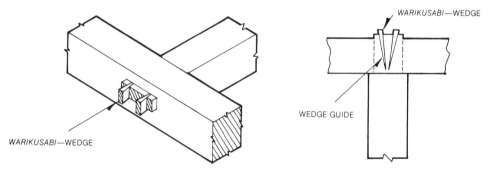

WARIKUSABI—WEDGE

WARIKUSABI—WEDGE

WEDGE GUIDE

The wedge guide is made by sawing with a slight angle.

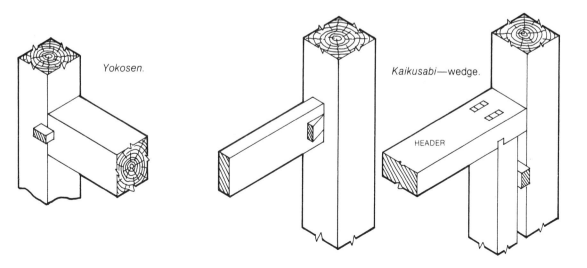

Yokosen.

Kaikusabi—wedge.

HEADER

4

Hikarikata—
Reproduction Methods

The word *hikaru* has many meanings; it can mean to shine, to collate, to sparkle, or to reproduce.

Architectural structures, especially wooden ones, when examined carefully, are not built with precise dimensions. The technique of reproducing or copying these inaccuracies so that corrections can be made without interstice or strain is called *hikari*. It may seem that *hikari* is an unnecessary skill, but in fact, it is required to work accurately and efficiently.

There are numerous examples of *hikaru* technique. Some major examples follow:

- The connection between a column and a grooved sill for various types of sliding doors and windows (*shikii*).
- The connection between a column and a grooved header, for various types of sliding doors and windows (*kamoi*).
- The connection between a combination of logs and their quality or grade (*sätsuke*).
- In the application of diagonal bracing.
- In measuring the actual length. (This is called *tsuki nori*)

Hikarikata is probably not explained in many texts on architectural construction methods. However, as a technique it is very important because the skill and knowledge of the master carpenters as well as of the carpenters will be reflected in the actual work they do.

Hikarikate

When one piece is to connect to another, it is necessary to copy the exact shape of the one piece onto the other. This copying method is called *hikari*, and the copying board or guide board is called *hikari-ita*. When a member is being reproduced on another (*hikaru*), it is important to check the front, back, left, and right sides of the member to check if these correspond to the sequence noted on the drawing made before the actual work. It is important to not scribe angles on the wrong side of the *hikari-ita*. Always stay on the same side of it. You want a mirror image, not a shadow image.

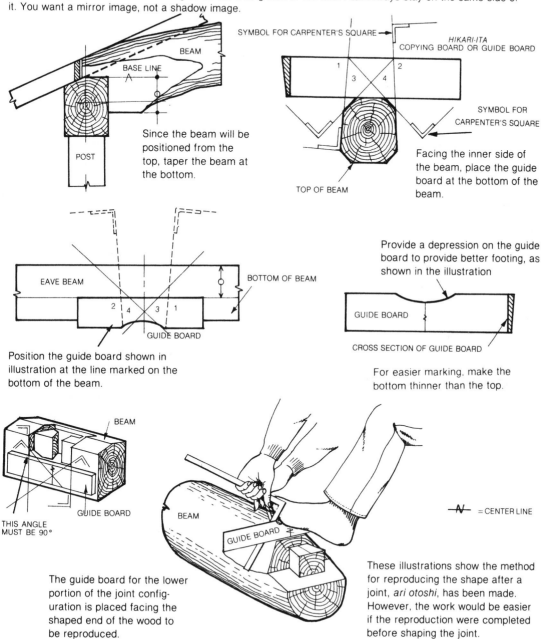

SYMBOL FOR CARPENTER'S SQUARE

HIKARI-ITA
COPYING BOARD OR GUIDE BOARD

BEAM

BASE LINE

POST

Since the beam will be positioned from the top, taper the beam at the bottom.

SYMBOL FOR CARPENTER'S SQUARE

TOP OF BEAM

Facing the inner side of the beam, place the guide board at the bottom of the beam.

EAVE BEAM

BOTTOM OF BEAM

GUIDE BOARD

Position the guide board shown in illustration at the line marked on the bottom of the beam.

Provide a depression on the guide board to provide better footing, as shown in the illustration

GUIDE BOARD

CROSS SECTION OF GUIDE BOARD

For easier marking, make the bottom thinner than the top.

BEAM

GUIDE BOARD

THIS ANGLE MUST BE 90°

BEAM

GUIDE BOARD

—N— = CENTER LINE

The guide board for the lower portion of the joint configuration is placed facing the shaped end of the wood to be reproduced.

These illustrations show the method for reproducing the shape after a joint, *ari otoshi*, has been made. However, the work would be easier if the reproduction were completed before shaping the joint.

Method for reproducing the beveled face of a beam at the top end of a post or pier.

In reproducing, always work from the center to the outside.

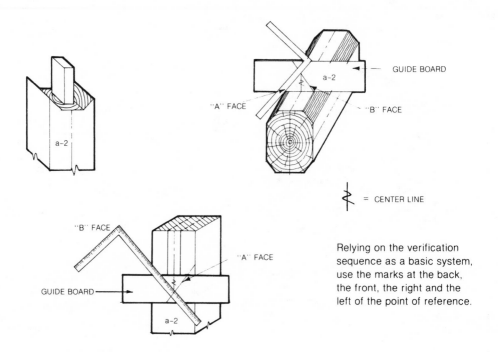

Relying on the verification sequence as a basic system, use the marks at the back, the front, the right and the left of the point of reference.

Method for reproducing cut-outs for a beam connection.

In order to reproduce, rely on the marked line on the bottom of the beam and the verification sequence of front, back, left and right as a standard.

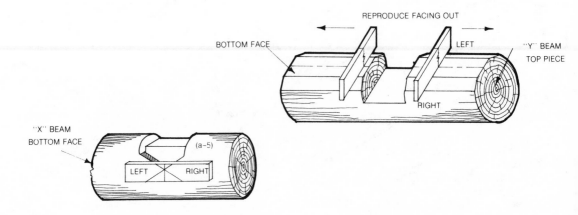

Kuchi-biki—Reproducing the curvature of a log onto a receiving member with a compass.

Always use a compass when reproducing the curvature of a log onto a receiving member, and take special care in handling it. It is important to remember that the lowest point of the curve drawn will become the reference point.

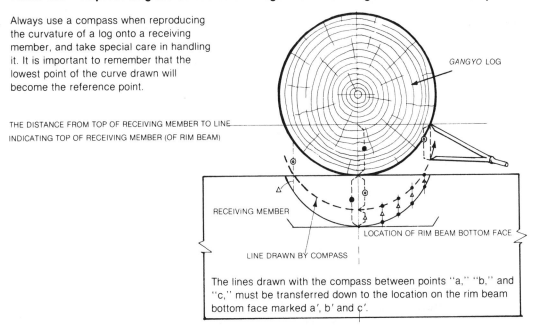

GANGYO LOG

THE DISTANCE FROM TOP OF RECEIVING MEMBER TO LINE
INDICATING TOP OF RECEIVING MEMBER (OF RIM BEAM)

RECEIVING MEMBER

LOCATION OF RIM BEAM BOTTOM FACE

LINE DRAWN BY COMPASS

The lines drawn with the compass between points "a," "b," and "c," must be transferred down to the location on the rim beam bottom face marked a', b' and c'.

Shaku gaeri—Check the reference distance.

When marking, locate a mark (*shaku gaeri*) 30 cm away from a point of reference. After the members have been set in position, check to see if they were correctly positioned.*

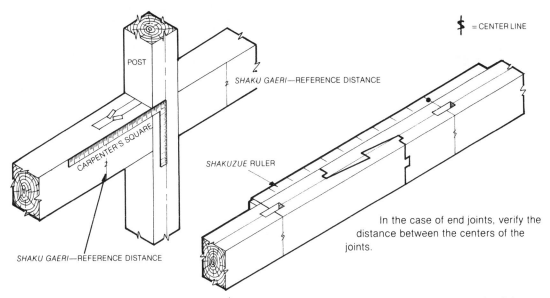

✚ = CENTER LINE

POST

SHAKU GAERI—REFERENCE DISTANCE

CARPENTER'S SQUARE

SHAKUZUE RULER

SHAKU GAERI—REFERENCE DISTANCE

In the case of end joints, verify the distance between the centers of the joints.

* *Shaku gaeri* ("return of measure") is an arbitrary reference mark about 30 cm from a reference point. It is used to check the accuracy of framing after the framing is completed, since the reference point itself will be covered over because of the joints.

Determining any peculiarity in a board member by using a carpenter's square or a parallel-sided board.

Place the carpenter's square on the surface against which a board is to butt. Mark the board on its top surface and use the marking as a reference line.

Reproducing the curvature onto a board with a compass.

Always draw evenly while facing towards the center of the wood.

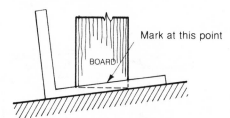

Mark at this point

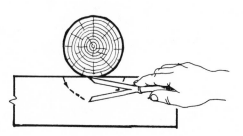

Reproduction of a curve using an *osa*—reed.

In the past, *hikari osa*, (the reproducing reed) was made using the bamboo reed from a loom. It is an instrument like a reed, where each stick comprising a reed is movable. Each reed stick butts against an object so as to take its exact shape. The thinner the *osa*, the better. (Normally the *osa* is 1 mm thick and 10 mm wide.) The following illustrations show the method of reproduction using the *osa*.

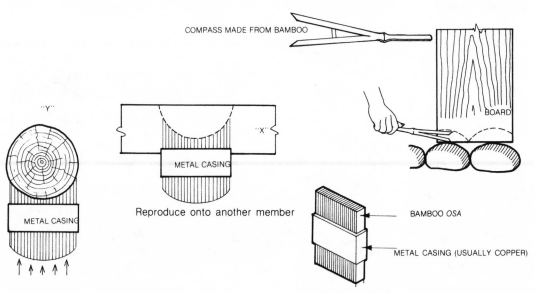

COMPASS MADE FROM BAMBOO

Reproduce onto another member

Tap gently and conform to shape.

Reproduction methods for the *shikii* and *kamoi*.

Shikii is a grooved or tracked sill for a sliding door or window. *Kamoi* is a grooved or tracked header for a sliding door or window. Because most work is never perfectly square, the reproduction method involves 5 steps, which are explained in sequence below.

First step

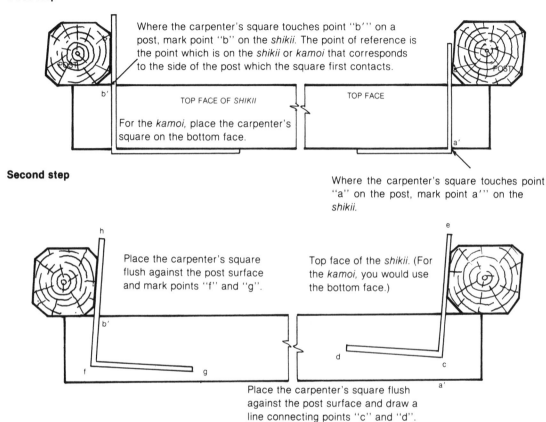

Where the carpenter's square touches point "b'''" on a post, mark point "b" on the *shikii*. The point of reference is the point which is on the *shikii* or *kamoi* that corresponds to the side of the post which the square first contacts.

TOP FACE OF *SHIKII*

TOP FACE

For the *kamoi*, place the carpenter's square on the bottom face.

Second step

Where the carpenter's square touches point "a" on the post, mark point a'" on the *shikii*.

Place the carpenter's square flush against the post surface and mark points "f" and "g".

Top face of the *shikii*. (For the *kamoi*, you would use the bottom face.)

Place the carpenter's square flush against the post surface and draw a line connecting points "c" and "d".

Third step

At the third step, the *dōtsuke* (reproduced lines transferring the obliqueness of column faces) on the *shikii* are determined.

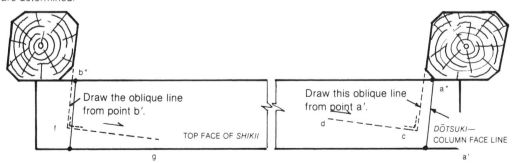

Draw the oblique line from point b'.

TOP FACE OF *SHIKII*

Draw this oblique line from point a'.

DŌTSUKI— COLUMN FACE LINE

Reproduction methods for the *shikii* and *kamoi* (continued).

Fourth step

Where there is a curvature or large bevel, it is reproduced as explained under steps four and five.

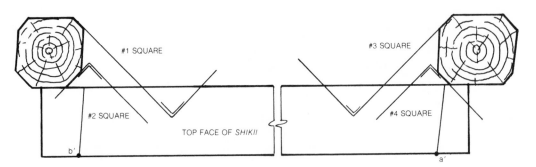

Reproduce the lines made with #1 and #2 squares on the top face of the *shikii*.

Reproduce the lines made with #3 and #4 squares on the top face of the *shikii*.

Fifth step

When transferring the measurements 1 and 2 of the post onto the *shikii*, use the center line of the post as a reference point, obtain the dimensions of the post face on both sides of the center line, and transfer them on to the appropriate *dotsuki* on the *shikii*.

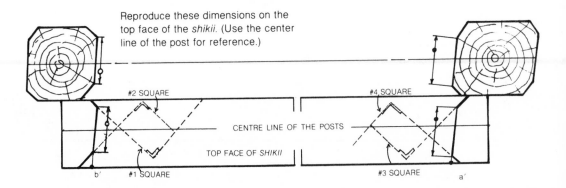

Reproduce these dimensions on the top face of the *shikii*. (Use the center line of the post for reference.)

Hikarikata or *kizukuri*—Wood shaping.

Method for transferring the center line to the opposite side from the side on which the warp has been corrected (squared surface).

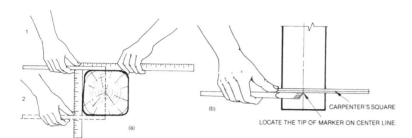

(b)

CARPENTER'S SQUARE

LOCATE THE TIP OF MARKER ON CENTER LINE.

(a)

Place the tip of the marker on the center line and hold it tightly with the finger tips where it meets the end of the carpenter's square. Then guide the marker along the carpenter's square edge from bottom to top and mark the wood below the other leg of the carpenter's square.

Method as shown in illustration (a): Transfer the dimension obtained as shown under (1) to the opposite end of the wood by using the edge of the carpenter's square as a guide as shown under (2). (There are many ways to transfer dimensions.)

Method as shown in illustration (b): This is for transferring dimensions to the bottom face of a piece by utilizing the right angle of the carpenter's square.

Method for locating the center line of faces adjacent to the squared surface.

Kane wo maku is a phrase describing the positioning of the carpenter's square on the center line. *Kaneba* is a position marked on the wood using the *kane wo maku* method to verify the squareness of a surface of a piece after its warp has been corrected.

Place the carpenter's square on the center line.

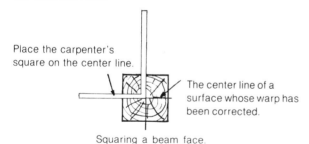

The center line of a surface whose warp has been corrected.

Squaring a beam face.

Gently move the carpenter's square up and down on the surface whose *kaneba* has been determined to verify its squareness.

The surface whose warp has been corrected.

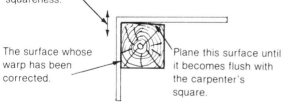

Plane this surface until it becomes flush with the carpenter's square.

The method of squaring a surface by checking for its squareness as illustrated is also called *kane wo maku*. After the surface has been squared, locate the *kaneba*.

A method using two sticks (*tsukinori*) for obtaining dimensions.

This is a method used, as illustrated, to obtain a dimension from a place where a ruler or measuring tools cannot be used.

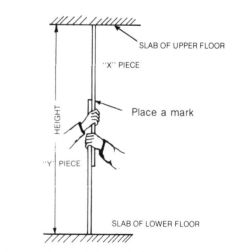

SLAB OF UPPER FLOOR

"X" PIECE

Place a mark

HEIGHT

"Y" PIECE

SLAB OF LOWER FLOOR

Determining any height or inside measurement.

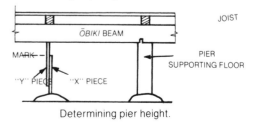

JOIST

ŌBIKI BEAM

MARK

PIER SUPPORTING FLOOR

"Y" PIECE   "X" PIECE

Determining pier height.

Method for checking and correcting warp.

Verification by placing carpenter's squares on the center line.

Illustration (a) shows a method which places the squares on the center line. If there exists a twist or warp as shown on (b), verification with only a single carpenter's square will result in an increased slope on the surface of the material. Therefore, decrease the twist from two opposite surfaces until two carpenter's squares align as illustrated on (c).

Space to be equally distributed

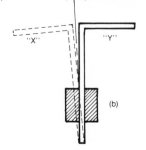

"X" "Y"

(b)

Illustrated is a method using two carpenter's squares to check the warp or twist in the wood. Place the squares 90° to the centerline of surface A.

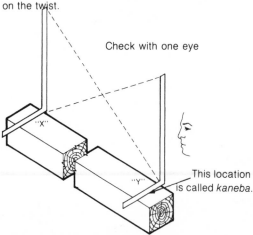

Check with one eye

(a)

Case where warp exists

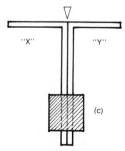

"X" "Y"

(c)

Once there is no twist or warp, "x" and "y" carpenter's squares will align.

Method of checking by using *kaneba* (the location where the carpenter's square has been placed).

As illustrated below, this method uses the two carpenter's squares and relies on the squareness of the tool to check on the warp and on the twist.

Check with one eye

"X"

"Y"

This location is called *kaneba*.

ABOUT 5 CM

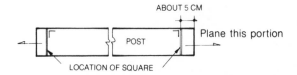

POST

Plane this portion

LOCATION OF SQUARE

The *kaneba* for a post: This is made by planing along the wood grain. The *kaneba* is located by placing the carpenter's square perpendicular to a piece and marking the position with the butt end of a marking tool (*sumi sashi*).

Arbitrarily select places to set the carpenter's squares. Always use the same places to check on the work of squaring a surface and for determining the center and the width of a piece. The method for correcting twist is to gradually plane the locations of both "x" and "y" carpenter's squares until the places are corrected. Maintain these two positions until the end of the work since they will be the reference points for locating the center line and to shape the wood.

GROOVED HEADER

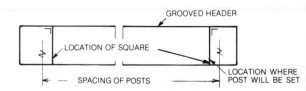

LOCATION OF SQUARE

SPACING OF POSTS

LOCATION WHERE POST WILL BE SET

The *kaneba* for a header (*sashi kamoi*): Locate the *kaneba* where the inside face of the column meets the header surface. (The distance equal to the column's depth.) To square the *kaneba*, plane across the grain. Mark the *kaneba* position which has been located by squarely placing the carpenter's square on the wood with the butt end of a marking tool (*sumi sashi*).

5

Jiku Gumi—Framing

After completion of the foundation work, parts of the architectural skeleton such as mud-sills, posts, beams, headers, etc., are put together. This is called framing (*jiku gumi*).

In order to construct the necessary joint cut-outs on the framing members, drawings (*eizu ita, kosakuzu* or *kanbanzu*),* rulers, and if necessary, *kanabakari* (detailed framing sectional drawings) are used.

There are two points which need to be carefully considered for actual construction work. One is to keep the joint cut-outs to a minimum so that a member's structural strength is not greatly reduced. The other is to keep the joint details as easy as possible to construct.

It is important that the framing will be able to resist various external forces and can maintain its shape without change. To achieve this, use diagonal braces and angle braces in equal quantities whenever possible. Also, form as many triangular connections for both horizontal and vertical framing as possible, and utilize bolts and other metal connectors to tighten connections.

* Note: *Eizu ita, kosakuzu* or *kanbanzu* are not architect's drawings. These are drawings made on wooden boards by the master carpenter showing the framing sequence in which to frame the skeletal structural members. The drawing, of course, does not alter the architect's design.

Ōkabe framing method.

The illustrations below show a portion of *ōkabe* framing. There are two different diagonal bracing methods, as shown on drawing (a).

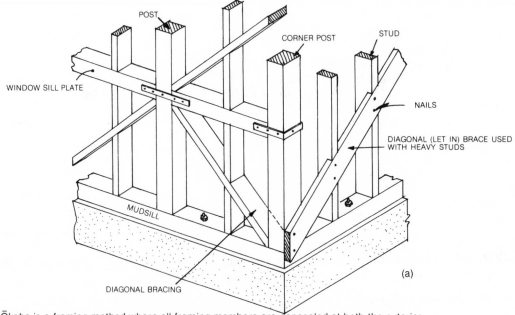

(a)

Note: *Ōkabe* is a framing method where all framing members are concealed at both the exterior and interior by the wall finishing materials (sheet rock or lath).

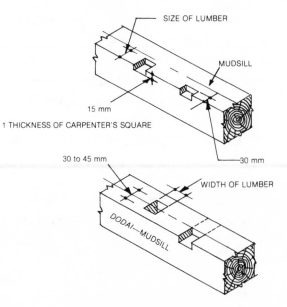

Cut-outs made on mudsill to receive studs.

Right angle joints of bridging for use with *kabe* (mud plastered walls).

At the corner post, use a blind and stub mortise and tenon joint (*kone hozo sashi*).

BRIDGING HASHIRA—POST

TENON ON BOTTOM ON *HARI* SIDE TENON ON TOP ON *KETA* SIDE

WEDGE

BRIDGING

The mortise portion of the blind and halved dovetailed stub mortise and tenon joint (*shitage kama*) must be made larger to accept the wedge.

Shinkabe framing method.

The illustration below shows the partial framing method of *shinkabe*.

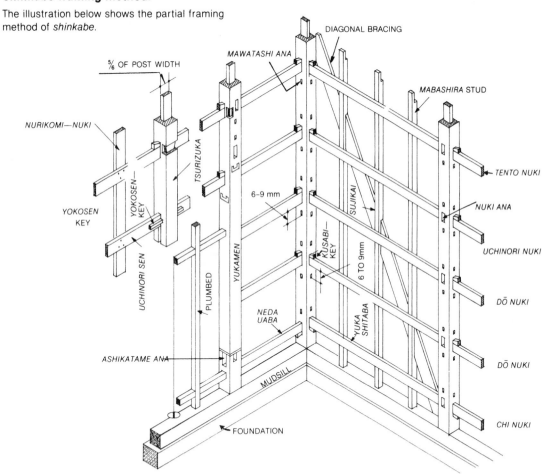

The wedge for *chi-nuki* (bottom bridging) is installed at the bottom edge of *chi-nuki*. For all other *nuki* (bridgings) the wedge is installed on the top edge. The *chi-nuki* on the *keta* (eaves beam which supports the rafters) side must be located lower than the subflooring boards. The *chi-nuki* on the *hari yuki* (rim beam which does not support rafters) side must be lower than the floor joists. Ideally, the *chi-nuki* should be placed as above, however this method is no longer practiced.

Note: *Shinkabe* is a framing method where some major structural members such as posts and beams are exposed and treated as finishing materials. This is similar to half timber construction.

Diagonal braces for *shinkabe* framing.

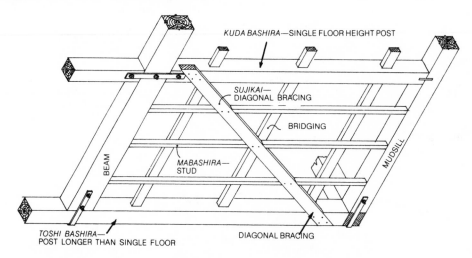

KUDA BASHIRA—SINGLE FLOOR HEIGHT POST

SUJIKAI— DIAGONAL BRACING

BRIDGING

MUDSILL

BEAM

MABASHIRA— STUD

TOSHI BASHIRA— POST LONGER THAN SINGLE FLOOR

DIAGONAL BRACING

When thin lumber is used as diagonal bracing, studs and bracing are connected by a cross-lap joint.

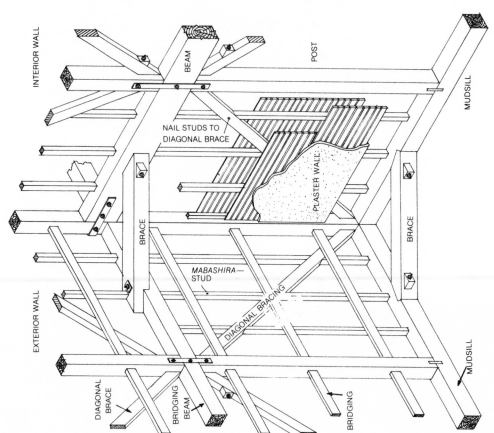

INTERIOR WALL

BEAM

POST

MUDSILL

NAIL STUDS TO DIAGONAL BRACE

PLASTER WALL

BRACE

BRACE

MABASHIRA— STUD

DIAGONAL BRACING

EXTERIOR WALL

MUDSILL

DIAGONAL BRACE

BRIDGING BEAM

BRIDGING

When thick lumber is used as diagonal bracing, all members such as the studs abutting it should be nailed to the bracing instead of it being notched or cut-out to receive other members.

Bridging for post and *mawatashi* holes.

Mawatashi holes are the holes drilled to accept the bamboo used as horizontal members of a lathing grid. Placing one *dō nuki* (intermediate bridging) between the chi nuki (bottom bridging) and the *uchinori nuki* (top bridging) is called *sandori nuki*. When two *dō nuki* are installed, it is called *yondori nuki*. *Uchinori* is made from lumber that is about 150 mm to 180 mm wide by 30 mm to 40 mm thick. The lesser quality *uchinori* are made from 120 mm wide by 25 mm thick pieces. Unless there is a space of 15 mm between the top of the *kamoi* and the bottom of the *uchinori nuki*, the plaster will easily come off.

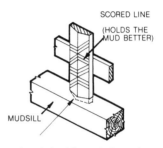

Insert about 6 mm to 9 mm deep. (Chisel out deep enough to allow droppage or sinking [of stud] with excessive load.)

b. *Nurikomi nuki.*

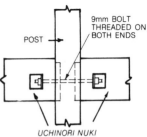

c. Method of connecting *uchinori nuki.*

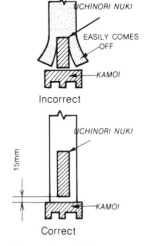

d. Leave about 15 mm space between *uchinori nuki* and *kamoi* to prevent plaster from easily being removed.

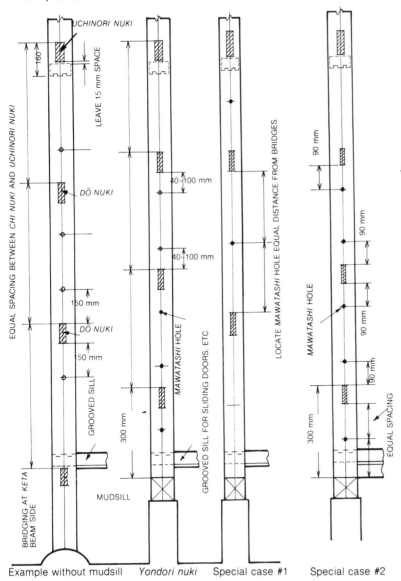

Example without mudsill   Yondori nuki   Special case #1   Special case #2

a. Method for locating the holes of *mawatashi.*

Sectional details: single floor residence.

SCALE UNIT—cm

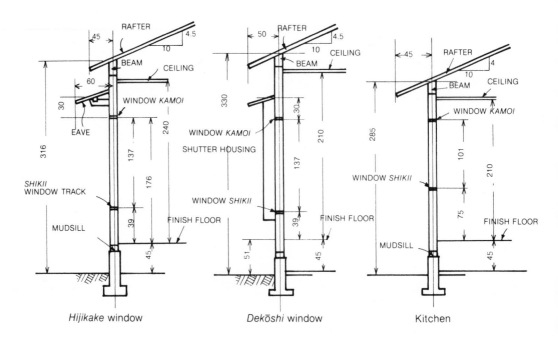

Hijikake window   *Dekōshi* window   Kitchen

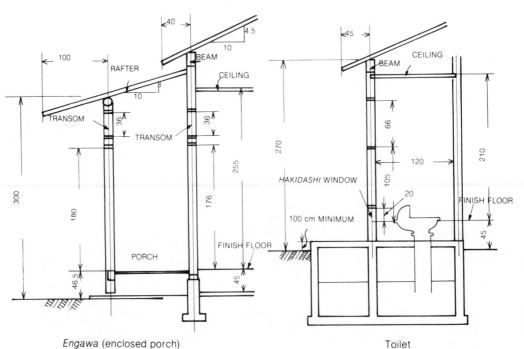

Engawa (enclosed porch)   Toilet

Sectional details: two storey residence.

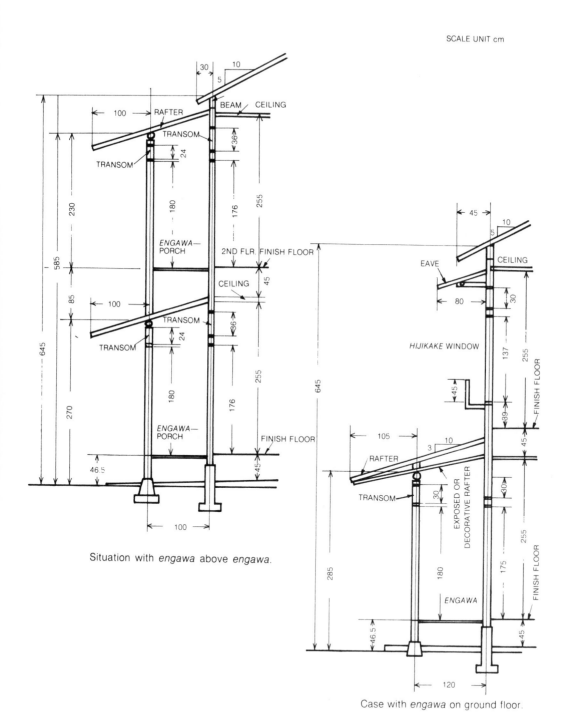

SCALE UNIT cm

Situation with *engawa* above *engawa*.

Case with *engawa* on ground floor.

Sectional detail: first floor portion of two storey residence.

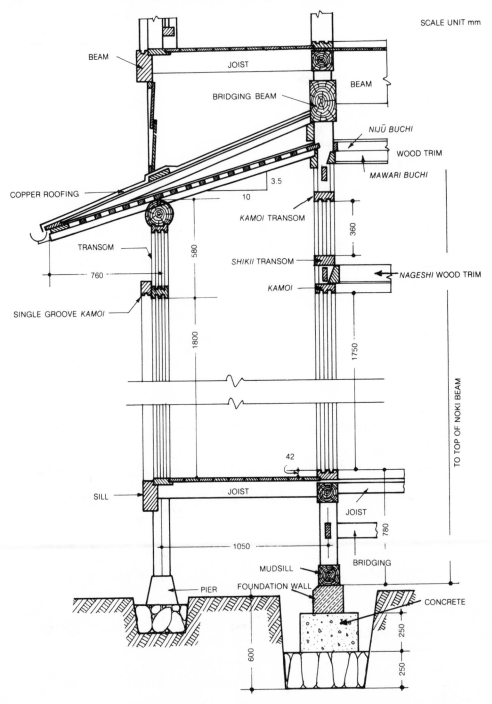

SCALE UNIT mm

BEAM

JOIST

BRIDGING BEAM

BEAM

NIJŪ BUCHI

WOOD TRIM

MAWARI BUCHI

COPPER ROOFING

3.5

10

KAMOI TRANSOM

580

360

TRANSOM

SHIKII TRANSOM

NAGESHI WOOD TRIM

760

KAMOI

1800

1750

SINGLE GROOVE *KAMOI*

TO TOP OF NOKI BEAM

42

SILL

JOIST

JOIST

780

1050

BRIDGING

MUDSILL

PIER

FOUNDATION WALL

CONCRETE

600

250

250

This illustration is also an example of a two storey residence with *engawa* above *engawa*.

Sectional detail: second floor portion of two storey residence.

SCALE UNIT mm

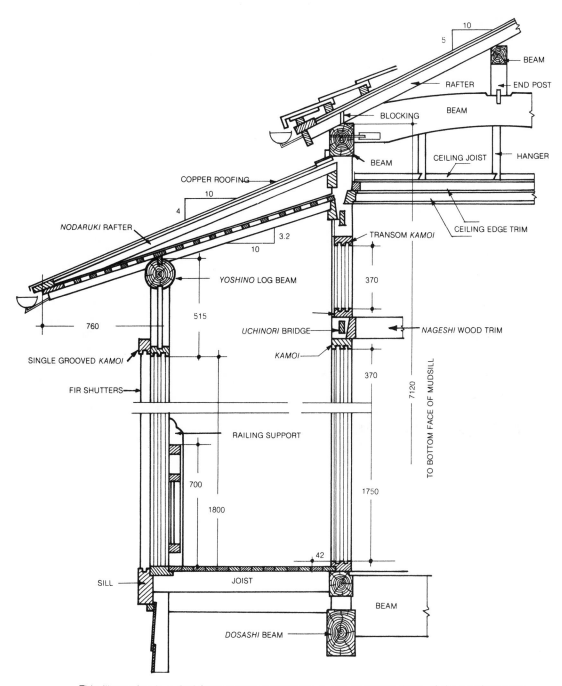

This illustration is a 2nd floor portion continuous to the sectional detail of the previous page.

Right angle joints of mudsill.

Right angle joints at the corner of the mudsill.

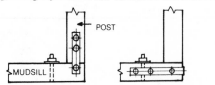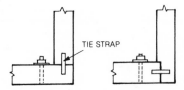

1. To determine the location for the anchor bolt, draw a guide line the width of the mudsill on the concrete surface of the foundation. Use the guide line to locate the anchor bolt.
2. As shown on the last illustration, when the sill is of thin material, use an end lap joint to connect the sill at the corner and use a full mortise and tenon joint to connect the column.

Right angle joints using straps.

In addition to the use of metal straps, clamps and pin anchors are commonly utilized.

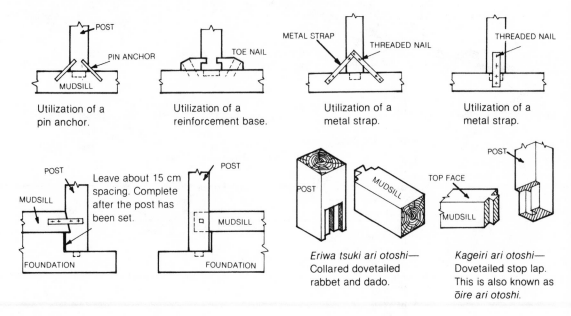

Utilization of a pin anchor.

Utilization of a reinforcement base.

Utilization of a metal strap.

Utilization of a metal strap.

Leave about 15 cm spacing. Complete after the post has been set.

*Eriwa tsuki ari otoshi—*Collared dovetailed rabbet and dado.

*Kageiri ari otoshi—*Dovetailed stop lap. This is also known as *ōire ari otoshi.*

Cross lap right angle joints.

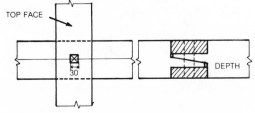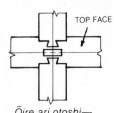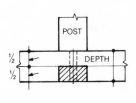

*Suberi hozo sashi—*Scarfed stub mortise and tenon joint. Stubs of the mudsill are secured by the stub of the post set perpendicular to them.

*Ōire ari otoshi—*Full half lap dovetail.

Cross lap; secured with stub of post.

Corner joints of mudsill.

End joints of mudsill.

1. For top quality work, use the *kanawa tsugi* joint.

2. For medium quality work, use the *koshikake kama tsugi* joint.

3. For low quality work, use the *koshikake ari tsugi* joint.

4. For lowest grade work, use the *aikaki tsugi* joint.

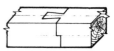
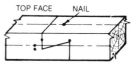

Kanawa tsugi—
Scarf joint or girder splicing.

Ari tsugi—dovetail joint.
Commonly used as an end
joint for mud sill walls.

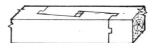
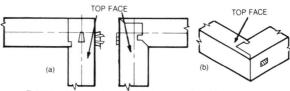

Kama tsugi—
Goose neck joint.

Arikaki tsugi—
Oblique surfaced half-lap joint.

Corner joints at end of mudsill.

1. The most commonly used and strongest joint is *eriwatsuki kone hozo sashi* secured by wedges. See illustration (a).

2. For top quality work, *sumidome hozo sashi* is used. See illustration (b).

3. Where there are aesthetic concerns, *daiwa dome* is used. See illustration (c).

4. Neither *bintadome*, illustration (d), nor *kiguchi hozo* and *aikaki* illustration (f), are commonly used.

5. The mortise for a column tenon must be fan-shaped.

6. The *kiguchi ari* joint, illustration (e), looks and is similar in function to *kiguchi hozo*. However, if the dovetailed stub is hard, the mortise could crack when joining, so insert if with care. It is not a strong joint.

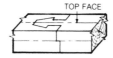

(a) *Eriwatsuki kone hozo sashi.*

(b) *Sumidome hozo sashi.*

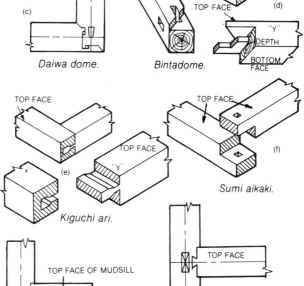

(c) *Daiwa dome.*

Bintadome.

(d)

(e) *Kiguchi ari.*

(f) *Sumi aikaki.*

Corner joints at the "T" junction of the mudsill.

Kageire ari otoshi, also called *ōire ari otoshi*, illustration (b), or *kageire hozo sashi*, also called *ōire hozao sashi*, see illustration (a), is used. However, for very rough work, an end lap joint is commonly used.

(a) *Kageire hozo sashi.*

(b) *Kageire ari otoshi.*
The thickness of the dovetail stud should be ½ to ⅔ the thickness of the wood.

Right angle joints of mudsill.

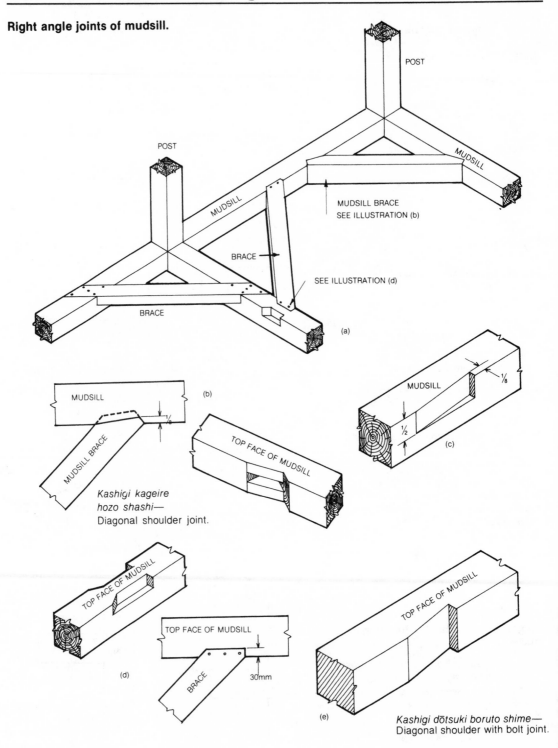

POST

POST

MUDSILL

MUDSILL

MUDSILL BRACE
SEE ILLUSTRATION (b)

BRACE

SEE ILLUSTRATION (d)

BRACE

(a)

(b)

MUDSILL

MUDSILL BRACE

*Kashigi kageire
hozo shashi—*
Diagonal shoulder joint.

TOP FACE OF MUDSILL

MUDSILL

$\frac{1}{8}$

$\frac{1}{2}$

(c)

TOP FACE OF MUDSILL

(d)

TOP FACE OF MUDSILL

BRACE

30mm

TOP FACE OF MUDSILL

(e)

Kashigi dōtsuki boruto shime—
Diagonal shoulder with bolt joint.

Securing of a post at its base.

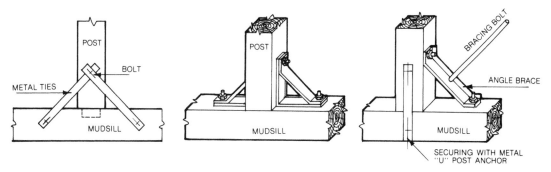

(a) Securing with metal ties.   (b) Securing with metal angle gussets.   (c) Case when bracing bolt is used.

Securing connection at base of independent post.

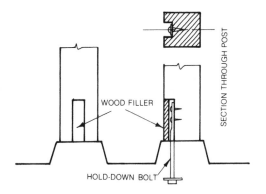

Posts which stand directly on the finished floor or in the entrance should be shaped as illustrated, and the post end joint face should be flush with the floor.

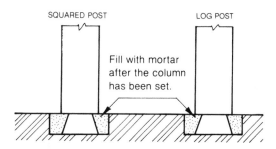

Hold-down bolts are imbedded in the concrete. The wood filler should be installed by adhesive onto the column face which is least exposed.

In cases where posts are to be installed on top of concrete, as on a porch or other similar locations, the tenon shape should be dovetailed as illustrated to resist pulling forces.

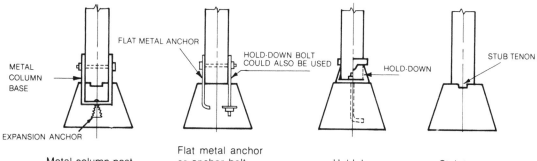

Metal column post.   Flat metal anchor or anchor bolt.   Hold-down.   Stub tenon.

Japanese framing—Exterior ōkabe.

In framing, special attention should be given to the following:

1. Use *kasugai-dome* at the connection of a post with the header beam and the mudsill.
2. Use a cross-lap joint where diagonal bracing connects with a post or with a stud. (Use at least four large nails at each connection.)
3. Secure *tōshi-nuki* (intermediate bridging) with a wedge at the top face.
4. Above the studs, the joint should be *hozo sashi* (mortise and tenon); at both top and bottom, the joint should be *dōtsuki tsukikaki dome* secured by nailing from the exterior.

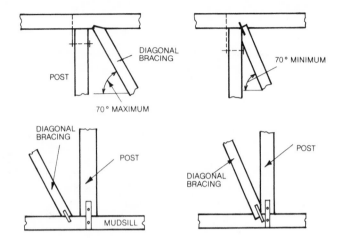

Connecting methods of diagonal bracing.

When connecting diagonal bracing, special attention must be given to the following:
1. Determining the location for diagonal bracing.
2. Determining the type of joints to be used.
3. Verifying if the foundation on which the diagonal bracing is to rest will be sufficient.
4. Verifying the strength of the diagonal bracing for the angle at which it will be set.

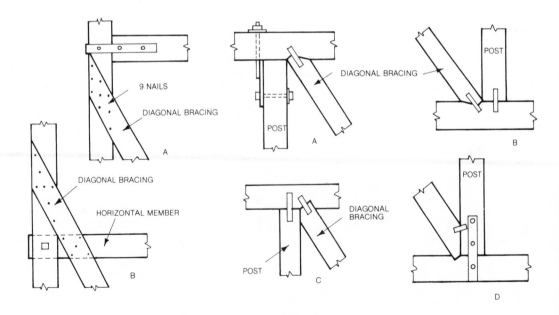

Example of right angle joints for diagonal bracing.

Right angle joint for thick diagonal bracing: the joint between a discontinuous post [two posts vertically aligned but separated by a beam] and a diagonal brace with its depth matching the post or more than half the depth of the post should be constructed as follows (with the width of the wood set to face up):

1. If the angle of the brace at the beam or mudsill is to be less than 70°, the brace should be connected in front of the post and onto the horizontal member using the joint ōire kasugai uchi. See illustration A (on previous page.)

2. Where the brace is to be set at an angle greater than 70°, the joint kasugi ōire is used to connect with the horizontal member, and the joint naname tsuki tsuke kasugai uchi is used at the post. See illustration B (on previous page).

Right angle joint for thin diagonal bracing (Hoso sujikai, also known as usui sujikai and hira sujikai.): the joint between a discontinuous post and a diagonal bracing with thickness less than ⅓ of the post's width should be constructed (with the width of the wood facing up) as follows:

1. The post and horizontal member to which the brace is to be connected are chiseled out to accept the brace forming a flush joint. The nail length should be 2½ to 3 times the thickness of the material and its size must be a minimum of 60 mm. A minimum of 4 nails is to be used where the brace is tied with a horizontal member, and 2 or more nails are to be used everywhere else.

2. The upper portion of the diagonal brace must be connected flush to the continuous post, which has been cut out as required to accept it. At each connection at least four nails are to be used. In a case where the post has to be exposed, the cut-out on it should be at least 40 mm deep and should be covered with a filler piece.

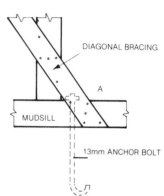

In the case where a diagonal brace is joined to the mudsill as illustrated under A, it is difficult to make the cut-out after framing has been begun. Here, a full scale form board is made and the mudsill, before it is set in place, is cut-out to accept the bracing.

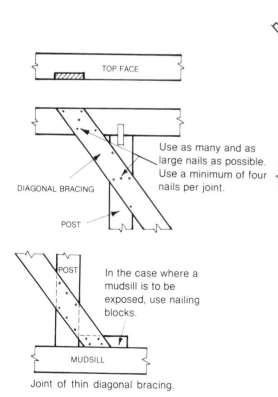

Use as many and as large nails as possible. Use a minimum of four nails per joint.

In the case where a mudsill is to be exposed, use nailing blocks.

Joint of thin diagonal bracing.

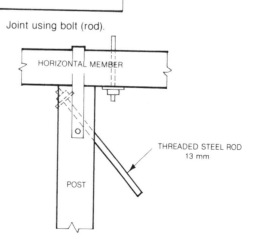

Joint using bolt (rod).

Wall types.

Framing methods vary according to wall types. The following illustrations show different types of framed walls.

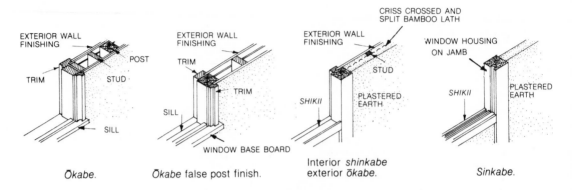

Ōkabe.

Ōkabe false post finish.

Interior *shinkabe* exterior *ōkabe.*

Sinkabe.

Western framing.

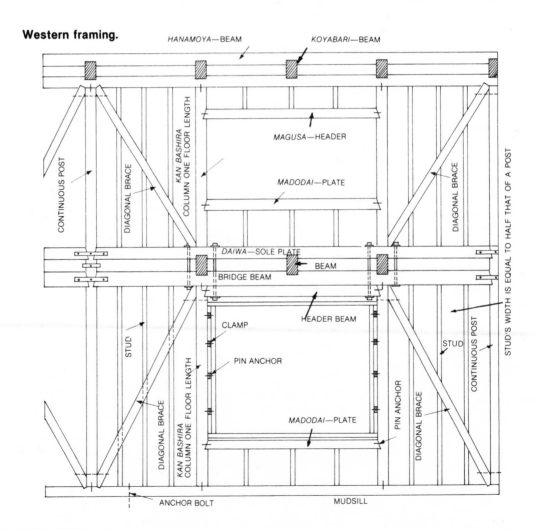

The right angle joint between diagonal bracing and studs, and between header and post.

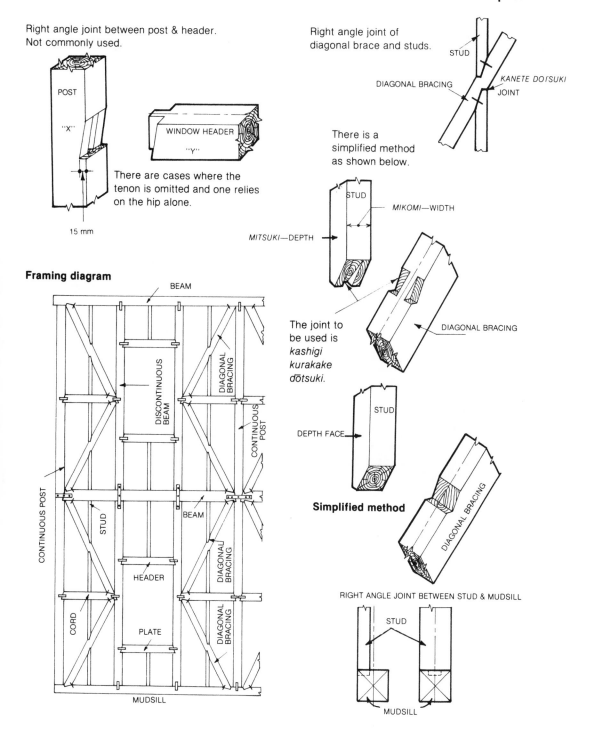

Right angle joint between post & header.
Not commonly used.

POST

"X"

15 mm

There are cases where the tenon is omitted and one relies on the hip alone.

WINDOW HEADER "Y"

Right angle joint of diagonal brace and studs.

STUD

DIAGONAL BRACING

KANETE DOTSUKI JOINT

There is a simplified method as shown below.

STUD

MIKOMI—WIDTH

MITSUKI—DEPTH

The joint to be used is *kashigi kurakake dōtsuki*.

DIAGONAL BRACING

Framing diagram

BEAM

DISCONTINUOUS BEAM

DIAGONAL BRACING

CONTINUOUS POST

CONTINUOUS POST

STUD

BEAM

HEADER

CORD

PLATE

DIAGONAL BRACING

DIAGONAL BRACING

MUDSILL

STUD

DEPTH FACE

Simplified method

DIAGONAL BRACING

RIGHT ANGLE JOINT BETWEEN STUD & MUDSILL

STUD

MUDSILL

Beveling of the post and hole for bamboo lath.

Beveling of the post.

In the case of *ōmendori* for the post, the standard practice is to take $\frac{1}{10}$ the depth of the wood trim (*nageshi*) over the grooved header (*kamoi*), grooved sill and header of the transom (*ranma no shikii kamoi*) and peripheral ceiling trim.

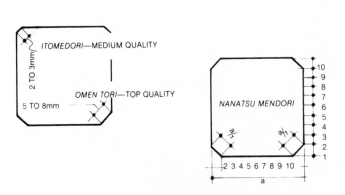

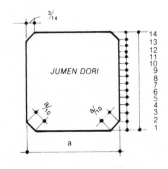

To construct *jumen dori*, common practice is to divide the depth of the column into 14 equal parts.

Holes for bamboo (for plastered mud walls).

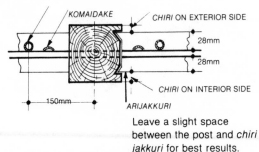

Leave a slight space between the post and *chiri jakkuri* for best results.

1. The hole for the bamboo lath should be located on the center line of the post.
2. The hole for the bamboo lath on a beam or on a mudsill should be chiseled out 150mm from the post's center line towards the exterior face of the post, or 90mm inside from the exterior face of the post.

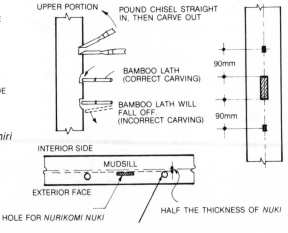

Kabe chiri and chiri jakkuri.*

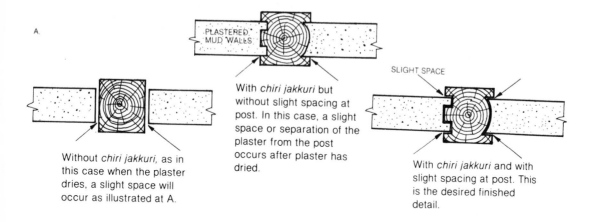

A.

PLASTERED MUD WALLS

SLIGHT SPACE

Without *chiri jakkuri*, as in this case when the plaster dries, a slight space will occur as illustrated at A.

With *chiri jakkuri* but without slight spacing at post. In this case, a slight space or separation of the plaster from the post occurs after plaster has dried.

With *chiri jakkuri* and with slight spacing at post. This is the desired finished detail.

Method of drawing center line of post which has been split—*sewari*.

Artificial check is wedged open to prevent random unwanted checking on visible surfaces.

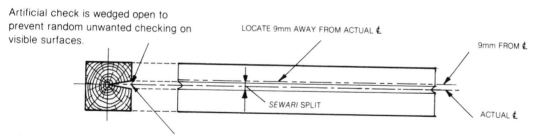

LOCATE 9mm AWAY FROM ACTUAL ₡

9mm FROM ₡

SEWARI SPLIT

ACTUAL ₡

For a post which has been split, mark a line 9mm away from the center point. This line will be the location for *nuki*'s face. *Nuki*'s face should be flush with the line.

Metric to English conversions:
1 mm = 0.04 inches; 10 mm = 0.4 inches; 100 mm = 4 inches; 1 metre = 39.3 inches.
To get approximate English dimensions, divide millimeters by 3 and multiply the answer by $\frac{1}{8}$.
For example $\frac{12\,mm}{3} = 4 \times \frac{1}{8} = \frac{1}{2}$ ".

* *Kabe chiri* and *chiri jakkuri* are finishing details of plaster butting to a post surface which has been cut to accept the plaster. This eliminates the need of trim at the point where the post and plaster edge butt.

Right angle joint between post and *nuki*.

In examples A through C, the *nuki* are joined at the outside of the hole for the *nuki* drilled on the post to accept[1] them, and then they are set inside the drilled hole. In example D, the single *nuki* is pushed into the hole, lowered, set at the position, and secured by wedges at the top.

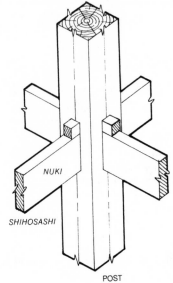

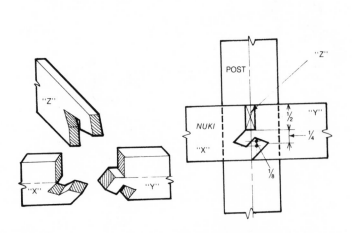

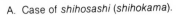

A. Case of *shihosashi* (*shihokama*).

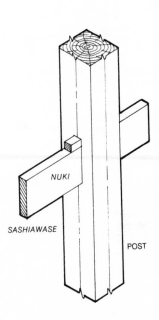

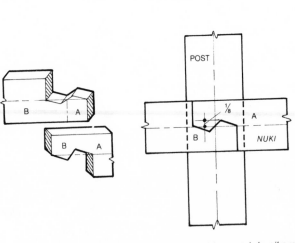

B. Case of *sashiawase* (*nimaikama*).

Kama or *sabaguchi*.

Right angle joint between post and *nuki* (continued).

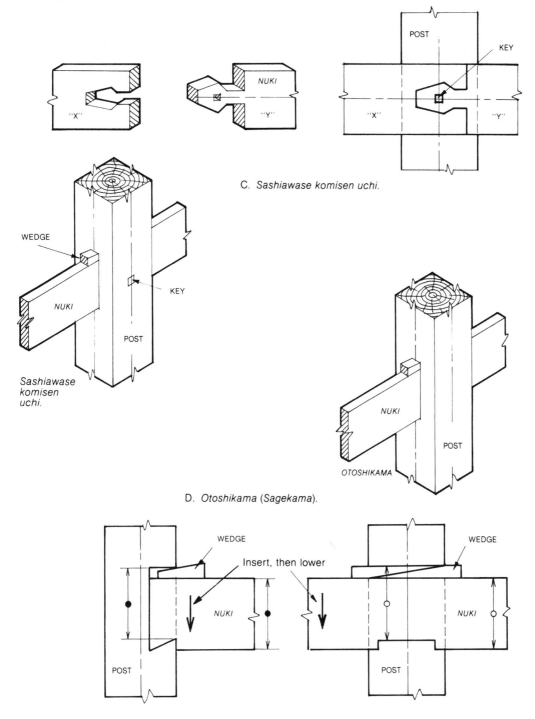

C. *Sashiawase komisen uchi.*

WEDGE

KEY

NUKI

POST

Sashiawase komisen uchi.

OTOSHIKAMA

D. *Otoshikama (Sagekama).*

WEDGE

Insert, then lower

WEDGE

NUKI

NUKI

POST

POST

Method of installing diagonal bracing.

Resistance factor of diagonal bracing according to angle at which it is framed.

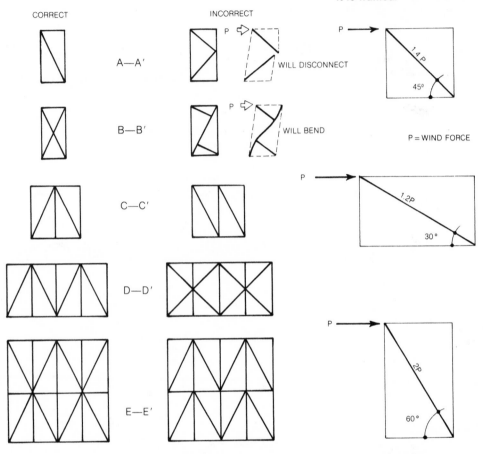

CORRECT   INCORRECT

A—A'   WILL DISCONNECT

B—B'   WILL BEND

C—C'

D—D'

E—E'

1.4P   45°

P = WIND FORCE

1.2P   30°

2P   60°

P = Wind force, earthquake force & other horizontal forces.

Tension diagonal bracing & compression diagonal bracing.

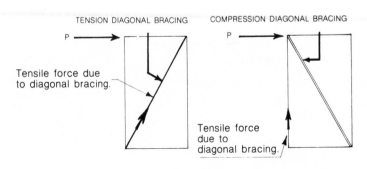

TENSION DIAGONAL BRACING   COMPRESSION DIAGONAL BRACING

Tensile force due to diagonal bracing.

Tensile force due to diagonal bracing.

1. Various pieces for *nuki* or small metal rods are used for tension diagonal bracing.
2. Compression diagonal bracing is commonly made of wood whose width is either equal to, half of, or a third of the column's width. However, to prevent buckling of the brace when resisting compressive force, pieces which are ½ or less of the column's width should not be used since they will be too weak.

Nailing method on tension diagonal bracing.

For the main thin diagonal bracing, use a minimum nail size of 60mm with a length 2.5 to 3.0 times the thickness of the brace. Use at least 4 nails at each joint.

QUANTITY OF NAILS	CORRECT	INCORRECT
2 NAILS	DIAGONAL BRACING 10cm x 1.5cm · POST 10cm x 10cm · 45°	
3 NAILS		
4 NAILS		
5 NAILS	BEST METHOD	

Installation method of tension diagonal bracing.

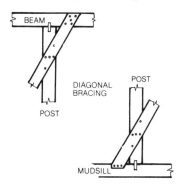

BEAM

DIAGONAL BRACING   POST

POST

MUDSILL

Spacing of nails

Spacing of nails acting parallel to forces	For the end of the board on which the force acts, use 10d nails; spacing of the nails is 10d. For the end of the board which is not affected by the force, use 5d nails.	5D / 10D / 10D D = SIZE OF NAIL
Spacing of nails acting perpendicular to force.	For the end, use 5d nails. Spacing of the nails is 5d.	5 D
At the shear plate	The spacing is 15d.	15 D

Right angle joint for diagonal bracing.

Provide cut-out on stud to
receive diagonal bracing.

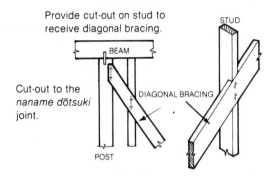

Cut-out to the
naname dōtsuki
joint.

Connection between *hira* diagonal bracing and stud.

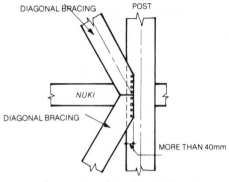

Connection of the diagonal bracing
with the same size as *ōnuki.*

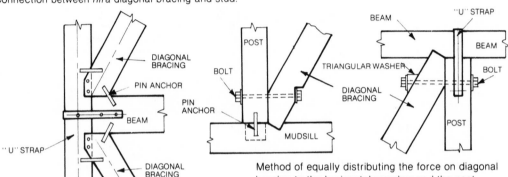

Reinforcement method with
diagonal bracing. Connection
using diagonal bracing which is
half as thick as the post.

Method of equally distributing the force on diagonal
bracing to the horizontal member and the post.

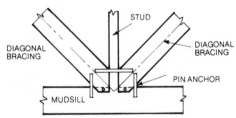

Joint for diagonal bracing which is half
as thick as the post.

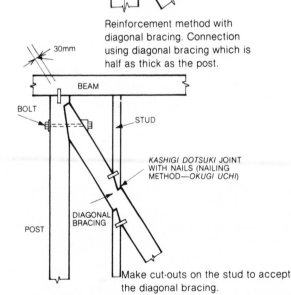

Make cut-outs on the stud to accept
the diagonal bracing.

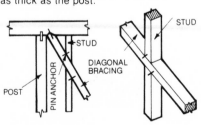

Right angle joint of *shin-mono* diagonal
bracing and stud.

When connecting a diagonal brace to a post's top end, use reinforcing ties such as a pin anchor, metal
tie strap, strap bolt, etc., at the connection between post and beam.

Hōzue—**Examples of right angle joint bracing.**

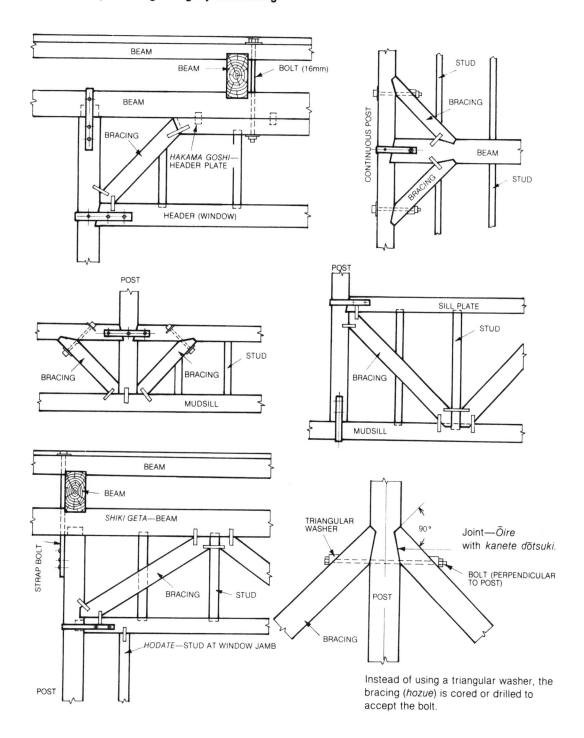

BEAM

BEAM — BOLT (16mm)

BEAM

BRACING

HAKAMA GOSHI—HEADER PLATE

HEADER (WINDOW)

STUD

BRACING

CONTINUOUS POST

BEAM

BRACING

STUD

POST

BRACING

BRACING

STUD

MUDSILL

POST

SILL PLATE

STUD

BRACING

MUDSILL

BEAM

BEAM

SHIKI GETA—BEAM

STRAP BOLT

BRACING

STUD

HODATE—STUD AT WINDOW JAMB

POST

TRIANGULAR WASHER

90°

POST

BRACING

Joint—*Ōire* with *kanete dōtsuki*.

BOLT (PERPENDICULAR TO POST)

Instead of using a triangular washer, the bracing (*hozue*) is cored or drilled to accept the bolt.

Right angle joint of *sashi kamoi.*

Shiguchi—**Common right angle joint.**

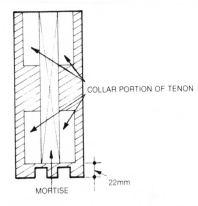

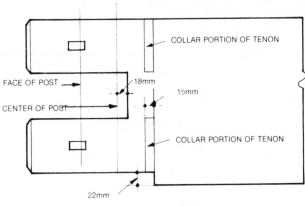

COLLAR PORTION OF TENON

FACE OF POST

CENTER OF POST

18mm

15mm

COLLAR PORTION OF TENON

22mm

COLLAR PORTION OF TENON

MORTISE

22mm

In the *Kansai district* (*Osaka* area), the gap depth is 18mm. The bottom of the tenon is located 22mm from the bottom of the beam in order to cover any rough work in the joint. (Nowadays, the gap depth is usually 15mm.)

SASHI KAMOI

Various collar tenons.

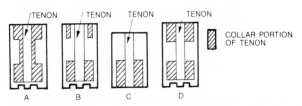

TENON TENON TENON TENON

COLLAR PORTION OF TENON

A B C D

1. Figures A and B show joint cut-outs of the female piece used to accept the tenon from opposite ends. Figure C is used for *dōsashi.*

2. When making the *eriwa* joint, consider the force acting on the post and its resultant torque when improvising to prevent weakening of the post.

ROUNDED

POST

COLLAR PORTION OF TENON

Collared tenon and mortise joint to a post with a rounded edge.

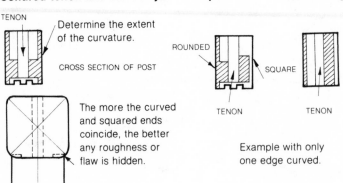

TENON

Determine the extent of the curvature.

CROSS SECTION OF POST

ROUNDED

SQUARE

TENON

TENON

The more the curved and squared ends coincide, the better any roughness or flaw is hidden.

Example with only one edge curved.

Example with two curved edges.

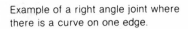

FACE OF POST

TOP FACE

Example of a right angle joint where there is a curve on one edge.

Right angle joint of eave beams. (Case 1)

Note: All the Japanese nomenclature indicates the different types of beams.

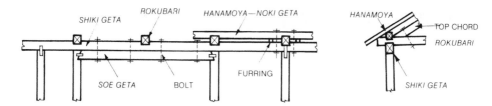

Noki geta—Eave beams.

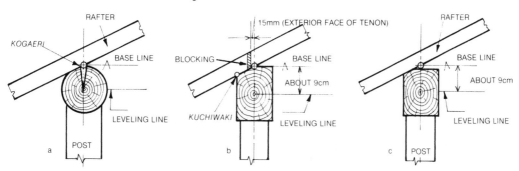

The baseline of a beam (*noki geta* or *hanamoya*) is the point of connection for the bottom face of a rafter and center of the post.

Since the baseline at times is offset slightly towards the exterior face of a beam as shown on illustration (c), a supplementary leveling line is drawn about 9mm below the pivot.

Kuchiwaki is the point of conection between the exterior face of a beam and the bottom face of a rafter.

Kogaeri are the beam cut-outs that accept the rafters. They are cut out in such a way that the bottom surface is at an angle parallel to the rafter slope.

Shiki geta—Rim beams.

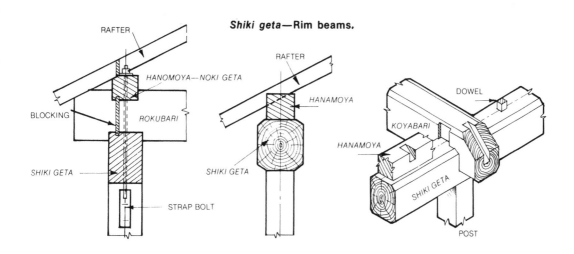

Right angle joint of eave beams. (Case 2)

A case where the top of a beam and the pivot of the beam are at the same point.

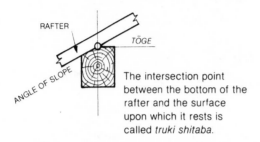

The intersection point between the bottom of the rafter and the surface upon which it rests is called *truki shitaba*.

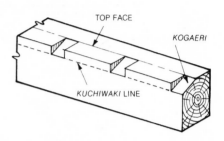

A case where the beam's top face is at a lower position than the beam *tōge*.

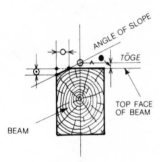

A simple method of determining the *kuchiwaki* line.

1. Draw a line at approximate location of the pivot at the top face of the beam.

2. Draw the width of the top face of the beam above beam's front face. (Actual difference between the beam's top face and the pivot.)

3. Connect the points of the intersecting lines to determine the angle of slope line.

4. The *kuchiwaki* line is located by transferring the distance of "a"—"b" on the top face to the side face. The distance shown as line "a"—"b'". (The distance between "c" and "a" is the width of *kogaeri*.)

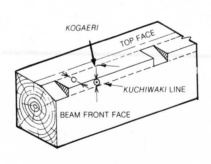

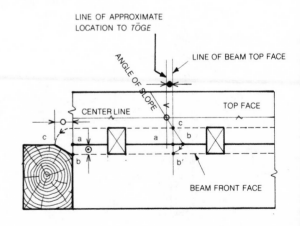

Right angle joint of eave beams. (Case 2 continued)

Method of drawing the *kuchiwaki* line.

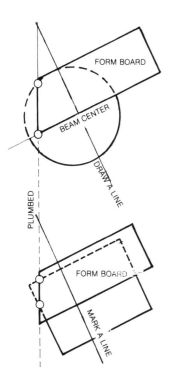

1. The *kogaeri* line for *kuchiwaki* has to be drawn plumbed. Special care must be taken when drawing on logs or on wood with rounded edges.

2. It is important to be able to draw the line in a slope without having to use a template.

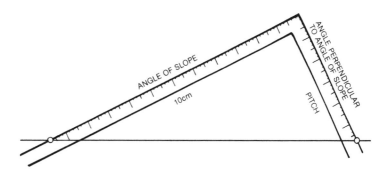

Special right angle joint of eave beams.

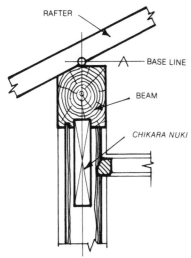

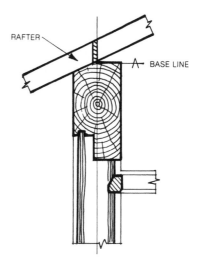

The above illustration shows an example of a beam with insufficient depth. The beam is reinforced with *chikara nuki* at its bottom.

The above illustration shows an example where, due to the heavy load, only a certain portion of the beam is enlarged. To align this large beam with other small beams, the exterior portion of the beam only is cut to the depth to match the others.

Right angle joint of eave beam. (Case 3)

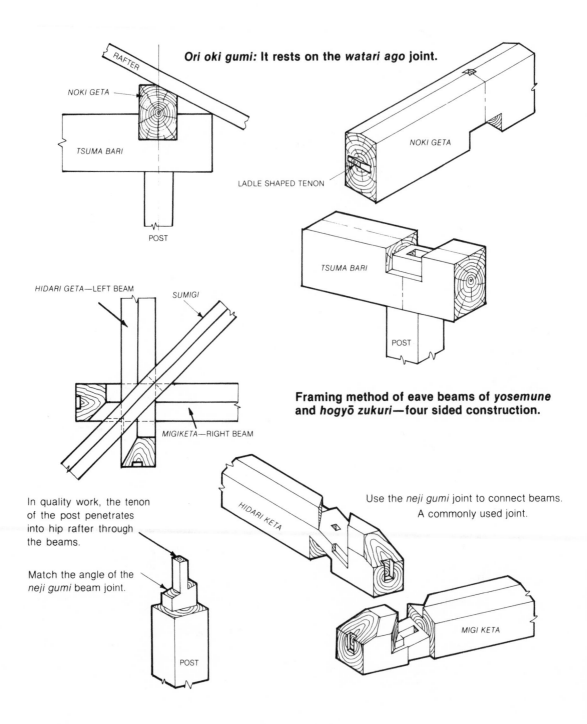

Ori oki gumi: It rests on the *watari ago* joint.

RAFTER

NOKI GETA

TSUMA BARI

POST

NOKI GETA

LADLE SHAPED TENON

TSUMA BARI

POST

HIDARI GETA—LEFT BEAM

SUMIGI

MIGIKETA—RIGHT BEAM

Framing method of eave beams of *yosemune* and *hogyō zukuri*—four sided construction.

In quality work, the tenon of the post penetrates into hip rafter through the beams.

Match the angle of the *neji gumi* beam joint.

POST

Use the *neji gumi* joint to connect beams. A commonly used joint.

HIDARI KETA

MIGI KETA

Noki beam and *tsuma* beam. (Case1)

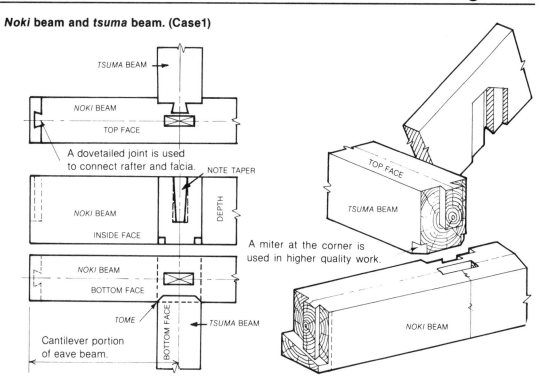

TSUMA BEAM

NOKI BEAM

TOP FACE

A dovetailed joint is used to connect rafter and facia.

NOTE TAPER

NOKI BEAM

INSIDE FACE

DEPTH

NOKI BEAM

BOTTOM FACE

TOME

BOTTOM FACE

TSUMA BEAM

Cantilever portion of eave beam.

TOP FACE

TSUMA BEAM

A miter at the corner is used in higher quality work.

NOKI BEAM

Noki beam and *tsuma* beam. (Case 2)

In many cases, in order to install blocking, the lap portion of the *tsuma* beam is cut off at the point where the inside face of the blocking is to align.

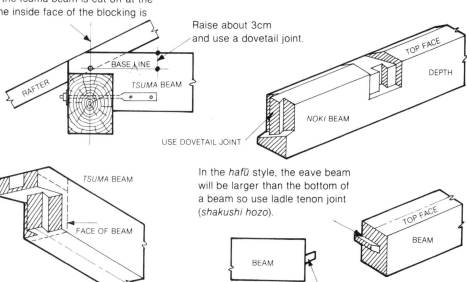

Raise about 3cm and use a dovetail joint.

BASE LINE

RAFTER

TSUMA BEAM

TOP FACE

DEPTH

NOKI BEAM

USE DOVETAIL JOINT

TSUMA BEAM

FACE OF BEAM

In the *hafū* style, the eave beam will be larger than the bottom of a beam so use ladle tenon joint (*shakushi hozo*).

TOP FACE

BEAM

BEAM

SHAKUSHI HOZO

6

Flooring Construction

Flooring construction consists of first floor flooring and second floor flooring. Among the first floor floorings are *korobashi* planks and *tsubadate* planks. *Tansho* and *fukusho* planks are some among the second floor flooring.

The function of flooring is to support loads and transmit them to the structural framing members and the foundation. The loads on first floor flooring are generally supported by piers (*yuka zuka*). The beam and joist sizes which can support the required live and dead loads acting on the floor must be calculated. The sizing of beams and flooring is no longer dependent, as in the past, upon intuition developed with practice.

It is important to rest the beam (*ōbiki*) for the first floor onto the pier in such a way that the beam will not warp upwards at its ends. Were this to happen, there would be no way to correct the separation of beam from post.

When installing the floor joists, place flooring members across several joists to check their levelness. Of course the two end joists must be level, having been verified at the outset with a level.

First floor framing method. Case 1: right angle joint of the *ashikatame* beam.

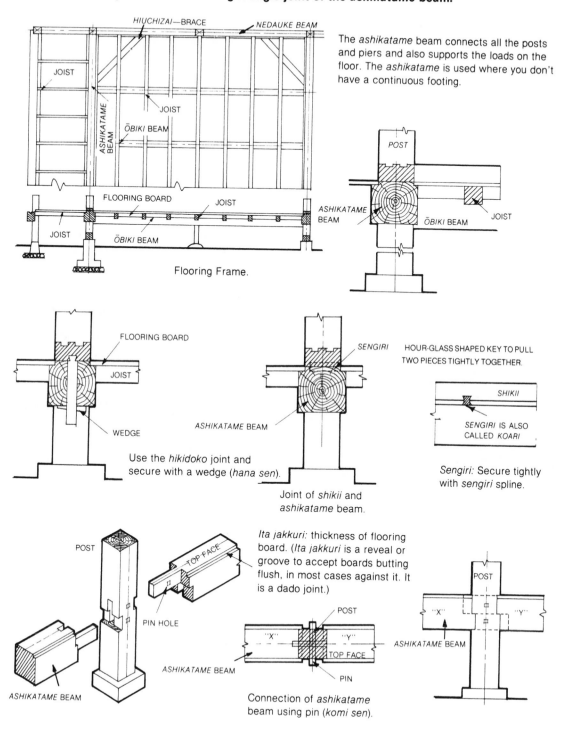

The *ashikatame* beam connects all the posts and piers and also supports the loads on the floor. The *ashikatame* is used where you don't have a continuous footing.

Flooring Frame.

Use the *hikidoko* joint and secure with a wedge (*hana sen*).

Joint of *shikii* and *ashikatame* beam.

HOUR-GLASS SHAPED KEY TO PULL TWO PIECES TIGHTLY TOGETHER.

SENGIRI IS ALSO CALLED *KOARI*

Sengiri: Secure tightly with *sengiri* spline.

Ita jakkuri: thickness of flooring board. (*Ita jakkuri* is a reveal or groove to accept boards butting flush, in most cases against it. It is a dado joint.)

Connection of *ashikatame* beam using pin (*komi sen*).

First floor framing method. Case 2: right angle joints for footing.

Installation of flooring board at the edge.

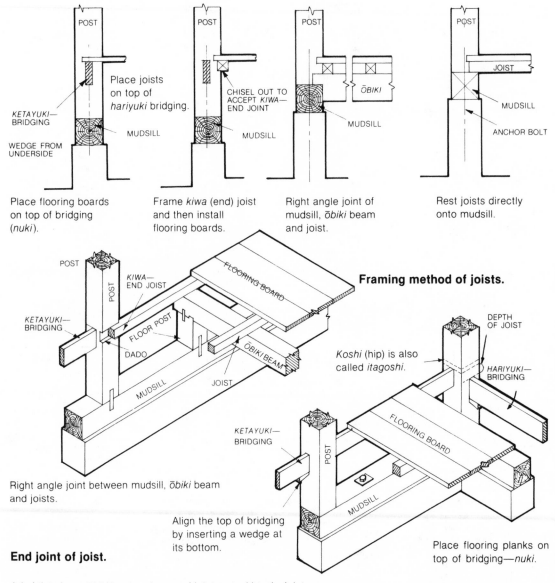

Place flooring boards on top of bridging (*nuki*).

Frame *kiwa* (end) joist and then install flooring boards.

Right angle joint of mudsill, *ōbiki* beam and joist.

Rest joists directly onto mudsill.

Framing method of joists.

Koshi (hip) is also called *itagoshi*.

Right angle joint between mudsill, *ōbiki* beam and joists.

Align the top of bridging by inserting a wedge at its bottom.

Place flooring planks on top of bridging—*nuki*.

End joint of joist.

Join joist above *ōbiki* beam using scarf joint or *tsuki tsuke* joint.

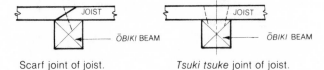

Scarf joint of joist.

Tsuki tsuke joint of joist.

First floor framing method. Case 3: four beams intersecting.

Four *ashikatame* beams intersecting joint.

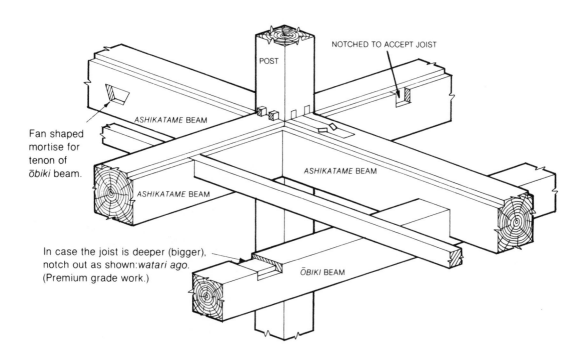

NOTCHED TO ACCEPT JOIST

POST

ASHIKATAME BEAM

Fan shaped
mortise for
tenon of
ōbiki beam.

ASHIKATAME BEAM

ASHIKATAME BEAM

ASHIKATAME BEAM

In case the joist is deeper (bigger),
notch out as shown:*watari ago*.
(Premium grade work.)

ŌBIKI BEAM

Right angle joint between *ashikatame* beam and *ōbiki* beam.

For the right angle joint, there is the *sashikomi* (inserting) type and *otoshi-komi* (dropping-in) type, however, in either case, the tenon for the *ōbiki* beam is fan shaped.

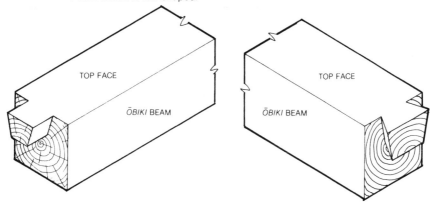

TOP FACE

ŌBIKI BEAM

TOP FACE

ŌBIKI BEAM

Otoshibomi type fan shaped tenon.   *Sashibomi* type fan shaped dovetail.

First floor framing method. (Case 3 continued)

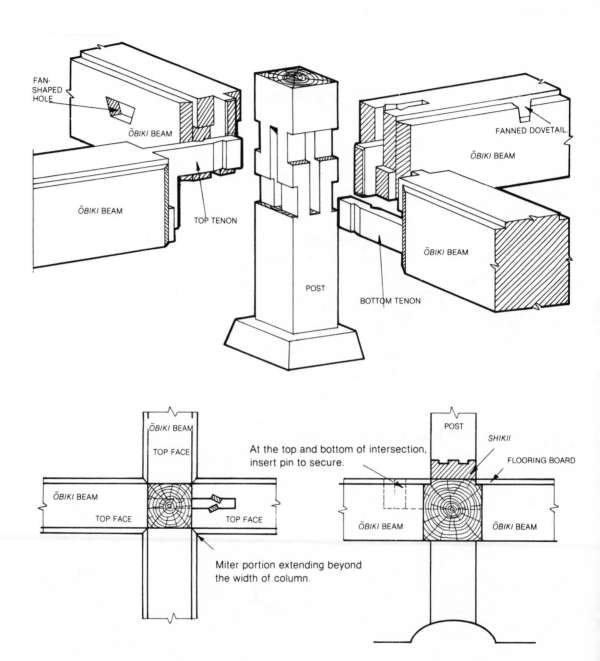

FAN-SHAPED HOLE

ŌBIKI BEAM

ŌBIKI BEAM

TOP TENON

FANNED DOVETAIL

ŌBIKI BEAM

ŌBIKI BEAM

POST

BOTTOM TENON

ŌBIKI BEAM

TOP FACE

ŌBIKI BEAM

TOP FACE

TOP FACE

Miter portion extending beyond the width of column.

At the top and bottom of intersection, insert pin to secure.

POST

SHIKII

FLOORING BOARD

ŌBIKI BEAM

ŌBIKI BEAM

First floor framing method. (Case 3 continued)

Yatoi hozo sashi—Four directional connection of *ashikatame* beam.

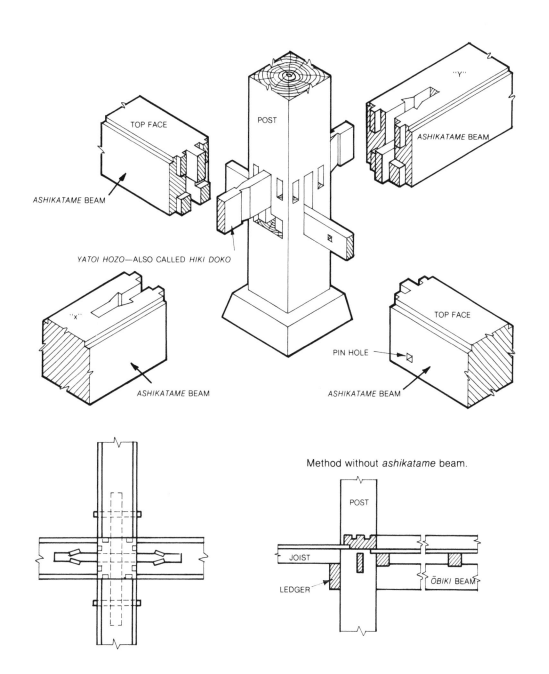

TOP FACE

POST

"Y"

ASHIKATAME BEAM

ASHIKATAME BEAM

YATOI HOZO—ALSO CALLED *HIKI DOKO*

"X"

ASHIKATAME BEAM

TOP FACE

PIN HOLE

ASHIKATAME BEAM

Method without *ashikatame* beam.

POST

JOIST

LEDGER

ŌBIKI BEAM

First floor framing method. (Case 4)

Hasami ashikatame beam.

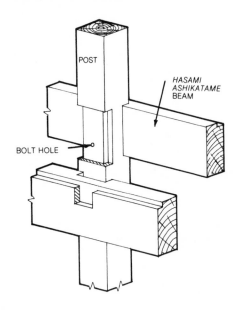

POST

HASAMI ASHIKATAME BEAM

BOLT HOLE

Michigiri tenon.

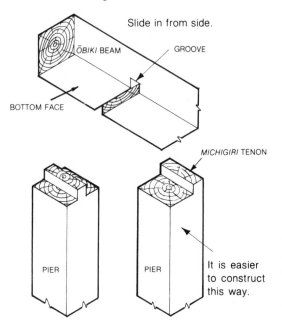

Slide in from side.

ŌBIKI BEAM

GROOVE

BOTTOM FACE

MICHIGIRI TENON

PIER

PIER

It is easier to construct this way.

Negarami bridging.

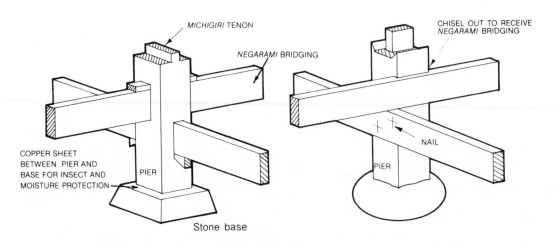

MICHIGIRI TENON

NEGARAMI BRIDGING

COPPER SHEET BETWEEN PIER AND BASE FOR INSECT AND MOISTURE PROTECTION

PIER

Stone base

CHISEL OUT TO RECEIVE NEGARAMI BRIDGING

NAIL

PIER

First floor framing method. (Case 5)

Piers for framing (*tsukadate* flooring).

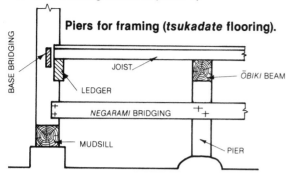

BASE BRIDGING

JOIST

LEDGER

ŌBIKI BEAM

NEGARAMI BRIDGING

MUDSILL

PIER

Framing method of ledger (*neda kake*).

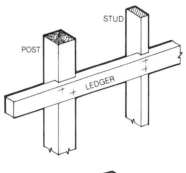

STUD

POST

LEDGER

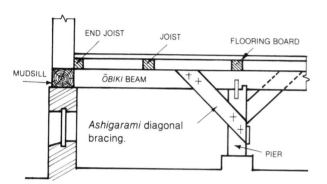

END JOIST

JOIST

FLOORING BOARD

MUDSILL

ŌBIKI BEAM

Ashigarami diagonal bracing.

PIER

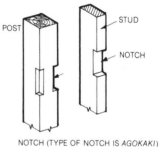

POST

STUD

NOTCH

NOTCH (TYPE OF NOTCH IS *AGOKAKI*)

Right angle joint for framing of *ōbiki* beam.

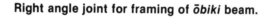

ŌBIKI BEAM

PIN

SOLE PLATE

MUDSILL

POST

DADO AND RABBET

ŌBIKI BEAM

PIER

PIN ANCHOR

MUDSILL

Example where the *ōbiki* beam and the post do not align.

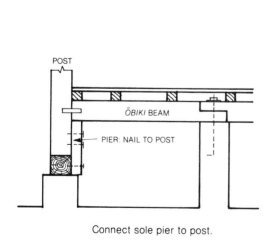

POST

ŌBIKI BEAM

PIER: NAIL TO POST

Connect sole pier to post.

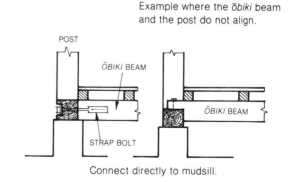

POST

ŌBIKI BEAM

STRAP BOLT

ŌBIKI BEAM

Connect directly to mudsill.

First floor framing method. (Case 5 continued))

Construction method of *yuka tsuka*—pier.

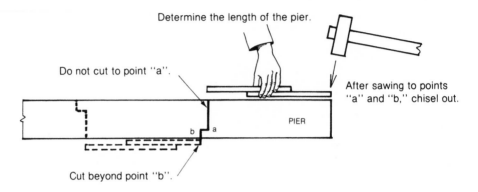

Determine the length of the pier.

Do not cut to point "a".

After sawing to points "a" and "b," chisel out.

PIER

Cut beyond point "b".

Using *ōbiki* as *taruki*.

Lay the wood in such a way that both ends will not warp up. Make sure that if any warpage occurs, it warps downward at the ends.

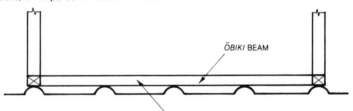

ŌBIKI BEAM

Place the wood with *sei* (back) facing down. (This will prevent upward warpage at the ends.)

Framing of *korobashi yuka*—planks.

Always treat lumber (Treat lumber against rot due to insects and weather.)

Korobashi yuka is commonly known as *ōbiki* beam. When the spacing between *ōbiki* beams is greater than 60cm, use planks thicker than 24mm.

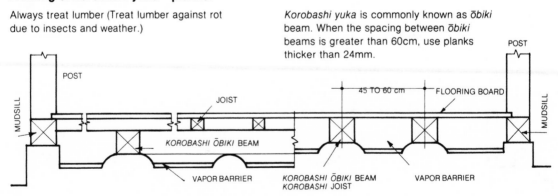

POST

MUDSILL

POST

JOIST

45 TO 60 cm   FLOORING BOARD

KOROBASHI ŌBIKI BEAM

MUDSILL

VAPOR BARRIER

KOROBASHI ŌBIKI BEAM
KOROBASHI JOIST

VAPOR BARRIER

Right angle joint between joists with _ōbiki_ beam, with beam, and with flooring planks.

Connection between pier and _ōbiki_ beam which has been extended with end joint.

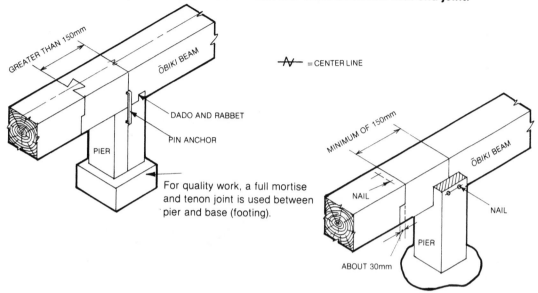

GREATER THAN 150mm

ŌBIKI BEAM

DADO AND RABBET

PIN ANCHOR

PIER

For quality work, a full mortise and tenon joint is used between pier and base (footing).

= CENTER LINE

MINIMUM OF 150mm

ŌBIKI BEAM

NAIL

NAIL

PIER

ABOUT 30mm

Right angle joint between joist and _ōbiki_ beam and between beams.

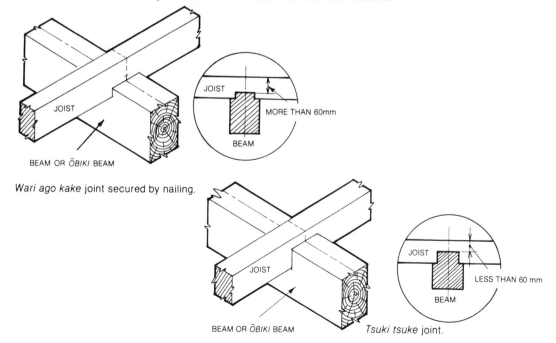

JOIST

BEAM OR ŌBIKI BEAM

JOIST

MORE THAN 60mm

BEAM

Wari ago kake joint secured by nailing.

JOIST

BEAM OR ŌBIKI BEAM

JOIST

LESS THAN 60 mm

BEAM

Tsuki tsuke joint.

Right angle joints between joists with *ōbiki* beam, with beam, and with flooring planks.

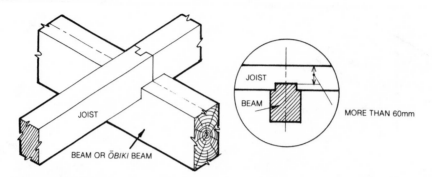

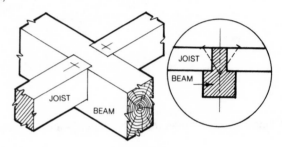

Mechigai tsugi joint. (This joint prevents twisting.)

Connection of joist and flooring planks.

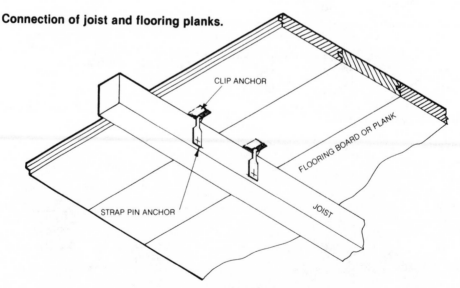

At the midpoint of boards width, secure by nailing strap anchor.

Installation method for flooring planks.

Tightening method when installing tongue and groove flooring planks.

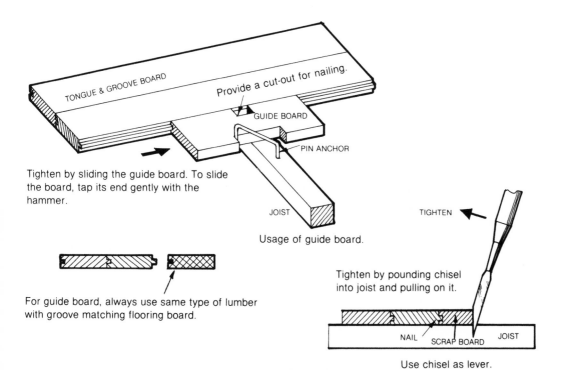

Provide a cut-out for nailing.

TONGUE & GROOVE BOARD

GUIDE BOARD

PIN ANCHOR

JOIST

Tighten by sliding the guide board. To slide the board, tap its end gently with the hammer.

Usage of guide board.

TIGHTEN

Tighten by pounding chisel into joist and pulling on it.

NAIL   SCRAP BOARD   JOIST

Use chisel as lever.

For guide board, always use same type of lumber with groove matching flooring board.

Nailing method.

When nailing, if nails are hammered forcefully, the tongue and groove may split, therefore hammer gently.

Always nail in such a way as to tighten the boards against each other.

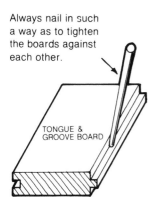

TONGUE & GROOVE BOARD

Right angle joint of the end plank.

1. For end plank installation, notch the post and reset the board to shape the mortise.
2. Once the mortise has been cut, realign the planks.
3. Insert fully into the notch on the post.

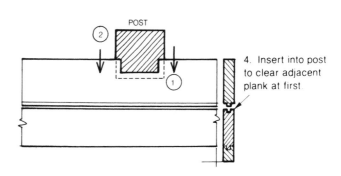

POST

2

1

4. Insert into post to clear adjacent plank at first

Installation of joists.

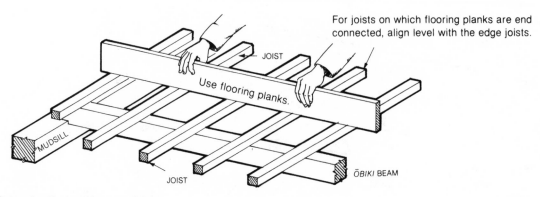

For joists on which flooring planks are end connected, align level with the edge joists.

Determine the level between joists by using floor planks as illustrated.

Allow 1.5 mm per tongue. Tighten planks simultaneously. Use maximum of five tongues at a time. As illustrated, nail the two end planks and with pressing board, push down on the planks and secure each plank with nails.

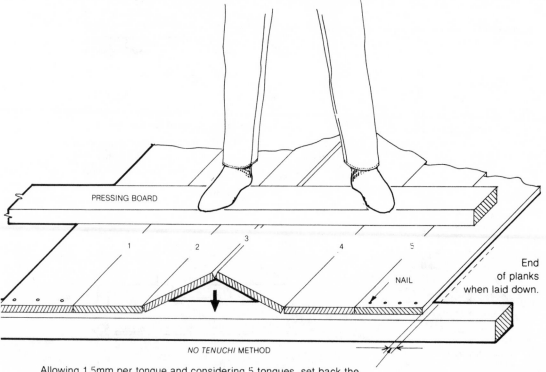

NO TENUCHI METHOD

Allowing 1.5mm per tongue and considering 5 tongues, set back the end plank 6mm and secure both end planks to the joists with nails.

Second floor framing. (Case 1)

Construction of floor.

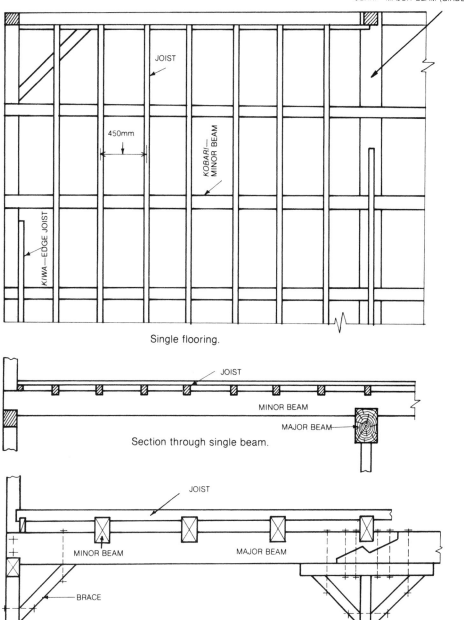

ŌBARI—MAJOR BEAM (GIRDER)

JOIST

450mm

KOBARI—MINOR BEAM

KIWA—EDGE JOIST

Single flooring.

JOIST

MINOR BEAM

MAJOR BEAM

Section through single beam.

JOIST

MINOR BEAM   MAJOR BEAM

BRACE

Section of multiple flooring.
(See illustration on page 116 for details.)

Second floor framing. (Case 1 continued)

Soe ita tsugi—Double shear end joint of *kobari* beam.

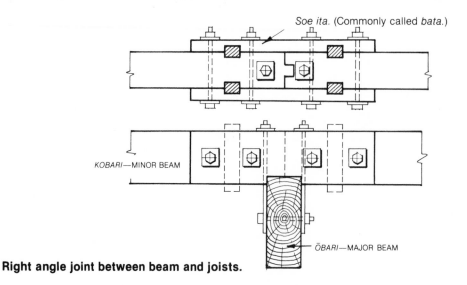

Soe ita. (Commonly called *bata.*)

KOBARI—MINOR BEAM

ŌBARI—MAJOR BEAM

Right angle joint between beam and joists.

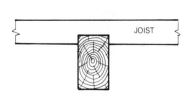

JOIST

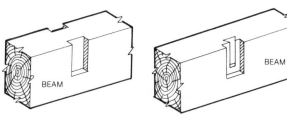

BEAM

BEAM

Ōire otoshibomi uwaba sasuri.

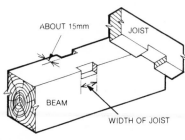

ABOUT 15mm

JOIST

BEAM

WIDTH OF JOIST

Fan shaped mortise.

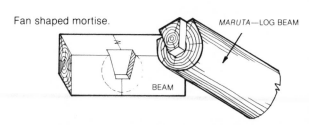

MARUTA—LOG BEAM

BEAM

Connect this to *ōgi ari* (fan shaped dovetail) to be effective.

Wide *ari kake* joint. (Enlarge the width as much as possible.)

WATARI AGO JOINT

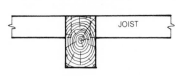

JOIST

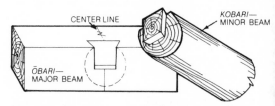

CENTER LINE

KOBARI—
MINOR BEAM

ŌBARI—
MAJOR BEAM

Where a log is used for the *kobari* beam, secure it by using a strap bolt.

Second floor framing. (Case 2)

Right angle joint of *nikai* beam with *dōsashi* beam & with *daiwa* beam

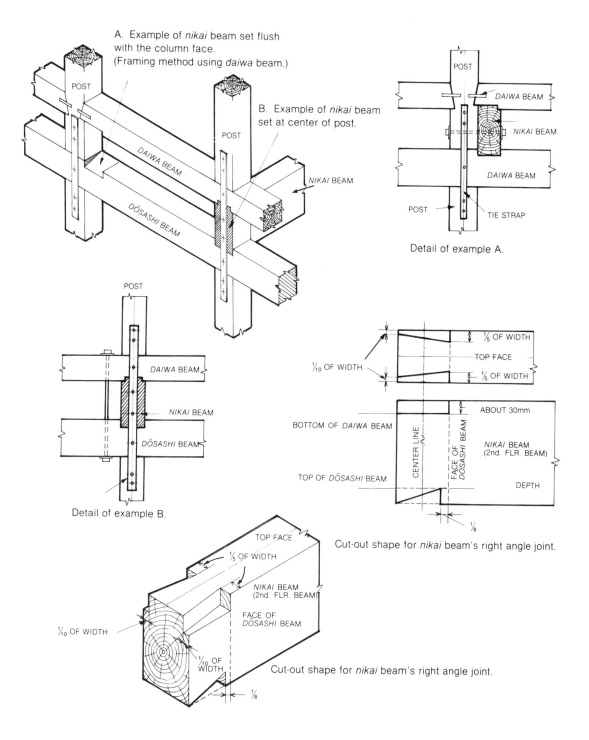

A. Example of *nikai* beam set flush with the column face. (Framing method using *daiwa* beam.)

POST

B. Example of *nikai* beam set at center of post.

POST

NIKAI BEAM

DAIWA BEAM

DŌSASHI BEAM

POST

DAIWA BEAM

NIKAI BEAM

DAIWA BEAM

POST — TIE STRAP

Detail of example A.

POST

DAIWA BEAM

NIKAI BEAM

DŌSASHI BEAM

Detail of example B.

⅕ OF WIDTH
TOP FACE
⅕ OF WIDTH
¹⁄₁₀ OF WIDTH

BOTTOM OF *DAIWA* BEAM

ABOUT 30mm

CENTER LINE

FACE OF DŌSASHI BEAM

NIKAI BEAM (2nd. FLR. BEAM)

DEPTH

TOP OF *DŌSASHI* BEAM

⅛

Cut-out shape for *nikai* beam's right angle joint.

TOP FACE

⅕ OF WIDTH

NIKAI BEAM (2nd. FLR. BEAM)

FACE OF DŌSASHI BEAM

¹⁄₁₀ OF WIDTH

¹⁄₁₀ OF WIDTH

⅛

Cut-out shape for *nikai* beam's right angle joint.

Second floor framing. (Case 3)

Right angle joint for beam and *daiwa* beam. (Using lateral ties.)

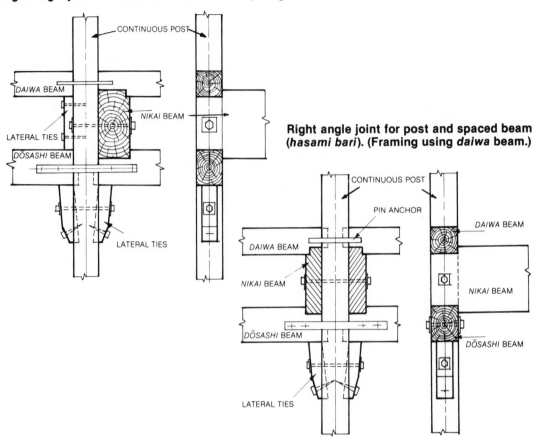

Right angle joint for post and spaced beam (*hasami bari*). (Framing using *daiwa* beam.)

Kashigi ōire tan hozo sashi **joint.**

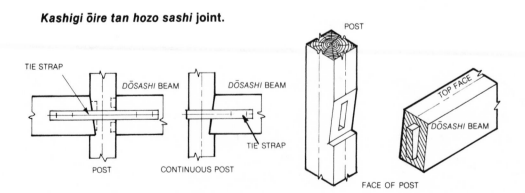

Second floor framing. (Case 3 continued)

Reinforcement with special clamps. (Examples of *oribeshiki* style)

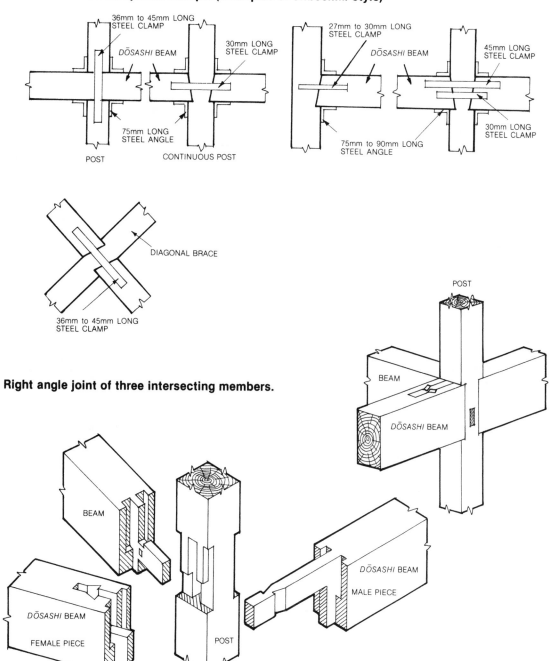

36mm to 45mm LONG STEEL CLAMP

DŌSASHI BEAM

30mm LONG STEEL CLAMP

75mm LONG STEEL ANGLE

POST

CONTINUOUS POST

27mm to 30mm LONG STEEL CLAMP

DŌSASHI BEAM

45mm LONG STEEL CLAMP

30mm LONG STEEL CLAMP

75mm to 90mm LONG STEEL ANGLE

DIAGONAL BRACE

36mm to 45mm LONG STEEL CLAMP

Right angle joint of three intersecting members.

POST

BEAM

DŌSASHI BEAM

BEAM

DŌSASHI BEAM

MALE PIECE

DŌSASHI BEAM

FEMALE PIECE

POST

Second floor framing. (Case 4)

End joints and right angle joints of *ōbari* beam and *kobari* beam.

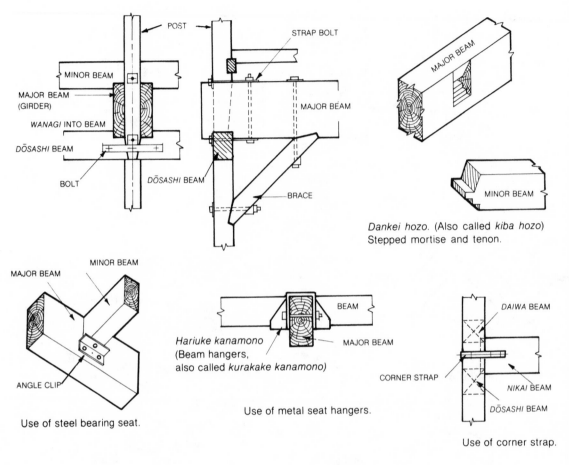

Dankei hozo. (Also called *kiba hozo*)
Stepped mortise and tenon.

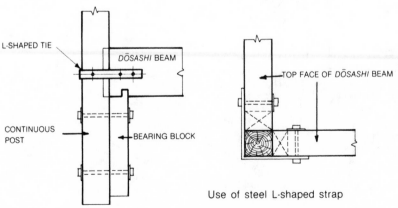

Use of steel bearing seat.

Hariuke kanamono
(Beam hangers,
also called *kurakake kanamono*)

Use of metal seat hangers.

Use of corner strap.

Use of steel L-shaped strap

Second floor framing. (Case 4 continued)

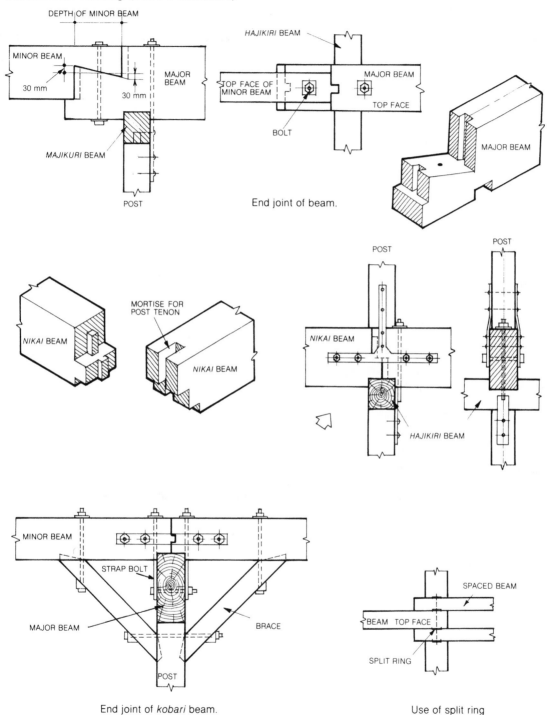

DEPTH OF MINOR BEAM

MINOR BEAM

30 mm

30 mm

MAJOR BEAM

MAJIKURI BEAM

POST

HAJIKIRI BEAM

TOP FACE OF MINOR BEAM

MAJOR BEAM

TOP FACE

BOLT

End joint of beam.

MAJOR BEAM

NIKAI BEAM

MORTISE FOR POST TENON

NIKAI BEAM

POST

POST

NIKAI BEAM

HAJIKIRI BEAM

MINOR BEAM

STRAP BOLT

MAJOR BEAM

BRACE

POST

End joint of kobari beam.

SPACED BEAM

BEAM TOP FACE

SPLIT RING

Use of split ring

Second floor framing. (Case 5)

Kashigi koshi tsuki tan hozo sashi joint.

Kiba hozo shashi joint—Stepped mortise and tenon.

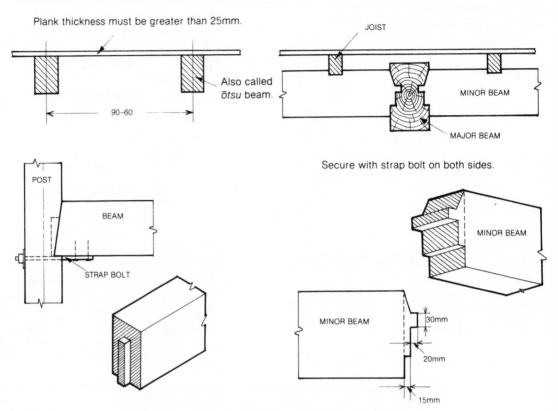

Plank thickness must be greater than 25mm.

Also called *ōtsu* beam.

90–60

JOIST

MINOR BEAM

MAJOR BEAM

Secure with strap bolt on both sides.

POST

BEAM

STRAP BOLT

MINOR BEAM

MINOR BEAM

30mm

20mm

15mm

Eriwa tsuki dōtsuki kimisen uchi joint—
Collared, haunched, and pinned through mortise and tenon.

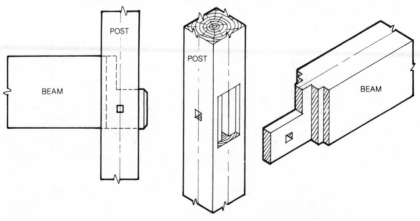

POST

BEAM

POST

BEAM

Second floor framing. (Case 5 continued)

Nikai bari sanpō sashi. (Three *nikai bari* beams intersecting joint.)

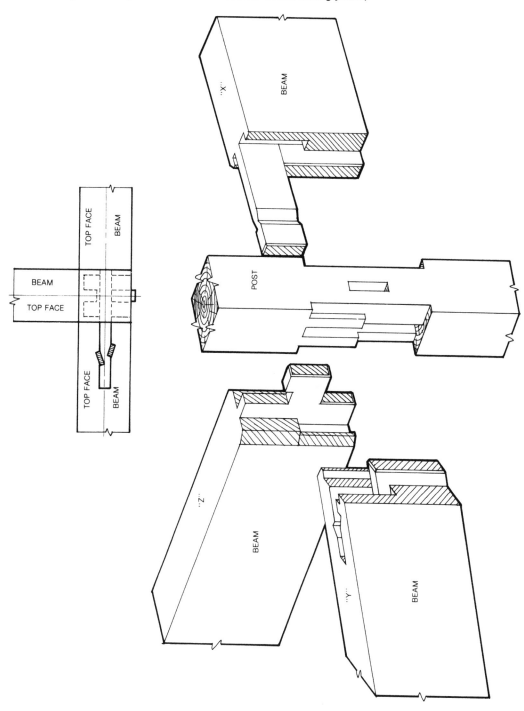

Second floor framing. (Case 6)

Right angle joint of *ōbari* beam and *kobari* beam.

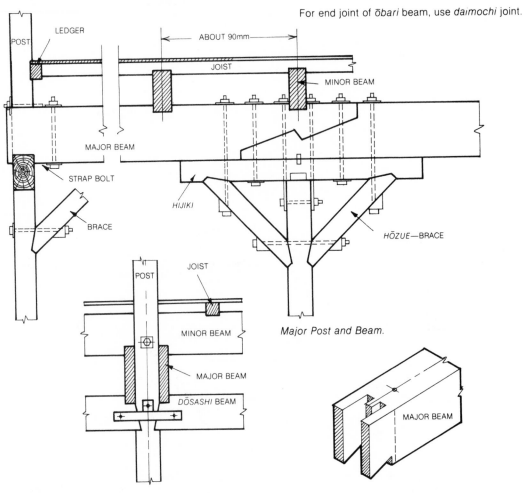

For end joint of *ōbari* beam, use *daimochi* joint.

LEDGER

POST

ABOUT 90mm

JOIST

MINOR BEAM

MAJOR BEAM

STRAP BOLT

HIJIKI

HŌZUE—BRACE

BRACE

POST

JOIST

MINOR BEAM

MAJOR BEAM

DŌSASHI BEAM

Major Post and Beam.

MAJOR BEAM

Example using beam hanger double, *Kurakake kanamono.*

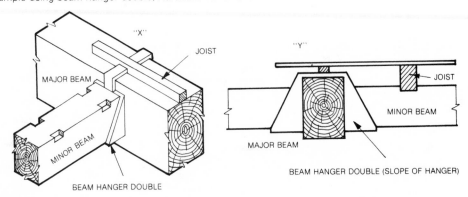

"X"

JOIST

MAJOR BEAM

MINOR BEAM

BEAM HANGER DOUBLE

"Y"

JOIST

MINOR BEAM

MAJOR BEAM

BEAM HANGER DOUBLE (SLOPE OF HANGER)

Second floor framing. (Case 6 continued)

Joint for *hiuchi bari* brace (horizontal brace).

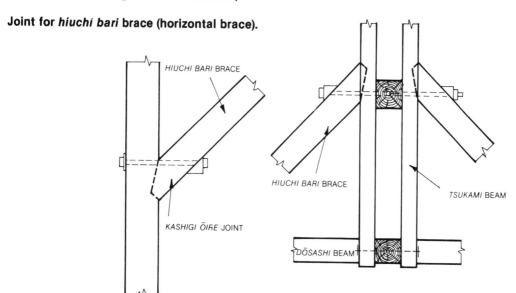

HIUCHI BARI BRACE

KASHIGI ŌIRE JOINT

TOP FACE OF *DŌSASHI* BEAM

HIUCHI BARI BRACE

TSUKAMI BEAM

DŌSASHI BEAM

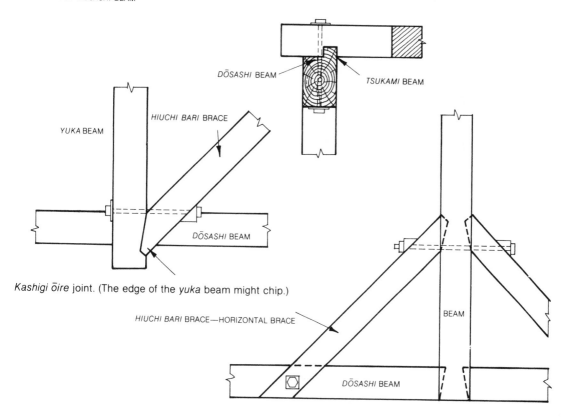

YUKA BEAM

HIUCHI BARI BRACE

DŌSASHI BEAM

TSUKAMI BEAM

DŌSASHI BEAM

Kashigi ōire joint. (The edge of the *yuka* beam might chip.)

HIUCHI BARI BRACE—HORIZONTAL BRACE

BEAM

DŌSASHI BEAM

Second floor framing. (Case 7).

Right angle joint of floor joist beam.

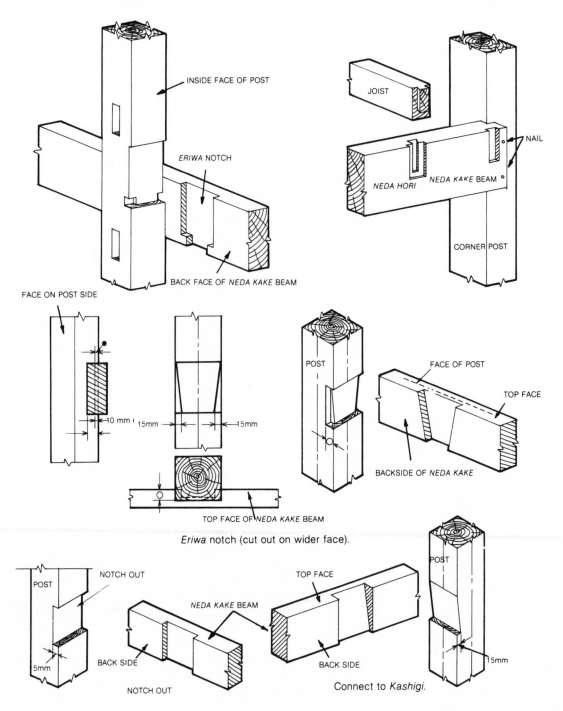

INSIDE FACE OF POST

ERIWA NOTCH

BACK FACE OF NEDA KAKE BEAM

JOIST

NEDA HORI   NEDA KAKE BEAM

NAIL

CORNER POST

FACE ON POST SIDE

10 mm   15mm   15mm

TOP FACE OF NEDA KAKE BEAM

POST

FACE OF POST

TOP FACE

BACKSIDE OF NEDA KAKE

Eriwa notch (cut out on wider face).

NOTCH OUT

POST

NEDA KAKE BEAM

TOP FACE

POST

5mm

BACK SIDE

NOTCH OUT

BACK SIDE

15mm

Connect to *Kashigi.*

7

Japanese Style Roof Framing

Japanese style roof framing is composed simply of placing the end post (*tsuka*) vertically on top of the beam, and connecting end posts at opposite ends horizontally with purlins and ridges (*mune*) on which rafters (*taruki*) are placed perpendicularly. Since the beams of Japanese style roof framing are simple beams which support all the concentrated loads from the end posts, they must be be strong enough to resist the bending moment.

The Japanese style of roof framing, due to its ease and simplicity of construction is used mainly on small buildings where beam spacing is short. Lumber becomes uneconomical and unstable as the spacing of beams becomes larger. In cases where the spacing of beams is large, western style framing is used.

Beams, whether they are made of logs, curved lumber or regular lumber, can easily be framed. However, it is important to set the lumber in such a way that when warpage occurs, the top face of the beam curves up or else the beam will have a negative bend.

Beams used in the *yojirō koya* framing method and *nobori* beams which are placed at a steep slope, are usually placed in such a way that when warpage occurs, the top surface will curve down, and beams will have a positive bend. This is done because of fear that the force will push out the *noki bari* beam rather than fear of it not being able to resist the loads.

Method of using a large carpenter's square to mark cutouts, etc. for a *nobori bari* beam.

This is a simple method where markings are directly drawn on the beams. The method of marking is as follows:

1. In order to mark for *nobori bari* beam, first determine the location of the *munashita bari* beam. (It is commonly called *ushi bari* beam.)
2. Place the large carpenter's square on top of the beam and consider the height difference between the baseline of the *noki geta* beam and the *munashita bari* beam. Then determine the angle or pitch of the *nobori bari* beam and position it.
3. Placing another large carpenter's square on the horizontal member of the large carpenter's square, mark center lines of each purlin (*moya* beam).
4. Mark the location of the baseline of the purlin. (In order to mark the line horizontally, use two large carpenter's squares.)

At the second end post (*tsuka*), determine the height along the center line. At the center point, using the *hikari ita* (guide board), determine the angle at the bottom of the end post (*tsuka*).

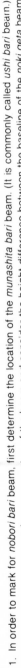

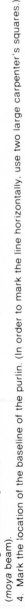

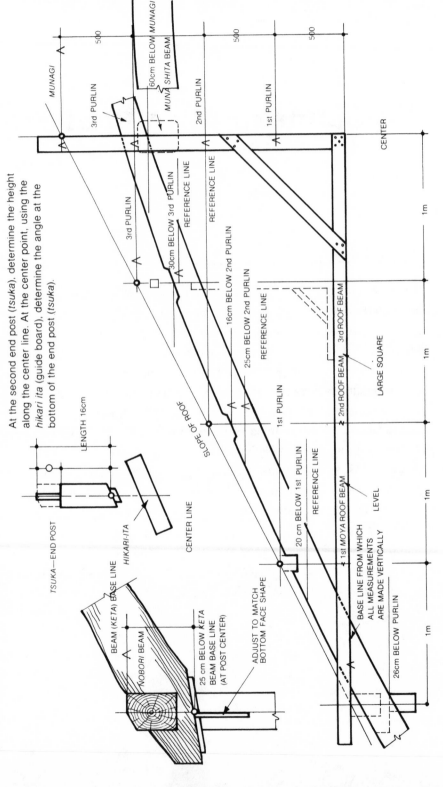

Right angle joint between eave blocking and joist.

In both 1 and 2, the blocking is secured by nailing from the building's interior, however there are many cases using the *tsuki tsuke kugi uchi* nailing method, where the blockings are flush mounted and nailed. In the case of a *soba noki* (*soba* eave), eave blocking is not used.

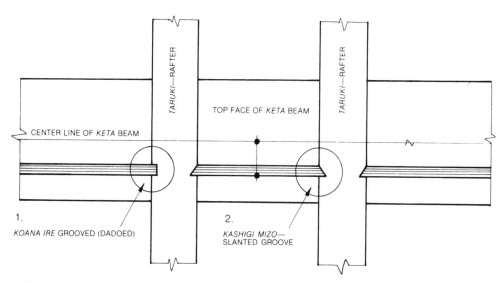

1.
KOANA IRE GROOVED (DADOED)

2.
KASHIGI MIZO—
SLANTED GROOVE

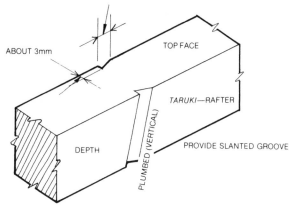

Adjusting the slanted groove for the various thicknesses of board is easier than for 1.

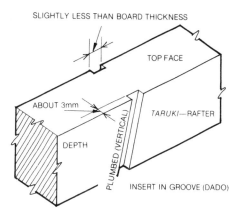

Adjusting the groove (dado) for the various board thicknesses is more difficult than for 2.

Installation of eave blocking.

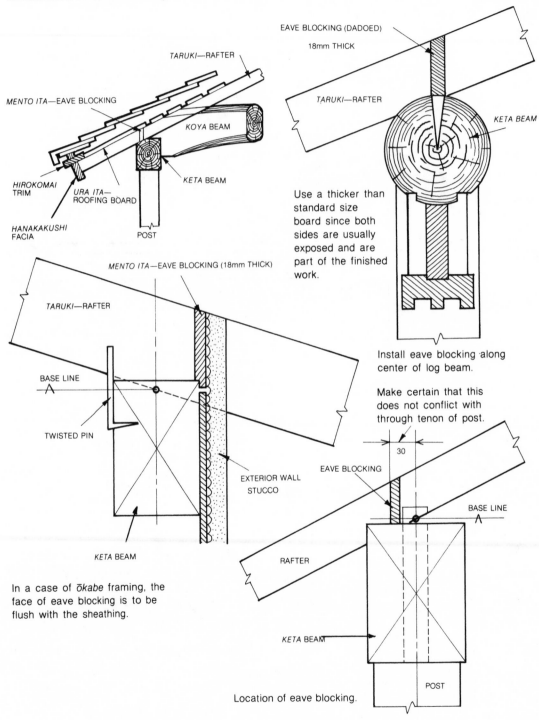

TARUKI—RAFTER

MENTO ITA—EAVE BLOCKING

KOYA BEAM

HIROKOMAI TRIM

URA ITA— ROOFING BOARD

KETA BEAM

HANAKAKUSHI FACIA

POST

EAVE BLOCKING (DADOED)

18mm THICK

TARUKI—RAFTER

KETA BEAM

Use a thicker than standard size board since both sides are usually exposed and are part of the finished work.

Install eave blocking along center of log beam.

Make certain that this does not conflict with through tenon of post.

MENTO ITA—EAVE BLOCKING (18mm THICK)

TARUKI—RAFTER

BASE LINE

TWISTED PIN

EXTERIOR WALL STUCCO

KETA BEAM

In a case of ōkabe framing, the face of eave blocking is to be flush with the sheathing.

30

EAVE BLOCKING

BASE LINE

RAFTER

KETA BEAM

POST

Location of eave blocking.

Kyoro gumi **framing method.**

Roof framing.

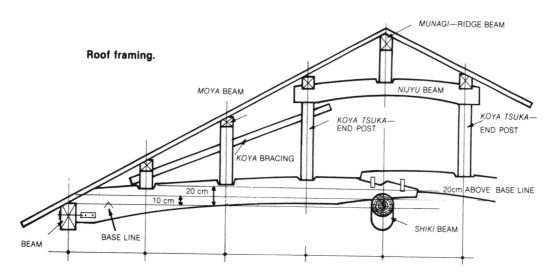

MUNAGI—RIDGE BEAM

MOYA BEAM

NIJYU BEAM

KOYA TSUKA—
END POST

KOYA TSUKA—
END POST

KOYA TSUKA—
END POST

KOYA BRACING

20 cm

10 cm

20cm ABOVE BASE LINE

SHIKI BEAM

BASE LINE

BEAM

Right angle joint of beam and *koya* beam. (Case 1)

The joint used for connecting two members is the *ari tsuki watari ago* joint.

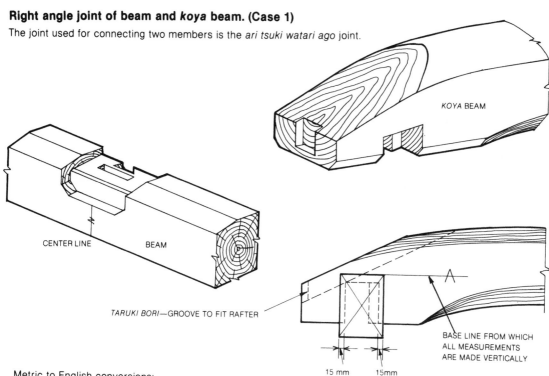

KOYA BEAM

CENTER LINE

BEAM

TARUKI BORI—GROOVE TO FIT RAFTER

A

BASE LINE FROM WHICH
ALL MEASUREMENTS
ARE MADE VERTICALLY

15 mm   15mm

Metric to English conversions:

1 mm = 0.04 inches; 10 mm = 0.4 inches; 100 mm = 4 inches; 1 metre = 39.3 inches.

To get approximate English dimensions, divide millimeters by 3 and multiply the answer by $\frac{1}{8}$.

For example $\frac{12 \, mm}{3} = 4 \times \frac{1}{8} = \frac{1}{2}$ ".

Kyoro gumi framing method (continued).

Right angle joint of beam and *koya bari* beam (Case 2).
In this case, the *kabuto ari* joint is used.

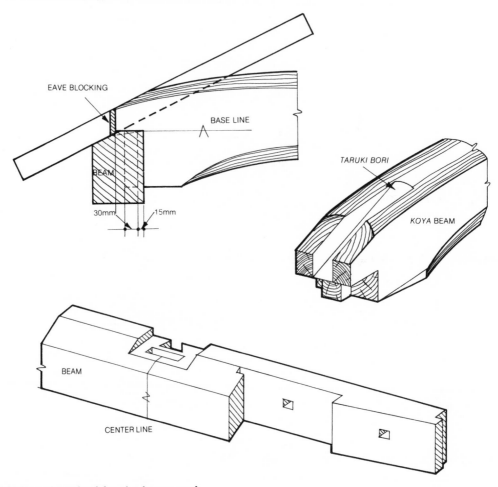

EAVE BLOCKING

BASE LINE

BEAM

30mm   15mm

TARUKI BORI

KOYA BEAM

BEAM

CENTER LINE

Guide board method for the beam end.

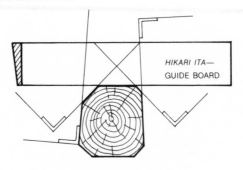

HIKARI ITA—
GUIDE BOARD

Ori oki kumi framing method.

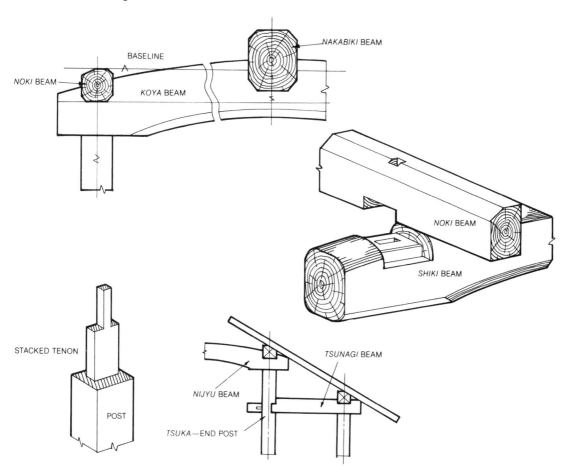

Right angle joint of koya beam and nakabiki beam.

For the method of copying the beam shape to provide for the notches, see pages 55–56.

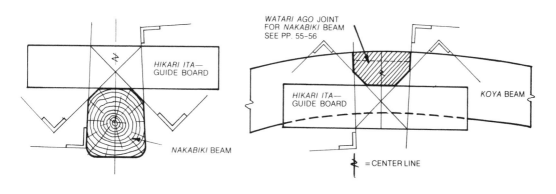

Ori oki kumi framing method.

Right angle joint of *tsunagi bari* beam and *tsuka* end post.

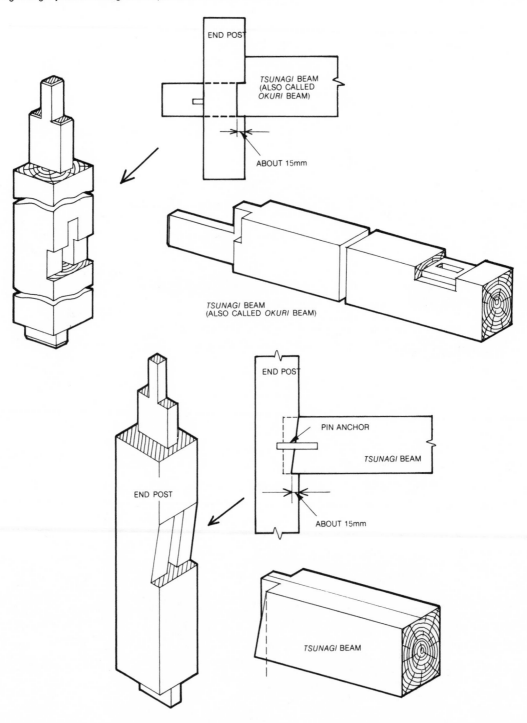

END POST

TSUNAGI BEAM
(ALSO CALLED
OKURI BEAM)

ABOUT 15mm

TSUNAGI BEAM
(ALSO CALLED *OKURI* BEAM)

END POST

PIN ANCHOR

TSUNAGI BEAM

ABOUT 15mm

END POST

END POST

TSUNAGI BEAM

Method of framing the ridge beam.

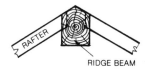

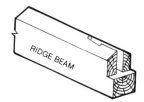

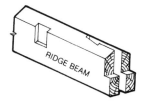

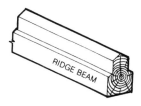

Ogami awase joint
(common use).

Taruki bori joint
(for exposed and finish work).

Mento kaki joint
(for exposed and finish work).

Framing method of *shiki* beam.

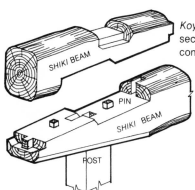

Koyadai uchi joint, reinforced and secured with bolts. *Koya* beam is connected using *watari ago* joint.

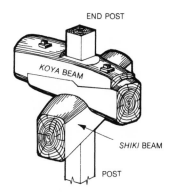

This type of end joint is *koyadaimochi tsugi* joint or *dan* joint. Both joints are reinforced and secured with bolts.

Framing method of *okuri* beam.

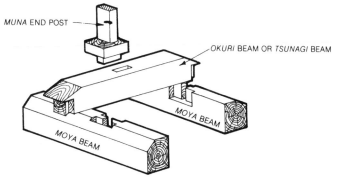

***Yojirō gumi* framing method.**

Roof framing.

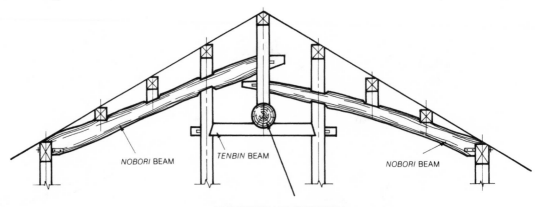

NOBORI BEAM

TENBIN BEAM

NOBORI BEAM

NAKABIKI BEAM OR *JIMUNE* BEAM

Right angle joint of *nobori bari* beam.

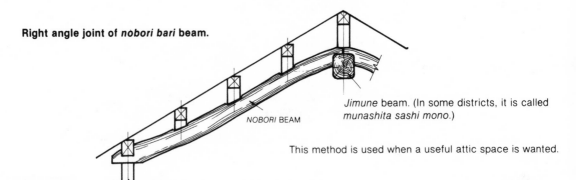

NOBORI BEAM

Jimune beam. (In some districts, it is called *munashita sashi mono*.)

This method is used when a useful attic space is wanted.

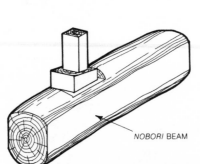

NOBORI BEAM

Base plate of the end post on *nobori bari* beam. The bottom face is slightly sloped so as not to weaken the *nobori bari* beam.

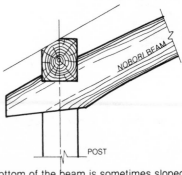

NOBORI BEAM

POST

The bottom of the beam is sometimes sloped in order not to weaken the end of the beam.

Yojirō gumi framing method (continued).

Right angle joint of *muna tsuka* (end post) and *nobori bari* beam is a method used by *Yojirō Gumi* (the *Yojirō* Sect).

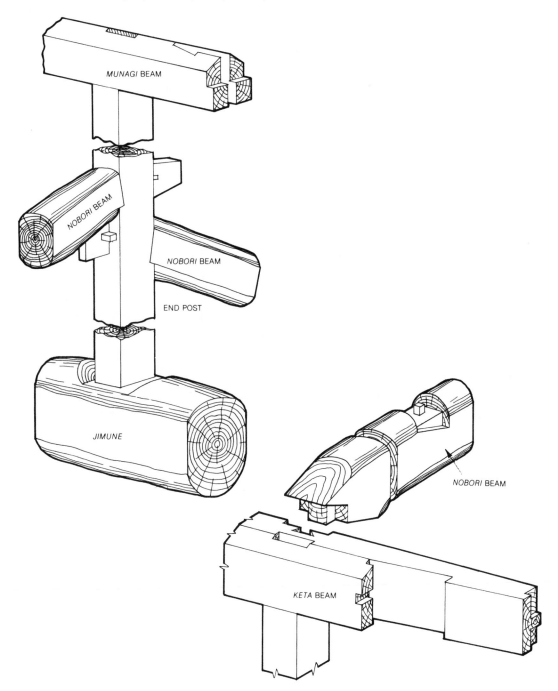

The right angle joint at the *nobori bari* beam should be a *kabuto ari* joint.

8

Finishing Eave Ends

In designing eaves, problems arising from rain, snow, strong wind, and freezing must be considered. As well as preventing damage caused by natural elements, eave design is further complicated by the aesthetic considerations that must be given to the relationship between roofing materials, which are numerous and the finishing of the eave's end—one of the main exterior design elements. Whether the gutter will be exposed or hidden also affects the design. Finally, problems of intensity and functional differences between western and Japanese styles must be considered.

Since the finishing of the eave ends is an important aspect of a structure's facade design, there are many design variations. Only one example is covered in this book.

Finishing of the eave's end.

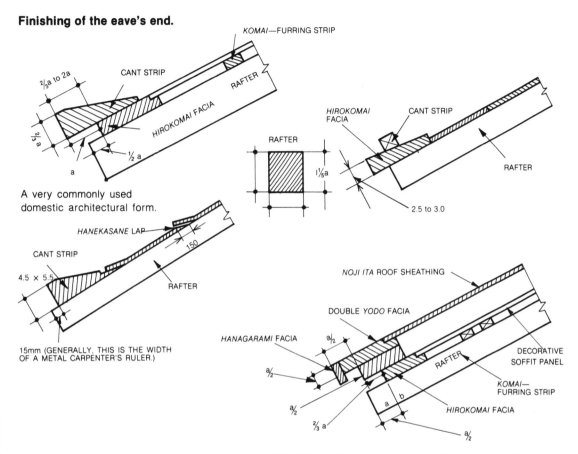

KOMAI—FURRING STRIP

CANT STRIP

RAFTER

HIROKOMAI FACIA

2/3a to 2a

2/3 a

1/2 a

a

A very commonly used
domestic architectural form.

HANEKASANE LAP

CANT STRIP

150

4.5 × 5.5

RAFTER

15mm (GENERALLY, THIS IS THE WIDTH
OF A METAL CARPENTER'S RULER.)

RAFTER

1⅕a

HIROKOMAI
FACIA

CANT STRIP

RAFTER

2.5 to 3.0

NOJI ITA ROOF SHEATHING

DOUBLE YODO FACIA

HANAGARAMI FACIA

a/2

a/2

a/2

2/3 a

RAFTER

a   b

a/2

DECORATIVE
SOFFIT PANEL

KOMAI—
FURRING STRIP

HIROKOMAI FACIA

The dimension of "a"—"b": If the yodo facia is single, the dimensions should
be equivalent to the thickness of the hirokomai facia. If the yodo facia
consists of double layers, the dimension should be approximately the width of
the bottom face of the rafters.

Roof tile guide of kawaraza.

When there is a hirokomai facia, the throat height of the roof tile guide should
be about 2cm. When eave blocking is to be installed above the rafters, the
depth of the throat should be about 5 cm.

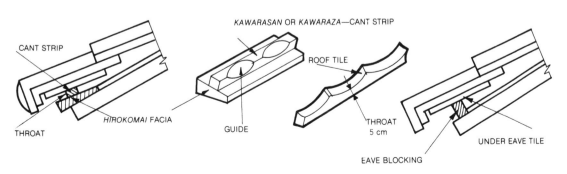

CANT STRIP

KAWARASAN OR KAWARAZA—CANT STRIP

ROOF TILE

THROAT

HIROKOMAI FACIA

GUIDE

THROAT
5 cm

UNDER EAVE TILE

EAVE BLOCKING

Framing of the eave end.

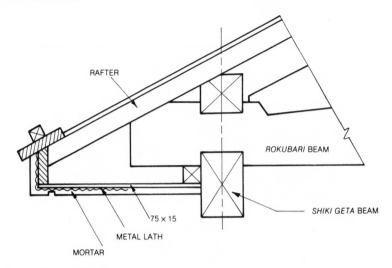

RAFTER

ROKUBARI BEAM

SHIKI GETA BEAM

75 × 15

METAL LATH

MORTAR

Plastered soffit.

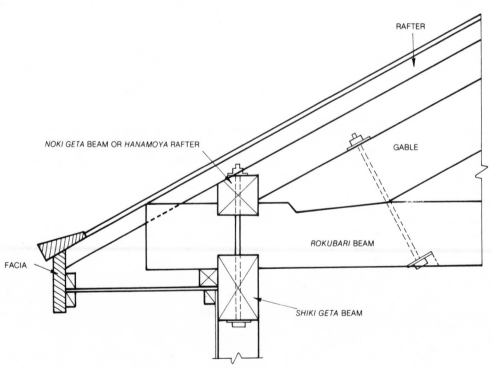

RAFTER

NOKI GETA BEAM OR *HANAMOYA* RAFTER

GABLE

ROKUBARI BEAM

FACIA

SHIKI GETA BEAM

Slate soffit or wood plank soffit.

Framing of the eave end (continued).

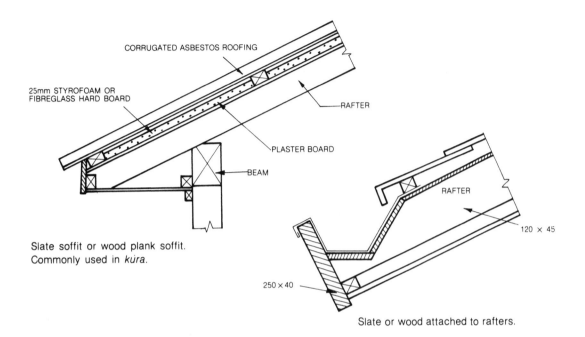

CORRUGATED ASBESTOS ROOFING

25mm STYROFOAM OR
FIBREGLASS HARD BOARD

RAFTER

PLASTER BOARD

BEAM

RAFTER

120 × 45

250 × 40

Slate soffit or wood plank soffit.
Commonly used in *kura*.

Slate or wood attached to rafters.

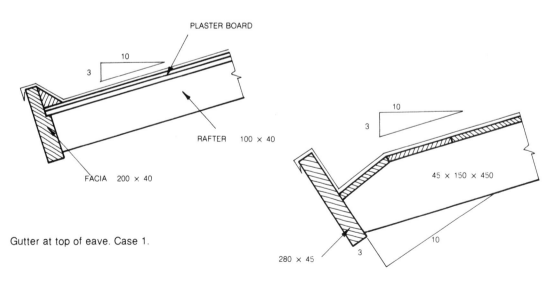

PLASTER BOARD

10

3

RAFTER   100 × 40

FACIA   200 × 40

Gutter at top of eave. Case 1.

10

3

45 × 150 × 450

10

280 × 45

3

Gutter at top of eave. Case 2.

End joint of *hirokomai* **and** *yodo* **facias.**

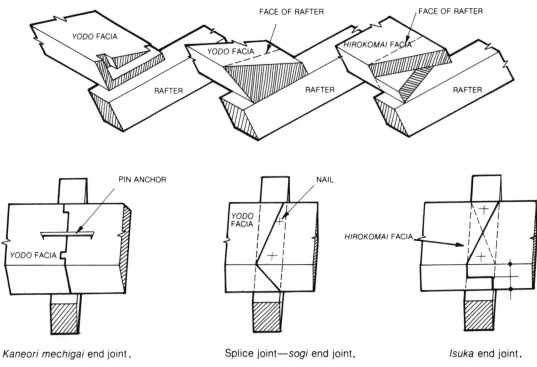

Kaneori mechigai end joint.

Splice joint—sogi end joint.

Isuka end joint.

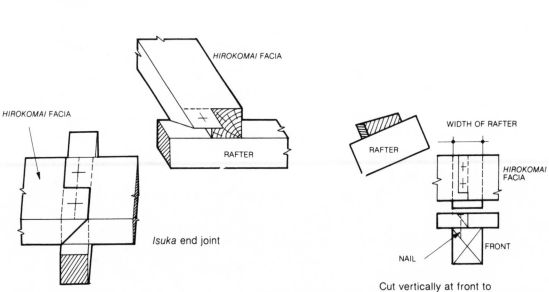

Isuka end joint

Cut vertically at front to
prevent exposure of angle cut.

Dividing or proportioning of a hip rafter.

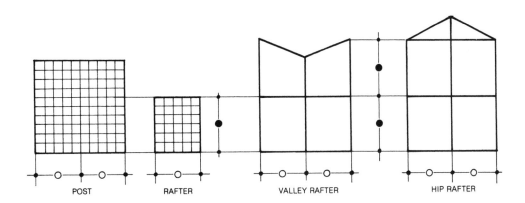

POST   RAFTER   VALLEY RAFTER   HIP RAFTER

Installation of facia.

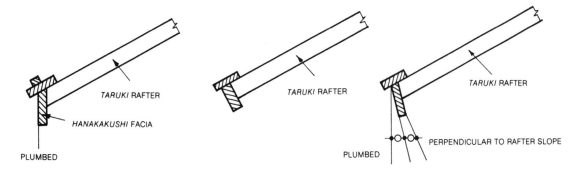

TARUKI RAFTER

HANAKAKUSHI FACIA

PLUMBED

TARUKI RAFTER

TARUKI RAFTER

PLUMBED

PERPENDICULAR TO RAFTER SLOPE

Metric to English conversions:
1 mm = 0.04 inches; 10 mm = 0.4 inches; 100 mm = 4 inches; 1 metre = 39.3 inches.
 To get approximate English dimensions, divide millimeters by 3 and multiply the answer by $\frac{1}{8}$.

For example $\frac{12 \, mm}{3} = 4 \times \frac{1}{8} = \frac{1}{2}''$.

9

Hip Rafter Assemblies

With the introduction of two angles, as in the *yosemune* (hip) roof and in the *irimoya* (hipped gable) roof, a corner or *sumi* is made. The type of roof may be ridge or hip, which divide the roof area for the water flow or the valley type which collects water. (The first type is called outside corner or *desumi* or simply *sumi;* the second type is called valley corner or *tanisumi* or *tani*.)

To construct the corner, a hip rafter is provided. Hip rafters are classed into two large groups, *shinzumi* and *fure sumi*. *Shinzumi* has *noki geta* beams intersecting perpendicularly to each other and both sides of the roof slope equally. A variation of *shinsumi, shakaku shinsumi,* has the *noki geta* beams intersect at an angle and the roof slope on both sides at an equal angle. Depending on the intersecting angle of the *noki geta* beams, *shaku shinsumi* is called *hishiya sumi* and *takakukei sumi*. *Fure sumi* has the *noki geta* beams intersecting perpendicularly, with roof slopes at a different angle on each side. When the roof slope angles are different and *noki geta* beams intersect at an angle, it is known as *shakaku fure sumi*.

Hip rafter slope and the Japanese square.

The back side of the Japanese square is used to lay out the hip rafter slope. The relationship between the back and the front of the square is demonstrated below.

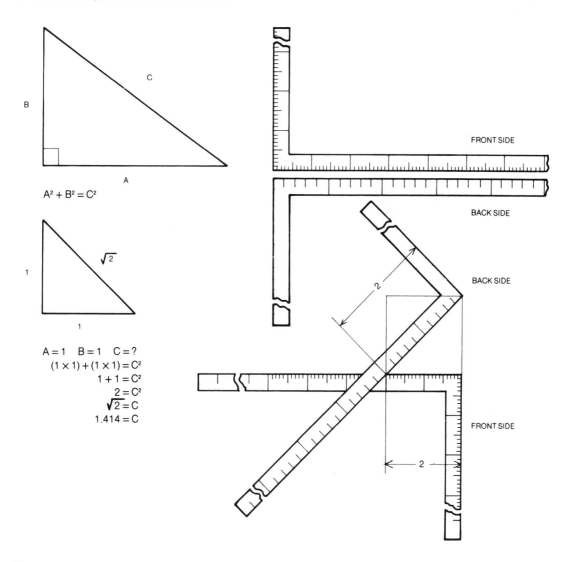

$A^2 + B^2 = C^2$

$A = 1$ $B = 1$ $C = ?$
$(1 \times 1) + (1 \times 1) = C^2$
$1 + 1 = C^2$
$2 = C^2$
$\sqrt{2} = C$
$1.414 = C$

Chogen

Chogen is used with laying out jack rafters and *hirokomai*. *Chogen* is one of the bisecting lines of a bisected triangle which represents the main roof slope.

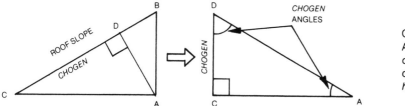

CD = *Chogen*
Angle CDA is the cut angle of the top of the jack rafters and *hirokomai*.

Roof Corner.

Since the eave corners of hip roofs and *irimoya* roofs have two directional flows, there is a ridge which divides the flow of water. This ridge is the *desumi* or outside corner. The valley where the water is collected is called *irisumi* or inside corner. See page 164 for further clarification between outside and inside corners.

Variations of roof corners.

1. *Shin sumi*—The *noki geta* beams intersect perpendicularly and the roofs on both sides slope at an equal angle.
2. *Shakaku shin sumi*—The *noki geta* beams intersect at an angle and the roofs on both sides slope at an equal angle.
3. *Fure sumi*—The *noki geta* beams intersect perpendicularly and the roofs on both sides do not slope at an equal angle.
4. *Shakaku fure sumi*—The *noki geta* beams intersect at an angle and the two slopes of the roof are not equal.
5. *Takakuke no sumi*—*Noki geta* beams are used to frame pentagonal or hexagonal shaped roofs. The slope the roofs on all sides are equal, and in the same direction as in *shakaku shin sumi*.

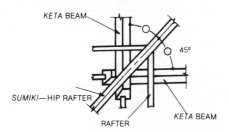

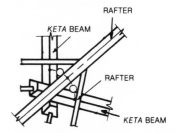

Shin sumi. The *keta* beams are perpendicular to each other. The hip rafter is placed at the corner dividing the *keta* beams equally and is at an angle of 45° to the face of the *keta* beams. The rafters are placed perpendicularly to the *keta* beams.

Shakaku shin sumi. The *keta* beams intersect each other at an angle. (The illustration shows an obtuse angle). The hip rafter is offset from the center line towards the roof with the steeper slope. The rafters are perpendicular to the *keta* beams.

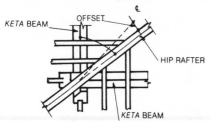

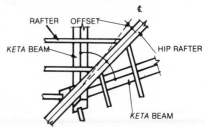

Fure sumi. The *keta* beams intersect each other perpendicularly. The hip rafter is offset from the center line towards the roof with the steeper slope. The rafters are perpendicular to the *keta* beams.

Shakaku fure sumi. The *keta* beams intersect at an angle to each other. (This is illustrated with an acute angle.) The hip rafter is off-set from the center line towards the roof with the steeper slope. The rafters are perpendicular to the *keta* beams.

For construction of the corners (especially the Japanese style) knowledge of *kikujitsu* (the use of the carpenter's square) is essential. The Japanese square is particularly designed for this use.
1. For *shin sumi*, the space between *sumichi* must be $\sqrt{2}$ or 1.414 of the space between the *heichi*. This is equivalent to 10 on the front scale and 10 on the back scale of the [Japanese] carpenter's square.
2. In *fure sumi*, the hip rafter is curved. In this case, the scale on the back of the carpenter's square cannot be used, unless a line describing the hip rafter slope is the reference point.
   Only the essential points will be covered in this book.

Proportioning of periphery members at eave corners.

The illustrations below depict the proportions used on shrine and temple architecture. In residential architecture, simplified proportions are used. Though proportioning is based on the size and spacing of rafters, this size and spacing is based on a method called *shaji shiwari hō*. Since this method is devised strictly for shrines and temples, it will be simplified here. The text illustrates the most common simplified version.

Ryaku ki wari—Ryaku proportioning

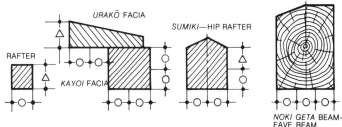

RAFTER · URAKŌ FACIA · SUMIKI—HIP RAFTER · KAYOI FACIA · NOKI GETA BEAM—EAVE BEAM

Plan of eave corner periphery.

The extension or depth of the eave is determined by the proportioning of the rafters. According to the determined rafter spacing (rafter width + rafter spacing) the depth of the eave is decided. (This is because the rafter spacing is measured from the face of the hip rafter. Extension of depth = (total number of spaces between rafters) + (½ hip rafter measured on back scale of carpenter's square) − (½ the width of rafter).)

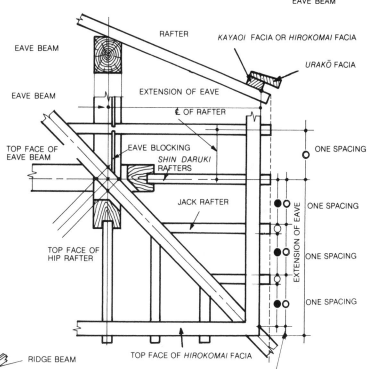

EAVE BEAM · EAVE BEAM · RAFTER · KAYAOI FACIA OR HIROKOMAI FACIA · URAKŌ FACIA · EXTENSION OF EAVE · ℄ OF RAFTER · TOP FACE OF EAVE BEAM · EAVE BLOCKING · SHIN DARUKI RAFTERS · JACK RAFTER · TOP FACE OF HIP RAFTER · ONE SPACING · EXTENSION OF EAVE · TOP FACE OF HIROKOMAI FACIA · BACK SIDE OF ½ OF THE HIP RAFTER WIDTH

Hip Roof

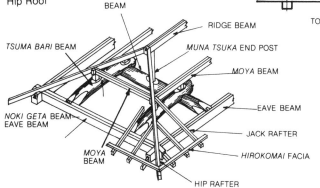

BEAM · RIDGE BEAM · TSUMA BARI BEAM · MUNA TSUKA END POST · MOYA BEAM · NOKI GETA BEAM—EAVE BEAM · EAVE BEAM · JACK RAFTER · MOYA BEAM · HIROKOMAI FACIA · HIP RAFTER

Determining the slope of the crown of the hip rafter.

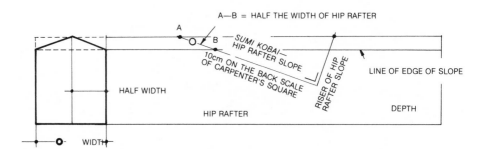

SLOPE = $^{4.5}/_{10}$

A—B = HALF THE WIDTH OF HIP RAFTER

A

B

SUMI KOBAI—
HIP RAFTER SLOPE

10cm ON THE BACK SCALE
OF CARPENTER'S SQUARE

RISER OF HIP
RAFTER SLOPE

LINE OF EDGE OF SLOPE

HALF WIDTH

HIP RAFTER

DEPTH

WIDTH

1. From point "A" on the corner of the top face, draw the slope of the hip rafter. (Hip rafter slope is equivalent to 10cm on the back side of the carpenter's scale × rafter slope.)
2. The distance along the hip rafter slope between points "A" and "B" is equal to ½ hip rafter width.
3. The lower point of the crown slope is located by extending a line parallel to the edge from point "B" to the end of the beam.

Cutting the end of the hip rafter.

There are two ways to determine the extent of projection of the hip rafter end. One is called *tsurami tōshi* (it is also called *tsurami koshi*) and another is *shinmi tōshi* (it is also known as *shinmi koshi*). Where the facia covers the rafter ends, *tsurami tōshi* is used.

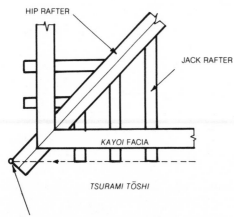

HIP RAFTER

JACK RAFTER

KAYOI FACIA

TSURAMI TŌSHI

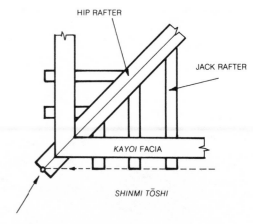

HIP RAFTER

JACK RAFTER

KAYOI FACIA

SHINMI TŌSHI

Extend the line of the rafter ends to the hip rafter face on the side opposite the rafters used as reference. Cut the tip of the hip rafter along this line. Used only with very long eave overhangs due to weathering.

Cut from an intersecting point of the hip rafter's center line and the extended line of the rafter ends.

Cutting the end of the hip rafter (continued).

Below are illustrated two methods to determine the cutline of the hip rafter end when a facia is not incorporated.
1. Cut at reverse slope of raft slope in relation to the horizontal line.
2. Cut at *nage sumi* line.

Hanamashi = $\frac{2}{10}$ (Translator's note: *hanamashi* is equal to $\frac{1}{10}$ of the depth of the notch made at the end of the hip rafter to receive the *kayaoi* facia. *Kayaoi* facia depth is equal to twice the depth of the above notch plus *hanamashi*.)

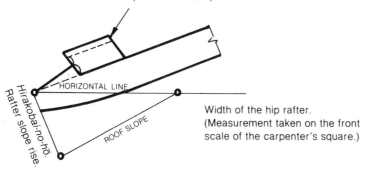

HORIZONTAL LINE

Hirakobai-no-hō.
Rafter slope rise.

ROOF SLOPE

Width of the hip rafter.
(Measurement taken on the front scale of the carpenter's square.)

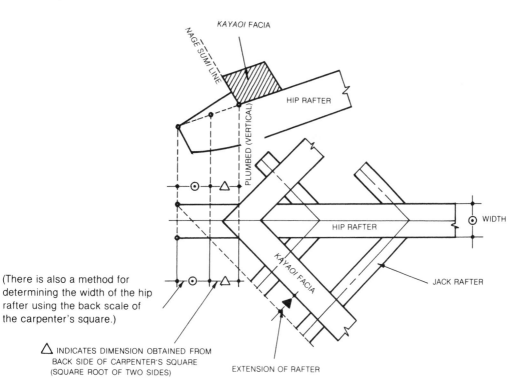

NAGE SUMI LINE

KAYAOI FACIA

HIP RAFTER

PLUMBED (VERTICAL)

HIP RAFTER

WIDTH

KAYAOI FACIA

JACK RAFTER

(There is also a method for determining the width of the hip rafter using the back scale of the carpenter's square.)

△ INDICATES DIMENSION OBTAINED FROM BACK SIDE OF CARPENTER'S SQUARE (SQUARE ROOT OF TWO SIDES)

EXTENSION OF RAFTER

Determining the cut line on the hip rafter for accepting the facia perpendicular to the rafters.

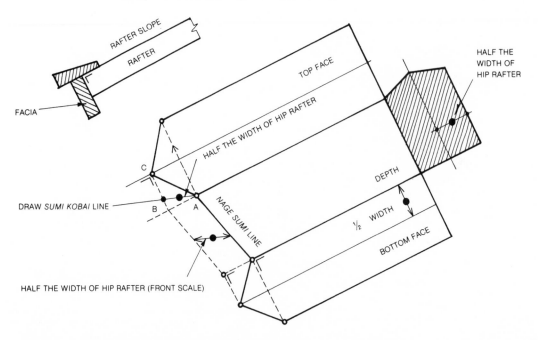

The angle of slope for the top surfaces is equal to the reverse slope of *chogen*. From point "A" draw the rafter slope line. The distance between points "A" and "B" is equal to ½ the hip rafter width. On the face of the hip rafter, place a carpenter's square toward point "C". Connect points "A" and "C".

The shape of the bottom surface is determined by drawing a horizontal line a distance equivalent to ½ the hip rafter's width from the *nage sumi* line and carrying this line underneath to the bottom surface.

Simple method for drawing the *nage sumi* line for cutting end of hip rafter.

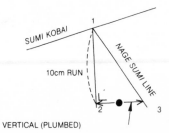

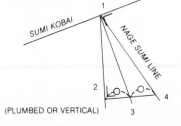

First method: From point 1, draw a vertical line. Locate point 2 10cm below point 1. From point 2, extend a horizontal line perpendicular to line 1—2 for a distance equal to the length of the vertical member of the rafter slope to obtain point 3. Line 1—3 is the *nage sumi* line.

Second method: Draw a vertical line from point 1 and also from the same point, draw a line perpendicular to the hip rafter slope. From point 2 at any point of the vertical line, draw a perpendicular line. Point 3 is the intersected point of this line and the line perpendicular to the hip roof slope. Locate point 4 on the horizontal line equal to twice the distance of 2—3. The *nage sumi* line connects points 1 and 4.

Determining the cut line on the hip rafter for accepting the vertical facia.

The slope of the top face is equal to the reverse slope of *chogen*. *Chogen* × slope run = line drawn on *chogen* side. Run of slope × *chogen* = line drawn on run of slope.

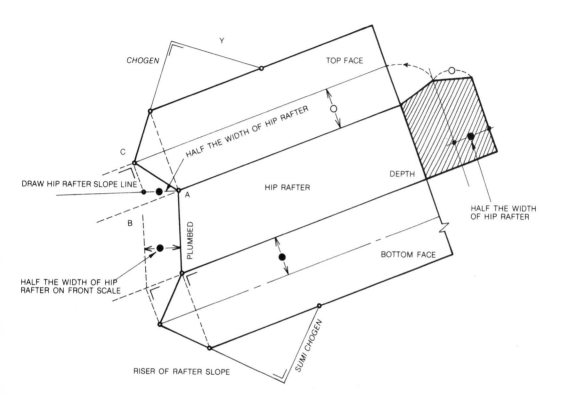

From point "A", draw hip rafter slope line. The distance "A"—"B" should be equal to half the width of the hip rafter. On the hip rafter, place the carpenter's square toward point "C". Connect points "A" and "C".

The slope on the bottom surface is equal to that of *chogen*. Extend horizontally and vertically a distance equal to ½ the hip rafter's width and carry the resultant to the bottom side. This forms the shape on the bottom surface.

Metric to English conversions:
1 mm = 0.04 inches; 10 mm = 0.4 inches; 100 mm = 4 inches; 1 metre = 39.3 inches.
    To get approximate English dimensions, divide millimeters by 3 and multiply the answer by ⅛.
For example $^{12\,mm}/_3$ = 4 × ⅛ = ½ ".

Determining the cut line on the hip rafter where it connects to a beam.

Determining the cut line on the top face.

Since there is a crown on the top surface of the hip rafter, the cut line is not a rectilinear shape but is shaped more like a blade.

Transfer the distance "A"—"B", on the hip rafter end to the side, line "A"—"B", and draw a line parallel to it on the top surface. Place a carpenter's square at the top surface corner "C" to determine the width 1—2. Transfer the distance on to center line of the top surface shown 1'—2'. Connect point 2' to the ends of the parallel line to obtain the cut line on the top surface.

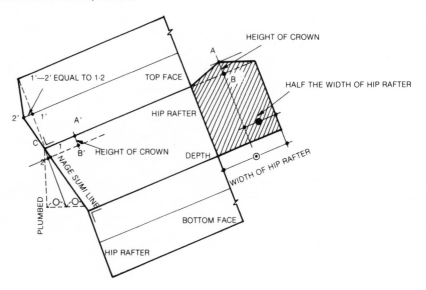

Method for determining the insertion length of the hip rafter.

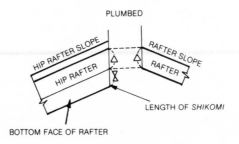

Determining the cut line on the hip rafter where it connects to a beam (continued).

Since the beam's center line will be marked on the face of the hip rafter, there will be three center lines, *nyūchū*, *shuchū* and *honchū*. (For example, see "Plan of eave corner periphery" on page 00.)

Nyūchū: A line determined by measuring the depth of the eave or the spacing of rafters. (The line can be drawn horizontally or vertically.) It is used as the basic reference in measuring the length of the hip rafter.

Shuchū: A line returned on a horizontal plane a distance equal to the width of the hip rafter (front side) from the *nyūchū*. It is used as a basic reference in determining rafter spacing (*taruki kubari*).

Honchū: The center line in the space between *nyūchū* and *shuchū*. It is also the center line of the space between the hip rafter and the *keta* beam that will be placed on top of the hip rafter.

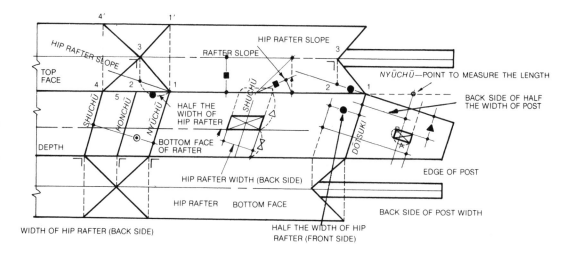

Uwaba sumi—top line. This line is also called *uma nori sumi*. However a line connecting points 3—5 is also called *nori sumi* by some people

1. Draw the rafter slope line from point 1 of *nyūchū*. Locate point 2 along the rafter slope line at a distance equal to half the hip rafter width.
2. From the side face of the hip rafter, place a carpenter's square toward the top face and locate point 3 on the center line of the top face.
3. When points 1—3, 4—3, 1'—3 and 4'—3' are connected, they form the *uwaba sumi* line (*uma nori sumi*).

Shitaba sumi—bottom line, also called *tasuki sumi*. Place a carpenter's square from *nyūchū* and *shuchū* across the bottom face of the hip rafter. Connect the ends forming X shape. These lines form *tasuki sumi*. The slope of the X is the slope of *chogen*.

The terms commonly used by Japanese carpenters instead of the original Chinese terms used in this book are as follows:

honchū = *honaka*
nyūchū = *irinaka*
schūchū = *denaka*

Determining the mortise cut line for the hip rafter tenon on the post and end post.

△ = Plumbed or vertical depth of rafter at hip rafter.
X̄ = Dimension which hip rafter penetrates into post.

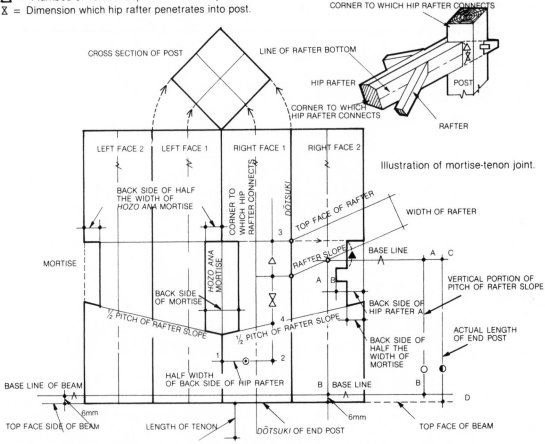

Illustration of mortise-tenon joint.

The dimension A—B is the pivot height of the end post. For the *tsuka-jiri* (end post), another 6mm must be added In other words, the actual length from the pivot point of the mortise to the *tsuka-jiri* is the C—D distance.

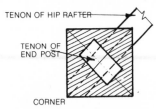

The tenon of the end post must be perpendicular to the mortise for the hip rafter.

1. Draw the rafter slope line from the intersected point "A" between the pivot point of the mortise and the center line of right face 2, and locate a point rafter depth away from it to obtain the lines for the rafter top.

2. Continue the line of the rafter slope and the top face of rafter at points "E" and "F" horizontally to the number 1 face of the end post.

3. Determine the *dōtsuki* line by obtaining the distance 1—2 which is half the width of the hip rafter on the back scale from the first face of the mortise corner.

4. Determine the location from the bottom face of the hip rafter by obtaining the distance 3—4 which is the dimension for the hip rafter *dōtsuki* △ and X̄ (the vertical depth of the hip rafter) from the line of the rafter top of the first surface.

5. Draw ½ pitch line of the rafter slope from point 4 and continue on to the second face (corner from which tenon protrudes out). This is the line for the bottom face of the hip rafter.

6. The top of the mortise is located by continuing a horizontal line from point "F." (Also the top face of the hip rafter tenon.)

7. The size of the mortise should be equal to the back side of the tenon. The hole for the wedge should be the width of the back side of the wedge determined on the hip rafter and on the post corner where the tenon is to protrude out.

8. The location of the wedge should be equivalent to the dimension of hip rafter ▲ and thickness B.

Method of joining hip rafter to *keta* beams. (Case 1)

This method uses *agokaki* notching on the bottom of the hip rafter since the *keta* beam's inserted portions are shared equally with the hip rafter, half a piece using *kiri kaki* notching. There are numerous methods of this type.

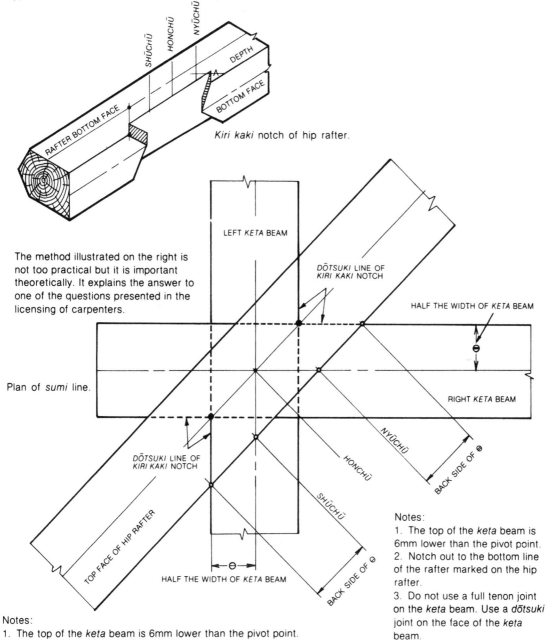

Kiri kaki notch of hip rafter.

The method illustrated on the right is not too practical but it is important theoretically. It explains the answer to one of the questions presented in the licensing of carpenters.

Plan of *sumi* line.

Notes:
1. The top of the *keta* beam is 6mm lower than the pivot point.
2. Notch out to the bottom line of the rafter marked on the hip rafter.
3. Do not use a full tenon joint on the *keta* beam. Use a *dōtsuki* joint on the face of the *keta* beam.

Notes:
1. The top of the *keta* beam is 6mm lower than the pivot point.
2. Notch out to the bottom line of the rafter marked on the hip rafter.
3. Do not use a full tenon joint on the *keta* beam. Use a *dōtsuki* joint on the face of the *keta* beam.
4. ⊖ and ⊖ symbols refer to width of *keta* beam shown on drawing.

Method of joining hip rafter to *keta* beams. (Case 7 continued.)

Cut line of the *keta* beam on the bottom face of the hip rafter.

The line connecting points 6—3—6′ and parallel lines 5—7—5′ is equal to the parallel lines of *tasuki sumi.*

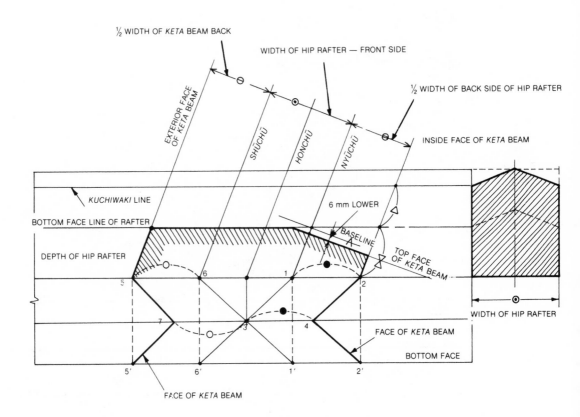

Method for obtaining the *dotsuki* line of the *keta beam* on the bottom face of the hip rafter.

The length 1—2 obtained by taking half the width of the *keta* beam from *nyūchū* should be equal to the distance 3—4, where point 3 is the intersected point of the *tasuki* line of the bottom face of the hip rafter. Connect points 2—4 and 4—2′. The length 5—6 obtained by taking half the width of the *keta* from *shūchū* should equal the distance 3—7, where point 3 is the intersected point of the bottom face of the hip rafter. Connect points 5—7 and 7—5′.

Method for joining the hip rafter to the *keta* beams. (Case 2)

In this method, the hip rafter is joined with the *watari ago* notch on the *keta* beam. For both the hip rafter and *keta* beam, the location of the notch is determined by doubling the distance a—b, which is the depth of insertion at the face of the hip rafter. The notch is made immediately below it.

The exterior side of the *watari ago* notch is cut out in shape of *kaneori* and the interior side is cut perpendicular to the hip rafter. (The illustration shows an example where the connection is initiated from corner No. 4.)

Framing method for the *noki geta* beam.

Where the *keta* beam's top is lower than the pivot point, the reference line of the *keta* beam's top for notching is to be located below this line an amount equal to the difference between the *keta* beam's top and the pivot point.

Hang perpendicular to the hip rafter.

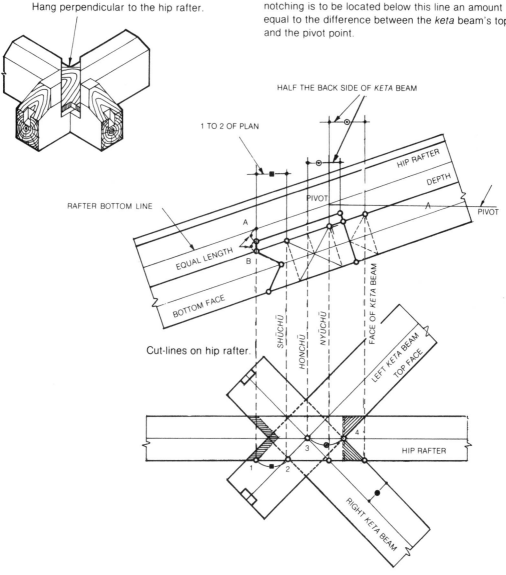

Method for joining the hip rafter to the *keta beams* (Case 2 continued).

Framing method for the *noki geta* beam.

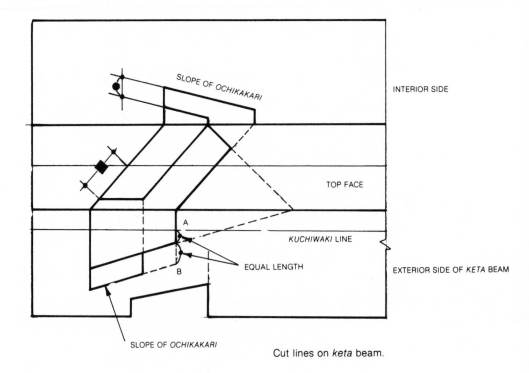

Cut lines on *keta* beam.

Detail of notch on hip rafter.

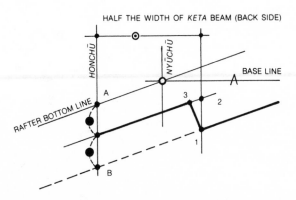

For notching the bottom face, there are methods where 1—2 is cut vertically (plumbed) and 1—3 is cut perpendicular to slope. In the case where the 1—3 cut is used, the notch on the top face of the *keta* beam has to have the slope of 2—3.

Method for hanging the hip rafter on the *keta* beam. (Case 3)

In this method both front and inside faces of the *keta* beams are *kaneori* notched for their connection. The depth of the notch should be 15mm from the face of the *keta* beam. Its location must always be measured from the center line "C" or "D", and not from the face of the *keta* beam. For the hip rafter, either measure A—B on the back scale of the carpenter's square or use the length 1—2.

Notch on the top face of the hip rafter.

LENGTH OF 1'—2'
C'—D' FROM BACK SCALE

SHŪCHŪ
HONCHŪ
NYŪCHŪ

LENGTH OF 1—2
C—D FROM BACK SCALE

RAFTER BOTTOM LINE

BASE LINE

A

B

HIP RAFTER
BOTTOM FACE

Cut-line on hip rafter.

C'
D'
LEFT *KETA* BEAM

3

TOP FACE OF HIP RAFTER

1   2   2'   1'

Notch for *keta* beam.

RIGHT *KETA* BEAM

For the cut lines on the bottom face of the hip rafter, refer to the drawings on pages 147 and 148. In short, the notch lines are parallel to the *tasuki* lines.

NYŪCHŪ
HONCHŪ

RAFTER BOTTOM LINE
BASE LINE
RAFTER TOP LINE
EQUAL LENGTH
BASE LINE

The top face of the hip rafter is lower than the pivot.

Example of top face of hip rafter below the pivot.

NYŪCHŪ
HONCHŪ

3   2
BASE LINE
1

BASE LINE

Base line aligned with the top face of the hip rafter.

Where the base line and the top face of the hip rafter correspond, there are ways of notching the top face where 1—2 is cut vertically (plumbed), and where 1—3 is cut perpendicular to the slope. When cut 1—3 is used, the notch on the *keta* beam top has to be cut with the slope of 1—3.

Ochi kakari—Right angle joint of hip rafter.

There are many methods for accomplishing this, especially where *ochi kakari* depth is determined on the interior side. The method described here is only one such example.

1. Determine the *kuchiwaki* line.
2. Locate the center of another *keta* beam on the top surface of the *keta* beam, then draw the hip rafter center line and the hip rafter width line.
3. Continue the center and width lines of the hip rafter drawn on the top surface of the *keta* beam to its front side.
4. Draw the rafter slope line from point "A", the intersected point of the *kuchiwaki* line, and the center line of the hip rafter. On the rafter slope line, measure a distance equal to the depth of the rafters and erase the remaining.
5. From point 1, an intersected point of the *kuchi waki* line and the line of the interior side of the hip rafter, obtain the insertion dimension 1—2.
6. From point 2, draw a ½ pitch of the rafter slope line to obtain the depth of the *ochi kakari* joint.
7. Another method for obtaining the cut lines for the *ochi kakari* joint is as follows: Locate point "B", which is the intersected point of the rafter slope line and the line of the exterior face of the hip rafter. From point "B", obtain insertion dimension B—3. The depth of the *ochi kakari* joint is the distance 3—2.

To make the *ochi kakari* joint on the interior side:

1. Continue the *ochi kakari* line to the top face of the *keta* beam and obtain point 4.
2. Obtain point 5 by going 45° on the top face of the *keta* beam from point 4. From point 5, draw a ½ pitch of the rafter slope line to locate point 6. The distance 5—6 is the depth of the interior side of the *ochi kakari* joint.

Neji kumi—Twist joint of the *keta* beam.

Make an *aikaki* notch on the slope which connects the center point of a distance equal to the dimension below the line of the *ochi kakari* slope which has been transferred to both the front and back ends of the *keta* beam. This applies to both the interior and exterior sides of the *keta* beam. To connect the *keta* beams, there are the *oiire* and *mengoshi* methods which connect only a small portion of the corners.

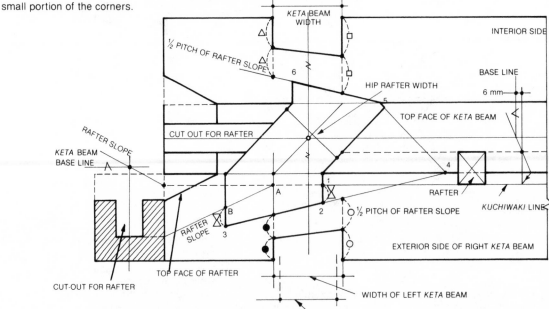

In the actual example, since it will be notched to accept a full tenon, the notch will be cut at this width.

Connection method for the *keta* beams.

The common uniting joint between the *keta* beams is the *neji kumi* joint. Besides the superior quality joint shown on the illustration below, the commonly used joints for the bottom faces use the *oiire* and the *mengoshi* method, where portions of corners are connected.

There is another method of joining the *keta* beams without using the uniting joint. This method uses the four directional *ari kake* joint, (dadoed, half lapped, half blind dovetail with full mortise and tenon), which consists of the third *keta* beam and the outrigger portion, called *kake hana*. *Kake hana* is made of a separate piece. The lower *keta* member is not determined by whether it is on the right or left side, but instead by whether it is in a *keta yuki* beam (a *keta* beam which is a major structural member).

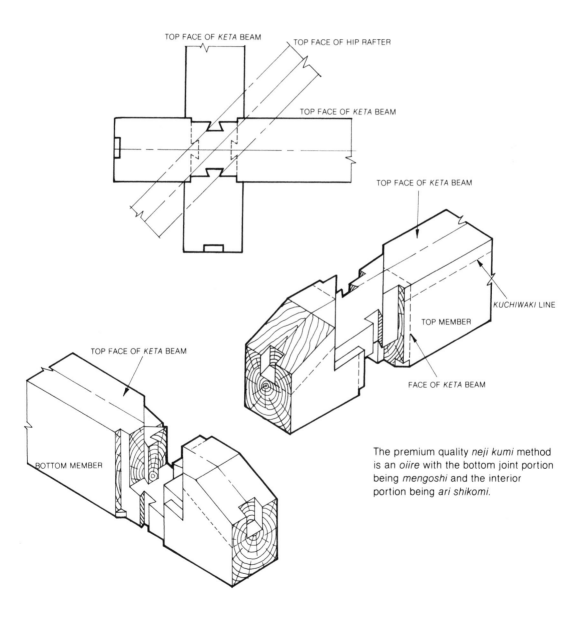

TOP FACE OF *KETA* BEAM

TOP FACE OF HIP RAFTER

TOP FACE OF *KETA* BEAM

TOP FACE OF *KETA* BEAM

KUCHIWAKI LINE

TOP MEMBER

FACE OF *KETA* BEAM

TOP FACE OF *KETA* BEAM

BOTTOM MEMBER

The premium quality *neji kumi* method is an *oiire* with the bottom joint portion being *mengoshi* and the interior portion being *ari shikomi*.

Connection method for the *keta* beams (continued).

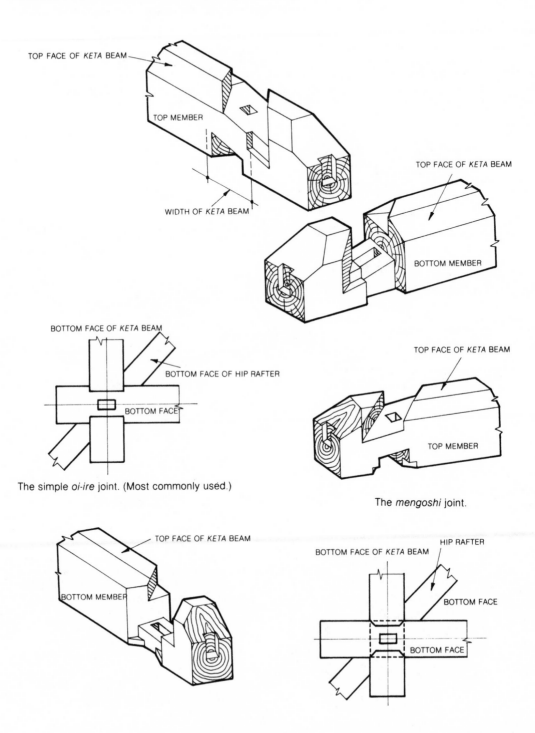

TOP FACE OF *KETA* BEAM

TOP MEMBER

WIDTH OF *KETA* BEAM

TOP FACE OF *KETA* BEAM

BOTTOM MEMBER

BOTTOM FACE OF *KETA* BEAM

BOTTOM FACE OF HIP RAFTER

BOTTOM FACE

The simple *oi-ire* joint. (Most commonly used.)

TOP FACE OF *KETA* BEAM

TOP MEMBER

The *mengoshi* joint.

TOP FACE OF *KETA* BEAM

BOTTOM MEMBER

BOTTOM FACE OF *KETA* BEAM

HIP RAFTER

BOTTOM FACE

BOTTOM FACE

End cut line for the *kayaoi* facia and the *hirokomai* facia (Case 1).

Members such as the *kayaoi* facia, *hirokomai* facia and *mizukiri* facia, all slope in two directions and cannot be joined at a corner simply with a 45° cut. The corner which is sloped in two directions is called the *shihō korobi*. The cut lines at the corners of the members are obtained as noted below.

Uwaba tome line at the *shihō korobi* corner.

This is the reversed slope of *chogen*. *Kayaoi* facia, *hirokomai* facia, and *mizukiri* facia all use the *uwaba tome* line.

1. Draw the rafter slope line from point 1.
2. Transfer the top width dimension A—B on to the rafter slope line to obtain point 2. On the edge of the facia, place the carpenter's square and align with point 2 to obtain point 3.
3. Line 1—3 is the *uwaba tome* line.

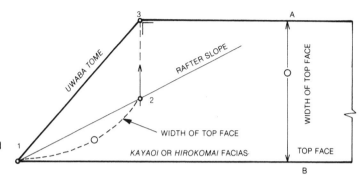

The *mukō tome* line (cut line along the vertical surface) at the *shihō korobi* corner.

This is the reverse slope of the median rafter slope.

1. From point 1, draw the reverse slope of the rafter slope.
2. Transfer the depth dimension of A—B along the reverse slope of the rafter slope to obtain point 2.
3. Obtain point 3 by aligning the carpenter's square on the edge of the facia to point 2.
4. Line 1—3 is the *mukō tome* line.

Uwaba sumi—top face line

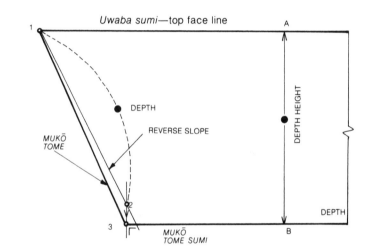

The *dōtsuki* cut line on the top surface of the *korobi* member.

The *dōtsuki* cut line on the top surface of the *korobi* member is the reverse slope *tangen*.

1. Draw the reverse slope of the rafter slope from point 1.
2. Transfer the top surface dimension a—b along the reverse slope of the rafter slope to obtain point 3.
3. Draw a perpendicular line from the side intersecting point 3 to obtain point 4.
4. Line 1–4 is the *dōtsuki* cut line.

A slope where its run is proportional to the width of the top surface. The width in this case is set at 1.

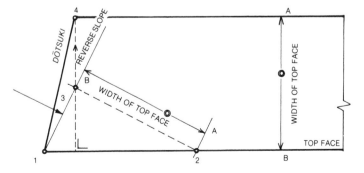

Uwaba dōtsuki—dōtsuki of top face

The end cut line of *kayaoi* facia and *hirokomai* facia (Case 2).

Determining *mukō dome* with *uwaba tome (upper surface miter).*

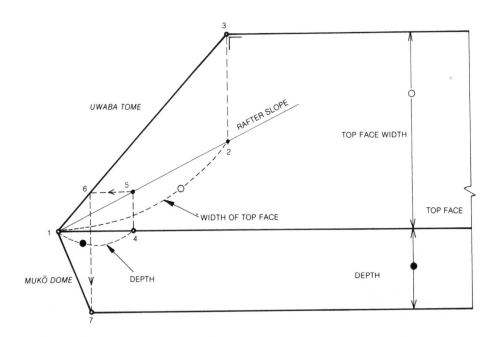

With thin *hirokomai* facia, it is difficult to obtain accurate *mukō dome* using its depth. Thus, the cut lines of *mukō dome* are best determined by using the cut lines of *uwaba tome.*

1. The cut lines of *uwaba tome* are determined as follows:

a. Draw the rafter slope line from point 1.

b. Locate point 2 on the rafter slope line by transferring the distance of the top surface width from point 1. Place a carpenter's square on the edge and align with point 2 to determine point 3 on the edge.

c. Line 1—3 is the *uwaba tome* line.

2. Cut lines of *mukō dome* are determined as follows:

a. At the top surface corner 1, locate point 4 on the edge by transferring the depth dimension on it.

b. On point 4, place a carpenter's square. Point 5 is where it intersects the rafter slope line. Point 6 is the intersected point on the *uwaba tome* line and a line drawn from point 5 parallel to the edge.

c. From point 6, place a carpenter's square vertically (plumbed) and continue the line to the depth's face. The point intersected by this line at the opposite edge is point 7.

d. Line 1—7 is the *mukō dome* line.

The end cut line of *kayaoi* facia and *hirokomai* facia (Case 2 continued).

Determining the *uwaba tome* line with the depth dimension.

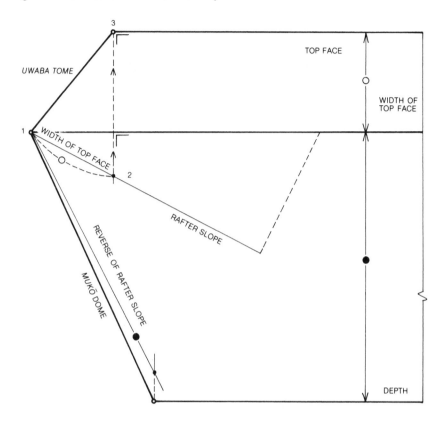

Usually the method on the previous page for determining the *uwaba tome* line is sufficient. However, in cases where the top face width is narrow, the *uwaba tome* line is determined by continuing the cut lines from the depth face to the top face as shown on the above illustration. To draw the *uwaba tome* line refer to the illustration.

Metric to English conversions:
1 mm = 0.04 inches; 10 mm = 0.4 inches; 100 mm = 4 inches; 1 metre = 39.3 inches.
    To get approximate English dimensions, divide millimeters by 3 and multiply the answer by $\frac{1}{8}$.
For example $\frac{12\,mm}{3} = 4 \times \frac{1}{8} = \frac{1}{2}$ ".

Cut lines on the top face of the *kawaraza* (cant strip or nailer for Japanese roofing tiles).

The *uwaba tome* line of *kawaraza*.

This method is used when slopes of the *kawaraza* and rafters are not the same, and the cross section of *kawaraza* is not rectangular. If the slope of the rafter and that of the top surface of the *kawaraza* are parallel, then the cut line of the *kawaraza* is equal to the reverse slope of *chogen*. However, if the above mentioned slopes are not parallel, the rafter slope becomes irrelevant and the reverse of *chogen* of the *kawaraza* top surface slope becomes the *uwaba tome* line.

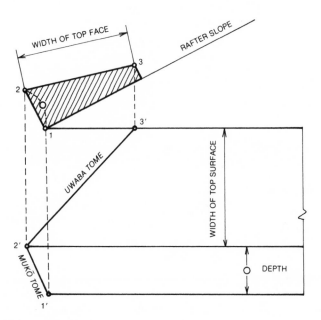

Determining the top surface slope of *kawaraza*.

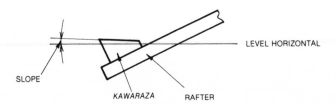

The illustration above shows a diagrammetic method for obtaining the *uwaba tome* line. By using the *kawaraza* top surface slope with a horizontal line, the *uwaba tome* line can be obtained by the ordinary method. Also, *uwaba tome* can be obtained by using the actual slope of the top surface with a horizontal line as shown on page 155.

Cut lines on the top of the *kawaraza* (continued).

Cut line for the *uwaba tome* line of the *hirokomai* facia at the valley corner (*tanisumi*) or inside corner (*irisumi*).

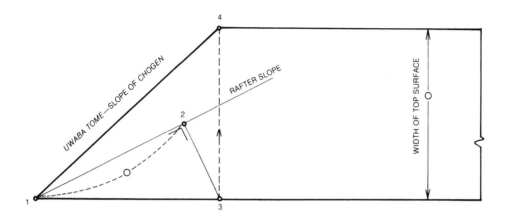

The *uwaba tome* line of the *hirokomai* facia is the reverse slope of *chogen* at either the valley or hip corner, inside or outside corner. The hip jack rafter's *uwaba tome* line is the slope of *chogen* for the hip corner.
The illustration above shows the *kinomi-gaeshi-hō* method.
1. Draw the rafter slope line from point 1.
2. Locate point 2 on the rafter slope line. Point 2 is located a distance equal to the width of the top surface from point 1.
3. Point 3 is obtained at the intersected edge of the perpendicular line to the rafter slope line at point 2.
4. Point 4 is the opposite end perpendicular to point 3.
5. Line 4—1 is the *uwaba tome* line (slope of *chogen*).

This method is also used to obtain the *dōtsuki* of the hip jack rafter at the *bō* corner. Though this method can be used on the hip jack rafter at the *bō* corner, it is easier to use a different method.

Method for determining the length of the hip jack rafter.

This method using *gangi gane* (a special carpenter's square) counts each spacing unit determined by the carpenter's square, reflecting the rise and run of the slope as shown in the illustration. If the unit space ends in a partial unit, such as 7cm or 5cm, this partial unit is to be considered the run of the slope and the rise is then determined by a proportional method or with carpenter's square. The illustration below is an example using a slope of $\frac{5}{10}$ or 5 rise for every 10 of run.

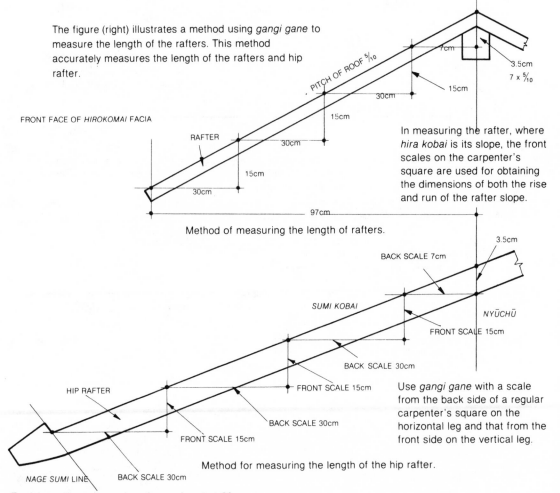

The figure (right) illustrates a method using *gangi gane* to measure the length of the rafters. This method accurately measures the length of the rafters and hip rafter.

FRONT FACE OF *HIROKOMAI* FACIA

In measuring the rafter, where *hira kobai* is its slope, the front scales on the carpenter's square are used for obtaining the dimensions of both the rise and run of the rafter slope.

Method of measuring the length of rafters.

Use *gangi gane* with a scale from the back side of a regular carpenter's square on the horizontal leg and that from the front side on the vertical leg.

Method for measuring the length of the hip rafter.

To enlarge the unit spacing, the run is set at 30 cm.
(run × 3) = 30cm.
(rise × 3) = 15cm.
In other words, by using 30cm × 15cm of *gangi gane* three times the remaining run is 7cm. The rise is thus 7 × $\frac{5}{10}$ = 3.5cm. The figure above illustrates a method for determining the length of the hip rafter by using the *gangi gane*. The *gangi gane* used for measuring the hip rafter uses the scale on the back side of a common carpenter's square on the horizontal leg, while the vertical leg uses the scale from the front side of a carpenter's square.

Method for determining the length of the hip rafter.

The figure below illustrates a way to determine the length of the hip rafter using the method called *ko-hira-okoshi*.

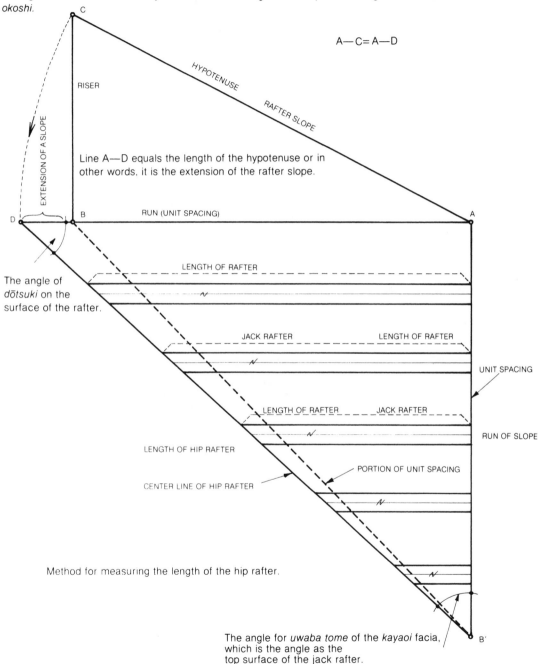

A—C= A—D

RISER

HYPOTENUSE

RAFTER SLOPE

EXTENSION OF A SLOPE

Line A—D equals the length of the hypotenuse or in other words, it is the extension of the rafter slope.

RUN (UNIT SPACING)

D   B   A

LENGTH OF RAFTER

The angle of *dōtsuki* on the surface of the rafter.

JACK RAFTER   LENGTH OF RAFTER

UNIT SPACING

LENGTH OF RAFTER   JACK RAFTER

RUN OF SLOPE

LENGTH OF HIP RAFTER

PORTION OF UNIT SPACING

CENTER LINE OF HIP RAFTER

Method for measuring the length of the hip rafter.

The angle for *uwaba tome* of the *kayaoi* facia, which is the angle as the top surface of the jack rafter.

B'

Cut line on the hip jack rafter (using *kinomi gaeshi hō* method).

From the point "C" on the vertical surface of the side (depth) of the hip jack rafter, obtain point "D" at a horizontal distance equal to the width of the top surface. Transfer point "D" to the top edge to obtain point "E". Place a carpenter's square along line E—G and connect points F—A to obtain the *dōtsuki* line.

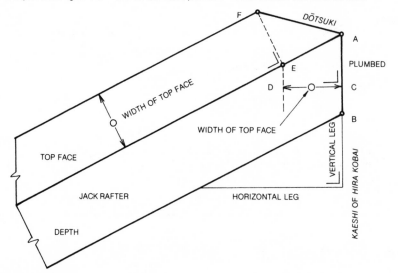

Tenon for the hip jack rafter.

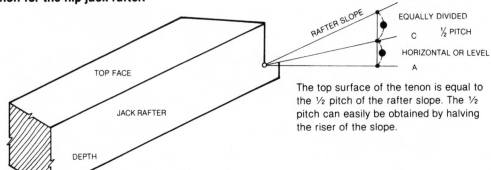

The top surface of the tenon is equal to the ½ pitch of the rafter slope. The ½ pitch can easily be obtained by halving the riser of the slope.

Mortise for the hip rafter.

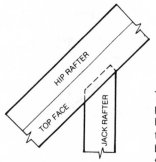

The top surface of the mortise is perpendicular to the depth side of the hip rafter. In other words, the cut-out is to be horizontal. The slope of the bottom surface of the mortise matches the *kuchiwaki* slope.

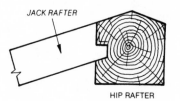

HIP RAFTER

Length of the jack rafter.

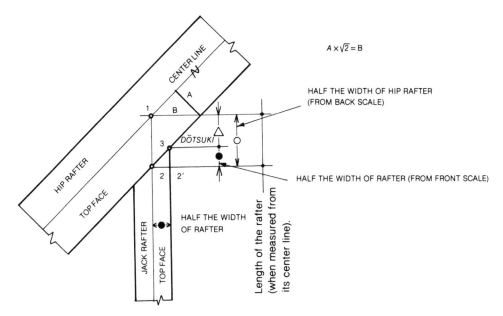

$$A \times \sqrt{2} = B$$

HALF THE WIDTH OF HIP RAFTER
(FROM BACK SCALE)

HALF THE WIDTH OF RAFTER (FROM FRONT SCALE)

Relationship between the jack rafter and the hip rafter.

Dōtsuki is the point derived by subtracting the remaining dimension which resulted from ½ the rafter width measured on the front ●, from ½ the hip rafter width measured on the back scale □, from the length measured from the rafter's center.

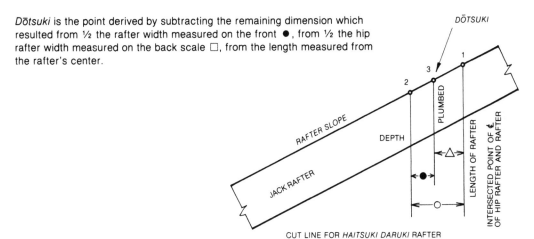

CUT LINE FOR *HAITSUKI DARUKI* RAFTER

□ = ½ width of hip rafter obtained with the back scale. Length of 1—2)
● = ½ width of rafter (obtained with the front scale.)
■ = (½ width of hip rafter obtained with the back scale) − (½ width of rafter obtained with the front scale). Subtracting the ■ dimension from the length of the cut line will result in the *dōtsuki* line. In other words □ − ● = ■ (*dōtsuki* line).

Cut line of the valley rafter at the inside corner.

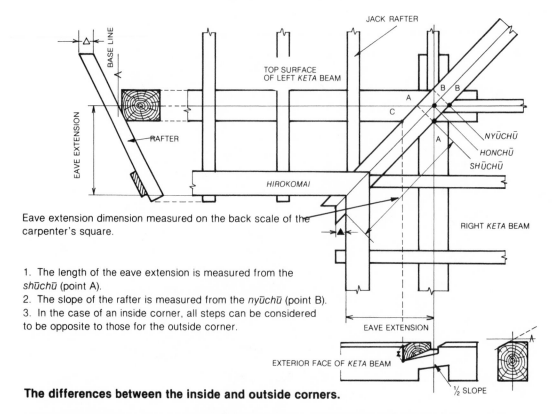

Eave extension dimension measured on the back scale of the carpenter's square.

1. The length of the eave extension is measured from the *shūchū* (point A).
2. The slope of the rafter is measured from the *nyūchū* (point B).
3. In the case of an inside corner, all steps can be considered to be opposite to those for the outside corner.

The differences between the inside and outside corners.

Conditions (a)	Outside corner (b)	Inside corner (c)
Form of top surface.	Crowned.	Valleyed.
The basic point for proportioning of rafter at the face of hip rafter.	Measure from *shūchū*.	Measure from *nyūchū*.
Point from which the eave extension and the length of the hip rafter is measured.	Measure from *nyūchū*	Measure from *shūchū*
Ochikakari joint of hip rafter at the face of the *keta* beam.	The insertion dimension is taken from the inside of the *kuchiwaki* line. One cuts the bottom surface of the slot into which the hip rafter fits into the *keta* at ½ the main roof slope.	The insertion dimension is taken from the outside of *kuchiwaki*. One cuts the bottom surface of the slot into which the hip rafter fits into the *keta* at ½ the main roof slope.
Height of the hip rafter at the end post.	The height of pivot is located on the two faces adjacent to the insertion face.	The height of its contact is located on the insertion face.
Top surface miter of the *kayaoi* and *hirokomai* facia.	Reverse slope of *chogen*.	Reverse slope of *chogen*.
Cut lines for hip jack rafter.	Slope of *chogen*.	Slope of *chogen*.

Cut line for the valley rafter.

Method for determining the slope of the valley on the valley rafter.

The slope of the valley on the top of the valley rafter is ½ the main rafter slope.
1. Draw the valley rafter slope line on the face of the valley rafter. If the top face of the valley rafter is placed along the valley rafter slope, the cut line becomes horizontal (level).
2. From point 1 locate point 2 at a distance of ½ the valley rafter's width.
3. The valley bottom line is located through point 2 running parallel to the edge of the top face.

The terms commonly used by Japanese carpenters instead of the original Chinese terms used in this book are as follows:

honchū = honaka
nyūchū = irinaka
schūchū = denaka

The depth of the rafter measured at the vertically cut face.

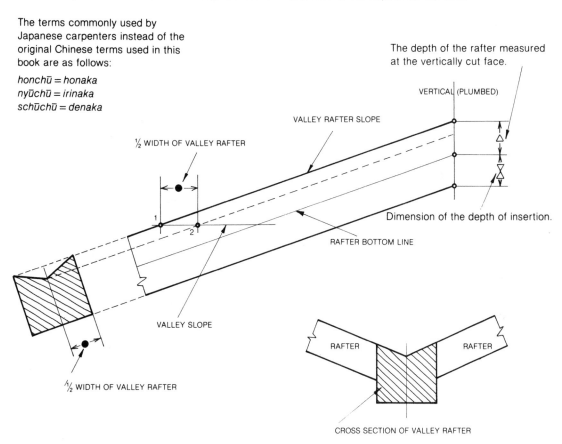

VERTICAL (PLUMBED)

VALLEY RAFTER SLOPE

½ WIDTH OF VALLEY RAFTER

Dimension of the depth of insertion.

RAFTER BOTTOM LINE

VALLEY SLOPE

½ WIDTH OF VALLEY RAFTER

RAFTER   RAFTER

CROSS SECTION OF VALLEY RAFTER

The length of the valley rafter is measured from *shūchū*. (The slope of the rafter is measured from *nyūchū*.)
1. On the face of the valley rafter, draw the valley bottom line.
2. From *shūchū* locate *nyūchū* at a distance of the width of the hip rafter.
3. *Honchū* is the center between *shūchū* and *nyūchū*.

Cut line for the valley rafter (continued).

Method for determining *umanori* and *tasuki* cut lines.

Method of cutting the end of valley rafter.

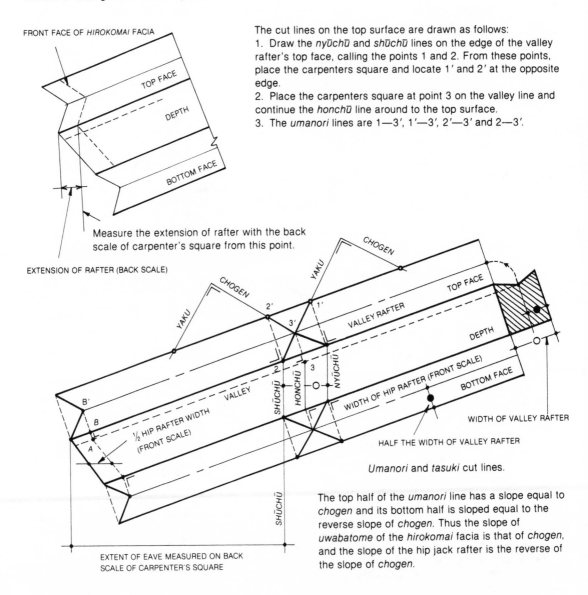

FRONT FACE OF *HIROKOMAI* FACIA

Measure the extension of rafter with the back scale of carpenter's square from this point.

EXTENSION OF RAFTER (BACK SCALE)

EXTENT OF EAVE MEASURED ON BACK SCALE OF CARPENTER'S SQUARE

The cut lines on the top surface are drawn as follows:
1. Draw the *nyūchū* and *shūchū* lines on the edge of the valley rafter's top face, calling the points 1 and 2. From these points, place the carpenters square and locate 1' and 2' at the opposite edge.
2. Place the carpenters square at point 3 on the valley line and continue the *honchū* line around to the top surface.
3. The *umanori* lines are 1—3', 1'—3', 2'—3' and 2—3'.

Umanori and *tasuki* cut lines.

The top half of the *umanori* line has a slope equal to *chogen* and its bottom half is sloped equal to the reverse slope of *chogen*. Thus the slope of *uwabatome* of the *hirokomai* facia is that of *chogen*, and the slope of the hip jack rafter is the reverse of the slope of *chogen*.

Cut line should be the *nage* line up to point "A". From point "A" place a carpenter's square on the valley bottom line to obtain point "B" at the edge. Continue the line on to the top surface to locate point "B" which will create a slope on the top surface equal to that of *chogen*, or cut it straight across at 90° and make vertical cut on the *nage sumi*.

The cut lines on the *keta* beam for accepting the valley rafter.

1. Determine the *kuchiwaki* line. The method is the same as that for a rafter at an outside corner.
2. On the top surface of the *keta* beam, draw the valley rafter's center line and width line at 45°.
3. On the front face of the *keta* beam, locate point 1, which is the intersected point of the exterior face of the valley rafter and the *kuchiwaki* line. Using point 1 as the reference point, determine the insertion dimension ● as 1—2. At the outside corner, the insertion dimension is taken on the inside line of the hip rafter, but at the inside corner, the dimension is taken on the outside line.
4. From point 2, if the ½ pitch line of the *ochikakari* slope is drawn as 2—4, the depth of the *ochikakari* slope is obtained at the front face of the *keta* beam.
5. To obtain the depth of the *ochikakari* slope on the inside face of the *keta* beam, place a carpenter's square on point 3, which is 45° of the hip rafter, to obtain line 3—5, and on the front face of the *keta* beam, transfer the dimension 4—a to b—6, and then from point 6 draw the ½ pitch line.
6. The *neji kumi* joint of the *keta* beam is the same as for those at the outside corner.

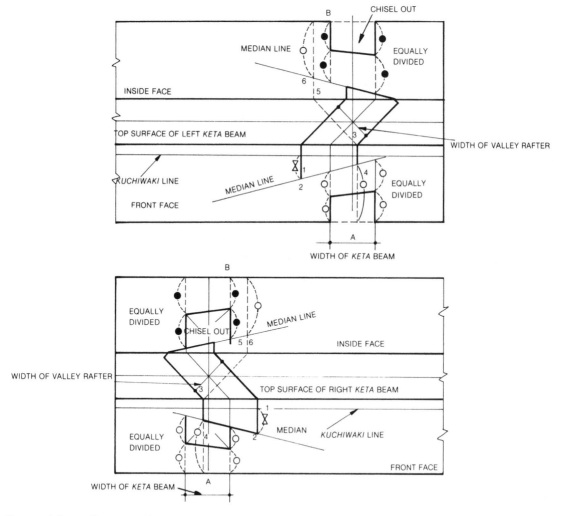

Or extend the median to outside top corner (not *noki kado* [*kuchiwaki*]). At that point double back at 45° to either hip rafter slot on top of *noki geta* or to back inside top corner of *noki geta*. If you get to back top miter corner of *geta* go half roof slope down from there to where you cross the hip rafter vertical cuts again.

10

Western Style Roof Framing

Since western roofs are framed with beams, rafters, end studs, braces, and other members constructed into trusses, or in other words, as a single unit, they can be categorized into two major types, the *shinzuka* truss with a vertical center web and the *tai zuku* truss without a vertical center web.

Since western roof framing is completely different from Japanese roof framing in resistance to forces and loads, the strength of each member of the truss must be considered. The roof framing as a unit is constructed quite logically, but the braces to resist torque, diagonal bracings, and spaced beams to resist wind and external forces, and other structural members, each have to be framed to form a monolithic structure. The supporting members such as webs, and tie pieces such as bolts are shaped and constructed after the actual dimensions required have been determined.

Corner of hip roof.

UNIT OF SCALE: mm

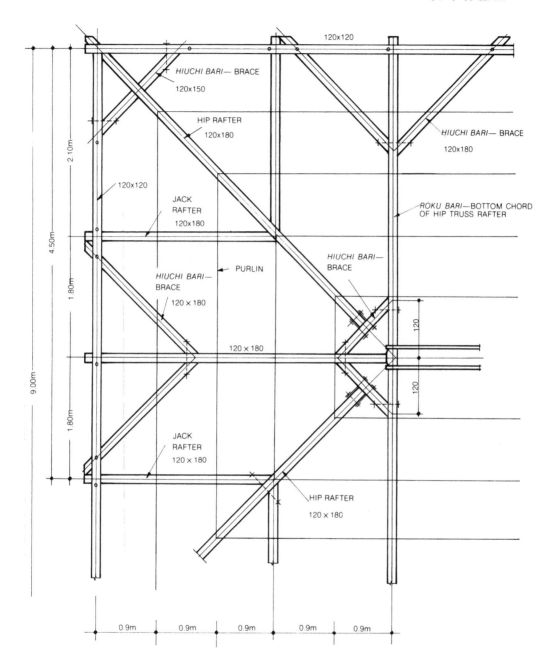

Metric to English conversions:

1 mm = 0.04 inches; 10 mm = 0.4 inches; 100 mm = 4 inches; 1 metre = 39.3 inches.

To get approximate English dimensions, divide millimeters by 3 and multiply the answer by $\frac{1}{8}$.

For example $^{12\,mm}/_3 = 4 \times \frac{1}{8} = \frac{1}{2}''$.

Shinzuka truss roof framing (Case 1).

The roof framing in illustration below uses a method which decreases the number of *hōzue* webs required by replacing the vertical web member with a *hasami zuka* web after the roof and ceiling load have been considered. In this case, the *hasami zuka* web, a tensional member, is enlarged and is connected not only with bolts but also with a split ring. It is better to employ a split ring at the connection of the spaced *hōzue* web which ties the truss to the post.

Force diagram (distinction of compression and tension members).

—— Thick line: member in compression.

— Thin line: member in tension.

The roof framing, illustrated on the right, depicts a method where vertical webs are connected with a reinforcing tie strap and a steel "U" strap at the tension points. Sometimes metal rods are installed. A common method for resisting tensional forces is to use metal rods or the *hasami zuka* web. When using a *hasami zuka* web, it is desirable to use a split ring.

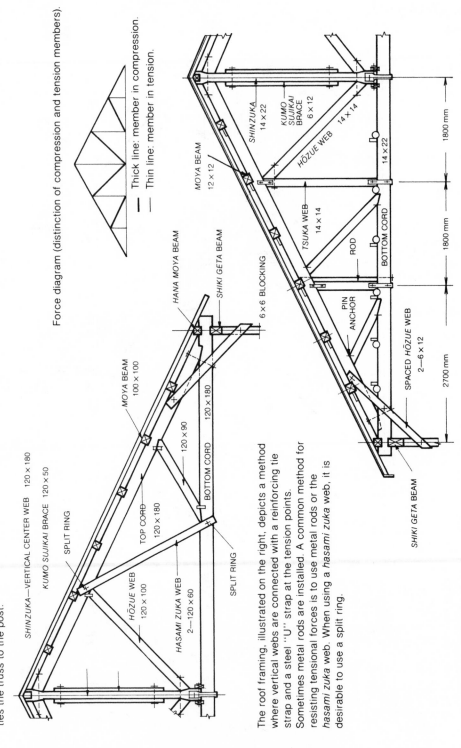

SHINZUKA—VERTICAL CENTER WEB   120 × 180

KUMO SUJIKAI BRACE   120 × 50

SPLIT RING

MOYA BEAM   100 × 100

HANA MOYA BEAM

SHIKI GETA BEAM

6 × 6 BLOCKING

TOP CORD   120 × 180

120 × 90

120 × 180

BOTTOM CORD

HŌZUE WEB   120 × 100

HASAMI ZUKA WEB   2—120 × 60

SPLIT RING

SHINZUKA   14 × 22

KUMO SUJIKAI BRACE   6 × 12

HŌZUE WEB   14 × 14

MOYA BEAM   12 × 12

14 × 22

TSUKA WEB   14 × 14

ROD

BOTTOM CORD

PIN ANCHOR

SPACED HŌZUE WEB   2—6 × 12

SHIKI GETA BEAM

1800 mm

1800 mm

2700 mm

Shinzuka truss roof framing (Case 2).

1. Draw top and bottom line of the bottom chord of the truss.
2. Draw the center line of the post. (The size of the bottom chord should be about 210mm–250mm.)
3. The depth of the *watari ago* notch on the *noki geta* beam (also called *hanamoya*) is to be 30mm. Locate pivot 1 on the side of the *noki geta* beam.
4. From the center line of the post, measure 4.5m, ½ the beam span, and draw the vertical center line of the *shinzuka* web.
5. On the center line of the *shinzuka* web, locate point 2 at the intersected point of a horizontal line extended from the pivot of the *noki geta* beam.
6. Locate 2—3, the height of the ridge pivot, from point 2. (4.5m × 0.5 = 2.25)
7. Connecting points 1 and 3 will form the roof slope (line of the rafter bottom).
8. Draw the size of the *shinzuka* web (180mm wide).
9. Make the depth of the *watari ago* notch on the bottom face of the *moya* beam. Draw the lines of the top chord's (*gasshō*) bottom and top surfaces.
10. Make the distance 7—8 about 35mm—28mm and 6—7 into a *kashigi dōtsuke* joint to connect the *shinzuka* web with the top chord.
11. Point "a" of the *kurakake hozo* mortise and tenon joint for the top chord end should be about 200mm from the center line of the post.
12. Locate the required quantity of *moya* beams spaced equally between points 1 and 3. (The illustration shows 5 equal spaces.)
13. Point 9, located by the sign ● about 150mm—180mm above the top face of the bottom chord on the *shinzuka* web's lower portion, is determined by dividing the distance 9—8' equally to obtain point 11. The bottom of the *hozue* web is determined by connecting 9—11'.

Points 4 and 5 are intersected points of line for the bottom of the *moya* beam with the post's center line and with the *shinzuka* web's center line respectively.

The strap ties and steel plates to be installed at bottom and top of the *shinzuka* web are not included.

1. The unit of measurement for the members is the millimeter.

2. To simplify the explanation, strap ties and steel plates have been omitted from the drawing.

BEAM SPAN 9m = SLOPE ⁵⁄₁₀

NOKI GETA BEAM

SHINZUKA WEB

HOZUE WEB

BOTTOM OF MOYA BEAM

TSURI ZUKA WEB

MOYA BEAM
100 × 120

BOTTOM CHORD 120 × 180

TOP CHORD

120 × 180

120 × 180

120 × 150

120 × 180

1.20 × 100

2.25m

4.50m — HALF THE SPAN

EQUAL

Shinzuka truss roof framing (Case 3).

Right angle joint of the bottom chord and end of the top chord.

There are many varieties of right angle joint for the end of the top chord, but in almost all cases, faces A and B as shown on the top center illustration must be able to resist the compressive force, N_1, of the top chord. Also faces B and C must be able to resist the tensional force, N_2, of the bottom chord. The joint must be constructed to meet these conditions.

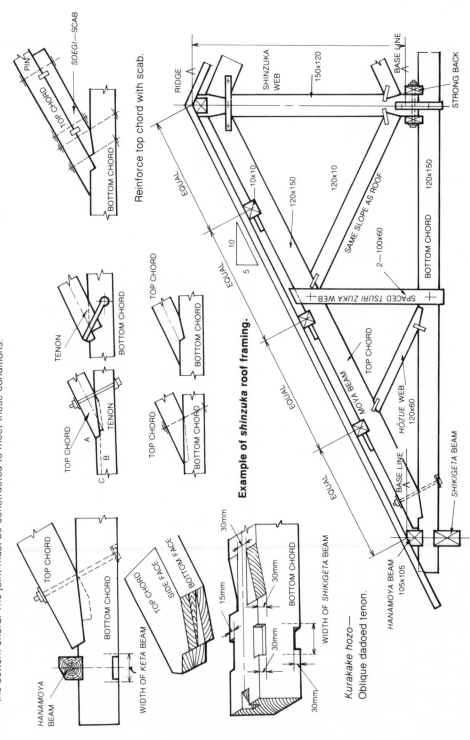

SOEGI—SCAB

PIN

TOP CHORD

BOTTOM CHORD

Reinforce top chord with scab.

TENON

BOTTOM CHORD

TOP CHORD

BOTTOM CHORD

TENON

TOP CHORD   A   TENON

C   B

BOTTOM CHORD

TOP CHORD

BOTTOM CHORD

Example of shinzuka roof framing.

RIDGE

SHINZUKA WEB

BASE LINE

STRONG BACK

150x120

10x10

120x150

120x10

EQUAL

EQUAL

10

5

SAME SLOPE AS ROOF

2—100x60

BOTTOM CHORD

120x150

SPACED TSURI ZUKA WEB

MOYA BEAM

TOP CHORD

HŌZUE WEB 120x60

EQUAL

EQUAL

BASE LINE

SHIKIGETA BEAM

HANAMOYA BEAM 105x105

HANAMOYA BEAM

TOP CHORD

BOTTOM CHORD

WIDTH OF KETA BEAM

TOP CHORD

SIDE FACE

BOTTOM FACE

SIDE FACE

30mm

15mm

30mm

30mm

30mm

30mm

BOTTOM CHORD

WIDTH OF SHIKIGETA BEAM

Kurakake hozo—
Oblique dadoed tenon.

Shinzuka truss roof framing (Case 4).

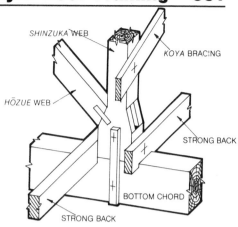

Right angle joint of *shinzuka* and bottom chord.

The *tan hozo* mortise and tenon joint is used to connect the *shinzuka* web and the bottom chord. (The tenon joint of *shinzuka* web must prevent movement and therefore is short. It is also short in order to prevent weakening the bottom chord.)

The slope of the *hōzue* web.

The slope of the *hōzue* web is generally matched to the slope of the roof.

Right angle joint of *shinzuka* web end

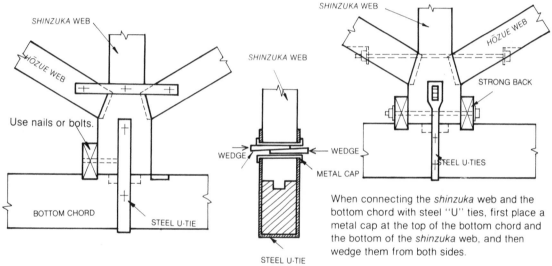

Use nails or bolts.

When connecting the *shinzuka* web and the bottom chord with steel "U" ties, first place a metal cap at the top of the bottom chord and the bottom of the *shinzuka* web, and then wedge them from both sides.

Right angle joint for strong back (*fure tome*).

For premium grade work, a strong back is joined to the bottom chord with a *watari ago* notch, and it is also bolted to the *shinzuka* web. For medium and lower grade work, the strong back is connected with a *watari kaki* notch and bolted or nailed to the *shinzuka* web.

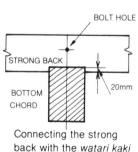

Connecting the strong back with the *watari kaki* notch (medium or lower grade).

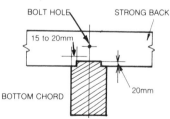

Connecting the strong back with the *watari ago* notch (premium grade).

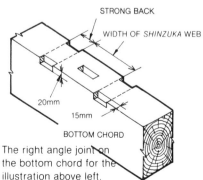

The right angle joint on the bottom chord for the illustration above left.

Shinzuka truss roof framing (Case 5).

Right angle joint of shinzuka web and top chord.

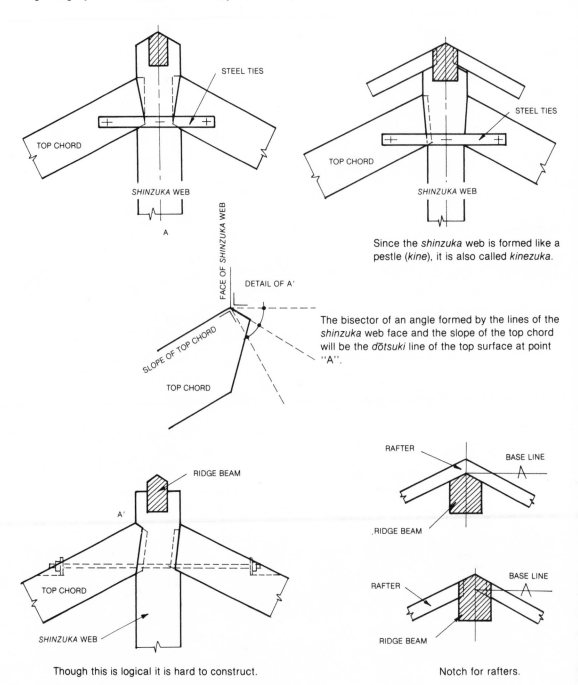

STEEL TIES

TOP CHORD

SHINZUKA WEB

A

STEEL TIES

TOP CHORD

SHINZUKA WEB

Since the shinzuka web is formed like a pestle (kine), it is also called kinezuka.

FACE OF SHINZUKA WEB

DETAIL OF A'

SLOPE OF TOP CHORD

TOP CHORD

The bisector of an angle formed by the lines of the shinzuka web face and the slope of the top chord will be the dōtsuki line of the top surface at point "A".

RIDGE BEAM

A'

TOP CHORD

SHINZUKA WEB

Though this is logical it is hard to construct.

RAFTER

BASE LINE

RIDGE BEAM

RAFTER

BASE LINE

RIDGE BEAM

Notch for rafters.

Shinzuka truss roof framing (Case 5).

Simple right angle joint of *shinzuka* web and bottom chord.

Join the bottom chord members to the bottom end of the *shinzuka* web.

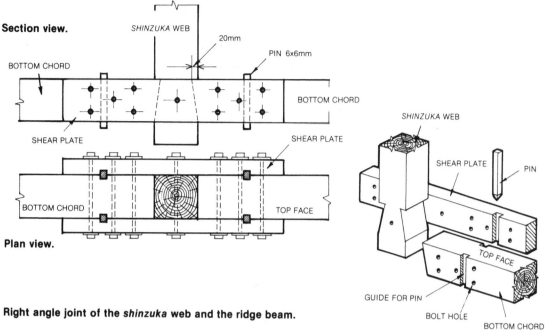

Section view.

SHINZUKA WEB

20mm

PIN 6x6mm

BOTTOM CHORD

BOTTOM CHORD

SHEAR PLATE

SHEAR PLATE

BOTTOM CHORD

TOP FACE

Plan view.

SHINZUKA WEB

SHEAR PLATE

PIN

TOP FACE

GUIDE FOR PIN

BOLT HOLE

BOTTOM CHORD

Right angle joint of the *shinzuka* web and the ridge beam.

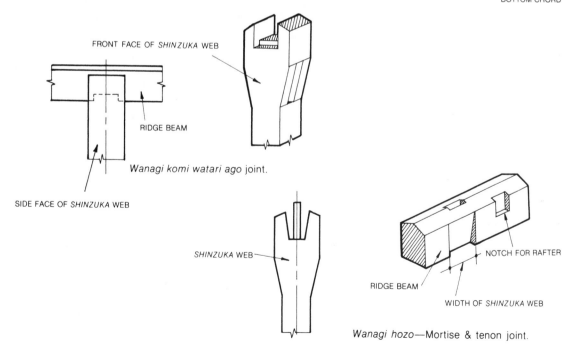

FRONT FACE OF SHINZUKA WEB

RIDGE BEAM

Wanagi komi watari ago joint.

SIDE FACE OF SHINZUKA WEB

SHINZUKA WEB

RIDGE BEAM

NOTCH FOR RAFTER

WIDTH OF SHINZUKA WEB

Wanagi hozo—Mortise & tenon joint.

Shinzuka truss roof framing (Case 6.)

○ Dimension from point 9 to the center line of the *shinzuka* web.

● Dimension from point 10 to the center line of the *shinzuka* web.

⊖ Top surface width of the common surface *dōtsuki*.

⊖ Bottom surface width of the common surface *dōtsuki*.

◉ Distance from the center line of the *shinzuka* web to the common surface point.

⊖ (○ × back of face of 2) − (○ × 2)

⊖ (● × back face of 2) − (● × 2)

◉ Top face width of the top chord × (1.207 [constant]) or ½ width of the *hira* top chord back face × ½ width of the *hira* top chord front face.

There are cases such as the one shown on page 171, where the slope of the *hōzue* web is ½ pitch of slope 8–9. There are also cases where the slope of the *hōzue* web is equal to that of the roof.

Bottom face of the hip *hōzue* web (the hip top chord slope of the *hira hōzue* web slope).

Method for obtaining the cross sectional shape of the hip *shinzuka* web.

Using the radius of 1–2, draw an arc and determine the *dōtsuki* position. In other words 1–2, 1–3, 1–4, 1–5 and 1–6 are equal.

When the *hira hōzue* web is inserted at a slope equal to that of the roof, it becomes the hip slope.

Section of hip *shinzuka* web.

Section of *shinzuka* web

Shinzuka truss roof framing (Case 7).

The length of the hip top chord and the *tsuma* top chord are measured from *nyūchū*. However, *honchū* is used as the reference point to determine their line of *dōtsuke* and their common surface.

First, measure the distance to *nyūchū*, then measure back on the back scale, half the width of the hip top chord or the *tsuma* top chord to determine the *honchū* location.

To determine the hip top chord *dōtsuki* common surface point, ⊙ either follow directions as illustrated or determine by adding ½ the width of the *hira* top chord (on the front scale of the square) and ½ the width of the hip top chord (on the back scale of the square). The common surface point of the *tsuma* top chord is obtained by adding ½ the width of the *hira* top chord (on the back scale) and the *tsuma* top chord (on the front scale).

Usually the width of the *tsuma* top chord matches the *hira* top chord.

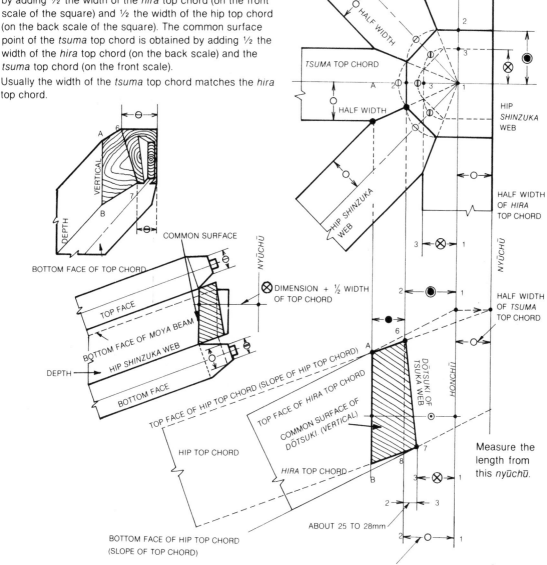

The front width of corner post is same as ◉

Dōtsuki line of the hip jack top chord.

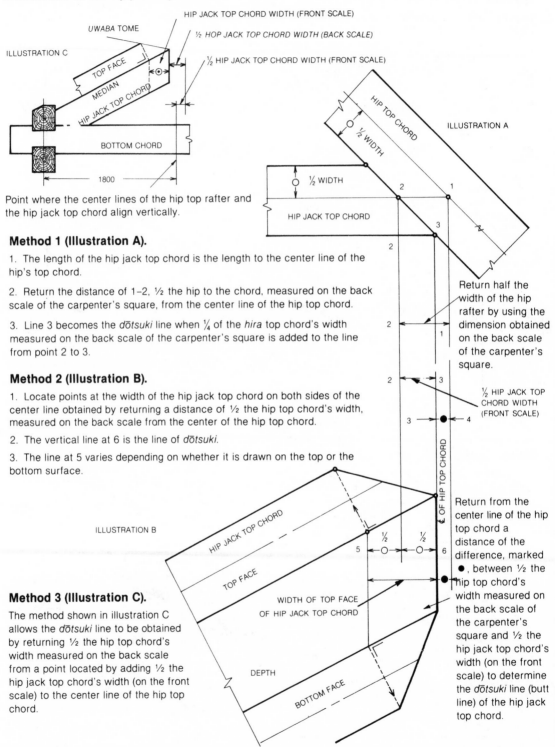

ILLUSTRATION C

UWABA TOME

TOP FACE

MEDIAN

HIP JACK TOP CHORD

BOTTOM CHORD

1800

HIP JACK TOP CHORD WIDTH (FRONT SCALE)

½ HOP JACK TOP CHORD WIDTH (BACK SCALE)

½ HIP JACK TOP CHORD WIDTH (FRONT SCALE)

HIP TOP CHORD

½ WIDTH

ILLUSTRATION A

½ WIDTH

HIP JACK TOP CHORD

Point where the center lines of the hip top rafter and the hip jack top chord align vertically.

Method 1 (Illustration A).

1. The length of the hip jack top chord is the length to the center line of the hip's top chord.

2. Return the distance of 1–2, ½ the hip to the chord, measured on the back scale of the carpenter's square, from the center line of the hip top chord.

3. Line 3 becomes the *dōtsuki* line when ¼ of the *hira* top chord's width measured on the back scale of the carpenter's square is added to the line from point 2 to 3.

Method 2 (Illustration B).

1. Locate points at the width of the hip jack top chord on both sides of the center line obtained by returning a distance of ½ the hip top chord's width, measured on the back scale from the center of the hip top chord.

2. The vertical line at 6 is the line of *dōtsuki*.

3. The line at 5 varies depending on whether it is drawn on the top or the bottom surface.

ILLUSTRATION B

HIP JACK TOP CHORD

TOP FACE

Method 3 (Illustration C).

The method shown in illustration C allows the *dōtsuki* line to be obtained by returning ½ the hip top chord's width measured on the back scale from a point located by adding ½ the hip jack top chord's width (on the front scale) to the center line of the hip top chord.

WIDTH OF TOP FACE OF HIP JACK TOP CHORD

DEPTH

BOTTOM FACE

₵ OF HIP TOP CHORD

Return half the width of the hip rafter by using the dimension obtained on the back scale of the carpenter's square.

½ HIP JACK TOP CHORD WIDTH (FRONT SCALE)

Return from the center line of the hip top chord a distance of the difference, marked ●, between ½ the hip top chord's width measured on the back scale of the carpenter's square and ½ the hip jack top chord's width (on the front scale) to determine the *dōtsuki* line (butt line) of the hip jack top chord.

Location line for bolts.

Location line for bolt on hip top chord.

Locate the center of the bolt at a distance 1–2, ½ the width of hip jack's top chord measured on the back scale of the carpenter's square, from *shūchū* 1 which is also the center line of the hip jack rafter. Locate the distance A–B to suit. The bolt holes on each side of the hip top chord are located identically.

Plan of hip top chord & hip jack top chord.

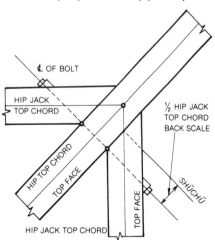

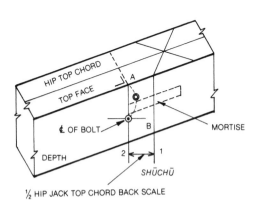

½ HIP JACK TOP CHORD BACK SCALE

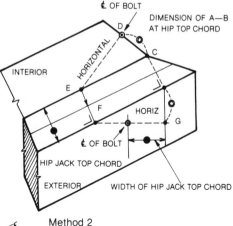

Dōtsuki line and location for bolt on hip jack top rafter.

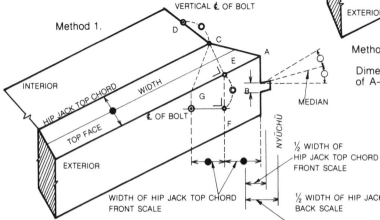

Method 2

Dimension of C—D is same as that of A—B on above illustration.

Dimension of E—P is same as that of A—B on above illustration.

Hip top chord and *tenbi moya* beam (Case 1).

Notch out the *tenbi moya* beam after aligning
it to the top face of the hip top chord.

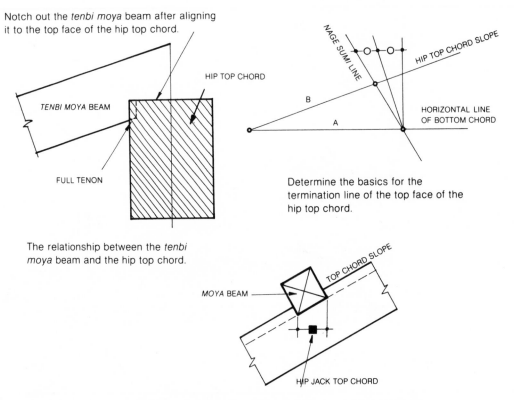

Determine the basics for the
termination line of the top face of the
hip top chord.

The relationship between the *tenbi
moya* beam and the hip top chord.

Method to determine the dimension of the *tenbi moya* beam.

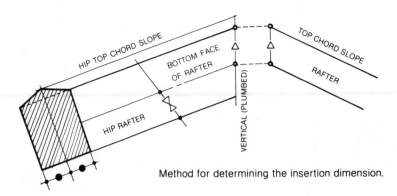

Method for determining the insertion dimension.

Hip top chord and *tenbi moya* beam (Case 1 continued).

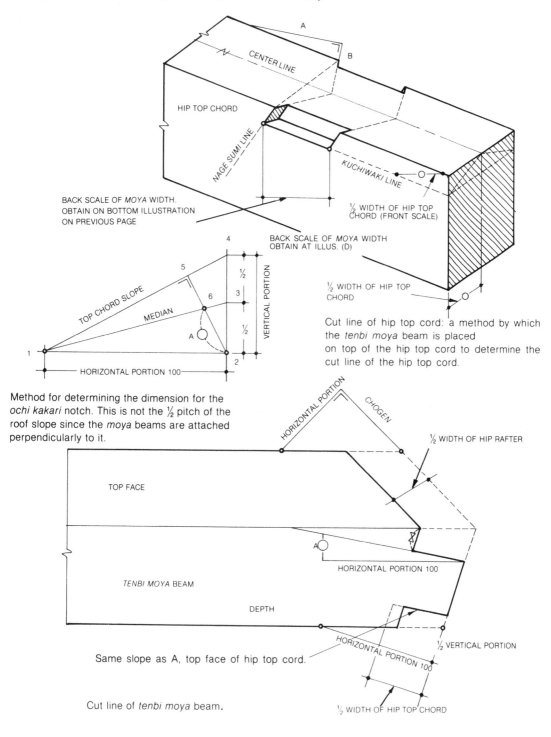

BACK SCALE OF *MOYA* WIDTH.
OBTAIN ON BOTTOM ILLUSTRATION
ON PREVIOUS PAGE

BACK SCALE OF *MOYA* WIDTH
OBTAIN AT ILLUS. (D)

½ WIDTH OF HIP TOP CHORD (FRONT SCALE)

½ WIDTH OF HIP TOP
CHORD

Cut line of hip top cord: a method by which
the *tenbi moya* beam is placed
on top of the hip top cord to determine the
cut line of the hip top cord.

Method for determining the dimension for the
ochi kakari notch. This is not the ½ pitch of the
roof slope since the *moya* beams are attached
perpendicularly to it.

½ WIDTH OF HIP RAFTER

Same slope as A, top face of hip top cord.

Cut line of *tenbi moya* beam.

Hip top chord and *tenbi moya* beam (Case 2).

This is a method in which the bottom portion on the *tenbi moya* beam is dadoed into the top face of the *tsuma* top chord. For details, see next page.

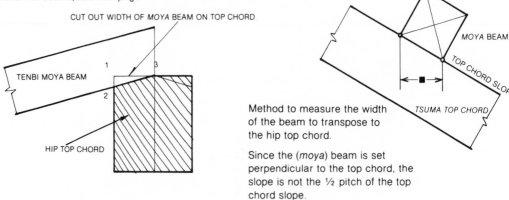

Method to measure the width of the beam to transpose to the hip top chord.

Since the (*moya*) beam is set perpendicular to the top chord, the slope is not the ½ pitch of the top chord slope.

The relationship between the hip top chord and the *tenbi moya* beam: Since point 3 on the top surface of the hip top chord will also be the point for one bottom edge of the *tenbi moya* beam, its other edge will be at the *kuchiwaki* line. Cut out 1–2–3 to form a sloped notch. (The slope will be ½ pitch.)

Method for determining the slope of the top surface. (This is not the reverse of *chogen*.) Using the slopes of A and B, draw on the side of slope of B.

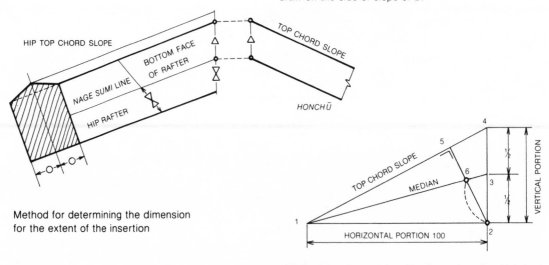

Method for determining the dimension for the extent of the insertion

Method for determining the dimension of *ochi kakari*.

Hip top chord and *tenbi moya* beam (Case 2 continued).

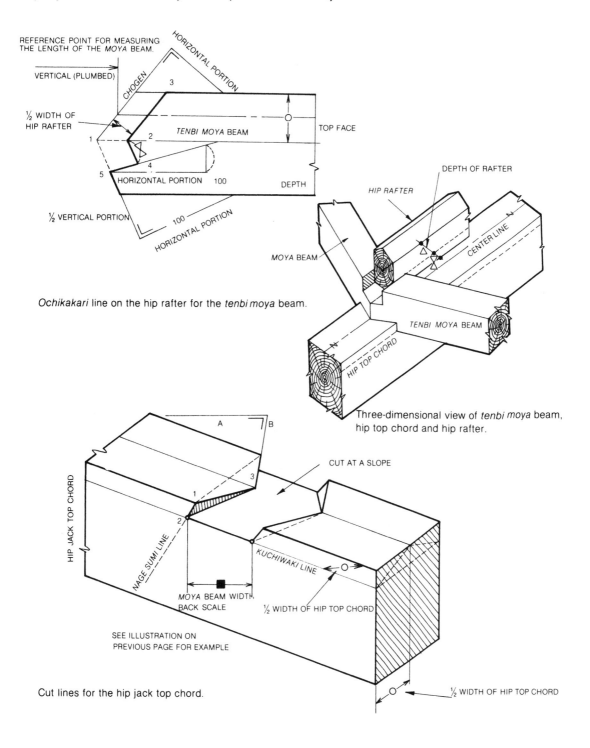

REFERENCE POINT FOR MEASURING
THE LENGTH OF THE *MOYA* BEAM.

VERTICAL (PLUMBED)

HORIZONTAL PORTION

CHOGEN

3

½ WIDTH OF
HIP RAFTER

TENBI *MOYA* BEAM

TOP FACE

1

2

4

5

HORIZONTAL PORTION   100

DEPTH

½ VERTICAL PORTION

100

HORIZONTAL PORTION

DEPTH OF RAFTER

HIP RAFTER

CENTER LINE

MOYA BEAM

Ochikakari line on the hip rafter for the *tenbi moya* beam.

TENBI *MOYA* BEAM

HIP TOP CHORD

Three-dimensional view of *tenbi moya* beam,
hip top chord and hip rafter.

A   B

CUT AT A SLOPE

3

1

HIP JACK TOP CHORD

2

NAGE SUMI LINE

KUCHIWAKI LINE

MOYA BEAM WIDTH,
BACK SCALE

½ WIDTH OF HIP TOP CHORD

SEE ILLUSTRATION ON
PREVIOUS PAGE FOR EXAMPLE

Cut lines for the hip jack top chord.

½ WIDTH OF HIP TOP CHORD

Hip top chord and *tenbimoya* beam (Case 3).

The following are methods for determining the cut lines on the hip top chord mentioned on the previous page (leaving the bottom face of the *moya* beam as is and the dado into the hip top chord).

Determining the slope of the cut lines on the top face.

Since the *moya* beam is set perpendicular to the top chord, this will not be the reverse slope of *chogen*.

It will be the same as the *nage sumi* line of the hip rafter.

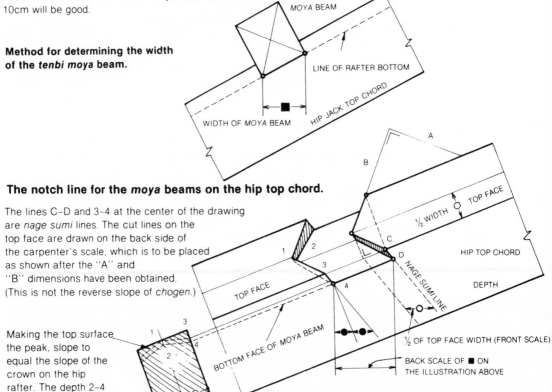

Method for determining the dimensions for "A" and "B": Draw the top chord slope as desired. Then measure the dimension of "A" horizontally. Though this dimension could be an arbitrary measure, about 10cm will be good.

With the dimensions of "A" and "B" obtained for illustration above left, determine the slope line of the notch on the top surface of the hip top chord.

Method for determining the width of the *tenbi moya* beam.

The notch line for the *moya* beams on the hip top chord.

The lines C–D and 3–4 at the center of the drawing are *nage sumi* lines. The cut lines on the top face are drawn on the back side of the carpenter's scale, which is to be placed as shown after the "A" and "B" dimensions have been obtained. (This is not the reverse slope of *chogen*.)

Making the top surface the peak, slope to equal the slope of the crown on the hip rafter. The depth 2–4 is the actual depth.

The bottom face of the *moya* beam on the hip rafter sits on a slope equal to that of the hip rafter's crown. In other words, on the edge of the top chord, the notch has the depth 3–4 but at the center line of the top face, it becomes shallow to the depth 1–2.

Note: As illustrated, match the actual depth of the *moya* beam on the slope drawn on the cross section of the hip top chord by using the same method to obtain the slope of the hip rafter crown.

Roof framing method using the *tai zuka* web truss.

Since *tai zuka* web truss roof framing was developed with the idea of utilizing the underside of the roof, it became a roof with greater spacing than the one with a *shinzuka* web. As shown on the illustration below left, the top chord terminates at the *nijū bari* beam (SB). Beyond that, common rafters (CR) are used to shape the roof. However, since it is not practical today in our country, the altered version as shown on the illustration below right is used. This is called *nijū goya* roofing. The portion above SB has been framed as in *shinzuka* truss roofing, and below SB braces are added to reinforce point 1.

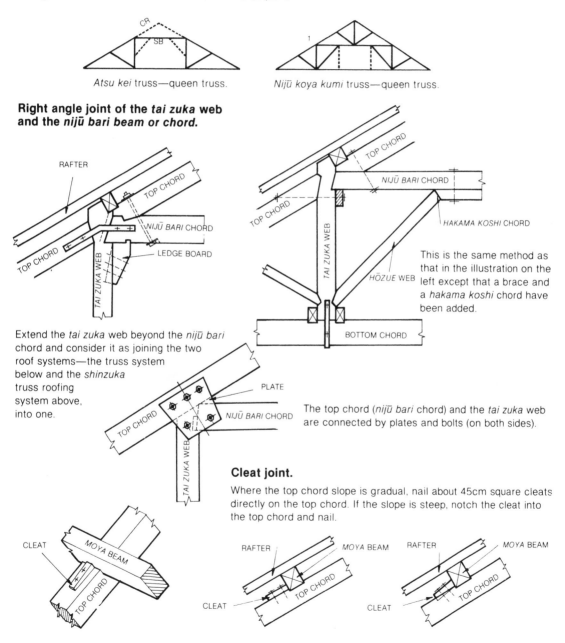

Atsu kei truss—queen truss.

Nijū koya kumi truss—queen truss.

Right angle joint of the *tai zuka* web and the *nijū bari* beam or chord.

This is the same method as that in the illustration on the left except that a brace and a *hakama koshi* chord have been added.

Extend the *tai zuka* web beyond the *nijū bari* chord and consider it as joining the two roof systems—the truss system below and the *shinzuka* truss roofing system above, into one.

The top chord (*nijū bari* chord) and the *tai zuka* web are connected by plates and bolts (on both sides).

Cleat joint.

Where the top chord slope is gradual, nail about 45cm square cleats directly on the top chord. If the slope is steep, notch the cleat into the top chord and nail.

An example of a saw tooth roof.

The saw tooth roof has been widely used as a factory roof but more recently, due to the increase in steel framing, light weight steel framing, and due to the ease of satisfying light and ventilation requirements, use of the saw tooth roof to obtain light has decreased. Thus, in this text, only one example will be shown.

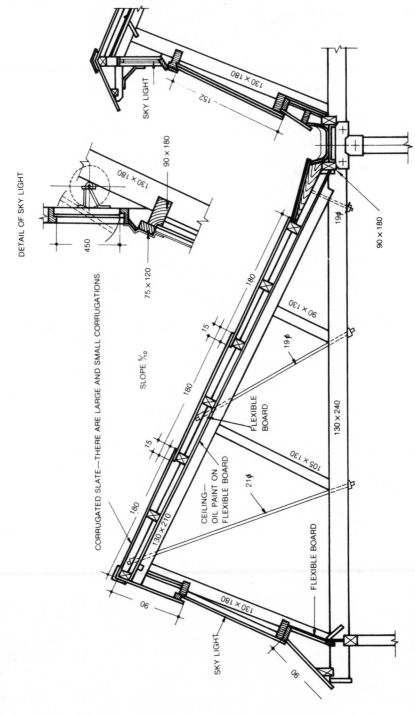

DETAIL OF SKY LIGHT

SKY LIGHT

130 × 180

152

90 × 180

130 × 180

450

75 × 120

CORRUGATED SLATE—THERE ARE LARGE AND SMALL CORRUGATIONS.

SLOPE ⁵⁄₁₀

180

15

180

15

180

130 × 210

90

130 × 180

SKY LIGHT

90

19ø

90 × 180

180

90 × 130

19ø

FLEXIBLE BOARD

130 × 240

105 × 130

21ø

CEILING—
OIL PAINT ON
FLEXIBLE BOARD

FLEXIBLE BOARD

Note: ø refers to diameter.

11

Gable Construction

The eave at the end of the gable roof is called the *soba noki* eave or *keraba*.

Among details of the gable roof, there are those with the ends of the *moya* beam and *keta* beams exposed, some with a *taruki kei* facia (facia piece with a depth twice that of the rafter) covering the ends of the *moya* beam, and others with a *hafū ita* facia covering the *moya* beam ends.

The further the *soba noki* eave extends out, the better it looks. An especially large roof requires a deep eave. The depth of the eave is determined by the types of roofing materials used, such as Japanese clay shingles (*kawara*), cement roofing, and metal standing seam roofing. In cases where the eave ends are designed to give a light feeling, the *soba noki* eave has the ends of the *moya* and *keta* beams exposed and either painted white to prevent dry rot or are covered with metal caps. At the overhang of the roof, the rafter ends are exposed.

On some mansions and large country houses, *gegyo* (an ornamental piece) and *hafū* facia are used. These decorations are slightly different from those seen on shrine and temple architecture.

Framing and detailing methods for gable roofs.

The roof end portion which extends beyond the wall is called the *soba* eave or *keraba*. Though the deeper the *soba* eave the better the form, the most common depths used are from 45cm to 75cm. The depth of the *keraba* or *soba* eave is determined by the total width of the roof (total width of the roofing material) and the size of the Japanese clay tiles. In other words, no partial tiles are used. Where there are clay tiles, there is a little margin for play with the dimensions. But in the case of thick cement tiles, the dimensions, especially for the forming work of the roofing, have to be accurate since there is hardly any margin.

Soba eave of the gable roof.

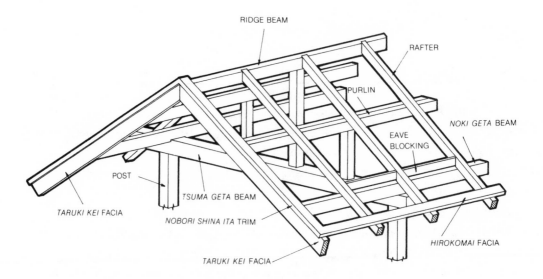

Example where the ends of the *keta* beams are to be hidden.

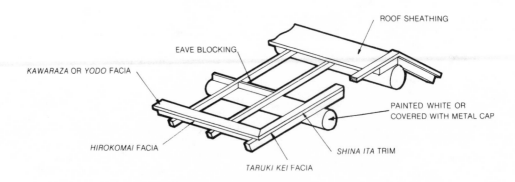

Example where the ends of the *keta* beams are to be exposed.

Framing and detailing methods for gable roofs (continued).

Joint for *yodo* facia and *nobori yodo* facia.

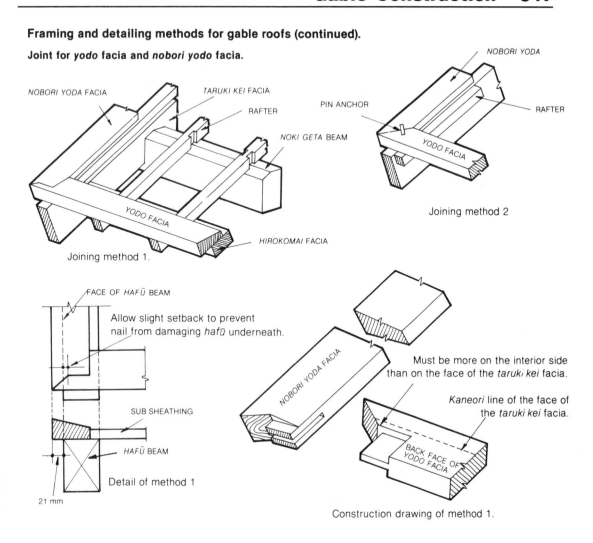

NOBORI YODA FACIA

TARUKI KEI FACIA

RAFTER

NOKI GETA BEAM

YODO FACIA

HIROKOMAI FACIA

Joining method 1.

NOBORI YODA

PIN ANCHOR

RAFTER

YODO FACIA

Joining method 2

FACE OF *HAFŪ* BEAM

Allow slight setback to prevent nail from damaging *hafū* underneath.

SUB SHEATHING

HAFŪ BEAM

Detail of method 1

21 mm

NOBORI YODA FACIA

Must be more on the interior side than on the face of the *taruki kei* facia.

Kaneori line of the face of the *taruki kei* facia.

BACK FACE OF YODO FACIA

Construction drawing of method 1.

Taruki kei facia and hirokomai facia.

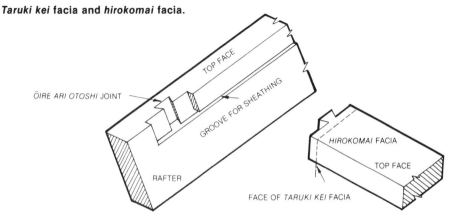

ŌIRE ARI OTOSHI JOINT

TOP FACE

GROOVE FOR SHEATHING

RAFTER

HIROKOMAI FACIA

TOP FACE

FACE OF *TARUKI KEI* FACIA

Framing and detailing methods for gable roofs (Case 2).

Though the deeper the *soba* eave the better the form, the most common depths used are between 45cm to 75cm. A depth equalling the rafter spacing is also used. In cases where the *soba* eave extension is greater than 45cm, an addition of 1 rafter has to be included at the midpoint of the eave extension.

Method to determine the depth of the *soba* eave.

The basic rule for determining the depth of the *soba* eave is as stated above, but a more accurate method is to make the total length of the roof including the *soba* eave to be a multiple of the roof tile dimension (unit dimension of roofing material). This method is also used to determine the total width of the roof.

Total width of roof—(Left tile width + Right tile width) divided by the exposed dimension of the main or field tile equals the total width, such that it will be evenly divided.

Note: The Japanese clay tile's exposed width is 250mm but it is calculated at 255mm with the addition of a margin. For thick cement tiles (English tile), their standard dimension of 303mm is used as the unit dimension.

Example with Japanese clay tiles.

Note that the width of a tile may vary at different places. When a roof is to be tiled, its length must be divided by the exposed dimension of a tile. Also, the location of the *hirokamai* and *hafū* facia must be decided with consideration given to the tile overhang.

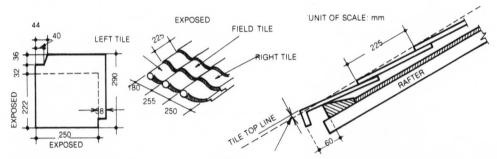

Dimension of exposed portion of tile. The actual dimension of the exposed portion of a shingle is used as a unit multiplier to determine the roof length.

Tile closure to be 20mm higher.

The finish of the rafter and overhang of a shingle at the eave end. The end starter shingle is raised slightly above the others by using a higher cant strip. (Sometimes, *hirokomai* or *yodo* facias are raised higher.)

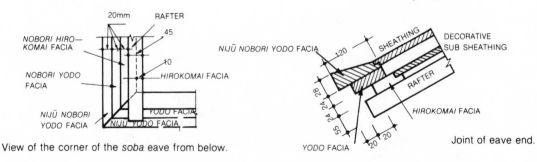

View of the corner of the *soba* eave from below.

Joint of eave end.

Examples with Japanese clay tiles (continued).

The tiles' overhanging dimension for the finishing work at the eave's end is determined by the tile layout, therefore the spacing between them and the *nobori yodo* facia is not constant. If the spacing becomes too narrow, the effect at the eaves end is not desirable, so the roof framing work must be done with care.

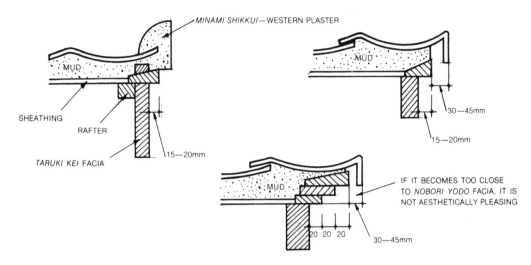

Example with thick cement tiles (similar to English tiles).

There are four types of thick cement tiles: the flat type, S-shaped type, Japanese type, and Western type. There are two flat types of tile: the first and the second type. The flat types are commonly seen on residences. In order to determine the length of a gable roof and the *soba* eave, the dimension shown on the illustration below is used as a modular. However for the total width of the roof, 150mm (5 *sūn*) must be added to it. (The exposed dimension of tile to be used is 303mm or 1 *shaku*.)

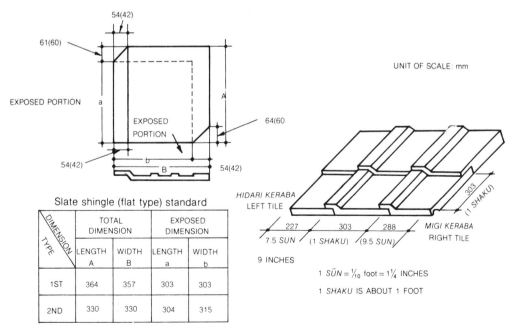

Slate shingle (flat type) standard

DIMENSION / TYPE	TOTAL DIMENSION		EXPOSED DIMENSION	
	LENGTH A	WIDTH B	LENGTH a	WIDTH b
1ST	364	357	303	303
2ND	330	330	304	315

UNIT OF SCALE: mm

HIDARI KERABA LEFT TILE

MIGI KERABA RIGHT TILE

1 *SŪN* = $\frac{1}{10}$ foot = $1\frac{1}{4}$ INCHES

1 *SHAKU* IS ABOUT 1 FOOT

Metal roofing.

The construction method for metal roofing is discussed below.

1. The materials used for metal roofing are tin, aluminum, stainless steel, Monel, zinc, copper, and others.

2. There are wood framing systems with and without rafters.

a. Framing systems using rafters: Rafters are placed with the same spacing as the ribs for the seams on metal roofing. When this is done the ribs are prevented from sliding because they are nailed onto the rafters. The sheathing is most often nailed on but when done with care it is grooved in. Since not all the nails for the ribs can be expected not to hit the rafters, the sheathing used should have a minimum thickness of 12mm. Wood planks are not the only materials used for sheathing. There are insulation board, plywood, particle board, and cement board. Where the sheathing is of planks, insulation boards are installed for thermal protection. On top of these is placed the waterproofing membrane, such as building paper and felts.

b. Framing systems without rafters: In this method the sheathing is secured directly to the *moya* beam. The spacing of the *moya* beams should be about 60mm, less than in the situation where rafters are used. The thickness of the sheathing should be at least 18mm–20mm and should be tongue and grooved. The nails used should be long. The *hanagarami* used must be greater than 40 × 20mm, or else the top and the bottom of the eave will not align.

Varieties and applications of metal roofing.   UNIT SCALE: mm

Type	Working dimension	Application
Stock item	419	Residences and small buildings
Special 1	364	Factory—warehouse—gymnasium
Special 2	321	Special structure at location with high altitude and strong wind.

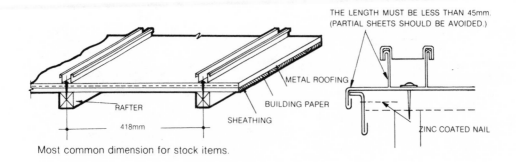

THE LENGTH MUST BE LESS THAN 45mm.
(PARTIAL SHEETS SHOULD BE AVOIDED.)

METAL ROOFING

BUILDING PAPER

SHEATHING

RAFTER

418mm

ZINC COATED NAIL

Most common dimension for stock items.

Taruki kei facia.

The *taruki kei* facia is a finishing piece which covers the ends of the purlin (*moya*) and main (*keta*) beams like the *hafū* facia which will be discussed later. The *taruki kei* facia is not just shallower than the *hafū* facia. *Taruki kei* facia originated during the *Edo* period when farmers and merchants were not permitted to incorporate the *hafū* facia on their roofs. They installed a piece which was narrower and straighter and called it *taruki kei* facia. *Taruki kei* facia has a depth twice that of the common rafter, and a width equal to that of the rafter. It is joined to the *noki keta* beam with an *oiire ariotoshi* joint and to the *moya* beam with a ladle shaped tenon. Another method for determining the size is to take .05–.06 of its length for the depth, and allow the top and bottom width to be ½ of the depth.

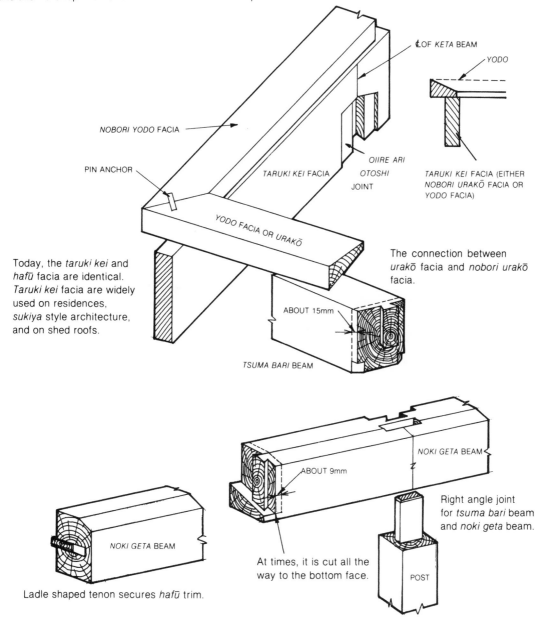

⅊OF *KETA* BEAM

YODO

NOBORI YODO FACIA

PIN ANCHOR

TARUKI KEI FACIA

OIIRE ARI OTOSHI JOINT

TARUKI KEI FACIA (EITHER *NOBORI URAKŌ* FACIA OR YODO FACIA)

YODO FACIA OR *URAKŌ*

Today, the *taruki kei* and *hafū* facia are identical. *Taruki kei* facia are widely used on residences, *sukiya* style architecture, and on shed roofs.

The connection between *urakō* facia and *nobori urakō* facia.

ABOUT 15mm

TSUMA BARI BEAM

NOKI GETA BEAM

ABOUT 9mm

NOKI GETA BEAM

Right angle joint for *tsuma bari* beam and *noki geta* beam.

Ladle shaped tenon secures *hafū* trim.

At times, it is cut all the way to the bottom face.

POST

Hirokomai facia.

The method for cutting lumber to obtain a certain grain (wood selection) (*kitori*) for the *hirokomai* facia is usually *hira masa* (similar to the common quarter sawed cut), but for quality work on the lower roof the method is *nihō masa* (close to radial cut of quarter sawed).

The shape of the *hirokomai* facia:

When the post is 105mm square (3.5 *sun*), the *hirokomai* shape should be 24 × 12 × 90 (mm).

When the post is 120mm (4.0 *sun*) square, the size of the *hirokomai* facia should be 28 × 12 × 105 (mm).

The thickness of the back end is 12mm, matching the thickness of the sheathing. In the case of clay shingle roofing, the *yodo* facia or *kawaraza* cant strip is added to make the total height equal to the thickness of the clay shingle. However, due to an optical illusion, the clay starter shingle will appear to be drooping, so sometimes the starter shingle end is raised about 25mm. Though *fukido* cant strips are usually used to adjust the height, it would be better to use an about 35mm deep *hirokomai* facia and adjust the difference with a *kawaraza* or *fukido* cant strip, or with a *yodo* facia. In the *Kinki* district, *kawaraza* cant strips and *hirokomai* facia are used together, and this combination is called the *kawaraza* cant strip. The size of the exposed dimension used is from 50mm to 55mm thick.

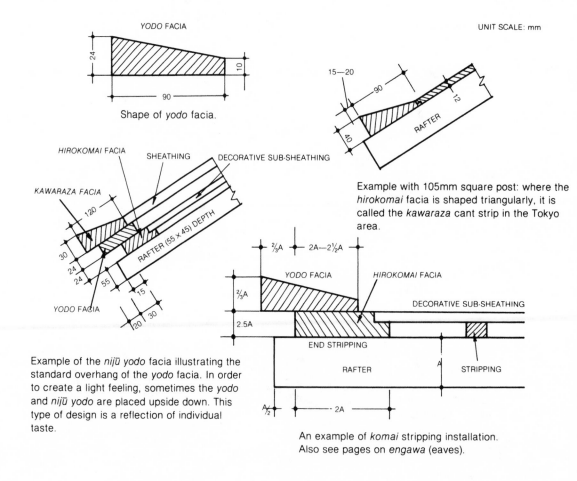

Shape of *yodo* facia.

Example with 105mm square post: where the *hirokomai* facia is shaped triangularly, it is called the *kawaraza* cant strip in the Tokyo area.

Example of the *nijū yodo* facia illustrating the standard overhang of the *yodo* facia. In order to create a light feeling, sometimes the *yodo* and *nijū yodo* are placed upside down. This type of design is a reflection of individual taste.

An example of *komai* stripping installation. Also see pages on *engawa* (eaves).

Hafū facia.

A decorative panel which accentuates the shape of the gable roof, and which has a depth similar to that of the *taruki kei* facia is called a *hafū* facia. It is used as ornamentation on shrine and temple architecture and on custom designed residences.

1. *Kirizuma* (cut) *hafū* facia, *sugu hafū* facia, *sori* (curved) *hafū* facia, *mukuri* (arched) *hafū* facia, *nagare* (sagging) *hafū* facia, *irimoya* (hip gable) *hafū* facia, *kara* (Chinese) *hafū* facia, and *chidori* (temple) *hafū* facia.

Kirizuma hafū facia.

The *mukuri hafū* facia.

Shape of the *hafū* facia.

1. Locate *koshi haba* at midpoint of the *hafū* facia's length. There are cases where *koshi haba* is located at $\frac{2}{5}$ or $\frac{3}{7}$ of the length from *ogami* end.

2. The depth of *koshi haba* should be $\frac{6}{100}$ or $\frac{8}{100}$ of the total length.

3. *Mukuri*'s depth should be $\frac{1.5}{100}$ to $\frac{2}{100}$ of the total length. (*Mukuri* is the height of the curve or arc from an imaginery straight line between two furthermost end points. For roofs of shrines, temples, and other large roofs, the *mukuri* should be about $\frac{3}{100}$ of the total length.)

4. *Ogami* (also called *hafū gashira*) should be 1.2 times the depth of *koshi haba*.

5. *Kijiri* (also called *hafū jiri*) is to be 1.1 times the *koshi haba* depth.

Note: The carpenters say *nanbu* for *nanwari*.

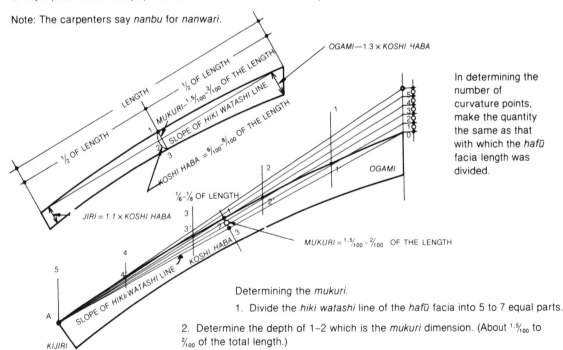

In determining the number of curvature points, make the quantity the same as that with which the *hafū* facia length was divided.

Determining the *mukuri*.

1. Divide the *hiki watashi* line of the *hafū* facia into 5 to 7 equal parts.

2. Determine the depth of 1–2 which is the *mukuri* dimension. (About $\frac{1.5}{100}$ to $\frac{2}{100}$ of the total length.)

3. On the vertical line of *ogami*, place an equal amount of points to the amount the facia was divided, and space the points a distance of 1–2 apart.

4. Connect point "A" at the *kijiri* end with points 0 to 5 at the vertical extension line of the *ogami* end. Connect the points of the vertical lines 1 through 4, which equally divide these lines and the length of the *hiki watashi* line, with points 1' through 4'.

5. Connected points 1'–4' forms the curvature of the *hafū* facia's top surface. To mark the actual curves use a thin defect-free piece of wood and bend it.

Sori hafū facia or *teri hafū* facia.

This facia is used mostly on shrines, temples, castles, and palaces, and hardly ever on residences. In shrine and temple architecture, the *ippon sori* facia, which has a sharp curvature is used, while on other structures, the curvature is not as sharp.

Shaping of the *sori hafū* facia.

1. Locate *koshi haba* at the midpoint of the *hafū* facia length. There are cases where *koshi haba* is located at $\frac{2}{5}$ or $\frac{3}{7}$ of the length from the *ogami* end.

2. The depth of *koshi haba* should be between $\frac{7}{100}$ to $\frac{10}{100}$ of the length. (It is recommended that the *sori hafū* facia be made thinner.)

3. The *tarumi* depth should be between $\frac{4}{100}$ to $\frac{3}{100}$ of the length.

4. The depth of *ogami* should be 1.1 to 1.3 times that of *koshi haba*.

5. The depth of *ogami* should be 1.1 times that of *koshi haba*.

Determining the shape of the *sori hafū* facia.

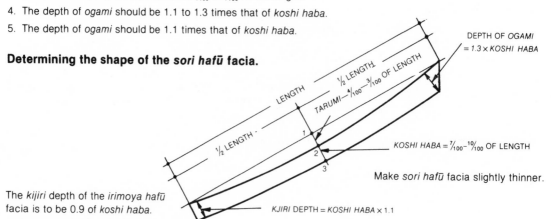

DEPTH OF *OGAMI* = 1.3 × *KOSHI HABA*

½ LENGTH

LENGTH

½ LENGTH

TARUMI − $\frac{4}{100}$−$\frac{3}{100}$ OF LENGTH

KOSHI HABA = $\frac{7}{100}$−$\frac{10}{100}$ OF LENGTH

Make *sori hafū* facia slightly thinner.

The *kijiri* depth of the *irimoya hafū* facia is to be 0.9 of *koshi haba*.

KJIRI DEPTH = *KOSHI HABA* × 1.1

Determining the *tarumi* depth.

1. Divide the *hiki watashi* line of the *hafū* facia equally (5 to 7 equal parts).

2. Determine the *tarumi* depth 1–2. (About $\frac{4}{100}$ to $\frac{3}{100}$ of the length.)

3. At the vertical line of *ogami*, place the same number of points as the amount the facia was divided into, and space the points a distance of 1–2 apart.

4. Connect point "A" at the *kijiri* end with points 0 to 5 at the vertical extension line of the *ogami* end. Connect the points of vertical lines 1 through 4 which equally divide these lines and the length of the *hiki watashi* line with points 1′ through 4′.

5. Connected points 1′—4′ form the curvature of the *hafū* facia's top surface.

If the length is divided into five parts, then the depth should also be divided into five parts.

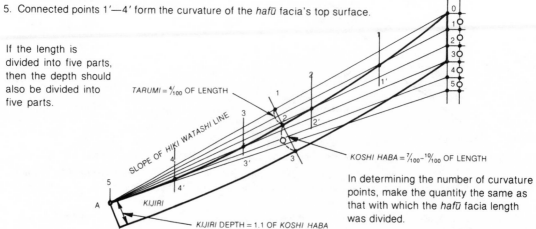

TARUMI = $\frac{4}{100}$ OF LENGTH

SLOPE OF HIKI WATASHI LINE

KOSHI HABA = $\frac{7}{100}$−$\frac{10}{100}$ OF LENGTH

KIJIRI

KIJIRI DEPTH = 1.1 OF *KOSHI HABA*

In determining the number of curvature points, make the quantity the same as that with which the *hafū* facia length was divided.

Finishing of the *kiritsuma hafū* facia.

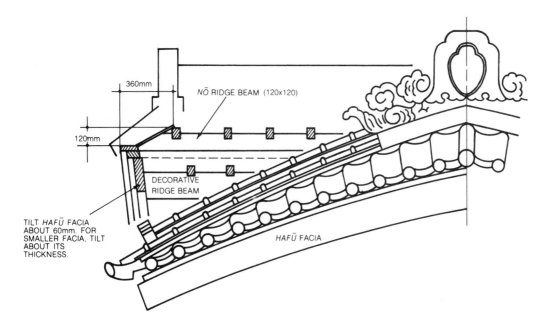

Kamuri of the *hafū* facia.

Tilting the *hafū* facia forward is called *kamuri* of the *hafū* facia. If the *hafū* facia is installed vertically, it gives the appearance of being turned upward when seen from below. To counter this optical illusion, the upper portion of the *ogami* end is turned slightly forward.

Kamuri's dimension is determined by the height it is positioned and by the location from where it is viewed. For example, the angle of vision is different when seeing the *hafū* facia on a main roof or on an entrance canopy. Also the facias are located at a different height. Thus the *kamuri* dimension is determined with consideration to these conditions. Try to set the *kamuri* as perpendicularly as possible visually. The general rule is as follows:

1. In the case of a small *hafū* facia, tilt it about 1.5 times its thickness. This is called *ichimai* (one board) or *ichimai han* (one and one half boards) tilt by the carpenters.

2. For large *hafū* facias and for those positioned high the tilt should be about 90 to 100mm.

3. The tilt is also about 2cm for every 30cm of the *hafū* facia depth. (Depth measured vertically.)

Hafū facia and *nobori yodo* or *nobori urakō* facia.

Regarding the amount of overlap of *nobori yodo* or *nobori urakō* facias over *hafū* facia will appear too prominent. But if the overhang is increased slightly, so that their shadows will fall on the *hafū* facia, they will appear more elegant.

Kamuri of the roof.

If the *nobori urakō* or *nobori yodo* facia's overhang is small on a large roof, the *hafū* facia will appear too strong, therefore, they should extend out about 60mm to 100mm so as to cast their shadows on the *hafū* facia giving it a serene appearance.

Framing of the *irimoya* roof.

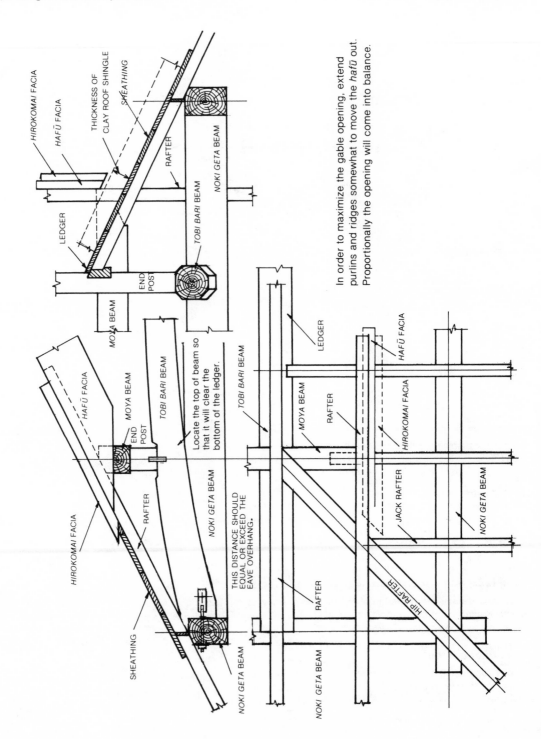

In order to maximize the gable opening, extend purlins and ridges somewhat to move the *hafū* out. Proportionally the opening will come into balance.

HIROKOMAI FACIA

HAFŪ FACIA

THICKNESS OF CLAY ROOF SHINGLE

SHEATHING

RAFTER

NOKI GETA BEAM

TOBI BARI BEAM

LEDGER

END POST

MOYA BEAM

LEDGER

HAFŪ FACIA

MOYA BEAM

END POST

TOBI BARI BEAM

TOBI BARI BEAM

Locate the top of beam so that it will clear the bottom of the ledger.

RAFTER

HIROKOMAI FACIA

NOKI GETA BEAM

RAFTER

JACK RAFTER

HIROKOMAI FACIA

NOKI GETA BEAM

THIS DISTANCE SHOULD EQUAL OR EXCEED THE EAVE OVERHANG.

RAFTER

HIP RAFTER

SHEATHING

NOKI GETA BEAM

NOKI GETA BEAM

Irimoya hafū facia.

The method for determining the *tarumi* (slack—convex shaped *hafū* facia) and *mukuri* (bow—concave shaped *hafū* facia) of the *irimoya hafū* facia is the same as that of the aforementioned common *hafū* facia. The main difference is that the width of the *kijiri* end is 0.9 of its *koshi haba* depth, instead of the 1.1 used for the common *hafū* facia. Give careful consideration to the following:

1. If the width of *koshi haba* is made slightly narrower than the common *hafū* facia, the *irimoya hafū* facia will appear better proportioned.

2. To determine the *koshi haba* location (point of *tarumi* or *mukumi*), divide the length of the *irimoya hafū* facia into 5 equal lengths. If the *koshi haba* is located at $\frac{2}{5}$ of the length away from the *ogami* end, the facia will appear strong at the point of *tarumi* or *mukuri*.

3. For a *sori hafū* facia, increase the *tarumi* slightly. If it is not enough, the curve line will appear straight.

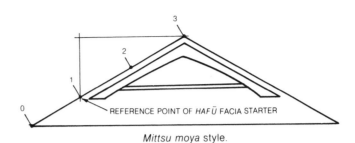

Mittsu moya style.

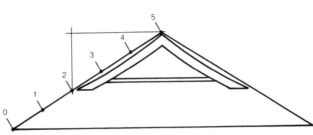

Itsutsu moya style.

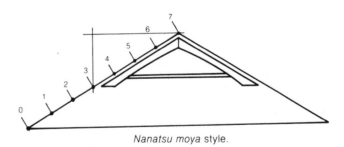

Nanatsu moya style.

Mittsu (three) moya style: The total length from the ridge to the eave ends of the roof is divided into three equal parts. The end of the first space from the eave is the reference point for the lower end of the *hafū* facia (front face). This style is the largest and most commonly used among the *irimoya hafū* facias.

The mittsu han (three-and-a-half) moya style: Divide the roof length into seven equal spaces, and locate the reference point at the second point.

The itsutsu (five) moya style: This is a style with the starter reference point located at the second point of the spaces which equally divide the roof into five.

The nanatsu (seven) moya style: This is a style with the starter reference point located on the third point of the spaces which equally divide the roof into seven.

The shape of the *irimoya hafū* facia.

The length of the *hafū* facia is determined by the *moya* style shown in the illustration.

The *mukuri hafū* facia.

1. The location for *koshi haba* is either at the midpoint of the length or at a point $\frac{2}{5}$ of the total length from the *ogami* end.
2. The depth of *koshi haba* should be $\frac{8}{100}$ to $\frac{10}{100}$ of the length.
3. *Mukuri* should be $\frac{1.5}{100}$ to $\frac{2}{100}$ of the length.
4. The depth of *ogami* should be 1.3 of *koshi haba*'s depth.
5. The depth of *kijiri* should be 0.9 of *koshi haba*'s depth.

Sori hafū facia.

1. The location for *koshi haba* is either at the midpoint of the length or at a point $\frac{2}{5}$ of the total length from the *ogami* end.
2. The depth of *koshi haba* should be $\frac{8}{100}$ to $\frac{10}{100}$ of the length.
3. *Tarumi* should be $\frac{1}{100}$ to $\frac{2}{100}$ of the length.
4. The depth of *ogami* should be 1.3 of *koshi haba*'s depth.
5. The depth of *kijiri* should be 0.9 of *koshi haba*'s depth.

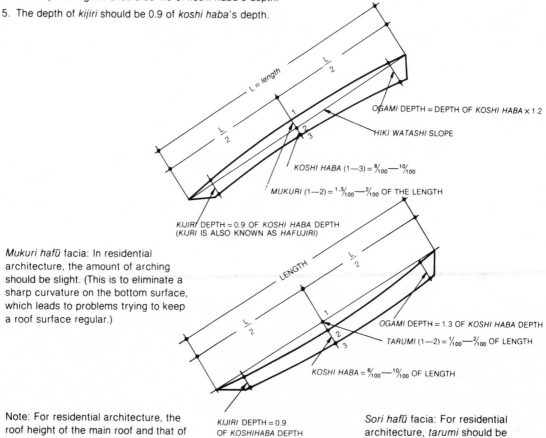

L = length

OGAMI DEPTH = DEPTH OF *KOSHI HABA* × 1.2

HIKI WATASHI SLOPE

KOSHI HABA (1—3) = $\frac{8}{100}$ — $\frac{10}{100}$

MUKURI (1—2) = $\frac{1.5}{100}$ — $\frac{2}{100}$ OF THE LENGTH

KIJIRI DEPTH = 0.9 OF *KOSHI HABA* DEPTH
(*KIJRI* IS ALSO KNOWN AS *HAFUJIRI*)

LENGTH

OGAMI DEPTH = 1.3 OF *KOSHI HABA* DEPTH

TARUMI (1—2) = $\frac{1}{100}$ — $\frac{2}{100}$ OF LENGTH

KOSHI HABA = $\frac{6}{100}$ — $\frac{10}{100}$ OF LENGTH

KIJIRI DEPTH = 0.9
OF *KOSHIHABA* DEPTH

Mukuri hafū facia: In residential architecture, the amount of arching should be slight. (This is to eliminate a sharp curvature on the bottom surface, which leads to problems trying to keep a roof surface regular.)

Note: For residential architecture, the roof height of the main roof and that of the entrance canopy are not the same, therefore take special care.

Sori hafū facia: For residential architecture, *tarumi* should be somewhat accentuated and the width narrowed.

Mayukaki carving on the hafū facia board.

This carving is also called *mayujakkuri*.

The example shown of *mayukaki* carving here has proportions which are used mainly on shrine and temple architecture. For general work, refer to the example and make it with one or two carvings. It is important that the carving be deep, since shallow ones will appear weak. Make the cut at least 2cm deep.

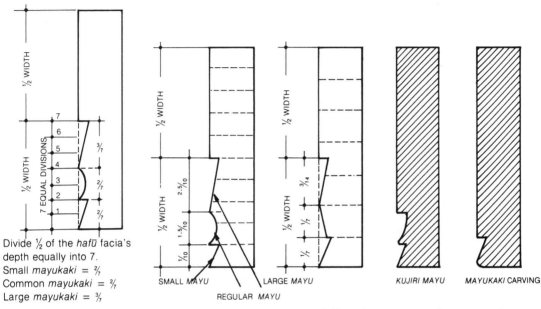

Divide ½ of the *hafū* facia's depth equally into 7.
Small *mayukaki* = 2⁄7
Common *mayukaki* = 2⁄7
Large *mayukaki* = 3⁄7

Method of *mayukaki* carving.   10 *Mayukaki* carving.   7 *Mayukaki* carving.   Common carving.

SMALL MAYU   LARGE MAYU   KUJIRI MAYU   MAYUKAKI CARVING
REGULAR MAYU

Right angle joint of the kijiri end.

The section of the *hafū* facia originally was the simple rectangle of a flat board, but later, ornamental carvings were added on the back. *Kijiri*, like the *hafū* facia, was originally simply cut square but later became decorative. Look at the *sode giri mayukaki* carvings on the *koryo* beams of shrine and temple architecture as a reference for *kijiri* decorations.

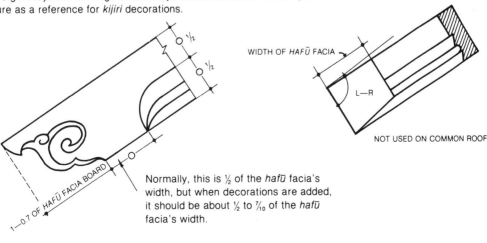

WIDTH OF HAFŪ FACIA

L—R

NOT USED ON COMMON ROOF

1—0.7 OF HAFŪ FACIA BOARD

Normally, this is ½ of the *hafū* facia's width, but when decorations are added, it should be about ½ to 7⁄10 of the *hafū* facia's width.

Kikai keibiki—Machine marking guage.

The marking guage illustrated below which can be easily made is used for laying out the *mayukaki* carving on the *hafū* facia board.

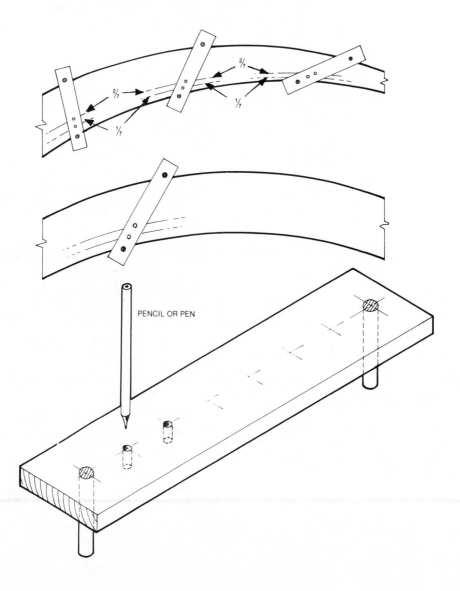

PENCIL OR PEN

Always keep the wooden pegs in contact with both edges of the *hafū*. The holes for marking are set at $\frac{1}{7}$ and $\frac{2}{7}$ of the distance between positioning pegs. Move the marking guage up the *hafū* (after it has been properly shaped) and the guage will automatically mark for *mayu* cuts at $\frac{1}{7}$ and $\frac{2}{7}$ of its span.

Right angle joint of the *ogami* of the *hafū* facia (Case 1).

Example using a *daimochi shachi* pin.

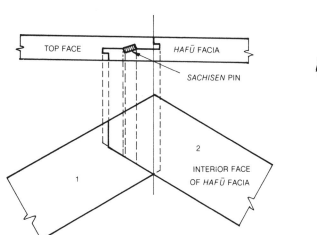

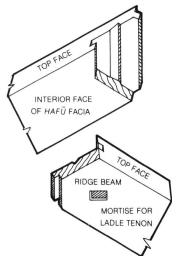

This is a joint at the *ogami* end commonly used on *mukuri hafū* facia. At the inside face of the joint, one *hafū* facia is extended out and interlocked with a *mechigai hozo* mortise and tenon joint at its end. Then they are tied at the top surface with a *shachisen* pin.

Example using *suitsukisan* (wood scab) and a *shachisen* pin.

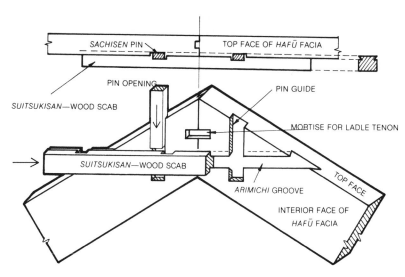

Commonly used right angle joint for the *ogami* of the *sori hafū* facia. On the inside face, install the wood scab (*suitsukisan*) and secure it from the top face with a pin. The pin should be installed in such a way as to pull the *ogami* tightly together.

Note: In order to pull the *ogami* together, consider the relationship of the pin cutout between the pin guide and *suitsukisan*.

Right angle joint of the *ogami* of the *hafū* facia (Case 2).

This method is the most appropriate one when the thickness of the *hafū* facia is greater than 45mm.

Depending on the thickness of the *hafū* facia, a 9mm bolt can be sufficient. The cut out shape as shown in the illustration for the washer may have to be enlarged at a certain place, depending on the thickness of the *hafū* facia. The *mechigai hozo* tenon at the *ogami* is about 24mm wide by 24mm long, but adjust this accordingly, as the thickness of the *hafū* facia dictates.

Joint using steel rod (bolt).

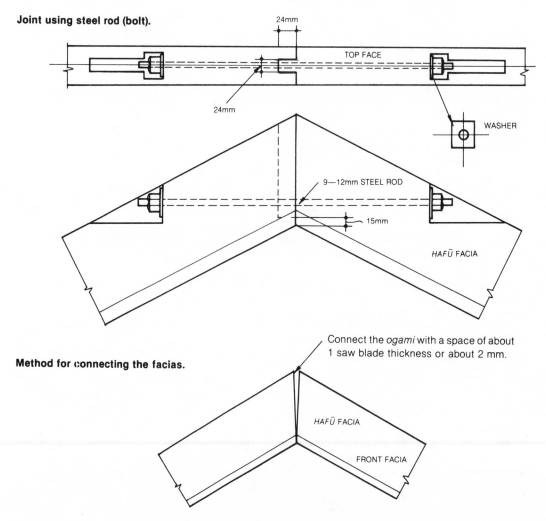

Method for connecting the facias.

This space is provided so that when a load is applied, it will close.

Finishing of the *irimoya hafū* facia.

The slope of the *urakō* facia.

1. *Mukuri hafū* facia.
It is difficult to determine the slope of the *urakō* facia. Do not make the slope steep.

2. *Teri hafū* facia.
Align the top face of the *urakō* facia with that of the ridge beam.

Kamuri of the *hafū* facia is 60mm from the *hafū* board. *Kamuri* of the roof is 90mm from the *hafū* board.

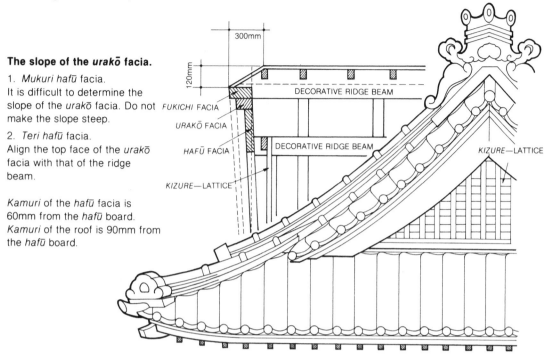

Kizure lattice work. This is used where the end wall is large or when a *chidori hafū* facia is used. There are many methods used to construct *kizure koshi* lattice.

The end of the *irimoya* (portion of the roof to which the *hafū* facia is attached) should have a slope about $\frac{5}{100}$ less steep than the rafter slope. This results in a *fure sumi* corner on the lower roof, as well as the *hafū* facia's becoming larger and there being more leeway at the end wall.

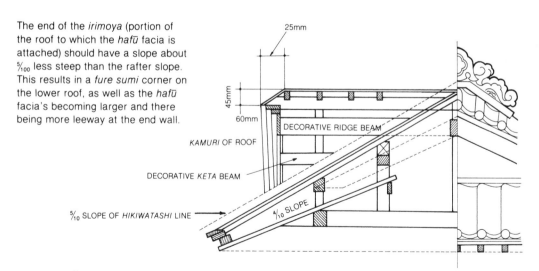

Note on *hafū* facia: On ordinary buildings, especially on residences, *mukuri hafū* facias are widely used. *Teri hafū* facias are seldom used, but there are a few instances where they are used on an entrance canopy and on a small roof. *Kamuri* and *sori* are seldom incorporated on ordinary buildings, unlike for shrine and temple architecture.

Gegyo (Case 1).

Gegyo is an ornamental piece which covers the end of the ridge beam on shrine and temple architecture (except in the *shinmyo zukuri* style). It is also used on common houses. *Gegyo* is quite commonly seen on farm houses in the *Kinki* district. Unlike the symmetrical and ceremonious type seen on shrine and temple architecture, the *gegyo* on common houses has ornamentation which appears as a fragmented single motif of an arbor, of foliage, or a whirlpool (eddy). Many of the designs appear to be fragmented. There are also many *gegyo* with fins. The *gegyo* must be designed with consideration for the size and the length of the *hafū* facia, the type of *hafū* facia, such as *kiritsuma*, *irimoya*, and *kara*, and the steepness of the slope. The examples shown in the text will be mainly those used on shrines and temples.

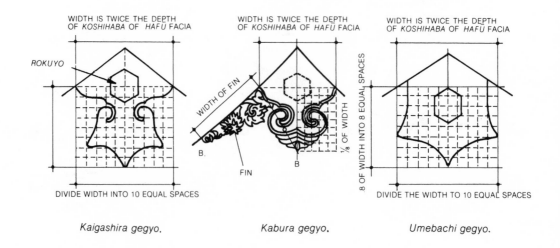

Kaigashira gegyo.   Kabura gegyo.   Umebachi gegyo.

It is necessary to change the proportion of the *gegyo* on houses with a slope less than $^{5.5}/_{10}$ because the illustrations show those used on shrines and temples whose roof slope is steep.

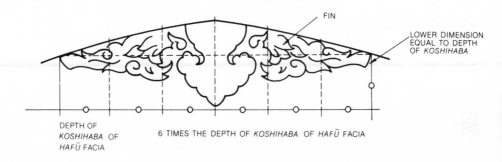

Gegyo (Case 2).

Those on shrines and temples are for roofs with a steep slope, therefore when *gegyo* is to be used on houses, decide on the decoration which would be most appropriate.

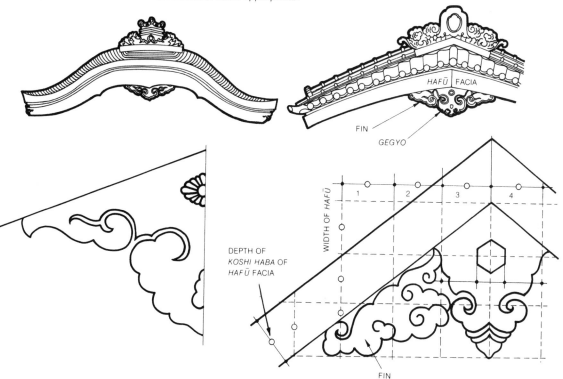

Gegyo for *kara hafū* facia.

These examples are not symmetrical. These types of *gegyo* are used mostly on houses. *Rokuba* is not incorporated.

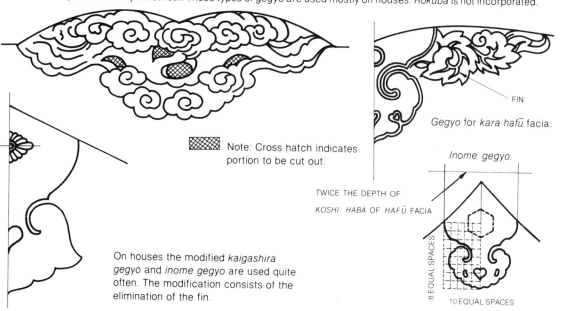

Note: Cross hatch indicates portion to be cut out.

Gegyo for *kara hafū* facia.

Inome gegyo.

TWICE THE DEPTH OF
KOSHI HABA OF HAFŪ FACIA

8 EQUAL SPACES

10 EQUAL SPACES

On houses the modified *kaigashira gegyo* and *inome gegyo* are used quite often. The modification consists of the elimination of the fin.

Gegyo (Case 3).

Rokuyo

Rokuyo is also called *taru no kuchi* by some people. This form of ornamentation is incorporated on shrines and temples, and also on some houses, and is frequently used to cover bolts or other unsightly hardware. some with a diamond shape. Shown below are these, parts of *rokuyo: rokuba* (6 leaves), *kikuza* (chrysanthemum seat), *maruza* (circular seat) and *taru no kuchi* (barrel mouth).

The size of the *rokuyo* should be ⅓ the size of *gegyo*. The thickness should be the same as that of the *hafū* facia or the bottom face of the rafter, or a half or third of *rokuyo*.

The *kikuza*'s size should be ½ of *rokuyo*, and its thickness ⅕ of *rokuyo*. If there is a *maruza*, then the thickness of the *kikuza* should be ½ or ⅓ of the *kikuza*'s width.

The *maruza*'s thickness should be ½ or ⅓ of its own width.

The *taru no kuchi*'s base should be ½ of the *kikuza*, or ⅙ of the *maruza*. Its head should be 1.25 of its base or ⅓ of *rokuyo*.

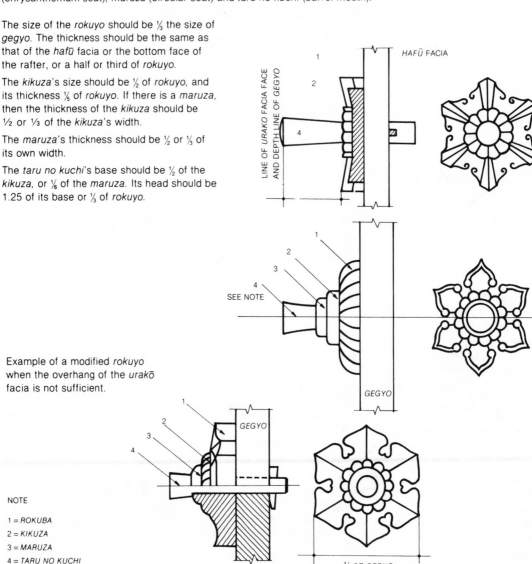

Example of a modified *rokuyo* when the overhang of the *urakō* facia is not sufficient.

NOTE

1 = *ROKUBA*
2 = *KIKUZA*
3 = *MARUZA*
4 = *TARU NO KUCHI*

Above are examples used on houses.

APPENDIX 1

Monjaku—Fortune Scale

Monjaku is a scale which divides 9 *sun* 6 *fu** into 8 equal parts, each named as listed below to determine the good or bad omen for a building of a given dimension. The dimension of a space is obtained with a regular scale which is then placed next to the *monjaku* scale on which the point to be transferred is read. Though not many modern scales include this scale, the names are given so they can be referred to in case the topic is discussed at the construction site.

> *Zai:* Happiness and wealth.
> *Byo:* A great amount of sickness in the family and the continuation of misfortune.
> *Ri:* Bad relationships within the family and family breakup.
> *Gi:* All wishes will come true, and there will be happiness.
> *Kan:* Much happiness and success achieved, except as a merchant.
> *Ko:* Many descendents and much happiness. However, the home will be burglarized and be unlucky.
> *Gai:* Much misfortune and death. The worst fortune.
> *Kichi:* Great fortune in everything with many descendents and a good family name.

Example: The width of a gate is 5 *shaku* (about 5 feet). According to the *monjaku* scale, this falls on *gi.* As explained above, this is a good omen, and as a dimension, the width of the gate is very good.

There was also a scale which gave the circumference of a circle after obtaining the circle's diameter. The diameter is read on the front edge of the scale—for example, 1 *sun.* The circumference scale is on the opposite edge. By transferring it reads 3.14; thus the circumference is 3.14 *sun.* (See example shown in Appendix Figure 1.)

*Translator's note: One *shaku* is about one foot, one *sun* is about one inch, and one *bu* is about ⅛ inch.

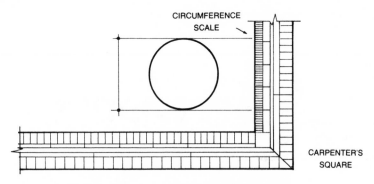

Appendix Figure 1. Circumference scale.

APPENDIX 2

The *Okane*—Large Carpenter's Square

(a) Before beginning the foundation work in the construction of a building, the leveling and setting up of the batter boards have to be done. For these jobs, the squareness and levelness of a structure are obtained using either the levels or the *okane*. Establishing squareness with the *okane* is called "3:4:5 *no hi*", or "43 *wo furu*" ("shake the 43"). This method utilizes the geometric relationships of a triangle with legs 3:4:5.

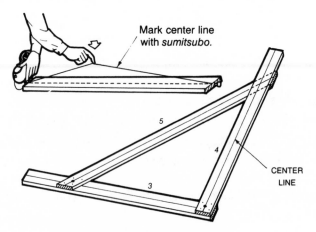

Appendix Figure 2. *Okane* (large carpenter's square).

Method for making the *okane.*

(i) Tools and materials: The materials needed are Japanese cedar boards: one board 1¼ in. thick, 4 in. wide, and 10 ft. long, and two boards 6 ft. long; and five to ten nails, 1½ in. long. A hammer, plane, carpenter's square, measuring tape, chalk line, and marker are the tools needed.

(ii) Construction sequence: Begin by planing the boards. The edges (sides) of the boards should be planed straight. Next, mark a center line on each board with the chalk line as shown in Appendix Figure 2. Place the boards on flat ground, the 6 ft. boards placed perpendicular to each other, and the 10 ft. board to be placed diagonally, forming a triangle. The distances between the intersecting points of the center lines should be in a ratio of 3:4:5, as shown. When the boards are arranged in this ratio, secure them with at least 4 nails at each point.

APPENDIX 3

Method for Making a *Kenzao* (Measuring) Scale

Kenzao, or *shakuzue* by its other name, is a scale for locating the position of a partition's center line, and of footings, beams, and other framing members. The scales, one for horizontal dimensions, the other for vertical dimensions, are made to simplify the work at the site.

The materials usually used are Japanese cedar boards with very few defects. The pieces should be planed on all four sides, measuring 1¼ in. × 1¼ in, and about 10 ft. to 13 ft. long.

On one side of the boards, marks are made 20 in. apart. The scales for horizontal and vertical measures are placed side by side so the marks on both scales are made at the same time in one motion. If the marks were made separately, due to the variation in thickness of the marked lines, differences would occur. Thus it is very important that the boards be placed side by side and marked simultaneously. Furthermore, never make two vertical or two horizontal scales. Always make one and always use that specific one. At the beginning mark, point "o," a protrusion should be made to prevent damage, as well as to act as an indicator. This projection is called *ishi tsuki.* (See Appendix Figure 3.)

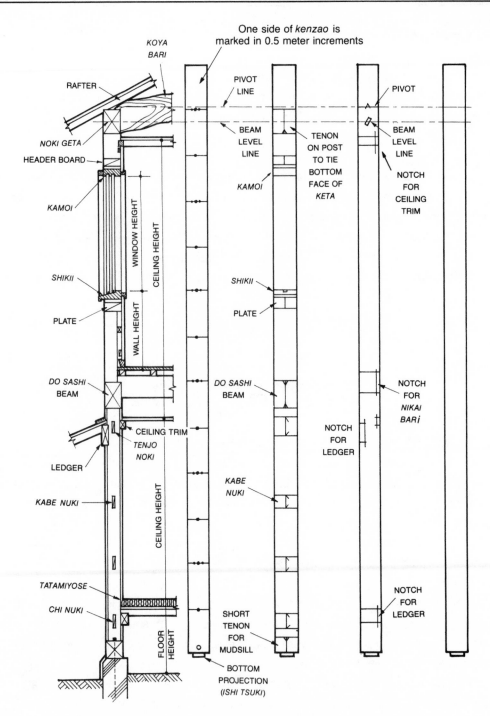

Appendix Figure 3. Markings on the *kenzao* (measuring) scale.

The scales for horizontal measurement are used to locate the center lines of partitions, and also for the center lines of beams and repeated posts. The use of this scale for constructing rooms with many *tatami* mats, such as *inaka ma* and *kyoma,* will keep errors to a minimum. (See Appendix Figure 4.)

The vertical scale can be considered as a tool to simplify the full scale drawing of details. As shown in Appendix Figure 5, markings on the scale are used to exactly locate and verify the position of mudsills, beams, and other members.

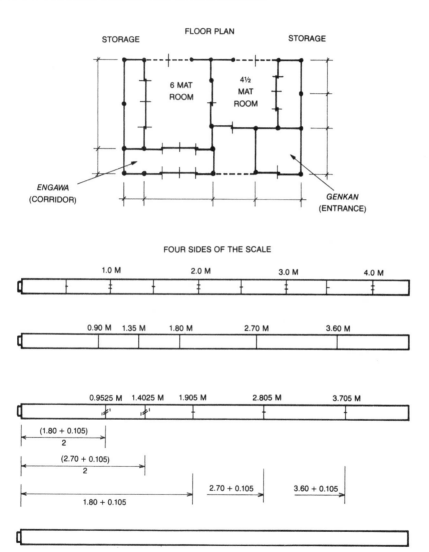

Appendix Figure 4. The horizontal scale.

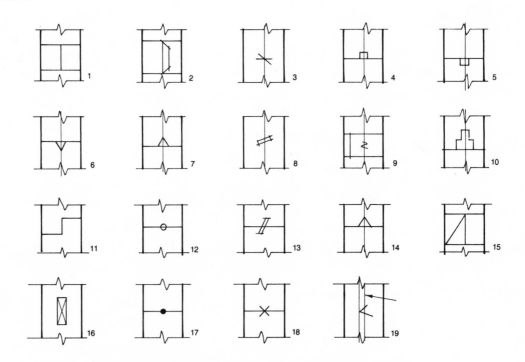

1. HORIZONTAL MEMBERS
   (MUDSILLS, BEAMS)
2. *DO NUKI*
3. WALL TRIM
4. BOTTOM OF *KAMOI*
5. TOP OF *SHIKII*
6. MORTISE MARK ON
   A BOTTOM SURFACE
7. MORTISE MARK ON
   A TOP SURFACE
8. CENTER LINE
9. SIDE SURFACE MORTISE
   FOR *DOTSUKE*
10. STACKED TENON
11. HAUNCH TENON
12. CUT LINE
13. BEAM LEVEL LINE
14. PIVOT
15. NOTCH
16. MORTISE
17. LINE TO BE USED
18. LINE TO BE DISREGARDED
19. *M'JRI* LINE

Appendix Figure 5. Forms of marking.

APPENDIX 4

Ceremonies

(1) Architectural ceremony recognizes that building one's own house is one of the major events of one's life. To some, such an event is impossible, but in this modern age, due to the various loans available, building a house has become a reality for many people. Nevertheless, it is an experience which cannot easily be repeated.

Since building a house is such an important event, it is natural to want everything to go well, so a ceremony is held at the start of construction. Over the ages various Shinto and Buddhist ceremonies have been performed. Here, only the most common ceremonies are described.

(2) The ceremonies.

(i) *Jichinsai:* It is said the origin of this ceremony was intended as a memorial for the numerous plants, various insects, and small creatures that would be destroyed during building on the property. It also asked the many gods of the property for their consent to the construction. Usually this was a Shinto ceremony, but there are also some similar Buddhist ceremonies.

This ceremony is held on a day especially selected for its auspiciousness.

The following information must be given to the priest for conducting the *jichinsai*:

- •Name of the ceremony.
- •Name of the construction (e.g., residence).
- •Name of the owner.
- •Name of the supervisor or contractor.

This information will be read into the rites. Appendix Figure 6 shows the position of the people at the site during the ceremony.

(1) Objects used in the ceremony: stands, a basket, plates, and the priest's tools for the ritual and the sacred tree.

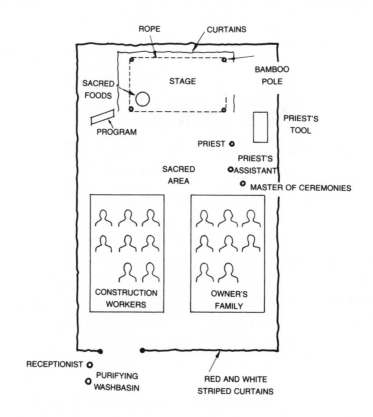

Appendix Figure 6. Seating for the *jichinsai* ceremony.

(2) Purified goods: rice, wine, sea salt, rice cake, spring water, and products of the sea, mountain, and fields, totaling either 5 or 7 (an odd number is preferable). Examples of mountain products: fruits, mushrooms. Field products: vegetables (but not onions). Sea products: fish, dried foods, shellfish. (The fish's head must be on its left side, with its belly facing the altar.)

The arrangement of these things will vary depending on the priest, so prior discussion with the priest will be necessary. If ritual digging is to be done, the shovels must be brand new, and their handles wrapped with white paper tied with sacred paper string.

(3) Sequence: The ceremony is carried out in the following sequence: opening ceremony, *shubatsu;* descent of god, *koshin-no-gi.* Reading of the following rites: *kensen, noritosojo, setsuma-sanma, tamagushi hoten, tessen,* ascent of god, and closing.

(ii) *Jotoshiki:* The ceremony of *jotoshiki,* widely known as *tatamae,* is performed for every building project. It is done where construction has reached the point when the ridge beam is about to be installed. With steel frame construction, it is performed when the last beam is about to be installed. *Jotoshiki* is intended to thank the gods for their protection, for the architectural construction, and for ensuring that the construction has progressed smoothly to the present stage, as well as to ask them for continuing favor until the completion of the work.

The ceremonial procedures are similar to those of *jichinsai.*

(1) The *munafuda*—ridge notice board. Since ancient times, the *munafuda* has been used to record the structure's particulars. It is tied to the south face of the *muna tsuka* (end post supporting the ridge beam) with hemp string. A Japanese cypress board is used, 6 ft. long, 12 in. wide at the top, 10⅝ in. wide at the bottom, and 1¼ in. thick. Today, a smaller version with the same proportions is used. (See Appendix Figure 7.)

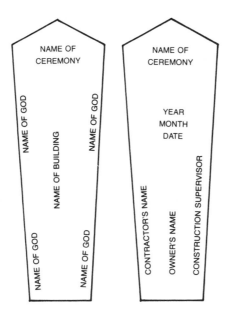

Appendix Figure 7. *Munafuda* (ridge notice board).

(2) The *heigushi heizuka, hei-no-kushi,* or *heishin* is called *sanpo* (three sticks) because three *heikushi* are used. Usually it is made of Japanese cypress board measuring ½ in. × ½ in. × 12 ft. (1 *jo* 2 *sun*). There are smaller ones with dimensions of ⅜ in. square and 9½ in. or 35 ½ in. long.

The *heigushi* is marked with lines in groups of 7, 5, and 3, starting from the bottom, and it is wrapped with *hosho* (sacred paper) and tied with *mizubiki* (sacred paper string) colored half red and half white. (See Appendix Figure 8.) The red side is on the right side and the white on the left side. A kerf is made on the top side of the ridge beam to accept the white paper offering to the god.

(3) The *goshikiginu* (five colored silks) and *asao* (hemp string): As shown in Appendix Figure 9, the five colored silks are draped on both left and right sides. Each side is hung in the following sequence starting from the center: blue, yellow, red, white, black (or purple). Beside the cloth, any number of hemp strings are hung. The five colored cloths can be of silk, cotton, or any other cloth.

(4) The *origuruma*—fan wheel. This is made of three opened fans tied together with red and white colored string, forming a circle. In the center is placed a metal mirror (plated with nickel) from about 9 7/16 to 12 in. in diameter.

In ancient times, it was believed to bring good fortune to carry the *heigushi* to the owner's and the master carpenter's homes, singing *kiyari bushi* songs—songs of construction workers. (At these homes the people were then rewarded with money.) Today this ceremony has been shortened and is held at the building site.

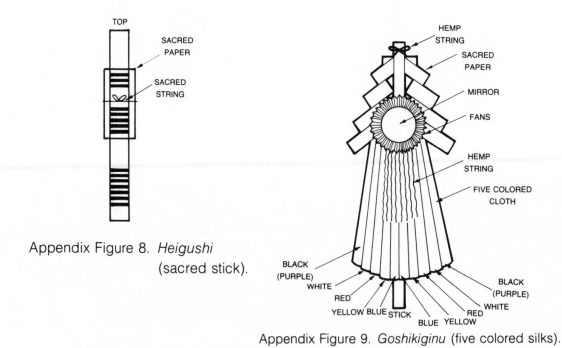

Appendix Figure 8. *Heigushi*
(sacred stick).

Appendix Figure 9. *Goshikiginu* (five colored silks).

Glossary

A

Agogaki: *Chin notch.* A type of notch made on a hip rafter to join the **keta** beam.

Ai jakkuri: *Harmonizing, fitting,* or *scooped line.* A shiplap joint. This joint is similar to the **aigati** except that the edge of the piece on the side parallel to the grain is removed. See also **Chigai hagi:** *Different patches.*

Aikaki: *Harmonizing* or *fitting of chipped parts.* An end (lap) joint where half of the piece's thickness is removed and the two such removed pieces are then joined.

Aikugi: Double pointed nails.

Amado: Shutters.

Amajimai: Weather proofing.

Ameosae: Dripboard.

Arashiko: A plane used as the primary shaver.

Arato: A whetstone made of sandstone.

Are kata: *Are* is a foreign word referring to a dumbbell.

Ari: A trapezoid shaped piece. (Dovetail.)

Ari hozo: *Ant tenon.* A dovetail tenon.

Arikabe: A type of trim.

Ari kake: *Hanging of ant shaped piece.* A dadoed, half lapped, half blind dovetail with full mortise and tenon. (**Ari kaki** refers only to the dovetail notch of the whole joint.) Also **Ari otoshi.**

Arikake tsugi: Obliqued surface half lap joint.

Ari kata: *Ant shape.* Butterfly spline.

Ari kata sanmai hozo: *Ant shaped three tenons.* Open or through single dovetail joint.

Ari kata sanmai hozo komisen uchi: *Driven pin ant shaped three tenons.* Through single dovetail with pin.

Ari michi: *Ant road.* Groove.

Ari otoshi: *Dropped ant.* Dadoed, half lapped, half blind dovetail with full mortise and tenon.

Ari otoshi kasugai uchi: A dadoed, half lapped, half blind dovetail joint, secured with a pin anchor.

Ari shikake: A dovetail joint.

Ari shikome: *Trained or broken-in ant.* Dado with dovetail mortise and tenon.

Ari tsugi: *Ant joint.*

Ari tsuki watari ago: *Crossing chin with ant.* Cross lap blind mortise and tenon with dovetail dado.

Asari: The outward flaring angle of certain sawteeth.

Asaridashi: A tool for aligning saw teeth at the proper angle.

Ashi: The protuberance on the back of the cap iron blade in a double blade plane.

Ashigarami: *Intertwined leg.* Diagonal bracing. Also **Naka nuki** or **ō nūki:** *Inside bridging* or *tie.*

Ashigatame: A bottom plate. (Beam.)

Ashikatame ana: *Hole for hardened feet.* One of the main holes for footing framing.

Ashikatame bari: *Harden feet.* Footing.

Asuka: *Flying birds.* Name of an historical period ca. 700 A.D.–800 A.D.

Atari: The butting faces of two joined pieces. (Literally "to hit.")

Atari kaki: Notch.

Ategi: A tightening board.

Atezai: Irregularly grained wood.

Atsu kei: *Thick* or *heavy shaped.* A type of truss.

B

Baka: A carpenter's square.

Banzuke (or **banzukemen**): The surface of a post which faces the main entry.

Bari: *Beam.* (**Hari** is the correct pronunciation when alone; **bari** is correct when following another word.) Any kind of beam, such as a girder, purlin.

Bintadome: *Side stop.* (**Binta** means *temple of head.* **Dome** means *miter.*) Haunched mortise and tenon with mitered lap joint.

Bintadome eriwa kone hozo sashi wari kusabi uchi: Haunched mortise and tenon with quarter-mitered joint secured with a wedge.

Bintatsuke ari otoshi: *Dropped ant with a side.* Dadoed quartered dovetail joint.

Boruto: Bolts.

Bô sumi: *Stick, rod,* or *pole.* A type of corner.

Bozu: A crane made of a tall log, ropes, and a pulley.

Byobu: A type of door.

C

Chidori hafū: *Thousand bird hafū facia.*

Chigiri tsugi: *Patching pieces of thorn.* Spline joints. Also **Kusabi tsugi:** *Wedge patch* or *wedge joint.*

Chikara daruki: *Power rafter.* A type of rafter found in temple architecture.

Chikara nuki: *Power bridging.* See also **Uchinori nuki.**

Chimune: A horizontal beam.

Chi nuki: *Ground bridging* or *tie.* A tie placed above the mudsills.

Chiri jakkuri: *Scattered,* or *dispersed and scooped-up.* A finishing detail of plaster dieing into a post which has been cut to accept the plaster.

Chogen: *Long line.* (See page 295.)

Chona: An adze.

Chushin giri: A center bit awl.

Chusiko: A plane used for the second stage in smoothing wood. (Medium plane.)

Chuto: A common whetstone for sharpening only slightly dull edges.

D

Dabo: *Pin.*

Daigashira: The toe of a plane.

Daimochi shachi: *Pedestal holding pin.*

Daimochi tsugi: *Pedestal holding joint.* Stub tenon scarf joint.

Dainaoshi: The checking for flatness of the sole of a plane.

Dainaoshi kanna: A plane used to manually correct the body of a plane.

Daisen: *Large pin.*

Daiwa: *Support ring,* or *pedestal ring.* Sole plate.

Daiwa dome: *Pedestal stop.* (**Tome** is the correct pronunciation when alone; **dome** is correct when following another word.) Full tenoned tongue and groove miter joint.

Dashi geta: *Stuck out beam.* (**Keta** is the correct pronunciation when alone; **geta** is correct when following another word.) An outrigger type of beam.

Dekôshi mado: *Stuck out latticed window.* A bay window with grating.

Desumi: *Stuck out corner.* Outside corner (refers to a line necessary for a rafter layout).

Dezumi no shigushi: Outside corner joints.

Dobuchi: A tie or bridge.

Dodai: A mudsill.

Dô nuki: *Trunk* or *body bridging.* (Or *tie* or *blocking.*) A tie placed between bottom bridging and ceiling bridging. (See illustration on page 223.)

Dô sashi (or **hariuke**): Subsidiary beams connecting discontinuous posts and supporting second floor joists.

Dô sashi bari: *Trunk* or *body beam.* (**Hari** is the correct pronunciation when alone; **bari** is correct when following another word.) A subsidiary beam below the main eaves beam.

Dôtsuki or **dô tsuke:** *With trunk.* The joint formed by two pieces of wood intersecting.

Do tsunagi: A combined fire stop and plate found only in Japanese framing.

Dozuki noko: A thin saw used for cutting joints which require perfectly flat surfaces.

E

Eddoko: A nail remover.

Edo: **Edo** is the old name for Tokyo. The name of an historical period ca. 1600–1860 A.D.

Eizu ita: *Drawing board.* Drawings on wooden boards by the master carpenter, showing the skeletal framing sequence.

Engamachi or **enkamachi:** Main external visible floor support.

Engawa: *Side of green.* An exterior corridor, or veranda.

Eriwa hozo: *Collar ring tenon.*

Eriwa kaki: *Collar ring.* A cross lap with collar, or a notch, like a lap joint, cut out of the back face of a **neda kaki** beam.

Eriwa kone hozosashi: *Collar ring small root tenon insert.* Collared haunch mortise and tenon joint.

Eriwa kone hozo sashi wari kusabi uchi: Collared haunch mortise and tenon joint with a wedge.

Eriwa tsugi: *Collar ring joint.* Dado and rabbet joint.

Eriwa tsuki ari otoshi: *Ant drop with collar ring.* Collared dovetail rabbet and dado joint.

Eriwa tsuki dotsuki komisen uchi: *Pin driven with collar ring and with trunk.* Collared, haunched, and pinned through mortise and tenon.

Eriwa tsuki kone hozosashi: *Collar ring small root tenon insert.* Wedged collared haunch mortise and tenon.

F

Fukido: A type of cant strip, as illustrated on page 352.

Fuki yose: *Gathered together breath.* A rafter spacing method.

Fukusho: *Double,* or *compound.* A type of second floor construction.

Fuku yuka gami: Multiple frame framing method.

Fumita uwaba koanahori oire: A type of dado joint.

Fumizura: Stair treads.

Funa kugi: An offset head nail.

Fure sumi: *Inclined corner.* One of two kinds of hip rafter other than 45 degrees.

Fure tome: *Inclined stop.* Strong back. (A type of tie.)

Fusama: A solid door.

G

Gangi gane: *Large metal.* (**Kane** is the correct pronunciation when alone; **gane** is correct when following another word.) A special carpenter's square.

Gasshō: *Praying hands.* The top chord of a truss.

Gaudo (or **sabanoko**): A cross cut saw used for rough cutting lumber or trees.

Gegyo: *Like a fish.* An ornamental piece of facia on some mansions and large country houses and generally found in temples.

Genno: Ball peen hammer.

Gyakume: Bent head nails.

H

Hafū: *Gable.* A type of facia on gable or end of gable roof.

Hafū gashira: *Gable head.* (**Kashira** is the correct pronunciation when alone; **gashira** is correct when following another word.)

Hafū ita: *Gable style board.*

Hafū jiri: *The way of hafū.* (Also **Ki jiri:** *The way of the tree.*) Refers to a grid on which the building is laid out parallel to a line across the width of the building.

Hagaeri: A bent burr on a blade after it has been sharpened.

Haitsuke daruki: *Distribution rafter.* (**Taruki** is the correct pronunciation when alone; **daruki** is correct when following another word.) Jack rafter.

Hakake (or **taruki kake**): A ledger.

Hakama koshi: *Hip of [a man's] kimono pants.* A chord of a truss.

Hakidashi mado: *Sweep out window.* A window at floor level to sweep out debris and dust.

Hako daimochi tsugi: *Holding box support joint.* Shipped and pinned and halved half lap joint.

Hako kaidan: Box stairs.

Hako mechigai tsugi: *Grain different box joint.* L-shaped shipped and tenoned half lap joint, or blind U-shaped stubbed mortise and tenon joint. **Hako mechigai** refers to the shape of the tenon, whether it is L-shaped or U-shaped.

Hakosen tsugi: *Box pin joint.* L-shaped dadoed and rabbetted scarf lap joint.

Hako shachi tsugi: *Box key joint.* L-shaped, dadoed and rabbetted and keyed lapped joint.

Hako tsugi: *Box joint.* Blind and stub diagonally cut half lap joint.

Hame komi: A dado joint.

Hana garami: *Entangled noses.* A type of facia.

Hanagi: *Nose wood.* A type of beam.

Hanakakushi: *Hide nose.* A type of facia.

Hanamashi: *Increase nose.* Set the depth in direct relation to the size of a notch to receive the **kayaoi** facia.

Hanamoya: *Nose rafter.* Eave beam. (Another name for **noki geta**.)

Hanasen: *Nose key.* Wooden keys used in traditional framing. Also **kusebi**.

Hanedashi: *Stuck out wing.* A type of beam.

Hanegi: *Wing wood.* (**Ki** is the correct pronunciation when alone; **gi** is correct when following another word.) Hidden cantilevered beam.

Hanegi osae: *Pressed down wing wood.* A type of blocking.

Hane jakkuoi: A notch for a nail.

Hanekasane: *Stacked wings.* A method of stacking or lapping.

Han tome: *Half stop.* Shoulder miter joint.

Hari: A style of ceiling.

Hariuke kanamono: *Beam receiving metal things.* Beam hangers.

Hari yuki: *Beam to go.* A term which refers to co-ordinates parallel with **hari**, usually across the width of the building.

Hasami: A beam.

Hasami bari: *Scissor beam.* (**Hari** is the correct pronunciation when alone; **bari** is correct when following another word.) Spaced beam.

Hasami zuka: *Scissors web* or *short post.* (**Tsuka** is the correct pronunciation when alone; **zuka** is correct when following another word.) End post.

Hashira: *Post.*

Hashiradate tobukuro: Complex shutter housing.

Hatsuri: A method of removing a piece from wood by chipping with a hatchet or an adze.

Hazuchi: A type of hammer used to set saw teeth.

Heichi: *Flat land.* A horizontal plane or the leg of a triangle.

Hibata: The space between the grooves for **shoji** (sliding doors).

Hibukura hagi: A V-grooved joint.

Hidari sode gawara: *Left sleeve tile.* (**Kawara** is the correct pronunciation when alone; **gawara** is correct when following another word.) A type of Japanese roof tile.

Hien daruki: *Flying swallow rafter.* (**Taruki** is the correct pronunciation when alone; **daruki** is correct when following another word.) A type of rafter.

Hijikake mado: *Elbow resting window.* A type of window.

Hikari ita: *Reflecting board.* A guide (board).

Hikarikata: *Reflecting way.* Duplicating method.

Hikari osa: *Reflecting reed.* A reproducing instrument made, from a reed in the past. Its sticks are movable and butt against an object so as to take its exact shape. Today they are made from bamboo or steel.

Hikaru: *Shine* or *reflect.*

Hikidoko: *Pulling peg.* Wood peg with French dovetail tenon and a key.

Hikikata: The main sawing actions (as compared to preliminary).

Hikikomi: The first cut in sawing a piece.

Hikimawashi (or **mawashibiki noko**): A jig saw.

Hikiowari: The final movements in sawing a piece.

Hikiwatashi: *Cross by pulling.* A type of slope (incline or angle).

Hirabaku: A square crosscut piece of core wood.

Hira hozo: *Flat tenon.* Full tenon.

Hira kanna: A jack plane.

Hirakobai: *Flat slope.* Main field rafter slope.

Hirakomai: A type of facia.

Hira masa: *Flat straight grain.* A cutting method.

Hira nomi: A chisel.

Hira sujikai: *Flat diagonal bracing.*

Hirakobai-no-hŏ: *Rafter slope rise.*

Hirakobai-no-yaku: *Rafter slope run.*

Hirawari: A rectangular shaped piece without pith, cut from a large tree.

Hira yarikata: A straight batter board.

Hisashi mawari: Eaves.

Hishiya sumi: *Diamond shaped roof corner.*

Hiuchi bari: A horizontal brace.

Hiuchi dodai: An angle brace for a mudsill.

Hiyodori sen: A type of key.

Ho: A blade of cutter.

Hodate: A framing member.

Hodate bashira: A small edge post.

Hogyo zukuri: *Four sided construction.*

Honba: The saw teeth nearest to the handle.

Honchŭ or **honaka:** *Basic center.* The center line in the space between **nyŭchŭ** and **shŭchŭ**. Also the center line of the space between the hip rafter and the **keta** beam that will be placed on top of the hip rafter.

Honshige wari: A type of rafter spacing.

Honzane hagi. Also **sane hagi**, or **inro jukkuri**. (**Jukkuri** means "scoop out.") Tongue and groove joint.

Hozo: Tenon.

Hozo ana: *Tenon hole.* Mortise.

Hozokiri: An electric router.

Hozo sashi: *Tenon insert.* Mortise and tenon joint.

Hozo sujikai: *Slim diagonal bracing.* Also **usui sujikai** (*thin diagonal bracing*), or **hira sujikai** (*flat diagonal bracing*).

Hŏzue: *Directional pole.* Brace.

I

Ichimai: *One board.* The extent of tilt of a small **hafŭ** facia.

Ichimai han: *One and a half board.* The extent of tilt of a small **hafŭ** facia.

Ikken: Single layered soffit.

Imohagi: *Potato edge joint.* Butt joint.

Inako: A pin.

Inako michi: Hole into which pin is inserted.

Inome gegyo: *Eye of boar gegyo.* A type of **gegyo** (ornamental facia piece).

Inrobame: A type of tongue and groove joint.

Inro tsugi: *Three or five pieces stacked small box joint.* Another name for a mortise and tenon joint.

Ippon sori: *Single warp.* A type of facia.

Irigawa: A piece of ingrown bark.

Irimoya: *Inside mother roof.* A type of roof (dutch gable or hipped gable).

Irimoya hafŭ: *Inside mother roof hafŭ.* A type of **hafŭ** facia.

Irimoya sashi mono: *Inside mother roof measuring thing.* A name used in the **Kansai** area (**Kyoto**) for a beam called **tobibari**.

Irizumi: *Inside corner.* (**Sumi** is the correct pronunciation when alone; **zumi** is correct when following another word.)

Irizumi no shigushi: Inside corner joint.

Ishi tsuki: The indicator on a **kenzao** (measuring) scale.

Isuka: A special shape of cut at the top of a stake.

Isuka tsugi: Halved scarf joint.

Ita hizashi: Eave board.

Itazu: Ink board drawings.

Itsutsu moya: *Five roofs.* A roof style. (See page 357.)

J

Jiberu: A split ring.

Jigoku hozo: *Hell tenon.* Blind mortise and tenon with dovetail mortise and tenon cut to receive wedge.

Jigoku hozo sashi: A "hell" tenon joint.

Jiku gumi: *Axial framing.*

Jimune: *Ground ridge beam.* (See illustration at top of page 286.)

Jobun: See **Kaneto.**

Jū hozo: A stacked tenon.

Juji toriai: A cross joint.

Juku gumi: Wall framing.

Jūmen dori: *Seize ten faces.* (**Tori** means "to take or seize.") (**Tori** is the correct pronunciation when alone; **dori** is correct when following another word.) The chamber at the edges is equal to one tenth of the square column's side.

Jyujikei: *Cross shape.* Crossed right angle joints.

Jyuji mechigai tsugi: *Different grain crossed joint.* Cross shaped mortise and tenon joint.

K

Kabe chiri: *Scattered wall.* A finishing detail of plaster dieing into a post which has been cut to accept the plaster.

Kabe nuki: Tie, or wall bridging.

Kabe shitaji: Wall sheathing.

Kabe tori: The name for the size of the dimension that a drip board is set in to a wall.

Kabuto ari: An end lap joint with a dovetail.

Kabuto ari kake: *Helmet ant hang.* End lap joint with a through single dovetail joint spanning a log.

Kaeshi kobai: The return slope of the face of beams on which rafters will be set.

Kageiri ari otoshi: *Dropped ant with shadow.* Dovetailed stop lap joint.

Kageiri hozo sashi: *With shadow tenon insert.* Pinned full or through mortise and tenon.

Kaidan: Stairs.

Kaigashira gegyo: *Shell head gegyo.*

Kaikusabi: A type of wedge.

Kai-no-kuchi tsugi: *Shell mouth connection.* X-shaped ship, or open end joint (French style).

Kakebana: *Nose hanging.* (**Hana** means "nose.") (**Hana** is the correct pronunciation alone; **bana** is correct when following another word.) A decorative outrigger.

Kaki hozowari: Split tenon.

Kaki hozowari kusabiuchi: Wedged mortise and tenon.

Kaku kugi: Offset head nail.

Ka kushi: Blind nailing.

Kakushi arikata sanmai hozo: *Hidden three ant shaped tenon.* Half blind dovetail joint.

Kakushi-dome ari sanmai hozo: *Hidden miter three ant joint.* Blind dovetailed miter joint.

Kakushi domekata sanmai hozo: *Hidden miter shaped three tenons.* Blind and stub miter joint.

Kakushi kanawa tsugi: *Hidden metal ring joint.* Blind dadoed and rabbetted scarf joint.

Kama tsugi: *Sickle connection.* Goose neck joint.

Kamoi: *Header for doors or windows.* Headers with grooves for two-paneled sliding doors.

Kamuri: Tilting the **hafū** facia forward.

Kanabakari: *Finely measured.* Detailed framing sectional drawings.

Kanawa tsugi: *Metal ring joint.* Mortised rabbetted oblique scarf joint.

Kanazuchi: Hammer.

Kanbanita: *Signboard.* A floor plan drawn on a wooden board.

Kan bashira: *Tube post.* (**Hashira** is the correct pronunciation when alone; **bashira** is correct when following another word.) Discontinuous post.

Kaneba: *Place of metal.* A position marked on the wood when the **kane wo maku** method is used. (See page 219.)

Kanegata sanmai hozo: *Metal shaped three tenon.* Ship, or open, mortise and tenon joint.

Kanejaku: A carpenter's square.

Kaneori mechigai tsugi: *Bent metal grain change tenon.* L-shaped half blind mortise and tenon joint.

Kanete dōtsuki: Mortise plane.

Kaneto (or jobun): A whetstone made of steel plate.

Kane wo maku: *To warp metal.* A phrase describin a position of the carpenter's square—on the center line. A method for marking with an ink line.

Kanna: A plane.

Kannadai: The body of a plane.

Kannamakura: The ridge formed where a plane has missed shaving.

Kara hafū: A type of Chinese facia (reverse curve).

Karakusa: *Arabesque.* A type of facia.

Kasaneba: A chipper blade for a plane.

Kasane bari: *Stacked beam.* Double stacked beam.

Kashigi dōtsuke: *Inclined plane.* A joint for connecting the **shinzuka** web with the top chord.

Kashigi dōtsuke boruto jime: *Inclined plane closed with bolt.* (**Jime** means "to close.") (**Shime** is the correct pronunciation when alone; **jime** is correct when following another word.) Diagonal shoulder with a bolt joint.

Kashigi dōtsuki tan hozo sashi: *Short tenon with inclined and hipped plain mortise insert.*

Kashigi kageire: *Shadowed incline.*

Kashigi kageire hozo sashi: *Incline with shadow mortise and tenon.* Diagonal shoulder joint.

Kashigi koshi tsuki tan hozo sashi: Short tenon with slanted hip mortise and tenon joint.

Kashigi kurakake dōtsuki: *Hung saddle with inclined plane joint.*

Kashigi ōire: *Large entry incline.* Obliqued dado.

Kashigi ōire hozo sashi: *Large entry inclined tenon insert.* Oblique dadoed full mortise and tenon joint.

Kashigi ōire tan hozo sashi: *Large entry inclined short* *tenon insert.* Oblique dado with blind stub mortise and tenon joint.

Kashiranuki: A type of beam.

Kasugae dome: *Metal pin anchor stop.* (**Tome** means "stop.") (**Tome** is the correct pronunciation when alone; **dome** is correct when following another word.) A joint using a pin anchor.

Kasugai: An anchor.

Kata ari: A half dovetail joint.

Kata ari suitsuki: A half dovetail dado joint.

Katageta: A stringer.

Katageta kaidan: A beam framed stair.

Katana yasuri: A file for sharpening saw-teeth.

Kawara: Japanese roof tile.

Kawaraza: *Seat of clay shingle.* Tile rest facia.

Kayaoi: A type of facia.

Kayaoi kama tsugi: *Kayaoi* facia sickle connection. Dadoed gooseneck joint with scarf.

Kazuridai: A planing table.

Kebiki: A cutting gauge which splits boards.

Kegaki: Ink markings.

Kegakisen: Cut lines.

Kenchiku Kijunho: Architectural Standards.

Kenzao: A scale for obtaining vertical measurements.

Keraba: *Wing of cricket-like insect.* A type of eave.

Keshō daruki: *Cosmetic rafter.* (**Taruki** is the correct pronunciation when alone; **daruki** is correct when following another word.) Visible finish rafter.

Keta: *Beam, crossbeam,* or *girder,* depending on the context. (**Keta** is the correct pronunciation when alone; **geta** is correct when following another word.) A girder or main beam.

Keta yuki: *Go beam.* Axis of a building parallel to its length.

Keta yuki sujikai: Roof bracings which run parallel to the beams.

Ki or **gi:** Wood.

Kiba hozo: *Fang tenon.* A type of tenon.

Kiba hozo sashi: *Fang tenon insert.* Haunched mortise and tenon.

Kidori: *Taking wood.* (**Tori** means "to take.") (**Tori** is the correct pronunciation when alone; **dori** is correct when following another word.) A method of cutting lumber to obtain a certain grain.

Kiguchi ari: *Tree cross-section ant.* Half blind dovetail-shaped mortise and tenon.

Kiguchi hozo: *Tree cross-section mortise.*

Kijiri: *Base of tree.* The lower end of a facia.

Kikaijakkuri: A combination plane.

Kikujyutsu: A method for obtaining the angle of the roof slope.

Kikuza: *Seat of chrysanthemum.* A part of a mortise.

Kine kata: *Pestle shape.* Bow-tie spline.

Kinomi gaeshi hō: *Return of tree body.* (**Kaishi** means

"return.") (**Kaishi** is the correct pronunciation when alone; **gaeshi** is correct when following another word.) Method used in constructing facia.

Kioi: A type of beam.

Kiomote: The front of a board.

Kiri: An awl for making small holes. Also, a type of wood (paulownia).

Kiri kaki: A method of notching, or cutting.

Kirizuma hafū: *Cut wife facia.* (**Tsuma** means "wife.") (**Tsuma** is the correct pronunciation when alone; **zuma** is correct when following another word.) A type of **hafū** facia.

Kiura: The back of a board.

Kiwa: A type of joist.

Kizamu: *Cutting up.* Cutting out the joints.

Kizukuri: *Making wood.* (**Tsukuri** means "to make.") (**Tsukuri** is the correct pronunciation when alone; **zukuri** is correct when following another word.) Making or shaping of wood, making lumber.

Kizure kōshi: A type of lattice work.

Koanaire: A dado and rabbet joint.

Kobari: *Small beam.* (**Hari** is the correct pronunciation when alone; **bari** is correct when following another word.)

Kodotsuki ariotoshi: A dovetail dado with a haunch on both sides.

Kogaisen: **Sen** means "key."

Ko-hira-okoshi: *Raise horizontally slightly.* The method for obtaining the length of the hip rafter.

Komagaeshi: *Return small space.* A type of spacing.

Komai: *Small dance.* Furring strip.

Komisen: *Stick in pin.* Pins used in traditional framing.

Kone hozo: *Small root tenon.* Haunch tenon.

Kone hozo sashi: *Small root tenon insert.* Blind and stub mortise and tenon joint.

Kongoto: A whetstone made of a powdered stone.

Koppa: The shavings produced in adzing.

Korobashi yuka: *Rolled floor.*

Korobi: *Tumble,* or *fall.* Member with a sloped surface, or twist.

Kōryo: *Red beam.* A temple outer eaves beam.

Koshi haba: *Hip width.* Depth at the center of the hafū facia. (See illustration on page 353.)

Koshi ire mechigai zuki ari tsugi: *Hipped offset ant joint.*

Koshikake: *Resting on chair seat.* A bench.

Koshikake ari tsugi: *Seated ant joint.* Lapped dovetail joint.

Koshikake kama tsugi: *Seated sickle joint.* Lapped gooseneck joint.

Koshi tsuki: *With hip.* Lap.

Koya: *Hut,* or *roof.* (**Koya** is the correct pronunciation when alone; **goya** is correct when following another word.)

Koya bari: *Hut beam.* A **hari** or a log beam.

Koyadaimochi tsugi: *Hut with support connection.* Tenon scarf joint, for logs usually.

Koya gumi: **Koya** means "roof," **kumi** means "to put together." Roof framing.

Koya sujikai: *Hut diagonal bracing.* A roof brace running parallel to the rafters.

Koya tsuka: *Hut post.* Short post to support purlin or ridge from main support beams.

Kuchibiki: *Pull with mouth.* (**Hiki** means "pull.") (**Hiki** is the correct pronunciation when alone; **biki** is correct when following another word.) Compass, used for scribing irregular shapes.

Kuchiwaki: *Side of the mouth.* Rafter slope cut into outer top edge of the eaves beam, purlin or ridge. Also **Noki kodo.**

Kuda bashira: A discontinuous post.

Kugi: Nails.

Kugiuchi: Nailing.

Kumi: *Framing.* (**Kumi** is the correct pronunciation when alone; **gumi** is correct when following another word.)

Kumite bari: *Erected or constructed beam.* Truss.

Kumo sujikai: *Cloud diagonal bracing.* A type of diagonal bracing.

Kurakake hozo: *Hung saddle tenon.* Oblique dadoed tenon.

Kurakake kanamono: *Hung saddle metal things.* Hangers.

Kusabi: *Wedge.*

Kutsuzuri: Baseboards.

Kuzuri: A wood lath wall underlayment.

Kyoro gumi: A framing method.

M

Ma bashira: *Spaced post.* Stud.

Mado: *Window.*

Madodai: *Window support.* Mudsill or sill.

Magusa: A type of a header.

Mai ita: A framing member.

Majikiri geta: A supporting beam.

Marugyo: *Round beam.*

Maru kanna: A plane for working rounded pieces.

Maruza: *Round seat.* Part of a motif. (See illustration on page 366.)

Maunen no kanoe zaru: Saru means "monkey." (Pronounced **zaru** when following another word.)

Mawari buchi: *Circumference trim.* Ceiling perimeter molding.

Mawarien: A ceiling trim.

Mawashibiki noko: A jig saw.

Mawatashi: *Cross over space.* Lath.

Mawatashi ana: *Cross over space hole.* Hole for lath.

Mayujakkuri: *Eyebrow groove.*

Mayukaki: *Eyebrow carving.* A type of carving in **hafū** facia on gable end of roof.

Meburi: See **Asari**.

Mechigai hozo: *Grain change tenon.* A type of tenon (short, generally up to 1 inch long).

Mechigai hozo tsuki kama tsugi: *Offset grooved sickle joint.*

Mechigai ire: *Grain change insert.*

Mechigai tsugi: *Grain change connection.* Short mortise and tenon joint.

Mechi hozo or **mechi:** Abbreviation of **mechigai hozo**. A very short tenon.

Mechi ire: Abbreviation of **mechigai ire**. The mortise portion of a joint.

Medate: Sharpening the sawteeth.

Mendo ita: *Too much trouble board.* Eave blocking.

Mengoshi: *Hip face.* A type of connection for the **keta** beam.

Mento kaki: *Door face carving.* Shaping of the top surface of the ridge beam.

Metchi: Short tenon.

Michikiri hozo: A rabbet.

Migi sode gawara: *Right sleeve shingle.* (**Kawara** means "shingle.") (**Kawari** is the correct pronunciation when alone; **gawari** is correct when following another word.)

Mikomi: *Estimate.* The rabbetted edge of a sliding door.

Mimi: Beveled corners of a plane blade.

Mitsuki: *Approach.* The visible surface.

Mitsuki dome: A blind miter joint.

Mitsume giri: An awl for making nail holes.

Mittsu han moya: *Three-and-a-half roofs.* A style of roof.

Mittsu moya or **mittsu:** *Three roofs.* A style of roof.

Miyajima tsugi: Rabbetted half scarf joint.

Mizo kanna (or **kamoi**): A plane used to make the groove in a sliding door sill.

Mizokiriban: An electric router.

Mizukiri: *Cut water.* A type of facia inserted into a vertical surface to prevent water penetration.

Mizumori: Leveling.

Mizunuki: Ties for batter boards.

Mizuso: A water tank used in leveling a site.

Mochi hozo: A tenon.

Moki ita: The front panel of a **tobukuro**.

Momoyama: Period of history ca. 1550 A.D.–1600 A.D.

Monjaku: A scale whose measures relate to good and bad omens for specific dimensions.

Moto: The base or butt of a tree.

Motoguchi: *Root* or *base.*

Moya: *Mother roof.* A purlin.

Muchidashi tsugi: A method where the end joint of a beam extends beyond the outer edge of a post.

Mukō dome: *Stop the other side.* (**Tome** is the correct pronunciation when alone; **dome** is correct when following another word.) A cut-line or referring to the far side of the building where it makes a 90° turn.

Mukumi: *Swelling.*
Mukuri: *Swelling.* Arched curve.
Mukuri hafū: *Swelling* **hafū**. A type of arched **hafū** facia.
Munagi: A ridge beam.
Munashita bari: Muna means "ridge." Shita means "below." **Bari** is **hari** and is "log beam." A large log beam parallel to the ridge but much below it.
Munashita shashi mono: *A ridge bottom different thing.* A type of beam.
Muna tsuka: End post which supports a ridge beam.
Muratogi: A term describing poorly done blade sharpening.

N

Naga hozo: *Long tenon.*
Naga hozo sashi: A long tenon.
Naga hozo sashi komisen uchi: A long tenon with pin.
Nagare hafū: *Flowing* **hafū**.. Sagging **hafū** facia.
Nagare hozo: *Flowing tenon.* Sloped tenon.
Nagekake bari: *Throw and hang beam.*
Nageshi: A wall molding.
Nageshibiki: A trapezoidal molding.
Nage zumi: *Throw ink.* (**Sumi** means "ink.") (**Sumi** is the correct pronunciation when alone; **zumi** is correct when following another word.) The name of a line, at cut off point on rafters, hip or otherwise.
Nagodai kanna: A plane used on thick boards where they will be butt joined.
Nakabiki bari: *Inside pulling beam.*
Naka gamoi: A header.
Nakanuki: Lathing for tile.
Namako kugi: Corrugated metal fasteners.
Nami gata: *Wave shape.* (**Kata** means "shape.") (**Kata** is the correct pronunciation when alone; **gata** is correct when following another word.) Corrugated metal fastener.
Naname dōtsuki (or **naname dōtsuki tan hozo sashi):** *Slanted plane.* An oblique dado mortise and tenon joint.
Naname tsukitsuke kasugai uchi: *Slanted thrust hit anchor flush mount and secure with anchor pin.*
Nanatsu moya: *Seven roofs.* A style of roof.
Nanbu: *What fraction.* X number of parts or divisions.
Nanwari: X number of parts or divisions.
Nawabari: Outlining the perimeter of a proposed building.
Neda: A joist.
Neda hori: *Joist cut-out.* Notch in which to rest joist.
Neda kake: *Hang joist.* A beam with notches cut out to receive a joist.
Neda shitaba: *Underside place of joist.* A name for **chi nuki** indicating that the top surface of it is to be equal to the bottom surface of the joist.
Negarami nuki: *Entangled root bridging or tie.* A type of bridging, or tie, used to support floor posts.

Neji gumi: *Twisted framing.* A two step tenon.
Nejire giri: An auger bit awl.
Nezumiha giri: A type of awl.
Nihō masa: *Two-directional center grain cutting method.*
Nijiri: A line parallel to the center line placed at a standard distance from it and used as a reference line in its place.
Nijū bari: *Double beam.* A spaced beam.
Nijū buchi: *Dougle edge or rim.* (**Fuchi** means "rim.") (**Fuchi** is the correct pronunciation when alone; **buchi** is correct when following another word.) A type of trim.
Nijū goya: *Double roofing.* (Abbreviation of **Nijū goya kumi.**) (**Koya** is the correct pronunciation when alone; **goya** is correct when following another word.) A type of truss.
Nijū goya kumi: *Double roof framing.* A type of truss.
Nijū noki saki: *Double eave end.* Double roof eave—two layers.
Nijū yodo: *Two layer* **yodo**. A type of **yodo** facia—one on top of another.
Nikai bari: *Second floor beam.*
Nikai bari sanpō sashi: *Second floor three-directional insert.*
Nimai banna: A double bladed plane.
Nimai hozo: *Two tenon.* Double tenon.
Nimai hozonuki kusabi uchi: A wedged mortise and tenon joint.
Nobori bari: *Climbing beam.* A type of log beam that slopes up in order to prevent the need to use progressively longer **tsuka**.
Nobori shina ita: *Climbing good board.* A type of trim.
Nobori urakō: *Climbing back shell*—as in turtle shell. A type of facia that goes up a **hafū**.
Nobori yodo: *Climbing* **yodo**. A type of **yodo** facia that goes up a **hafū**.
Noboriza: *Climbing seat.* Another name for **nobori yodo** that goes up a **hafū**.
Nobuchi: Ceiling joists.
Nodaruki: *Wild rafter.* A rafter that is rough and not visible.
Noge tsugi: Dadoed gooseneck joint with scarf.
No hi: Using the **okane** to establish squareness.
Noji: See **Noji ita.**
Noji ita: *Field ground board.* Roof sheathing.
Noki: *Eave.*
Noki bari: *Eave beam.*
Noki geta: *Eave beam.* (Another name for **hanamoya**.)
Nokogiri: A saw.
Nomi: A chisel.
Nosekake: A full tenon joint.
Notenuchi: Straight nailing.
Nuki: Bridging, or tie. Support for wall (most commonly plastered mud wall).
Nuki ana: Bridging or tie hole.

Nuki hozo: A through mortise and tenon.

Nuki hozosashi wari kusabi uchi: A blind and wedged mortise and tenon.

Nuri: A style of ceiling.

Nurikomi nuki: *Coat (painting or lacquering) in bridging or tie.* A type of **nuki**.

Nyūchū or **irinaka:** *Enter center.* A line determined by measuring the depth of the eave or the spacing of hip rafters.

O

Ōbari: *Large beam.*

Ōbiki: *Large pulling.* A girder which supports floor joists.

Ochi kakari: *About to drop.* A slope line.

Odome: Blind miter joint.

Odome mechigai ire: A large stop mortise and tenon.

Ogami: *Worship, bow, pray.* Depth of **hafū** facia at the ridge end.

Ōgi ari: *Fan shaped ant.* Fan shaped dovetail.

Ōgi hozo: *Fan tenon.* A through single dovetail secured with a pin anchor.

Oifushi: A type of planing.

Oiire: *Driven in.* A method of connecting wooden members by inserting the entire piece into another piece.

Oiire ariotoshi: *Driven in dropped ant* or **Kageire ariotoshi:** *Large entry dropped ant.* Full half lap dovetail joint.

Oime: A correct planing direction.

Oire ariotoshi: A full dado with dovetail.

Oire hozo sashi: *Large entry tenon insert.* Dadoed full (or through) mortise and tenon joint.

Ōire with **kanete dotsuki:** To cut obliquely.

Ōire kasugai uchi: *Large entry struck pin anchor.* Oblique dado with pin anchor.

Oire nonu: A finishing chisel with a thin blade.

Ōire otoshikomi uwaba sasuri: *Complete drop-in with top notched.* Blind dado with French dovetail mortise.

Oire tan hozo sashi: A dadoed full short tenon joint.

Ōkabe: *Large wall.* A framing method where members are concealed both on the exterior and interior commonly with a plastered mud wall.

Okake kari: A saw for rip cutting large lumber.

Okane: The large carpenter's square.

Okkake daisen tsugi: A dadoed and rabbetted scarf joint.

Okuri tsugi: A method of attaching two logs to each other.

Ōmendori: *Take large surface.* Big chamfer on post.

Omurato: See **Arato**.

Onnagi: *Female wood.* Female piece.

Ono: A hatchet.

Ōnuki: *Large bridging or tie.*

Oribe shiki: *Weave room style.* A method of placing a reinforcing clamp.

Orioki gumi: A framing method.

Osa: *Reed.* Contour gauge of split bamboo.

Osae gane: The securing rod in a plane.

Otoshigama: *Dropped sickle* or **Sagegama:** *Hung sickle.* (**Kama** means "sickle.") (**Kama** is the correct pronunciation when alone; **gama** is correct when following another word.)

Otoshikomi: *Dropped in.*

Ōtsu bari: *Second or latter beam.*

R

Rantsugi: Randomly placed joints.

Rasu: Western style lath underlayment.

Rasu bodo: Western style lath board underlayment.

Rokuba: *Six leaves.* Part of a motif.

Rokubari: A beam used in temple construction.

Rokuyō: *Six leaves.* (See illustration on page 366.)

Rokuzumi: The name of an ink line.

Ryaku ki wari: *Abridged wood splitting.* A type of proportioning.

Ryoba: A double edged saw.

S

Sabanoko: See **Gando**.

Sage furi: A handmade guide tool.

Sage kama: A dropped gooseneck joint.

Sakame: A planing direction where the blade gouges the surface.

Sandori nuki: *Three passing bridging or tie.* The placement of intermediate bridgings between bottom and top bridging.

Saobiki dokko: *Stacked tenon with keys.*

Saobuchi: A style of ceiling.

Saoen: Exposed ceiling joists.

Saotsugi shachisen uchi: A dado with a cross tenon lap joint secured with a key.

Saraita: A saddle piece.

Saraita tobukuro: A type of shutter housing.

Sasara hori: Routing of the stringers.

Sashi gamoi: *Jabbing header.* Also **Atsu gamoi:** *Thick header.*

Sashigane: *Ruler metal.* Carpenter's square. See also **Kanejaku**.

Sashikomi: *Insert.*

Sātsuke: *Application of quality.* Grading according to quality.

Segaishi: *Back (of a body).* Where the space between rafters must be equal to the depth of the rafters.

Sei: *Back (of a body).* The side of the tree not facing the sun (north side), where the distance from the outside surface of the log is closest to the pith.

Seichoku: *Properly straight.* Plumb.

Sewari: *Back splitting.* Controlled split in a natural round column (control joint).

Shachi ari: A dovetail secured by inserting keys.

Shachisen: *Key.*

Shachi tsugi: *Key connection.*

Shaji shiwari hŏ: A rafter proportioning method used in shrines and temples.

Shakaku fure zumi: *Shaking sloped corner.* The **noki geta** beams intersect at an angle and the roof slopes on both sides at an equal angle.

Shakaku shin zumi: *Sloping center corner.* The **noki geta** beams intersect at an angle and the roof slopes on both sides at an equal angle.

Shaku: A Japanese unit of measure equal to about one foot, based on a decimal scale. (A Japanese decimal foot.)

Shakugaeri: *Return a distance.* A reference mark, generally one **shaku** from a part that will be cut off.

Shakushi hozo: *Ladle shaped tenon.*

Shakuzue: See **Kenzao**.

Shiageko: A final finishing plane.

Shiageto: A fine whetstone made from pressurized particles.

Shiguchi: Right angle joints.

Shihŏ kama tsugi: *Four directional sickle joint.* Four directional gooseneck joint.

Shihŏ korobi: *Four directional roll.* Corner which is sloped in two directions.

Shiki bari: The bottom member in a triangular hip roof frame.

Shiki geta: *Laid beam.* A supporting beam.

Shikii: *Window sill.* Sliding door or window bottom track or sill.

Shiki men: *Spread surface.*

Shikomi: *Break in.* A distance as shown on an illustration.

Shina ita: *Article board.* A type of trim.

Shindaruki: *Center rafter.*

Shingaeri: *Center return.* A line running slightly to the inside of a center line, or off-set from a center line in reference to the location of a pin in relation to the center line.

Shingiri daimochi tsugi: *Cut heart with support connection.* Dadoed and rabbetted squared scarf joint.

Shinkabe: Exposed framing.

Shinkabe hirayadate: *Center wall, single floor construction.* (**Tate** means "construction.") (**Tate** is the correct pronunciation when alone; **date** is correct when following another word.)

Shinmata gaeri: *Double return to center.* Off set. See also **Shingaeri**.

Shinmi tŏshi or **shinmi koshi:** *Pass through looking at center.*

Shinmono: *Centered things.* A type of diagonal bracing.

Shinmyo zukuri: *Brighten God construction.* A style of temple and shrine construction.

Shin osame uchi: *Strike settled center.* Another name for **hanshigi wari** rafter spacing.

Shin tsugi: A center joint.

Shinuchi: *Center hit.* The location of a pin in relation to a center line.

Shinzuka: *Center end post.* A western style roof.

Shinzumi: *Center line.* Center line or a type of hip rafter.

Shippasami tsugi or **shiribasami tsugi:** *Sandwiched seat joint.* (Pronunciation varies in different regions.) Blinded and stubbed, dadoed and rabbetted scarf joint.

Shiraki zukuri: Natural wood finishing, where pieces are left in the planed condition.

Shitaba dome mechigai ire: A mortise and tenon locked at bottom joint.

Shitaba sumi: *Bottom surface ink marking.* The form of the cut line on a hip rafter.

Shitage kama: *Bottom sickle.* The mortise portion of the blind and halved dovetailed stub mortise and tenon joint.

Shitaji: The supports for interior finishing materials.

Shitajiki: *Bottom piece.*

Shobaku: A square shaped cross-section of wood with pith.

Shoji: A light, translucent door.

Shojiki: A type of carpenter's square used for foundation work.

Showari: A square shaped cross-section of wood without pith.

Shŭchŭ or **denaka:** *Entering center.* One of three center lines on a hip rafter.

Shunoma: The main room of a structure.

Soba noki: *Close to edge* (of eave). The eave at the end of the gable roof.

Sodegiri mayukaki: *Sleeve cutting eyebrow carving.* A type of **mayukaki**.

Soe ita tsugi: *Attach board connection.* Double shear end joint.

Sogi tsugi: *Sliced, sharpened, or shaved connection.* Scarf joint.

Soku ita: Stringers.

Sori hafŭ: A curved facia.

Suberiba: A scarf joint.

Sue (or **sueguchi**): The top of a tree.

Sueguchi: *End,* or *close.*

Sugu hafŭ facia: A **hafŭ** facia.

Suigui: A stake used for marking a building's placement.

Suijungi: A transit.

Suitoi: A level.

Suitsuki ari: A top face.

Suitsukisan: *Sucked in with a crosspiece.* Wood scab.

Sujikai: *Diagonal bracing.*

Sukiya: *To gather many roofs.* (**Suki** means "to like," **ya**

means "house.") A residental architectural style related to tea house architecture.

Sukui: The condition of a plane, where shavings clog the mouth.

Sumi: *Corner.* (**Sumi** is the correct pronunciation when alone; **zumi** is correct when following another word.) Corner, ink, or line.

Sumi aikaki: *Join carved corner.* End lap.

Sumibashira: *Corner post.*

Sumichi: *Corner land.* The hypotenuse of a 45° triangle.

Sumidome hozosashi: *Stop at corner tenon insert.* A haunch blinded and collared tongue and groove miter joint.

Sumidome hozasashi warikusabi uchi: A tongue and groove shoulder miter with wedge.

Sumigi: *Corner wood.* Hip rafter.

Sumi kanamono: *Corner metal thing.*

Sumikiri isuka tsugi: *Cut corner isuka connection.* Rabbetted halved scarf joint. (Same as **miyamima tsugi**.)

Sumi kobai: *Corner slope.* Hip rafter slope.

Sumi sashi: *To put ink.* Bamboo ink stick used to make lines and to write.

Sumitsubo: An ink container used for marking lines.

Sumi yarikata: A corner batterboard.

Sumizuke: Ink marking which serve as guide lines.

Sun: A unit of measure, approximately equivalent to an inch and a quarter.

Sunato: See **Arato**.

T

Tabasami uchi: A kind of rafter spacing. See **Segaishi**.

Taiko otashi: End joint for joining log beams.

Tai zuka: *End post versus.* The name of the end post.

Takakukei zumi: *Many shaped corners.* A type of rafter.

Tangen: *Short side.* The **dōtsuki** cut line on the top surface of the **korobi** member.

Tan hozo (or **tan hozosashi**): *Short tenon.*

Tan hozosashi kasugai uchi: A short tenon secured with a pin anchor.

Tanizumi: *Valley corner.* A roof which is divided in such a way as to collect water.

Tansho: *Single plank.*

Tan yuka gumi: A form of framing for small structures.

Taruki: *Rafter.* (**Taruki** is the correct pronunciation when alone; **daruki** is correct when following another word.)

Taruki bori: *Carved out rafter.* A notch cut in a **keta** or **hari** end grain to receive a rafter.

Taruki hisashi: An eave rafter.

Taruki kake: A ledger.

Taruki kei: *Like a rafter.* The name of a facia.

Taruki kubari: *Rafter distribution.* Rafter spacing.

Taruki shitaba: *Bottom place of taruki.* The intersection point between the bottom of a rafter and the surface upon which it rests or the bottom surface of the rafter.

Tarumi: *Slack.* The midpoint distance of an arc from an imaginary straight line connecting two ends of a concave arc. (See illustration on page 354.)

Taru no kuchi: *Mouth of barrel.* (See illustration on page 366.)

Tasuki kake watari ago: Double mitered cross lap joint.

Tasuki sumi: See **Shitaba sumi**.

Tataki nomi: A chisel used for rough work.

Tatami: A straw mat.

Tatamiyose: A base trim.

Tatebiki nokogiri: A rip saw for rough cutting.

Tatekata (or **tatemae**): The work of framing.

Tateokoshi: Plumbing posts to check verticality.

Teita: See **Itazu**.

Tenbi moya: *Rolled rafter.* A type of rafter.

Tenjo ita: A ceiling board.

Tenjō nuki: **Ten** means "heaven"; **jo** means "place"; **numi** means "bridging." Ceiling bridging.

Teri hafū: *Shining hafū.* The name of a **hafū** facia.

Tesaki tsuma udegi: A framing member.

Tobi bari: *Flying beam.*

Tobukuro: A shutter housing.

Tōge: *Crest, peak.* Baseline or layout of log beams. See also **Ten**.

Toishi: Whetstones.

Tokonoma: An alcove where a scroll is hung.

Tome: *Stop.* Plain miter.

Tome ari kata sanmai hozo: *Ant shaped stop three tenon.* Through single dovetailed miter.

Tomekata sanmai hozo: *Stop shaped three tenons.* Ship miter.

Tōshi bashira: *Through post.* Continuous post for more than one story.

Tōshi hozo sashi: *Through tenon insert.* Full, or through, mortise and tenon joint.

Tōshi nuki: *Through bridging or tie.* The name of a **nuki** that passes through (a post usually).

Tozugiri: A guide piece.

Tsubo giri: A type of awl.

Tsubureta: A dulled whetstone edge.

Tsuginoma: An annex.

Tsugite: *Grafting juncture.* An end joint.

Tsuka: *End post.* (**Zuka** is the correct pronunciation when alone; **tsuka** is correct when following another word.) Short post to support purlins or ridge.

Tsukadate: *Standing pier.*

Tsukadate yuka: *Standing end post floor.* A type of first floor construction.

Tsuka-jiri: End post.

Tsukegamoi (or **tsukekamoi**): A molding.

Tsuki nomi: A chisel for paring off thin pieces.

Tsukinori: *Measuring the actual length.*

Tsukitsuke: A butt joint.

Tsuki tsuke tsugi: *Put under connection.* Lap joint.

Tsukuri: *Construction.* (**Tsukuri** is the correct pronunciation when alone; **zukuri** is correct when following another word.)

Tsukuridashi: *Manufacture.*

Tsuma bari: *Wife beam.* Log or timber across width of building.

Tsuma geta: *Wife beam.* Hari yuki oriented beam, square timber or log.

Tsuma ita: Shutter housing end panel.

Tsumaitadate tobukuro: Standard shutter housing.

Tsuma udegi: Cantilevered outrigger for a shutter housing.

Tsuma yuki: Axial orientation; same as hari yuki.

Tsunaki bari: The name of a beam.

Tsuno nobashi: A form of mortise and tenon joint.

Tsurami toshi or **tsurami koshi:** *Pass through face looking.* A way to determine the size of the projection of a hip rafter end.

Tsuriki: A hanger.

Tsuriki uke: A hanger support.

Tsurizuka: A hanging post.

Tsuru: Laborious sawing.

Tsurubake noko: A saw for cutting hard woods.

Tsutsumi hozo sashi: *Wrapped tenon insert.* Blind and stub mortise and tenon joint.

Tsutsumi komi hozo: *Wrapped around tenon.* Same as tsutsumi hozo sashi.

Tsutsumi-uchi tsuki tsuke: *Wrapped bit put under.* Shoulder joint.

Tyi: A T-shaped joint.

U

Uaba: Top surface.

Uchidashi tsugi: *Sticking out connection.*

Uchikomi: Hitting with a hammer.

Uchinori: The finished framing around an opening.

Uchinori nageshi: A frieze trim.

Uchinori nuki: *On the inside bridging or tie.*

Udegi: *Arm wood.* A bracket that sticks out from the side of a building to support an external member or purlin.

Udegi hisashi: An eave.

Umanori: *Horse riding.* An ornament on a thatched roof.

Uradashi: A method of sharpening a chipped blade.

Uraga kireta: A condition of a pane blade where the back edge is flattened.

Uragane: Cap iron.

Uraita: Soffits.

Urakō: *Back of shell* (turtle shell). A type of facia.

Urasan: Ceiling joists.

Uraza: See **Uragane**.

Ushi bari: A type of beam.

Usunomi: A thin chisel.

Usuzoko: A type of surface.

Uwaba dōtsuki: *Top place plain.*

Uwaba tome: *Top place stop.* A miter on a top surface.

Uwaba zumi: *Top place ink.* Cut line on top surface.

Uwajiki: *Top piece.*

W

Wagaeshi: A method of connecting ceiling boards.

Wagoya: Japanese roof framing.

Wakari tsugi: *Divorce joint.* A form of connection between two logs where the butt ends connect.

Waki kanna: A finishing plane.

Wanagi hozo: A type of finger tenon.

Wanagi komi: *Insert wanagi, or shove through a ring.* Ship, or open, mortise and tenon joint.

Wanagi komi watari ago: *Wanagi insert crossing chin.* Half blind finger mortise and tenon joint.

Wanaida hozo: Finger tenon.

Warihada: *Split shin.* A type of surface.

Wari kamoi: A type of trim.

Wari kusabi: *Split wedge.* A type of wedge system where opposing wedges expand by sliding by one another.

Wari tsugi: *Split connection* or *split joint.* Another name for **okkake daisen tsugi**.

Watari ago: A dadoed cross lap joint.

Watari ago kake: *Cross over chin hanger.* A tongue and groove cross lap joint.

Watari kaki: *Cross over notch.* Stop dadoed cross lap joint.

Wo furu: See **No hi**.

Y

Yahazu: A way to shape the tops of stakes.

Yamamono: Trees from mountain regions transported on land.

Yanitsubo: Holes in wood where sap has collected.

Yarikata: Staking batter boards.

Yatoi hozo: *Employed tenon.* Right angle joint with spline tenon.

Yatoizane hagi: *Employed spline.* Spline joints.

Yodo: A type of facia.

Yogoya: Western style roof framing.

Yojiro goya: A person's name, referring to a roof system.

Yojiro gumi: A person's name, referring to a type of framing.

Yokobiki: Cross cutting.

Yokobiki nokogiri: A cross cutting saw.

Yokohozo sashi: A half blind mortise and tenon joint.

Yokohozo sashi: A half blind mortise and tenon joint.
Yokomechi: A groove.
Yokose: *Side pin.*
Yokosen: A spline joint.
Yondōri nuki: *Four post bridging or tie.*
Yonmai hozo: *Four tenon.* Quadruple tenon.
Yosemune: *Gathered roof.* Hip roof.
Yosemune hogyo zukuri: *Four sided construction.*
Yoshino: A person's name, referring to a log beam.
Yotsume giri: An awl for nail holes.

Yuka bari: *Floor beam.* Floor log beam, floor timber.
Yukamen: *Floor face.*
Yuka shitaba: *Floorunderside.*
Yuka shitaji: A subfloor.
Yuka tsuka: *Floor end post.* A short post supporting the floor from below.
Yukiai tsugi: A method of joining logs.

z
Zaishin: Pith.

Index